THIRD EDITION

HAIRDRESSING FOR AFRICAN AND CURLY HAIR TYPES

FROM A CROSS CULTURAL PERSPECTIVE

SANDRA GITTENS

with contributions from June Forbes and Patricia Livingston

CENGAGE
Learning®

Australia • Brazil • Japan • Korea • Mexico • Singapore • Spain • United Kingdom • United States

HABIA SERIES LIST

Hairdressing

Student textbooks

Hairdressing and Barbering The Foundations: The Official Guide to Hairdressing and Barbering NVQ at Level 2 7e *Martin Green*

Begin Hairdressing: The Official Guide to Level 1 REVISED 2e *Martin Green*

Hairdressing and Barbering The Foundations: The Official Guide to Hairdressing and Barbering VRQ at Level 2 1e *Martin Green*

Professional Hairdressing: The Official Guide to Level 3 REVISED 6e *Martin Green and Leo Palladino*

The Pocket Guide to Key Terms for Hairdressing *Martin Green*

The Official Guide to the City & Guilds Certificate in Salon Service 1e *John Armstrong with Anita Crosland, Martin Green and Lorraine Nordmann*

The Colour Book: The Official Guide to Colour for NVQ Levels 2 & 3 1e *Tracey Lloyd with Christine McMillan-Bodell*

eXtensions: The Official Guide to Hair Extensions 1e *Theresa Bullock*

Salon Management *Martin Green*

Men's Hairdressing: Traditional and Modern Barbering 2e *Maurice Lister*

African-Caribbean Hairdressing 2e *Sandra Gittens*

The World of Hair Colour 1e *John Gray*

The Cutting Book: The Official Guide to Cutting at S/NVQ Levels 2 and 3 *Jane Goldsbro and Elaine White*

Professional Hairdressing titles

Trevor Sorbie: The Bridal Hair Book 1e *Trevor Sorbie and Jacki Wadeson*

The Art of Dressing Long Hair 1e *Guy Kremer and Jacki Wadeson*

Patrick Cameron: Dressing Long Hair 1e *Patrick Cameron and Jacki Wadeson*

Patrick Cameron: Dressing Long Hair 2 1e *Patrick Cameron and Jacki Wadeson*

Bridal Hair 1e *Pat Dixon and Jacki Wadeson*

Professional Men's Hairdressing: The Art of Cutting and Styling 1e *Guy Kremer and Jacki Wadeson*

Essensuals, the Next Generation Toni and Guy: Step by Step 1e *Sacha Mascolo, Christian Mascolo and Stuart Wesson*

Mahogany Hairdressing: Step to Cutting, Colouring and Finishing Hair 1e *Martin Gannon and Richard Thompson*

Mahogany Hairdressing: Advanced Looks 1e *Martin Gannon and Richard Thompson*

The Total Look: The Style Guide for Hair and Make-up Professional 1e *Ian Mistlin*

Trevor Sorbie: Visions in Hair 1e *Trevor Sorbie, Kris Sorbie and Jacki Wadeson*

The Art of Hair Colouring 1e *David Adams and Jacki Wadeson*

Beauty therapy

Beauty Basics: The Official Guide to Level 1 3e *Lorraine Nordmann*

Beauty Therapy – The Foundations: The Official Guide to Level 2 VRQ 5e *Lorraine Nordmann*

Beauty Therapy – The Foundations: The Official Guide to Level 2 5e *Lorraine Nordmann*

Professional Beauty Therapy – The Official Guide to Level 3 4e *Lorraine Nordmann*

The Pocket Guide to Key Terms for Beauty Therapy *Lorraine Nordmann and Marian Newman*

The Official Guide to the City & Guilds Certificate in Salon Services 1e *John Armstrong with Anita Crosland, Martin Green and Lorraine Nordmann*

The Complete Guide to Make-Up 1e *Suzanne Le Quesne*

The Encyclopedia of Nails 1e *Jacqui Jefford and Anne Swain*

The Art of Nails: A Comprehensive Style Guide to Nail Treatments and Nail Art 1e *Jacqui Jefford*

Nail Artistry 1e *Jacqui Jefford*

The Complete Nail Technician 3e *Marian Newman*

Manicure, Pedicure and Advanced Nail Techniques 1e *Elaine Almond*

The Official Guide to Body Massage 2e *Adele O'Keefe*

An Holistic Guide to Massage 1e *Tina Parsons*

Indian Head Massage 2e *Muriel Burnham-Airey and Adele O'Keefe*

Aromatherapy for the Beauty Therapist 1e *Valerie Worwood*

An Holistic Guide to Reflexology 1e *Tina Parsons*

An Holistic Guide to Anatomy and Physiology 1e *Tina Parsons*

The Essential Guide to Holistic and Complementary Therapy 1e *Helen Beckmann and Suzanne Le Quesne*

The Spa Book 1e *Jane Crebbin-Bailey, Dr John Harcup, and John Harrington*

SPA: The Official Guide to Spa Therapy at Levels 2 and 3, *Joan Scott and Andrea Harrison*

Nutrition: A Practical Approach 1e *Suzanne Le Quesne*

Hands on Sports Therapy 1e *Keith Ward*

Encyclopedia of Hair Removal: A Complete Reference to Methods, Techniques and Career Opportunities, *Gill Morris and Janice Brown*

The Anatomy and Physiology Workbook: For Beauty and Holistic Therapies Levels 1–3. *Tina Parsons*

The Anatomy and Physiology CD-Rom

Beautiful Selling: The Complete Guide to Sales Success in the Salon *Rath Langley*

The Official Guide to the Diploma in Hair and Beauty Studies at Foundation Level 1e *Jane Goldsbro and Elaine White*

The Official Guide to the Diploma in Hair and Beauty Studies at Higher Level 1e *Jane Goldsbro and Elaine White*

The Official Guide to Foundation Learning in Hair and Beauty 1e *Jane Goldsbro and Elaine White*

Project Title: Hairdressing for African and Curly Hair Types from a Cross-Cultural Perspective, 3rd edition
Gittens, Sandra; Forbes, June; Livingstone, Pat

Publisher: Andrew Ashwin

Development Editor: Lauren Darby

Administrative Assistant: Claire Whittaker

Marketing Manager: Sally Gallery

Production Manager: Susan Povey

Print Buyer: Elaine Willis

Cover Designer: HCT Creative

Compositor: MPS Limited

For product information and technology assistance, contact us at
Cengage Learning Customer & Sales Support, 1-800-354-9706

For permission to use material from this text or product,
submit all requests online at **cengage.com/permissions**
Further permissions questions can be emailed to
permissionrequest@cengage.com

Library of Congress Control Number: 2007922480

ISBN-13: 978-1-4080-7433-6

Cengage Learning EMEA
Cheriton House,
North Way, Andover, Hampshire, SP1- 5BE,
United Kingdom

Cengage Learning is a leading provider of customized learning solutions with office locations around the globe, including Singapore, the United Kingdom, Australia, Mexico, Brazil, and Japan. Locate your local office at:
international.cengage.com/region

Cengage Learning products are represented in Canada by Nelson Education, Ltd.

Visit our corporate website at **cengage.com**

Printed in China by RR Donnelley
Print Number: 01 Print Year: 2014

Contents

PART ONE Salon Skills

PART TWO Styling

PART THREE Chemically Processing Hair

PART FOUR Cutting and Colouring

PART FIVE Natural Hair

16 Maintaining and styling natural hair 346

17 Cultivating and maintaining locks 368

PART SIX Barbering

18 Men's hairdressing 384

Foreword from Habia

Sandra was first choice many years ago to write this book and even after all these years Sandra shows why she's still at the top of African Caribbean hairdressing. This third edition highlights Sandra's keen skills in delving deeper and deeper into what makes African Caribbean type hair a must for everyone to learn.

This book is not just about the basics but gets right to the centre of what top class stylists have relied on for years. Taking Level 2 junior stylists through to Level 3 is central to Sandra's philosophy of learning; constantly pushing to get the best out of every learner.

I am delighted to provide this Foreword, having known Sandra for many years. Clearly in African Caribbean academia, there is no one that has more knowledge and ability to put that into writing.

As Director of Standards and Qualifications for Habia, I am delighted that this book reflects the standards and ethos of Habia.

Jane Goldsbro
Director of Standards and Qualifications

About our partners

Habia, the Hair and Beauty Industry Authority is appointed by Government to represent employers in the Hair and Beauty Sector. Habia's main role is to manage the development of the National Occupational Standards (NOS) for hairdressing, barbering, beauty therapy, nails and spa. They are developed by industry for industry and represent best practice to achieving skills and knowledge for a particular job role. The NOS are used as the building blocks for the development of all qualifications that are developed by Awarding Organizations and by Cengage to develop text books and support products for learners.

Habia is responsible for the development and implementation of Apprenticeship Frameworks and issuing the apprenticeship certificates. Habia also provides information to employers on Government initiatives that may affect the hair and beauty industry be it educational, environmental or financial. A central point of contact for information, Habia provides guidance on careers, business development, legislation, salon health and safety.

Habia is part of SkillsActive, the Sector Skills Council that covers Hair & Beauty, Sports and the Active Leisure Sector.

Vocational Training Charitable Trust (VTCT) is a Government-approved awarding organization offering vocational qualifications across the hairdressing and beauty sector. It is the first non-unitary awarding body accredited to offer Principal Learning for the new Diploma in Hair and Beauty Studies. VTCT's full qualification package includes complementary therapies, sport and leisure, business skills, hospitality and catering. VTCT is involved in many new initiatives being introduced into the education system, including the embedding of general education skills and online assessment.

About the Author

My Mother, Mrs Beryl Gittens reminded me on completion of the first edition of the book, that my early experience of writing a journal of hairdressing was when I was at primary school. All of this was very much influenced from growing up in a hairdressing environment, after hearing my mother, who was also a hairdresser, advise clients on how to care and look after their hair, it was of course, very easy for me to decide on a career in hairdressing. I trained at the Morris Institute of Hairdressing in Shaftesbury Avenue, London and then the Christine Shaw School of Beauty in Bond Street. My Mother closed down her salon in Streatham and opened a family-run hair salon in Guyana. It was here that I developed and honed my hairdressing skills on a diverse range of hair types including men's hairdressing. In 1981 I decided to return to England to study Trichology (the study of the hair) at the London College of Fashion (LCF). In 1984 I started teaching part-time at City & East London College (now Tower Hamlets College). In 1986 I applied for a full time position at LCF (now University of the Arts) and was appointed hairdressing tutor.

Sandra Gittens

I became co-ordinator of the hairdressing courses at NVQs Levels 2 & 3 and was an external moderator for City & Guilds and consultant for Habia in the development of NVQ awards. I progressed to Director of Programmes for Further Education (FE) at LCF with responsibility for a suite of fashion/media hair and make up, history of fashion and photography courses. I have worked as a consultant with several large multinational product companies in the UK, South Africa and Ghana and acted as a judge at hairdressing competitions both in the UK and internationally. I completed a BA honours in education in 2003. Currently I am working as a consultant and teaching part-time and lecturing on the history of hairdressing. I have been involved in several hair related projects and given talks at the Fitzwilliam Museum, Petrie Museum and V&A Museum. I still teach hairdressing part-time to keep my skills current as I have been involved in the hairdressing industry for over 40 years.

Sandra Gittens

I became a hairdresser at the age of 24 having first qualified as a nurse and midwife. Upon deciding to pursue my passion I completed my initial training at Alan International School of Hairdressing in London with the ambition of one day owning a West End salon. Burnett Forbes opened on Wells Street, London W1 in 1998 and went on to become a multi award winning salon. Throughout my hairdressing career I have always believed in the importance of education and have been committed to maintaining high professional standards within the Afro Hairdressing Industry. I also worked as a technician for Soft Sheen Products for several years, which as well as exposing me to hairdressing on an international level; gave me an invaluable insight into hair the science and chemistry behind hairdressing.

June Forbes

I was first introduced to Sandra Gittens in the 1980s while she was teaching at the London College of Fashion and eventually employed several junior members of staff directly through her. I always knew that Sandra's students were trained to work and conduct themselves impeccably within the salon environment. Since then I have worked with Sandra on several other projects relating to the history of hairdressing. These include talks given at the Fitwilliam Museum and the Wycombe Museum. I am currently working as a freelance stylist whilst studying for my DTTLS qualification which will enable me to teach hairdressing at Further Education Level. My work is represented in the first and second editions of this text book and more recently I have worked with Sandra on several other projects relating to the history of hairdressing. These include talks given at the Fitwilliam Museum and the Wycombe Museum. I am currently working as a freelance stylist whilst studying for my DTTLS qualification which will enable me to Teach hairdressing at Further Education Level.

June Forbes

Patricia Livingstone

Patricia has worked in the hairdressing industry for over 25 years. She came into it by default when, having finished her degree in education qualifying with a B.Ed. Honours, she moved back to London from Newcastle upon Tyne to the news that her father, who had a salon and barbers in Hackney, was not well. Patricia stepped in to run the salon and did not look back. Her qualification was later put to good use when she started teaching part time at the London College of Fashion. She later worked as part of the European styling team for D'orum International (Leisure Curl Brand) and took part in many hair shows both nationally and internationally.

In 1990 she and her husband started a publication, with Patricia as the editor, entitled *Afro Salon News,* a magazine dedicated to the professional black hair care industry. The magazine not only brought news of what was happening in the industry but was educative with practical articles from industry specialists on areas such as taxation, health and safety, and accounting, to name but a few. In 1992, concerned with the increasing number of requests from salon owners for salon management training and for reliable and well trained staff, Patricia decided to start her own Consultancy and Employment Bureau which she ran for a number of years.

In 1994 Patricia became Chair for Specialist Hair & Beauty Associates (an organization concerned with the progression of the African Caribbean Hairdressing Industry) and later became a contributor to the first and second publication of this textbook *African Caribbean Hairdressing*. Since 2004 she has been teaching at City of London Business College delivering NVQs Levels 2 & 3 in Combined Hair Types, teaching on the TAQA, CTLLS & DTLLS pathways and acting as Internal Quality Assurer for the Business Admin programme.

Patricia has also worked with Goldwell Cosmetics at their Academy in Mayfair as a platform artist and also delivering training programmes to their external clients and in-house staff on working with African-Caribbean hair types and colour. Patricia now runs her own salon in Ilford, East London.

Patricia Livingstone

Introduction by the author

African type hair requires knowledge and a range of excellent practical skills to be competent in dealing with this specialist hair type. Working on naturally curly hair and its range of styling options, can bring much satisfaction and a tremendous sense of achievement to the stylist as well as the client. As stylists we are working in the medium of hair and should be as diverse as possible in our skills of processing, styling hair and product knowledge; this new edition also celebrates working on European and Asian hair types. Always remember the adage 'it is only hair, have no fear'. Develop all the skills, knowledge and experience required to succeed as an all-round hair stylist, once this is your chosen goal. Some stylists prefer to specialize in the industry by working on natural hair, or as a barber. Whatever your chosen option, hone your skills and be one of the best in the field of hairstyling.

As a practitioner and hairstylist it is important to keep abreast of all the latest products, hairstyles, techniques, training and technology available. Attending college full or part time, taking short courses or gaining your training while on an apprenticeship is extremely important in developing the correct standard of skill and professionalism in preparation for working in industry.

Knowledge is enhanced on your chosen NVQ or VRQ in hairdressing, if you use this book to guide and walk you through each chapter and unit of study while training. It is a reference book that will support your learning by adding value to both new and existing knowledge or skills by covering all the aspects required to make you a competent and successful hairdresser.

Well done! You have taken one of the most vital steps in your career by purchasing the third edition. May you have a long, happy and successful future in the industry!

Yours truly,
Sandra Gittens

Acknowledgements

When writing such a detailed textbook as *Hairdressing for African and Curly Hair Types,* there are so many individual people who helped and supported us throughout the process that we must show our heartfelt appreciation by thanking them. First of all, I must thank contributing authors June Forbes and Pat Livingstone for their tireless effort and devotion to the book and all things hair. Nothing was too much for them to do, whether revisiting, updating, planning step-by-step sequences or making changes to chapters and continuing to uphold the legacy of high standards attributed to the book over the years.

In addition, I know both Pat and June would like to join me in thanking the following individuals:

Technical advisors for the barbering chapter; Pat Hope and barber Tyrone Chambers. Hakeem Lotty and Mark Johnson, created the men's hairstyles and shaving for the step-by-step images. Hairstylists Glenda Clarke, Lorraine Dublin, Lisa Edwards, Brenda Mcleod Ford and Natasha John-Lewis, for creating the hair looks for the new and updated step-by-step images. Nikki Bassy make-up artist and Mac products make-up artists, all of whom spent two gruelling days creating step-by-step images for this third edition.

The equipment and product companies, who helped with providing products for the step-by-step technical images and also supplied supporting images and tables to use within the text and chapters. They are as follows: Curlformers, Design Essentials, Goldwell products, Mizani L'Oreal products, Luster products, Sensationnel hair, Mac make-up products, Wella products and Hammersmith & Fulham College for the use of hair studios.

Above all, a big thank you goes out to Junior Green who for this third edition supplied both the creative and innovative front and back cover images, photographed by Gabor Szantai. Special thanks also to Desmond Murray who provides modern, clean fresh images within the book. Desmond – the faith and especially trust you displayed when you would hand me your collection saying, Sandra use the images you wish, I am ever appreciative. Thank you both for sharing your great gift, talent, creativity, case studies and for being an inspiration to all who read this book including us the authors.

Korell Williams, Charlotte Mensah, Dionne Smith and Kimberley Hay – who all provided supporting images for the book and also shared with us their personal case studies. Wow, what outstanding work from all of you, so fresh, diverse, creative and motivating, we thank you.

Not to be forgotten are the models who gave their precious time.

Individual thanks go out to all our families, nearest and dearest who encouraged, supported and put up with the weeks, months, and nights we have devoted to writing. Also, to Sharon Thompson and Winston Isaacs who encouraged the completion of the first, second and third editions and who would always find out how the book was developing and remind me how necessary such a text book is for the industry. A personal thank you to Alan and Jane Golosboro at Habia for their continual encouragement and support.

Finally, I remain eternally grateful to my parents who always encouraged us to choose whatever career we wanted, but always strive to be the best. To my Mum for instilling such high standards of hairdressing and allowing me to develop my hairdressing skills in any way I wanted. Thanks to my dear friends, sister Brenda Arno, brother Aubrey Gittens Uncle Edward Murray, niece Dawn Kendall, nephew Colin Gittens, the Murray and Gittens families for their interest and encouragement. I could not do it without you.

Sandra Gittens

The publisher would also like to thank the many copyright holders who have kindly granted us permission to reproduce material throughout this text. Every effort has been made to contact all rights' holders but in the unlikely event that anything has been overlooked please contact the publisher directly and we will happily make the necessary arrangements at the earliest opportunity.

Special mention must also be accredited to content editor Cathy Lake, picture researcher Sarah Smithies at Luped Media Research, photographer Nathan Allan, content experts Samantha Golding and Tina Arey, Lynda Whitehorn at VTCT and Jane Goldsbro at Habia, for their tireless dedication to ensuring that this title is as comprehensive as possible.

Credits

Although every effort has been made to contact copyright holders before publication, this has not always been possible. If notified, the publisher will undertake to rectify any errors or omissions at the earliest opportunity.

Photos

The publishers would like to thank the following sources for permission to reproduce their copyright protected images:

Alamy pp 24m (Medical-on-Line), 23b (Image Source Plus), 35b (Medical-on-Line), 36t (MedicImage), 37t (Medical-on-Line), 39b (Medical-on-Line), 40t (BSIP SA), 41m(Medical-on-Line), 41b (Medical-on-Line), 42b (BSIP SA); BaByliss PRO pp 118b, 119t; Balmain pp 175c, 175bl, 176t, 191; Car-ron Grazette pp 256t; Charlotte Menash pp 64b, 73, 152, 180b, 228, 310, 334bl, 353; Chris Foster pp 397tr; Chubb Fire & Security pp 10r; Curlformers pp123 t, 123b, 354b, 355; Denman pp 102t, 102m, 102c, 102b, 103t, 103m, 103c, 103b, 103bl, 105tr, 119tl, 119b, 119,bl, 120t, 120b, 174b, 208t, 208mt, 208mb, 209c, 209b, 239mt, 239mb, 239ct, 239cb, 257, 258tl, 258t, 336c, 336b, 389bm; Desmond Murray pp 136t, 136m, 136bl, 136br, 139, 260, 261, 264, 348, 383; Dr John Gray pp 38m, 38c, 38b, 41c; Dreamstime pp 175tl 207b (Alexander Morozov), 354m (Dudarova), 389br (Micheloomen); E A Ellison & Co Ltd pp 12t, 17t, 17b , 18b; Ellisons pp 206m, 206br, 207br, 207m, 209m, 238mt, 238ttr, 238tbr, 238bbr, 239tl, 257, 336m; Fotolia pp 208bl; Goldwell pp 53bl, 206cr, 207tl, 207c, 238btr, 239t, 257tl, 257t, 337m, 337c, 390l; Habia pp 50t, 50m, 50c, 50b; Hair Tools Ltd pp119mt, 119c, 119mb, 208tl, 208cb, 208b,209t, 354tl, 354tr; HSE Health and Safety Executive pp 15; iStockphoto pp 35c (russaquarius), 44 (Vetta Stock Photo), 114 (Alejandro Rivera), 199t (Lorado), 200 (iconogenic), 276r (iconogenic), 278 (iconogenic), 346 (iconogenic), 392b (EyeJoy); Junior Green pp 96; Julette Burnett pp 164r; June Forbes pp 124br; Korell Williams pp 150b, 253b, 254, 330t, 387m; Kimberley Hay pp 372; Kizure Ltd pp 154; L'Oréal MIZANI pp 59b, 87, 89, 336tl, 337b; Luster pp 82, 117, 236, 239b, 239bl, 258m; Maksym Bondarchuk pp 14; Melissa McCullock pp 163r; Milady pp 180t, 181tr, 185b, 188tl, 223t, 380t; Patricia Livingston pp 125 br, 130br, 296b, 358b; REM UK Ltd pp 16, 68; Renscene Ltd pp 18t; Rex Features pp 313tl(Araldo Crollalanza), 313tr (Everett Collection), 313bl (Moviestore Collection); Sandra Gittens pp134; Sharpsafe® / Frontier Medical Group pp 12b; Science Photo Library pp 35t (DR M.A. Ansary), 35m, 36m (Biophoto Associates), 37m (Dr P Marazzi), 38bl (STEVE GSCHMEISSNER), 40b (DR. CHRIS HALE), 41t, 53br (Dr P. Marazzi); Seymour Weaver, III, M.D. pp 36c, 36b, 37tl, 371; Simon Jersey pp 257; Shutterstock pp 1t (Yaromir), 6 (Dragana Gerasimoski), 10l (Neil Donoghue), 22 (Jason Stitt), 30t (Jubal Harshaw), 31b (lekcej), 34t (Roblan), 34m (olavs), 34b (Maksym Bondarchuk), 37c (Adam Gregor), 37b (itanistock), 38t (rSnapshotPhotos), 39t (D. Kucharski K. Kucharska), 42t (Levent Konuk), 48tl (Aleksandar Bozhikov), 48t (Aleksandar Bozhikov), 48m (Aleksandar Bozhikov), 48c (Aleksandar Bozhikov), 48b (Aleksandar Bozhikov), 48bl (Aleksandar Bozhikov), 62 (MartiniDry), 64t (Paul Vasarhelyi), 66 (Mike Flippo), 76 (Nuzza), 79b, 84t (Peter Bernik), 137l (Jason Stitt), 137c (MartiniDry), 137r (Sanjay Deva), 139b(Africa Studio), 139bl (Micha Klootwijk), 140 (Yuriy Zhuravov), 144 (Valua Vitaly), 146b (Olga Ekaterincheva), 170 (MartiniDry), 174t (nito), 175t (Buida Nikita Yourievich), 175m (Buida Nikita Yourievich), 175b (photopixel), 176b (KKulikov), 179tr (Luba V Nel), 180c (Luba V Nel), 185t (photopixel), 190ml, 206l (Dan Kosmayer), 207tr (Peter Zijlstra), 213m (schankz), 226 (Svetlana Fedoseyeva), 238tl (Dan Kosmayer), 238btr (Peter Zijlstra), 256b (Valua Vitaly), 257tm (Peter Zijlstra), 257mt (EML), 258mb (EML), 258ct (Mariusz Gwizdon), 258cb (cretolamna), 267r (Subbotina Anna), 270br (Subbotina Anna), 280t (Blamb), 280b (kosmos111), 282 (Subbotina Anna), 290t (Subbotina Anna), 290b (Irina Okuneva), 300 (Ivory27), 313br (s_bukley), 314l (Luba V Nel), 314r (c12), 317b (Rido), 319c (Poznyakov), 319b (coka), 320t (snedelchev), 330b (Sundraw Photography), 333t (Helga Esteb), 335 (Sundraw Photography), 336t (97755089), 336m (Dan Kosmayer), 337t (Eillen), 337m (Madiz), 349 (J Hersh Photo), 358t (Luba V Nel), 359tr (Alan Bailey), 365 (Felix Mizioznikov), 368 (Laurin Rinder), 372t (Feature Flash), 373 (Everett Collection), 375 (Felix Mizioznikov), 386 (Jamie Rogers), 387t (szefei), 387c (Artmim), 387b (KAMONRAT), 388 (OZaiachin), 389t (schankz), 389m (Arva Csaba), 389c (hd Connelly), 389bl (Stephen Clarke), 390m (Peter Zijlstra), 393 (Eillen), 394tl (Roxana Gonzalez), 401l (Jaguar PS), 401ml (Jaguar PS), 401mr (Featureflash), 401r (Efecreata Photography); Viking pp 2; Wella pp 214b, 215tl, 215tr, 223tl, 281m, 281b, 292, 293, 296t.

About this book

Welcome to the textbook *Hairdressing for African and Curly Hair Types from a Cross-Cultural Perspective,* third edition.

The new edition of the book continues to celebrate African type hair as an art form and all the curl patterns within this unique hair type. Introduced to this edition are new step-by-step hair styles carried out on straighter hair types and men's barbering and hairstyling. The ever popular technical step-by-step guides and easy to follow text remain a mainstay of the book for all learners. Each chapter contains a short historical overview which puts into context the history of each technique, hairstyle or process and the evolution of hair throughout time.

This edition clearly identifies and signposts learning at NVQ, Level 2, junior stylist and NVQ, Level 3, senior stylist. It also contains new updated images and text, which reinforce new and prior learning. The text supports academic theory, health and hygiene, practical skills, science and underpinning knowledge. All of which will guide and support the reader in easy to understand hairdressing terms and language in preparation for working in industry.

The structure of the National Occupational Standards (NOS) are mirrored in many ways within this text:

◆ The book is broken into parts to provide the fastest possible navigation to the areas of learning that you need to know.

◆ Each chapter contains unit topics and learning objectives, related to the NOS, which you can use to help you work through your qualifications.

◆ A comprehensive glossary and index have been provided to help you find and understand key terminology.

How to use this book

You can use this book in a number of different ways:

1   College students can use the revised chapter structure to cover complete units as they encounter them within their training.

2   Professional stylists can use the book as a quick reference guide to hone their existing knowledge and skill to ensure they are kept abreast with the changes in industry.

Three tutors can use this book as a reference point and as a classroom teaching support tool. The new format of this book will help you read and use it more easily. Each part and chapter opens with a simple overview and then extends deeper by covering each aspect of your training, before finishing with revision questions.

Throughout this textbook you will find many colourful text boxes designed to aid your learning and understanding as well as highlighted key points. Here are examples and descriptions of each:

Level 2 and Level 3 Signposting

Indicate parts of the text that are more suited to Level 2 Junior Stylist or Level 3 Senior Stylist learning.

TOP TIP

Shares the author's experience and provides positive suggestions to improve knowledge and skills in each unit.

HEALTH & SAFETY

Draws your attention to related health and safety information essential for each technical skill.

ACTIVITY

Featured in the book to provide additional tasks for you to further your understanding.

Directional arrows point you to other parts of the book that explore similar or related topics, so you can expand your learning.

Web link boxes recommend certain supplementary sites that can be viewed online.

REVISION QUESTIONS

At the end of each chapter there is a useful revision section which has been specially devised to help you check your learning and prepare for your oral and written assessments.

Use these revision sections to test your knowledge as you progress through the course and seek guidance from your supervisor or assessor if you come across any areas that you are unsure of.

PART ONE
Salon Skills

Salon Skills are the functions we carry out in a hair salon or training environment on a day-to-day basis, that define our professionalism within the hair care industry. These skills enable us to provide the highest standards in health and safety, client care, salon organization and support for others. Understanding, identifying and observing safe working practices continuously, and particularly when dealing with non-infectious and infectious conditions, is of the utmost importance as we perform a variety of skills, and is the kite mark to our salon branding and our own personal standards.

ROLE MODEL

KIMBERLEY HAY Freelance Hairdresser specializing in locks and natural hair

" Kimberley Hay studied hairdressing at Amersham and Wycombe College and spent time working in local hair salons as a junior stylist. Having decided to grow out her relaxer and subsequently adopt the wearing of locks, she became frustrated by the lack of professional care and advice available to people who wanted to wear their hair without chemical enhancement. She made the decision to undergo specialist training at Essence Salon, London, in order to broaden her knowledge and develop her skills in this area.

With a keen eye for style Kimberley was able to quickly adapt locking and styling techniques to help her clients achieve individual and often chic looks for what has traditionally been regarded as a very casual way of wearing one's hair. It did not take long for word to spread and for Kimberley's skills to be in demand by a clientele ranging from young trendsetters to discerning professionals.

1 Health and safety

LEARNING OBJECTIVES

This chapter covers the following:

Level 2

◆ How to identify risks in your working environment

◆ What steps to take to minimize the risks to yourself and others

◆ Working in a way that maintains safe and effective practice

◆ Awareness of legislation pertaining to health and safety in your place of work

Level 3

◆ How to identify risks in your working environment

◆ Understanding what policies need to be put in place to minimize the risks in the working environment

Small business health and safety starter pack graphic image

◆ How to ensure that safe practices within the work environment are maintained

◆ Understanding the importance of keeping staff informed and educated with regard to current health and safety legislation

KEY TERMS

Blood borne

Emergency numbers

Legislation

Manual handling

Policy

Potential

PPE

Risk assessment

UVA

Working environment

INTRODUCTION

It is the duty of all stylists to maintain a clean and safe environment within the salon. This reflects the standard of service that you offer your clients. Health and safety is also important because there are certain standards that must be met by law. As you go about your daily activities it is essential that you observe what is happening around you and make sure that your actions do not compromise the health and safety of others. For example, a trailing electricity cord, an obstructed fire exit or poorly cleaned tools are all hazards that could cause harm to you, your clients and the people working around you.

The information and guidelines set out in this chapter will enable stylists at Levels 2 and 3 to maintain a safe working environment.

At Level 2, the focus is on identifying hazards and reducing risks. You need to be aware of your personal responsibilities and know who to report to about health and safety issues.

At Level 3, your responsibilities also include keeping up-to-date with current health and safety legislation. You need to make sure that policies are implemented and monitored, that staff understand who to report to and any incidents are dealt with promptly. If your establishment employs five or more people then it is a legal requirement to provide written records of any significant findings of the risk assessment. You will also ensure that stocks of products needed for use in the salon are ordered, replenished and stored safely. It is also your responsibility to ensure the safeguarding of all salon records.

Health and safety legislation

Health and Safety at Work Act 1974

Under the Health and Safety at Work Act 1974, every individual in a **working environment** is required by law to carry out their activities and practices in a way that does not pose a risk to themselves or those they come into contact with.

This law also requires that a safe working environment is maintained and monitored, including the safe handling of substances which may be dangerous or harmful.

Health and safety **legislation** is constantly being reviewed and updated. You need to keep abreast of any changes.

At Level 2 you should understand the difference between a risk and a hazard:

◆ A hazard is an object or a situation which can be potentially dangerous or could cause harm.

◆ A risk is the likelihood and nature of the harm that could arise.

You also need to know how to avoid **potential** accidents. You should be able to identify hazards and know who to report them to. You are responsible for your own actions with regard to maintaining a clean, healthy environment and must be fully aware of salon **policy** regarding health and safety.

At Level 3 you should be up-to-date on all current legislation that affects the salon environment and know how to access this information readily. It is your duty to see that this information is distributed or displayed appropriately among the staff. You are responsible for seeing that all other members of staff are kept up-to-date with salon health and safety policy and that those procedures are adhered to. You must also ensure that any training required by less senior members of staff is given and that first aid and emergency procedures are implemented. You are held responsible for the monitoring and recording of hazards and ensuring that action is taken to eliminate or reduce any possible risk.

The Health and Safety at Work Act 1974 is enforced by the local authority's Environmental Health Department, which authorizes environmental health officers to inspect local business premises. If the inspector recognizes a potential danger, the employer is issued with an improvement notice, which allows a designated time for improvements. If the improvements are not carried out, the inspector will then issue a prohibition notice, and could close the business until the dangers have been made safe for employees and the public.

Employers with five or more employees are required to carry out **risk assessment** and the findings need to be documented. As a Level 3 stylist, this could be part of your role. Upon carrying out an assessment the risks identified should then be considered in order of priority. For example, the likelihood of an incident occurring and its potential to cause damage or harm. This will enable you to rank the urgency of the risk as high, medium and low. You can then implement the necessary health and safety measures. To eliminate or minimise the risk.

Electricity at Work Regulations 1989

Each year about 20 people die from electric shock in the workplace and about 30 die at home. Electric shock can cause deep slow healing burns, muscle strain from sharp contraction during a shock, or injuries from falling when shocked. Most electric shocks are preventable if safety measures are followed.

There is more information about the topics covered in this chapter on the Health and Safety Executive's (HSE) site at www.hse.gov.uk/guidance/index.htm

You can find a current version of the Health and Safety at Work Act at www.legislation.gov.uk/ukpga/1974/39

TOP TIP

Any **emergency numbers** should be on display clearly in easily accessible areas such as by the reception desk, by the telephone, or on the staffroom noticeboard.

Further information can be accessed online through the HABIA website at: http://www.habia.org/healthandsafety/index.php?page=738
Habia also provide a health and safety pack designed for hairdressers.

ACTIVITY

This table shows hazards, risks and possible causes of action at Levels 2 and 3. Complete the table by adding any further hazards that you can find in your salon. Identify the risk they present, who might be affected and the action that should be taken.

Hazard	Risk	Who is at risk	Action at Level 2	Action at Level 3
Spillage of relaxer on the floor	Slipping on the product\n\nDamage to skin in contact with relaxer	Anyone in the salon	Wear gloves, clean up the relaxer immediately and dispose of appropriately.	Ensure that staff are aware of the potential dangers of spillage and the dangers associated with relaxer coming into contact with the skin.\n\nEnsure that staff are aware of the location of gloves and how to dispose of the relaxer.
Damaged cable on hairdryer	Electric shock or fire	Anyone using the dryer or anyone in the salon in the case of fire	Report to manager or senior stylist.	Discard dryer or have repair done by qualified electrician.\n\nEnsure that staff are aware of the location of fire fighting equipment and have been trained on how to use it. Ensure staff know the location of fire exits.
Use of oven for heating of curling irons	Burn to client or stylist\n\nFire from over-heating	Client and stylist using the oven\n\nAnyone in the salon in the case of fire	Ensure that oven is only switched on when in use. Only use oven if you have been properly trained to do so. Gown the client correctly placing a towel around their shoulders to protect them.\n\nPosition the client correctly when tonging the hair.\n\nDo not leave hot oven unattended. Switch off after use.	Ensure that the oven is kept in a place where it cannot be brushed against accidentally and where there is good lighting to be able to see clearly when using the tongs.\n\nEnsure stylists using the oven and tongs have been properly trained to do so.\n\n(See above for fire procedures.)
Exposure of skin to harmful products	Sensitivity dermatitis	All stylists and staff handling these products	Wear gloves while working with these products. Wash hands and apply barrier creams regularly.	Ensure that staff have been trained to use these products correctly. Educate staff on what dermatitis is and how to avoid it. Ensure availability of gloves and that stylists know where to find them. Ensure any staff suffering from dermatitis receives medical attention and that this has been documented.

The Electricity at Work Regulations 1989 state that regular professional checks should be carried out on all electrical equipment by a qualified electrician. The frequency of checking is determined by the number and level of faults found. However, a visual inspection can be carried out by staff on a regular basis. You can design your own checklist for this. It should include potential hazards such as:

◆ frayed cables;
◆ broken or cracked plugs;
◆ overloaded sockets;
◆ exposed wires in flexes.

TOP TIP

An example of a risk assessment table for hairdressing can be found at hse.gov.uk

As a junior or senior stylist, you should inspect your electrical tools regularly for damage and do not overload socket with appliances. While working, make a habit of checking for any faulty sockets, switches or electrical equipment. If you find any problems, report them immediately to your manager.

As a senior stylist, you should also carry out a risk assessment on all electrical fittings and appliances within the salon, document your findings, remove any faulty equipment from use and ensure that any necessary repairs are carried out by a qualified electrician. Portable appliance testing (PAT) is required by law in order to prevent danger. You should keep a checklist of all electrical equipment in the salon and arrange for regular testing (though no specified time frame is given, it is recommended annually). Keep a record of all testing dates and the age of equipment.

Hazardous substances

A hazardous substance can get into the body via:

- ◆ the skin;
- ◆ the eyes;
- ◆ the nose (breathed in);
- ◆ the mouth (swallowed).

Hazard labelling

Chemicals used in hairdressing range from everyday cleaning solutions to lightening agents and relaxers. Most of the products we come into contact with are safe, with only a few posing a threat if they are used or handled incorrectly. All hazardous substances should be clearly labelled by the manufacturer using universal symbols that indicate any potential harm they can do and it is important that you deal with them accordingly. It is the hairdressing product supplier's and/or manufacturer's responsibility to provide adequate information on how the materials should be used and stored and to comply with UK and EU product and manufacturing legislation. It is the duty of the hairdresser to protect themself and the client from unnecessary exposure and risk from harm by such substances.

Always ensure that you are working in an area that is properly ventilated. You should wear gloves and a protective apron at all times when dealing with chemicals. Clients must be gowned and protected according to the requirements of the service being carried out. If necessary the appropriate barrier cream should be applied (see Personal protective equipment PPE Page 8). When you use any hazardous substance, such as colour or relaxer, follow the manufacturer's instructions and record its use on the client's record card.

If any products accidentally come into contact with the skin or eyes, rinse them off immediately and report to your manager who will take any further action necessary. If chemical is ingested, take appropriate first aid measures which should be outlined in the manufacturers guidelines for use, or as outlined in your salon first aid policy. It is important that such intervention is only carried out by a trained first aider so as not to cause further harm. The salon environment should always be well ventilated to avoid unnecessary inhalation of dust and fumes.

Always clear away, close and return products to storage and dispose of any leftover products according to salon policy and manufacturer's instructions.

At Level 3, you should be aware of the chemicals contained in any products used. These should be listed in the ingredients by the manufacturer. You should assess the hazards that these products pose when in use and appreciate the importance of such issues as the timing and monitoring of relaxer application.

You should make sure that sufficient and correct storage for hazardous substances is available. Keep a listing of hazardous substances used within the salon in your salon handbook, stating what measures should be taken to prevent harm when using them. It is your responsibility to control and monitor the use of these substances by all staff, ensuring that training in their correct and safe use has been given where necessary. You should also make sure that protective clothing is provided for use when working with hazardous substances and ensure that the salon is always sufficiently ventilated.

You should know the correct first aid procedure for dealing with any accidents that may occur while working with any of these products. Finally, you should follow the correct procedure for documenting any incidents involving hazardous substances that may arise in your salon incident book.

Control of Substances Hazardous to Health Regulations 2002 (COSHH Regulations)

These Regulations help control employees' exposure to hazardous substances and help with the assessment of any possible risk.

TOP TIP

Any leftover chemical can be diluted with water to reduce its harmful potential. It may then be allowable to rinse small amounts down the sink. Check salon policy.

For more information see CHAPTERS 11, 12, 14 & 15.

Leaflets on hazardous substances can be found at www.hse.gov.uk /coshh/index.htm

HEALTH & SAFETY

Environmental protection Act 1990

All staff must be trained and shown the correct way to dispose of unwanted products or equipment in order to prevent environmental pollution.

You can find more information on PPE at http://www.hse.gov.uk /pubns/indg174.pdf

HEALTH & SAFETY

Sharps such as blades should be placed in a specially provided box and disposed of according to local authority instructions.

The Personal Protective Equipment at Work Regulations 1992 (PPE Regulations)

These Regulations ensure employers provide adequate personal protective equipment **(PPE)** for handling hazardous substances in the salon such as:

◆ acid solutions in different strengths;

◆ alkaline creams in different strengths;

◆ colouring agents;

◆ pressurized cans filled with flammable liquid.

Under these guidelines, handling of tools needs extreme caution and adequate training. Examples include:

◆ heated appliances;

◆ electrical appliances;

◆ sharp cutting tools.

At Level 2, you have a duty to yourself to ensure that you have been given proper training on the use of any product or piece of equipment in the salon before attempting to utilize it. You must also make sure that you are wearing proper protective clothing, such as an apron and gloves when necessary. You also have a duty to adequately protect the client from harm by using protective gowns/towels and barrier creams where necessary.

The employer has a responsibility to ensure staff are correctly trained to use PPE and know where to locate it. This responsibility is also part of the role of the Level 3 stylist. Proper protective clothing, such as gloves, gowns and aprons, must be provided for both staff and clients.

Provision and Use of Work Equipment Regulations 1988 (PUWER)

Under these Regulations, any equipment used at work, whether it was supplied by the employer or brought in for use by the employee, must be suitable for the purpose for which it is intended. This means that it must be in good working order, safe for use and have been properly maintained. All equipment brought in for use in the salon, whether new or second-hand, must be inspected to determine its level of safety and suitability for use. The person using the equipment must be properly trained to do so.

Manual Handling Regulations 1992

In hairdressing there are various situations that require the stylist to lift and move objects such as stock, upright hairdryers and trollies. There is a range of painful, long-term injuries that can occur through repeated lifting using incorrect techniques. The **Manual Handling** Regulations require that employers do not place employees at undue risk of such injuries through poor working practices. Risk assessment should be carried out and policies put in place to prevent this occurring.

Education on posture and how to lift properly should be carried out in all areas of work. The diagram shows the correct lifting technique.

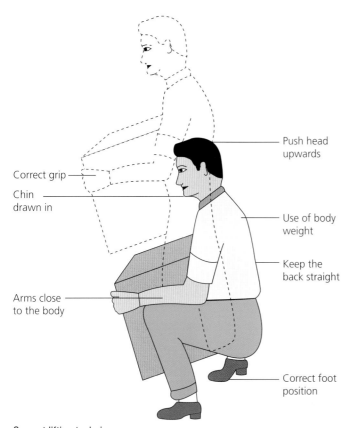

Push head upwards

Correct grip

Chin drawn in

Use of body weight

Keep the back straight

Arms close to the body

Correct foot position

Correct lifting technique

The HSE has provided guidelines on loads that may be safely handled at different heights. They come with the warning that these guidelines are not weight limits. They assume that you are working in good conditions. If this is not the case, you may not be able to handle as much safely.

TOP TIP

Instead of trying to move a heavy box, unpack it and move the contents in smaller amounts.

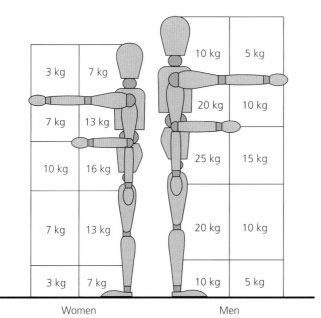

	Women		Men	
	3 kg	7 kg	10 kg	5 kg
	7 kg	13 kg	20 kg	10 kg
	10 kg	16 kg	25 kg	15 kg
	7 kg	13 kg	20 kg	10 kg
	3 kg	7 kg	10 kg	5 kg

Guidelines on loads that may be safely handled at different heights

Fire Precaution Act 1971

This Act states that all employees should receive adequate training in fire and emergency evacuation procedures. A premises requires a fire certificate when more than 20 people work in a building at one time, or when more than 10 people work on floors other than the ground floor. The emergency exit is the shortest and quickest exit for staff and clients to leave the premises. Emergency exits must be easily recognized and clearly sign posted. A smoke alarm should be fitted to alert staff to any fires. Fire doors where applicable must be fitted, to help contain the spread of fire from one area to the next.

Fire-fighting equipment should be stored accessibly throughout the premises. This should include fire blankets, fire extinguishers, sand, buckets and water hoses. Do not use fire extinguishers unless you have been fully trained. It is important to know which extinguisher to use on a fire – using the wrong type could make matters worse.

◆ Fire blankets smother small fires or a person's clothes.

◆ Sand absorbs spilt liquids – if it is the source of the fire, smother the flames.

◆ Water hoses extinguish large fires caused by paper.

Fire fighting equipment should be checked regularly and renewed according to the suppliers' instructions.

HEALTH & SAFETY

If a chemical application has been started on a client and the salon has to be evacuated because of fire, you will have to take the client to a neighbouring business to rinse the products. It is advisable to set up this arrangement in advance.

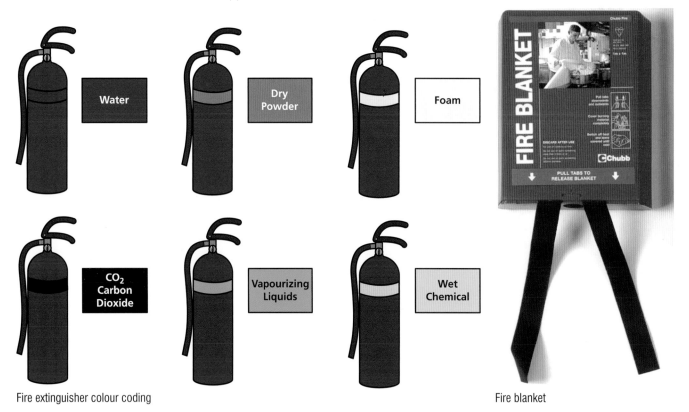

Fire extinguisher colour coding   Fire blanket

 At Level 2, you should be aware of salon evacuation procedures and know where all the fire exits are in the building. You should have been given fire prevention training and know how to use the relevant fire extinguishers safely.

 At Level 3, you should ensure that adequate fire training is provided for all staff, who must also be made aware of the salon evacuation procedures. All fire exits must be accessible and free from obstruction. You must also check that all fire fighting equipment is in good working order and keep a record of these checks.

Health and Safety (First-Aid) Regulations 1981

These Regulations require employers to provide adequate and appropriate equipment, facilities and personnel to ensure their employees receive immediate attention if they are injured or taken ill at work. These Regulations apply to all workplaces, including those with less than five employees, and to the self employed.

There should be a first-aid trained member of staff on the premises at all times during opening hours. Sufficient first aid boxes should be positioned in accessible locations, the contents of which should include the following according to current Health and Safety (First-Aid) Regulations 1981:

◆ basic first-aid guidance leaflet (1)

◆ individually wrapped sterile adhesive dressings (20)

◆ individually wrapped triangular bandages (6)

◆ safety pins (6)

◆ sterile eye-pads, with attachments (2)

◆ medium-sized, individually wrapped, sterile, un-medicated wound dressing – 10 cm × 8 cm (6)

◆ large, individually wrapped, sterile, un-medicated wound dressings – 13 cm × 9 cm (2)

◆ extra-large, sterile, individually wrapped, medicated wound dressings – 28 cm × 17.5 cm (3)

◆ gloves.

Anything removed from the first aid box should be replaced as soon as possible.

All incidents requiring first aid should be recorded in the salon incident book.

Never administer anything but basic first aid. If any further treatment is required then a health professional should be called.

At Level 2, you can administer basic first aid if you are trained to do so and competent. You should be aware of the location of any first aid boxes in the salon. If further assistance is required you should report the incident to the salon manager. Always ensure that the incident book is completed.

At Level 3, you should:

◆ ensure that adequate first aid boxes are provided within the salon and keep the contents well stocked and up-to-date;

◆ make all staff aware of the location of these boxes;

◆ ensure that there is a qualified first aider present in the salon during all opening hours;

◆ ensure that all first aid incidents are correctly documented and countersigned in the salon incident book.

Detailed information can be found online at: http://www.hse.gov.uk /firstaid/legislation.htm

HEALTH & SAFETY

Eyes can be rinsed out with tap water, or with sterile water contained in sealed containers.

TOP TIP

Check the first aid box regularly to make sure that items have not reached their expiry date.

TOP TIP

Cross contamination is the transfer of harmful bacteria from person to person and should be avoided or minimised as much as possible to lessen the risk of cross infection.

First aid box

Level 3

Further information is available online at: http://www.hse.gov.uk /pubns/indg453.pdf

Sharps container

Reporting of Injuries, Diseases and Dangerous Occurrences Regulations 2013 (RIDDOR Regulations)

This Regulation requires employers and other people who are in control of work premises to report and keep a record of:

◆ work related deaths;

◆ serious injuries;

◆ cases of diagnosed industrial disease or illness contracted at work causing incapacity to work for more than three calendar days;

◆ certain dangerous occurrences (near miss incidents).

Industrial disease such as dermatitis, a condition directly connected with hairdressing, is reportable. If a member of the public is injured while visiting the salon, this is also reportable.

Hairdressers work in close physical contact with their clients, often using sharp implements. It is therefore important to understand the principles of cross contamination in relation to life threatening **blood borne** diseases such as the human immunodeficiency virus (HIV) and Hepatitis B.

If a client is accidentally cut you must put on gloves and clean the area with damp cotton wool or antibacterial wipe. This will enable you to asses the severity of the cut. You should then give the client a piece of cotton wool or lint to apply pressure on the wound until the bleeding stops. This method is used because an individual will know the amount of pressure they can withstand which will avoid you applying undue pressure to the area and creating further damage. Next cover with a suitable dressing or plaster if necessary. Dispose of any contaminated gloves/plastic aprons/cotton wool/lint in a sealed plastic bag and dispose of following salon/HSE guidelines.

New clean sterile sharps such as razors must be used for each client and any used sharp must always be disposed of in an allocated sharps container. It is the salon owner's duty to find out from the local authority how this box is to be safely disposed of.

Reporting of accidents, injuries and damage

Salon incident book This is where all accidents and injuries occurring in the salon are recorded. In addition to this any serious confrontational issues between staff and clients or between different members of staff should be recorded in this book. It is a legal document and can be called upon by the authorities if there is any need for further investigation into an incident.

Damage to salon equipment, whether wilful or accidental, should be recorded in the incident book if applicable and/or in the equipment log for repairs or replacement.

The incident book must be kept up-to-date, signed and any follow up action taken where applicable.

It must be kept in a safe, secure but accessible place at all times.

The following information should be provided:

◆ the date and time of the incident;

◆ the name, age and address of the injured person;

◆ details of the injury or illness and the treatment given;

◆ what happened to the person following the treatment (e.g. whether they were well enough to leave without further medical attention).

The book should be signed by the person giving the treatment and be checked and countersigned by the manager working at the time of the incident.

Employers Liability (Compulsory Insurance) Act

All employers are bound by law to provide adequate insurance to compensate any member of staff who sustains an injury or becomes ill as a direct result of their work. An Insurance Liability Certificate should be visibly displayed in all salons.

Personal hygiene

As a hairdresser you will be working in close bodily proximity to your clients. The image that you project and your standards of hygiene must be immaculate. You will more than likely be working very long hours in active, warm environments so you must always pay attention to personal cleanliness.

Body care

Regular cleansing twice a day, together with antiperspirant deodorants, should prevent body odour and control perspiration. Showers are quicker than baths and more hygienic. While washing, you should concentrate on genital areas, under arms and the feet. The feet have a tendency to smell because they have more sweat glands, breed bacteria and, spend most of the day enclosed in shoes.

Skin   Keep your skin healthy by following these suggestions:

◆ Cleanse tone and moisturize skin regularly. Many moisturizers now offer protection against harmful **UVA** and UVB rays.

◆ Regular facials remove dead skin and control spots.

◆ Optionally, you can tidy eyebrows, facial hair and wear light make-up.

Hair care   Hair should be clean, trimmed, healthy and always neat. The style should be modern and current. Clients depend on their stylists to keep them up-to-date with the new trends. Unkempt hair could reflect a negative and unprofessional attitude to your trade.

For health and safety reasons, long hair should be tied back to avoid becoming tangled in equipment or coming into contact with clients. Wash your hair regularly to prevent it becoming lank and to reduce sebum on the forehead.

Oral care   Halitosis or unpleasant breath is more often than not a direct result of bad oral hygiene. It can be caused by:

◆ not cleaning the teeth and mouth sufficiently, leaving food trapped between teeth;

◆ eating strong-smelling or highly seasoned foods, such as garlic, onions, coffee;

◆ not visiting the dentist regularly to identify dental problems;

◆ smoking;

◆ digestive problems;

◆ not eating regularly.

Hands   Your hands must be well cared for at all times. Your nails should be regularly manicured to prevent nail breakage. Broken or damaged nails may scratch your clients and tear and pull their hair. Chipped nail varnish looks untidy and unprofessional and it is easy and quick to remove it. Cuts should be kept covered until healed. Warts should be medically removed.

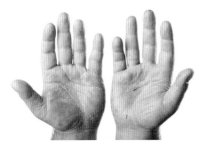

Dermatitis

Dermatitis   Continuous use of shampoos and hair-processing chemicals can cause contact dermatitis. The skin becomes inflamed with a dry, irritable rash that spreads rapidly, in extreme cases covering the entire body. This can permanently damage and discolour the skin and nails.

About 70 per cent of hairdressers suffer from dermatitis. It is a health and safety regulation (and also very sensible if you wish to engage in a long career in hairdressing), to protect your hands. Wearing protective gloves and the continuous use of barrier and hand creams can help. Also make sure that you dry your hands thoroughly.

Level 3

At Level 3, you should ensure policies and practices are put in place and implemented to combat dermatitis. Ensure that any members of staff with signs of dermatitis receive correct medical attention. Keep a record in the salon incident book.

The HSE poster shows the five steps which can be taken to avoid dermatitis and would be useful to display in your place of work.

Clothes

Clean, neat, comfortable and fashionable clothes help to complete the picture of a positive attitude and a person who pays attention to fashion. Natural fibres such as cotton and linen are preferable as they allow the skin to breathe and will not absorb body odour. Clothes should not be revealing and underarms should be covered. Some salons require stylists to wear a uniform to promote a corporate image. Wear your uniform with pride – do not give the impression that you resent it.

Jewellery Rings, chains and other jewellery should be kept to a minimum as they could catch on clients' hair or skin when carrying out salon services. Wearing rings also increases the risk of dermatitis because water can collect underneath them and they make it impossible to dry your hands properly. Chemicals used in the salon could also cause jewellery to tarnish.

Footwear The shoes you wear at the salon must be comfortable and easy to clean, low heeled and made of natural fibres such as leather, to allow the feet to breathe. Fashionable shoes are not always designed for comfort and can cause the feet to become increasingly painful after hours of standing.

High heels throw the body forward and can lead to bad posture and fatigue of the feet. Low or medium heels are more comfortable. The shoe should grip the heel and cover the instep and toes to prevent entry of stray hairs into the skin. Sensible footwear and possibly support tights, can help prevent your feet aching and ankles swelling after a long day spent standing. Remember to wash your feet regularly.

Bad hand days poster

Posture

Standing for long periods of time causes tired feet, swollen ankles and backache, among other things. These are all problems that hairdressers are familiar with. The way a person stands, sits and walks is known as posture, and you should be aware of your posture in order to reduce aches and permanent injury. An individual's posture depends on the skeleton, ligaments which hold it together and the muscles which help movement. Good posture means that the muscles do not tire easily and cause damage and injury.

While standing you should:

◆ stretch the body upwards;

◆ position the spine in a natural curl;

◆ contract the stomach muscles to keep the back erect;

◆ distribute the body weight onto both feet, shoulder width apart;

◆ wear low-heeled shoes to reduce pressure on legs and ankles.

Standing for long periods of time tends to cause swelling of feet and eventually varicose veins in the legs. When you are walking around, the action of your leg muscles helps to return circulation of blood and lymph from your feet and legs. However, this does not happen when you are just standing and blood and lymph tend to accumulate in your feet and lower legs, causing swelling.

Exercise is one way of controlling the swelling. Brisk walking and cycling strengthen muscles and also help improve your circulation. Whenever possible, always try to elevate your feet as this helps the blood flow.

Hygiene in the salon

In order to appear professional and organized, tools, products and equipment should be set up prior to the arrival of the client alongside the client's record card. The salon environment, including the areas that clients do not see, should be kept as clean as possible at all times. Regular and correct methods of cleaning will reduce the transfer of bacteria thus reducing the risk of cross infection between clients. All spillages should be cleared up immediately to avoid further accident or injury, i.e. slipping.

All floors should be:

◆ made of a non-slip surface, such as vinyl, which can be easily cleaned;

◆ clean at all times – regularly mopped, swept and/or vacuumed;

◆ marked by a visible notice when cleaning is in progress;

◆ cleared of hair, which should be swept up after each cut and placed in covered bins.

Chairs should be:

◆ made of a washable fabric, such as vinyl, or any fabric that is easily wiped;

◆ washed with a detergent daily;

◆ wiped with alcohol or disinfectant daily.

Trolleys should:

◆ be clean;

◆ have removable trays, preferably plastic;

◆ be washed with detergent daily.

Salon interior

Rollers and perm rods should be:

◆ cleaned after each use by removing hair and disinfecting or washing in detergent;

◆ sorted into colours, sizes and shapes or types, etc.

Mirrors should:

◆ be cleaned daily with glass cleaner and/or hot water.

All reading material (literature and magazines) should be:

◆ current and appropriate to suit clientele;

◆ kept tidy in a rack and free from damage if possible.

When sterilizing combs and brushes use the following procedure:

◆ remove all hair;

◆ wash in warm soapy water;

◆ soak in disinfectant;

◆ rinse and dry before use;

◆ always follow manufacturer's instruction on the use of disinfectants.

Gowns and towels   Gowns must be washed daily. Towels must be washed after every use in hot soapy water to remove soils and smells and to kill germs and thereby prevent the spread of infection. Ensure that there are enough clean gowns and towels to meet the demands of the salon day.

Tools   Ideally, tools should be used on just one client and then cleaned. All traces of hair should be removed and tools should be soaked in disinfectant before use with the next client. Tools that fall on the floor must be cleaned and sterilized before they are used again and placed in the tool bag to avoid contamination.

Metal surgical instruments, such as scissors and razors, are cleaned by wiping with an antiseptic swab or surgical spirit.

Sterilization

Sterilization is the complete destruction of all living organisms on an object. However, once sterilized items are exposed to the air they are no longer sterile. The process can be carried out with the use of heat, vapour, chemicals, and radiation.

Heat sterilization   Different methods of heat sterilization use dry or moist heat.

◆ **Dry heat.** Traditionally, a dry, hot air oven was used. The heat reached a temperature between 150°C and 180°C, and had to be maintained for 30–60 minutes without disturbance. Nowadays, a glass bead sterilizer is often used instead. This is excellent for small tools, which are placed on electrically heated small beads which channel the heat.

◆ **Moist heat.** This is the process of steaming tools under pressure in an autoclave, using the same principles as a pressure cooker. The units are automatic and increase the pressure on water to 32 lb/in^2 which raises the boiling temperature to 134°C. This means complete sterilization only takes 3–4 minutes and tools can be returned for use very quickly. Although this method is very effective it could cause rusting and distort plastics.

Vapour sterilization   The gases used in vapour cabinets included ethylene oxide and formaldehyde. These are too hazardous to use, and vapour sterilization has now been replaced with other methods.

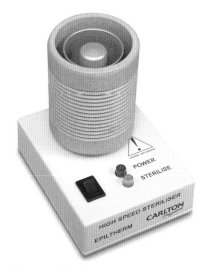

Glass bead sterilizer

An autoclave

Barbicide

Ultraviolet cabinet

Chemical sterilization

◆ **Disinfectants.** These liquids destroy a large majority of microorganisms. Solutions such as quaternary ammonium compound (quats) or glutaraldehyde (e.g. Barbicide) work against bacteria and fungi to remove contamination by coating them or drying them out. They are very suitable for salon use and chemicals can be added which inhibit rust, thus making disinfectants suitable for most tools.

◆ **Antiseptics.** These liquids prevent the rapid growth of microorganisms but are not permanent and do not kill microorganisms. They are kinder than disinfectants and effective enough to be used on the skin.

Radiation sterilization
Ultraviolet rays destroy microorganisms. They are produced artificially by mercury vapour lamps in an ultraviolet cabinet. However, the UV rays are harmful to skin and eyes. In modern cabinets, the UV lamp automatically switches off when the door is opened.

Germs absorb the radiation and die, but as ultraviolet light travels in straight lines, the tools must be turned after 20 minutes, and even then the rays do not get into the corners. Although anything can be sterilized by ultraviolet, it is time-consuming and not very effective. Before sterilization, tools must be washed to remove grease (which will protect germs) or any oils or product build up which may prevent full sterilisation and killing of all germs.

Ventilation

Ventilation is the process by which stale air is replaced by fresh air. Humans alter the composition of the air in the salon by breathing and perspiration. The oxygen in the air will be reduced while the carbon dioxide will increase. This leads to feelings of exhaustion and sluggishness. Ventilation in the salon also helps reduce the high levels of humidity which can prevent the body from cooling itself properly. Ventilation can be achieved naturally or artificially.

Natural ventilation
This makes use of the natural flow of air in the environment. The air should be changed three or four times an hour. The cool air must not enter the room below shoulder level and should be directed upwards.

Two methods provide natural ventilation without uncomfortable draughts:

◆ **A coopers' disc** provides some control of the incoming air. The inner disc is rotated so that its holes coincide with similar holes in the window.

◆ **Louvred windows** consist of movable strips of glass which may be used as air inlets or outlets according to their position.

Artificial ventilation
This is commonly known as air conditioning. The air moves freely by itself and does not need any special treatment. Efficiency is calculated by multiplying the room volume by the number of complete air changes required per hour.

Fans
Room fans do not ventilate, they only circulate air. Extractor fans remove fumes and dust from the air, but do not provide ventilation.

Security

As most salons have a high level of public access, diligence is required on the part of both staff and clients. Staff should be discouraged from bringing valuable personal property into work. However a lockable room or cupboard should be available for safe storage of handbags, purses etc. while at work. Clients should be advised to keep their valuable property with them at all times.

Cash should be kept in a locked till with limited access either through the receptionist, manager or a delegated member of staff. On busy days the till should be emptied regularly leaving only a cash float. The size of the float is usually determined by the proprietor. Any discrepancies in the till balance should be reported and investigated to check for error. If the discrepancy remains then this should be recorded and reported to the manager or senior in charge.

Insurance

There are a range of insurance products available that are beneficial to the hairdresser, depending on the type of business. Insurances can be tailored to meet the needs and size of the business. It is advisable to seek advice from a professional insurance broker. Independent hairdressers should also register with the Hairdressing Council to receive state registration which will provide access to advice on good insurance packages.

Public liability insurance
This covers any awards of damages given to a member of the public because of an injury or damage to their property caused by you or your business. It also covers any related:

- legal fees;
- costs;
- expenses;
- hospital treatment.

General health and well-being

Working in a salon can be physically exhausting and mentally draining. Hairdressers are often required to work long hours standing on their feet in humid, stuffy atmospheres. Regular breaks are important. If possible, leave the premises to get some fresh air.

A separate area for staff to eat and drink in should be provided away from chemicals and hair products. Uninterrupted breaks of 20 minutes should be taken at a minimum of every six hours according to Working Time Regulation 1998.

Working with a computer for sustained periods can give rise to problems related to poor posture, and headaches related to eyestrain can be caused by long hours in front of the screen. These are not problems commonly associated with hairdressing but they may need to be addressed if you have a permanent receptionist.

The salon handbook

The salon handbook allows the owner to communicate what is expected of each member of staff during the term of their employment. Each new member of staff should be issued with a copy.

The contents of the salon handbook are key to setting the standards that the workplace demands. It should be a well thought out document which is easy to read and understand.

The salon handbook should contain information on things such as:

- salon opening time and staff working hours;
- code of conduct;
- dress code;
- fire procedures;

TOP TIP

If you have an unsupervised cloak area, a notice should be posted in plain view stating that customers place their possessions there at their own risk.

You can find information about insurance through the hairdressing council at: http://www.haircouncil. org.uk/pages/whyreg.html

TOP TIP

A copy of the salon handbook should be kept at the reception.

TOP TIP

The salon handbook should be reviewed and updated regularly, taking into account any relevant changes to the way that the salon is run.

◆ emergency telephone numbers;

◆ location of first aid box (and possibly some basic first aid information);

◆ the accident/incident reporting procedure;

◆ some basic health and safety guidelines relating to everyday salon activities;

◆ salon cleaning schedules;

◆ correct reporting procedures;

◆ the chain of command within the salon;

◆ how disputes, problems and incidents will be settled within disciplinary procedures;

◆ salon security procedure;

◆ guidance on where to find further information on any of the above.

At Level 2 it is your responsibility to read and understand the contents of the salon handbook.

At Level 3 it is your responsibility to ensure that the salon handbook is current and up-to-date. You should also make sure that all staff are issued with a copy of the handbook and that they adhere to the policies, standards and procedures it contains.

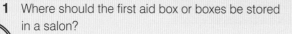

REVISION QUESTIONS

1 Where should the first aid box or boxes be stored in a salon?

1 In accessible locations throughout the salon

2 By reception

3 In the staff room

4 In the dispensary

2 Why is it important to keep hair swept up off the floor?

1 To keep the salon looking clean and tidy

2 Because someone could slip on it

3 To collect the hair for wig-making

4 To maintain a professional salon image

3 Why is it important to be observant of your salon environment from a health and safety point of view?

1 To learn new hairstyling techniques from other stylists

2 To be aware of when another stylist may need assistance

3 To be able to spot a potential hazard

4 To ensure the salon is kept clean and tidy

4 Why is it important to keep the salon incident book up-to-date, signed and in a safe place?

1 To keep a reminder of anything important that happened in the salon

2 To leave messages for the manager

3 Because it is a legal document that can be called upon in the case of an investigation

4 To provide information for other stylists in the salon

5 Which of these abbreviated regulations control the use, storage and disposal of harmful substances?

1 COSHH

2 HSE

3 RIDDOR

4 PPE

6 Which injury is most likely to be sustained as a direct result of an electrical shock?

1 Broken bones

2 Burns

3 Stomach cramps

4 Hair loss

7 Why is it important to follow manufacturer's instructions when using products?

1 To save time

2 To prevent waste of product

3 To reduce the risk of causing harm to the client

4 To look professional

8 Which one of the following fire extinguishers should be used on a 'class A' fire involving paper, hair and wood?

1 Foam extinguisher

2 Dry powder extinguisher

3 Water extinguisher

4 CO_2 extinguisher

9 Which one of the following is the employee's responsibility under the Health and Safety at Work Act 1974?

1 To keep the salon clean to prevent infection and cross contamination

2 To carry out risk assessments

3 To provide secure lockers for client's property

4 To ensure all electrical equipment is PAT tested

10 What is your employer's responsibility under the Personal Protective Equipment At Work Regulations 1992? (PPE Regulations)

1 To report low levels of PPE stock

2 To wear PPE when using chemicals

3 To provide PPE required for work

4 To dispose of PPE

11 What is the correct way to stand to maintain good posture?

1 Feet flat on the ground, shoulder width apart

2 Feet arched, spine curved

3 Legs bent, back straight

4 Weight shifted between both legs

12 Why is it important to keep up with current legislation?

1 So that you can keep up ahead of your competitors

2 Because the policies are always being reviewed and updated

3 So that you know how to present the salon in a good light

4 To be able to provide information to your clients

13 What is the purpose of a risk assessment?

1 To evaluate and ensure safe working practices

2 To record and check all electrical equipment

3 To measure and record stock levels

4 To train and document stylists' achievements

14 Which of the following should be covered in a fire risk assessment?

1 The contents of the first aid box

2 The security of the premises

3 The contents of the accident report book

4 Regular check and maintenance of fire fighting equipment

15 What colour is the label on a CO_2 extinguisher?

1 Yellow

2 Blue

3 Black

4 Red

16 Why is it important to maintain good posture?

1 To reduce aches, pains and permanent injury

2 To increase height when wearing flat shoes

3 To prevent portraying an unprofessional image

4 To make the clients feel comfortable

17 What is the employer's responsibility under the Provision and Use of Work Equipment Regulations 1988 (PUWER)?

1 To make sure that all equipment is PAT tested and results recorded

2 To ensure all equipment is suitable for the purpose for which it is intended

3 To ensure products are used and stored correctly

4 To ensure that risk assessments are documented

Level 3

2 Hair characteristics

LEARNING OBJECTIVES

This chapter covers the following:

◆ Analyzing the hair, skin and scalp

◆ Advising clients on hair maintenance and management

KEY TERMS

Arrector pili muscle
Consultation
Keloid
Melanin
Pediculosis capitis
Pityriasis capitis

Sebaceous gland
Seborrhoea
Sudoriferous gland
Tinea
Traction alopecia

◆ Provide client consultation

INTRODUCTION

This chapter provides the knowledge of hair characteristics that you will need when you undertake a consultation and analysis, which are covered in Chapter 3. In this chapter we will examine the structure of hair and how it grows. We will also look at a range of infectious and non-infectious conditions that you should be able to recognize.

The structure of the hair

Hairs are thin fibres which cover the majority of the skin surface with the exception of the palms of the hands, the soles of the feet, the lips, the eyelids and the area of skin between the fingers and toes. The main function of hair is to act as:

◆ a buffer to diffuse effects of blows and knocks;

◆ an insulating layer around skin when temperature drops;

◆ a warning mechanism – an indicator to any foreign objects on skin, in ears or nose;

◆ a sense organ – sensitive to touch due to nerve supply connected to each hair follicle;

◆ protection for delicate organs. In these areas hair is more dense, for example, around reproductive organs, brain and under arms.

The hair is made up of three layers: the cuticle, the cortex and the medulla.

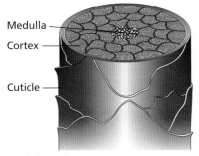

Medulla
Cortex
Cuticle

The hair shaft

The hair cuticle

The cuticle is the outer layer of the hair and its main function is to protect the cortex. The scales are elongated, flattened and overlap each other from the roots to the tips (like tiles on a roof). The scales are colourless, translucent and easily damaged. A healthy cuticle surface will reflect light, making the hair glossy and shiny. It will feel smooth when felt from roots to ends. An unhealthy cuticle will not reflect light, making the hair look dull. The cuticle scales are raised and feel rough when felt from roots to ends. This is the case with porous or over-processed hair. Curly hair may look dull and feel rough to touch. This is due to the cuticle scales not lying flat, as they follow the crests and waves of the curl contour some of the cuticle scales will be open, causing the rays of light to be diffused. Straighter hair types that have not been chemically processed may be better at reflecting light as the cuticle is flatter due to genetic make up.

The hair cuticle

The cortex

The cortex makes up the main bulk of hair and is home to all the chemical bonds (sulphur bonds, salt bonds and hydrogen bonds) and colour melanin/pigment (eumelanin and pheomelanin). The tensile strength and elasticity of the hair is also held in the cortex.

CORTEX
Contains natural colour pigments

CUTICLE
Can be many layers thick

MEDULLA
Not always present

Cross-section of hair

The cortical cells are long and thin and composed of small bundles of macrofibrils. These are made up of bunches of even smaller microfibrils, which in turn are made up of bunches of protofibrils, all held together by cross bonds. These bonds determine the elasticity, texture and curl of the hair.

A cross-section of African-Caribbean hair will show how flat the cortex is, in comparison with Caucasian and Asian hair. The flatter the hair, the faster it will absorb chemicals. The cortical thickness will also vary. This is why African-Caribbean hair is easily damaged.

African-Caribbean hair has both a para and ortho cortex.

Para cortex: the cortical fibres grow in an even, uniformed cylinder; the cells are tightly packed together. Present in straight hair, European and Asian hair. The hair will absorb liquids at an even rate.

Ortho cortex: the cortical fibres grow in an uneven formation following the contours of the wave and curl. Present in curly hair. The hair will absorb liquids at an uneven rate.

TOP TIP

The number of cuticle layers differs between ethnic groups. In Caucasian hair there are normally four to seven layers. Afro hair has seven to eleven layers. Asian hair has eleven or more, making it more resistant to chemicals.

Wavy hair has a partly para cortex. The cortex of African-Caribbean curly hair is a combination of para and ortho cortex – the para cortex develops on the outside of the curl and the ortho cortex is present on the inside of the curl. Close examination of a strand of curly hair clearly shows the para and ortho-cortex, in that some parts of a single strand will be thinner and other parts thicker.

'Para' cortex   'Ortho' cortex

African type hair structure

The cortex of African type hair

The medulla

The medulla is the central core of the hair, consisting of rigid tunnels of cells filled with air spaces running either continuously or intermittently through the hair. A medulla is present in most types of hair, with the exception of very thin hair. The medulla has no function that we know of, but may be responsible for how thick or thin the hair is.

Hair classification

In the past, hair was sometimes classified by ethnicity:

◆ **European hair**. Loosely waved or straight;

◆ **African type**. Tightly curled or wavy;

◆ **Asian hair**. Coarse and straight.

Hairdressers have long understood that the picture was more complicated than this and nowadays hair is classified according to its curl. Four main types of hair are recognized:

◆ straight hair;

◆ wavy hair;

◆ curly hair;

◆ very curly hair.

Within these broad types, you need to be aware of different types and textures of hair, as shown in the table. It is important to recognize these distinctions because they will affect how the hair behaves and how you should treat it.

In curlier type hair you will find differing degrees of curl patterns which may be more than type 2, 3, and 4 listed. For further information see CHAPTERS 16.

Type of hair	Thickness	Definition
Type 1: Straight hair	1a: Fine/Thin	Hair tends to be very soft, shiny, difficult to hold a curl. Hair also tends to be oily and difficult to manage.
	1b: Medium	Hair has lots of volume and body.
	1c: Coarse	Hair is normally extremely straight and will usually set well. Asian hair usually falls into this category.
Type 2: Wavy hair	2a: Fine/Thin	Hair has a definite 'S' pattern. Normally can accomplish various styles.
	2b: Medium	Hair tends to be frizzy and a little resistant to styling.
	2c: Coarse	Hair is resistant to styling and normally very frizzy; tends to have thicker waves.
Type 3: Curly hair	3a: Loose curls	Hair tends to have a combination texture. It can be thick and full with lots of body, with a definite 'S' pattern. It also tends to be frizzy.
	3b: Tight curls	Hair tends to have a combination texture, with a medium amount of curl.

Type of hair	Thickness	Definition
Type 4: Very Curly Hair	4a: Soft	Hair tends to be very fragile, tightly coiled and has a more define curly pattern.
	4b: Wiry	Also very fragile and tightly coiled; however with a less defined curly pattern – has more of a 'Z' pattern shape.

Every individual has different types of hair on their body:

◆ **Lanugo** is fine downy hair covering the foetus. This is usually lost around the 32nd week of pregnancy. Some babies are born covered with a lot of lanugo hair, but this is lost within the first few weeks.

◆ **Vellus hair** is fine, soft hair which replaces lost lanugo hair over most of the infant body, and remains throughout life. Its growth rate is excessively slow. This type of hair can be seen clearly on the faces of some women.

◆ **Terminal hair** is coarse hair which covers the scalp, eyebrows, eyelashes, in ears and nose, under arms, legs, pubic areas and, in men, the chest and face.

◆ **Virgin hair** is the name given to hair which has not been subjected to chemical processes.

Hair shape

Hair shape in cross-section varies according to the curl type. Asian hair is typically circular in cross-section. In European hair the shape varies from oval to kidney while African type hair tends to have more of a flat, oval shape.

The hair above and below the surface of the skin is known as the hair shaft. Resistant hair has over 12 layers of cuticle, tightly packed together, making penetration into the cortex by chemical agents more difficult.

The curl pattern of hair is genetically determined before birth. The more bent and coiled the hair follicle is, the tighter the curl pattern will be with the bulb being virtually upside down in very curly hair.

Industry recognizes over 32 different curl patterns in African type hair, ranging from a very tight spiral curl to a very loose wave. On close examination, there may be three or more varying curl patterns on one head. Areas to note are the hairline, crown, nape, occipital and temple areas. You will find a variety of curl patterns (from wavy to tight curly) throughout Africa and the Diaspora. Hair will also vary in curl pattern due to inter-racial union.

straight hair — round
wavy hair — flat, oval
curly hair — kidney

TOP TIP

Always try to determine the natural curl pattern prior to processing the hair. Different curl patterns respond to chemicals in various ways. Establishing the more resistant curl formation is an important factor when selecting suitable relaxer and perm products.

Shapes of Hair Follicles

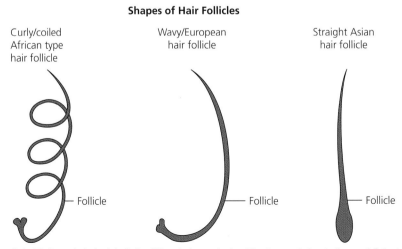

Curly/coiled African type hair follicle — Follicle
Wavy/European hair follicle — Follicle
Straight Asian hair follicle — Follicle

Spiral hair, curly hair, tight hair   Wavy hair or of mixed heritage   Asian Indian and Oriental type hair

The structure of the skin

The skin is composed of three main layers: the epidermis, dermis and subcutaneous layer.

Epidermis

The epidermis is the top layer of the skin that we see and touch. It differs in thickness depending on the area of the body that it supports. Epidermal skin is at its thinnest on the eyelids and is thickest on the palms of the hands and the soles of the feet.

Dermis

The central structure of the skin is called the dermis. Suspended in the dermis are blood vessels, nerve endings, hair follicles, sweat glands and their ducts, sebaceous glands and papillary muscles. The dermis is composed of collagen, elastin and fibroblast cells. The job of collagen is to support and add bulk to the skin. Elastin is there to give the skin its elasticity which allows the skin to expand and contract like an elastic band. Fibroblast cells manufacture the collagen and elastin fibres.

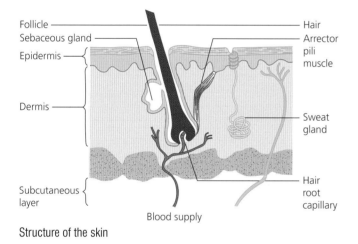

Structure of the skin

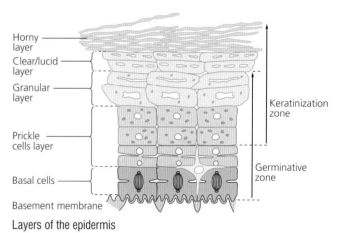

Layers of the epidermis

Subcutaneous layer

The third layer of the skin is the subcutaneous layer. This is a fatty layer which helps provide insulation.

Melanin

Melanin is a brown pigment found in the germinative layer of the epidermis (also found in the horny layer in African-Caribbean skin). When ultraviolet light stimulates the pigmented cells, the brown colour is transmitted to the skin's surface. Melanin acts as the skin's natural protector against the ultraviolet rays of the sun. It helps to filter the UVA and UVB rays that can be extremely damaging. UVA activates the melanin to produce a short-term, rapid tan and due to its deep penetration, premature ageing can be caused due to over exposure to sunlight. UVB activates vitamin D production and melanin, offering a more long-term tan, but is the cause of sunburn which can lead to forms of skin cancer, one of which is malignant melanoma.

HEALTH & SAFETY

Regardless of ethnicity, in very hot sunny conditions, sun protection should be used. The sun factor will depend on the conditions you are in. Some product companies also produce sun protection for the hair.

Chemical properties of the hair

Hair, nails and the horny outer layer of the epidermis are all made up of a protein called keratin. Smaller units called amino acids combine in various formulas, creating different types of protein. About 22 amino acids form proteins. They consist of atoms of the following elements in these proportions:

◆ carbon 50%;

◆ oxygen 21%;

◆ nitrogen 18%;

◆ hydrogen 7%;

◆ sulphur 4%.

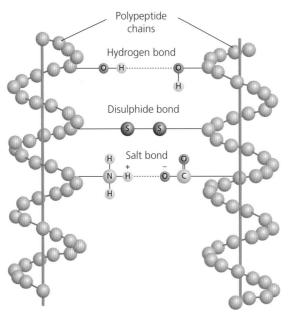

Polypeptide chains, showing linking bonds

For more information on the chemical properties of the hair, please see CHAPTERS 11 and 12.

Amino acids are joined together by peptide bonds to produce long polypeptide chains, which coil and fold like springs to form a spiral or alpha helix (α-helix). In the hair, these spirals lie parallel to each other.

Disulphide/sulphur and cystine bonds are the strongest bonds and they form the 'rungs' in a ladder-like structure, holding two polypeptide chains together. These are broken down by chemical relaxers and permanent waves (curly perms).

Hydrogen bonds

Hydrogen bonds are responsible for the elastic properties of hair. They break when the hair is stretched when set or blow-dried, and reform when it is dried, and the hair takes on the new shape from the blow-dry brush or rollers. When the hair is allowed to cool after any of these processes, the new shape curl or blow-dry movement locks into the hair, giving a more durable set or blow-dry. When the hair is in its natural condition before setting and blow-drying we call this state alpha keratin. When the hair has been stretched, set, blow-dried, thermally styled, tonged or straightened with electrical irons the hair takes on a new shape, and is described as being in a beta keratin state.

Hair is hygroscopic and can absorb moisture from the atmosphere, especially in moist and humid conditions, or when the hair becomes wet during shampooing or being in the rain. Once this happens the hair reverts back to its alpha keratin state.

You will find more information on what happens to the hair during styling in later chapters of this book.

Salt bonds

These bonds are easily broken by weak acid found in some shampoos or alkaline solutions. They are made up of two amino acids with opposite electrical charges.

> **TOP TIP**
>
> The more porous the hair is the more possible it is that the hair will not hold a curl for a long time. This is because the hair is damaged and lacks the ability to hold moisture. Setting and blow-dry lotions will assist in helping the hair to hold a curl better.

The formation of hair

The hair follicle grows from an indentation of the epidermis into the dermis. Follicles are normally found in clusters of three. Each follicle is about 4 mm deep and 0.4 mm wide, with the base widening out into a bulb. The walls of the follicle are made up of layers of connective tissue. Each follicle has its own **sebaceous gland** that opens into the follicle, lubricating the hair inside. Beneath the sebaceous gland is the arrector pili muscle that is connected to the nerve fibres.

The connective tissue sheath provides a constant blood supply to nourish the hair follicle. Attached just below the sebaceous gland is a network of nerve endings, surrounding and penetrating the connective tissue. These detect different types of stimuli, for example, temperature, pain and pressure.

Arrector pili muscle

The **arrector pili muscle** is a long tissue that extends from the outer root sheath about one third of the way up the hair follicle to the underside of the epidermis. In cold temperatures or when we experience fear, the muscle contracts and pulls the sloping hair follicle into an erect position. The erect hair traps a warm layer of air above the skin. The skin near to the follicle opening becomes raised, causing a 'goose bump' appearance. The muscle also acts as a warning device to detect the presence of small insects crawling on the skin.

Sweat glands

Sweat glands or **sudoriferous glands** cover the entire skin surface. Sweat is a watery secretion, consisting of 98 per cent water and 2 per cent salt. Perspiration occurs due to the discharge of the solution into long, slim ducts and then on to the skin through tiny openings called pores. The sweat cools the skin by evaporation.

There are two types of sweat glands. The smaller glands are called *eccrine glands*. They are independent of the hair follicle and open directly on to the skin surface. They produce a watery secretion, which can be controlled by regular washing and daily use of deodorants.

The larger glands are known as *apocrine glands*. These glands are attached to the follicle wall and open into the mouth of the follicle. They produce a waxy, milky emulsion, responsible for body odour. The odour can be controlled by regular washing and daily use of antiperspirant.

Sebaceous glands

Sebaceous glands are often referred to as *oil glands*. They are attached to the hair follicle and produce an anti-bacterial, waxy oil called *sebum* directly into the hair follicle, coating the surface of hair and skin.

A thin layer of sebum adds lustre and sheen to hair and skin. When the production of sebum is excessive the hair becomes lank and greasy, often seen in the nape area of wavy hair. However, under-production of sebum causes hair and skin to look and feel very dry and dull. This is more common in tight-curly hair, as sebum cannot successfully coat the hair when there are sharp bends and twists in the curl pattern. The curlier the hair, the longer it takes for sebum to travel up the hair shaft and lubricate the hair.

Hair growth

Terminal hair has three cycles: anagen, catagen and telogen.

Anagen　This is the growing stage and can last from two to seven years. The duration of anagen for each hair follicle is genetically predetermined. Hair grows approximately 1.25 cm per month. On an average adult head, 85 per cent of follicles are in anagen at any one time.

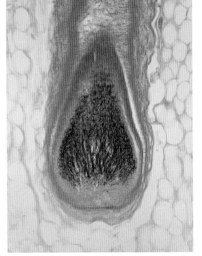

The hair papilla and germinal matrix

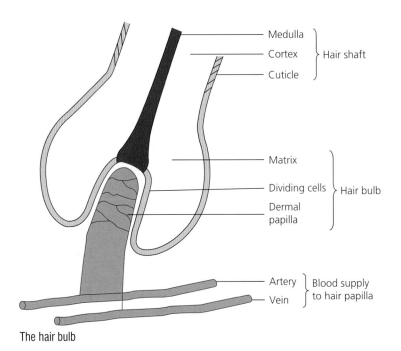

The hair bulb

The hair grows from the hair bulb, which contains the germinal matrix. The dermal papilla is the capillary network that provides the hair follicle with nourishment.

Catagen   This is the end of the growing period. All activity in the germinal matrix ceases. The blood supply from the dermal papilla is cut off. The lower part of the hair detaches from the base of the follicle, forming a club-ended hair, this stage normally lasts for a fortnight.

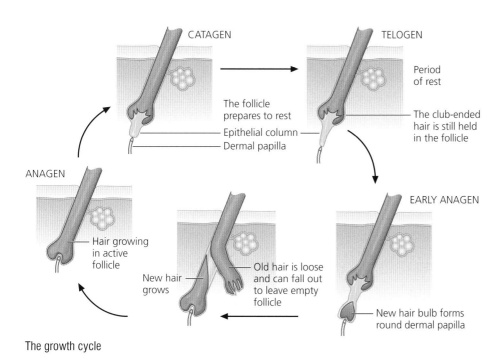

The growth cycle

Telogen   This is known as the resting stage. There is no activity in the hair follicle and this stage can last from three to four months. The dermal papilla will provide nourishment, while new cell division starts in the germinal matrix and the anagen cycle starts again. The new growing hair eventually loosens and pushes the old hair out of the follicle.

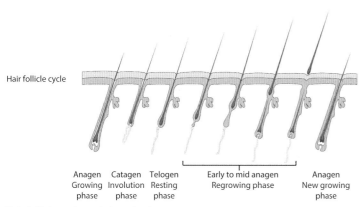

Hair follicle cycle

Hair follicle cycle and alopecia phases

TOP TIP

On average, 60–100 hairs are lost daily. One hair follicle may contain two or more growing hairs. One will be more dominant and larger than the others.

Hair colour

Natural hair colour is genetically predetermined before birth, but it can be lightened or darkened artificially by chemical treatments. Cells called *melanocytes*, which develop in the germinal matrix, produce granules of colour molecules called melanin or pigment. These colour molecules are evenly distributed throughout the cortex.

The colour largely depends on the amount of pigment production by the melanocytes. Pigments form the natural colour tones of the hair. They are usually yellow, brown, red, indigo or orange.

There are two main types of melanin:

◆ **Eumelanin** produces oval-shaped black and brown granules found in large quantities in dark hair.

◆ **Pheomelanin** produces long, thin, red and yellow granules found in small quantities throughout the cortex of fair hair.

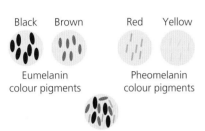

Black   Brown   Red   Yellow

Eumelanin   Pheomelanin
colour pigments   colour pigments

Natural dark brown hair

Hair colour pigments

Albinism

Failure of melanocytes to produce colour pigments in hair and skin results in a congenital condition called *albinism*. An albino has creamy white skin colour, yellowish-white to yellowish-red hair colour and pink eyes.

Grey hair

Grey hair is a mixture of coloured and white hair. This condition is normally a result of the ageing process, but can also occur as a result of medication and illness, leading to the absence of melanocytes in rejuvenated hair follicles, producing colourless hairs.

Albino male

Factors affecting hair growth and development

There are several factors that can affect the development of hair.

Diet   Our bodies depend on a balanced diet rich in vitamins A, B, C and proteins in order to produce healthy hair and nail growth. The hair shaft itself is dead. The actual nourishment from the dermal papilla goes directly to the newly forming hair cells in the germinal matrix.

Hereditary influences   The characteristics of hair largely depend on the genes passed on from our parents. An offspring receives 23 chromosomes from each parent. These chromosomes influence hair colour, length, texture, natural curl and baldness.

Age   Several changes take place in the hair follicles during our lifetime. At puberty the hair begins to thin, due to the onset of hormone production. Between the ages of 15 and 25, hair growth is at its most rapid, gradually slowing down as we become older. As new hairs replace old ones, they may differ in colour, texture, curl and thickness.

Climate   In warmer climates, where there is a greater amount of ultraviolet light (sunlight), growth will be accelerated. High, intense ultraviolet light will bleach and dry colour-treated hair.

See CHAPTER 14 Colouring hair using basic techniques.

Stress   Stress plays an important part in everyday life. It can have a negative effect on our general health and can result in hair loss (alopecia) and hair shaft disorders (e.g. monilcthrix).

Hormones   Hormones influence hair growth and sexual development. The levels of hormones change during pregnancy, puberty and menopause, all of which can cause diffuse hair fall. During pregnancy, many of the hair follicles which are due to enter catagen continue in anagen, therefore naturally increasing the density of the hair. When the levels of hormones fall after birth, these hair follicles all enter catagen at the same time, causing an excessive and potentially alarming hair fall.

Illness   Illness and diseases influence the hair growth cycle, by either slowing down or speeding up the growth rate. Such changes can cause hair and colour loss, and general thinning of the hair, which may occur a few months after the illness has passed. A microscopic examination of the hair shaft will reveal evidence of varying degrees of ill health.

Medication   Some drugs used to control illness can cause hair loss or baldness. For example, chemotherapy treatment for cancer can cause extreme hair loss.

Substance abuse   The continuous abuse of drugs and alcohol can cause premature hair loss, as vital organs and body systems function erratically and even start to shut down.

Hair and scalp conditions

You should be aware of conditions you may come across in the salon or during the **consultation** process. These include non-contagious conditions, contagious conditions and infestations that can be present in the hair or on the scalp or skin. Often the client will already be aware of the condition and may be quite sensitive about it, but you may also discover disorders that they are not aware of, or have not identified. Some of these disorders may require medical attention. Some may mean that you need to take extra precautions and others may mean that you should not proceed with any treatment. Advise clients to see their GP or relevant specialist.

TOP TIP

If you believe you have discovered a contagious hair, scalp condition or infestation, take care not to embarrass or alarm your client. Talk to them privately so that other clients cannot overhear. Do not try to diagnose their condition yourself. Refer the client to a GP or pharmacist. If you are unsure how to handle the situation, ask for help from a senior colleague. Ensure that the work station and any tools/gown/towel that have come in contact with the client are removed and washed/sterilised.

TOP TIP

Always comb the hair thoroughly as part of the consultation and analysis process from the nape upwards starting at the ends, up to the mid lengths through to the roots, until you reach the front hairline. Observe the scalp and hair carefully so that you do not miss something that could potentially affect other clients and staff.

TOP TIP

A trichologist treats conditions of the scalp and hair. A dermatologist treats conditions of the skin.

HEALTH & SAFETY

Cross infection is when a contaminated tool, towel or gown comes into contact with another client and they become infected.

The following tables provide a guide to the main conditions you are likely to come across.

As a stylist you will need to identify that there is something you are concerned about on the scalp or hair. Trying to become familiar with a range of non-infectious conditions will assist you in making a decision to refer a client to a GP, trichologist or dermatologist.

Non-infectious disorders of the scalp and skin

Name	Condition and symptoms	Cause	Treatment
Pityriasis capitis Dandruff	Excessive production of epidermal cells which triggers the onset of bacterial or fungal infections. Dry itchy flakes in patches on the scalp.	A dry scaling scalp caused by yeast-like fungal or bacterial infection that causes the epidermis layer to shed. Symptoms can be temporary, permanent or intermittent.	Regulate and control epidermal cell production by shampooing with mild anti-dandruff shampoos that work by removing the upper layer of the epidermis. In severe cases seek medical attention.
Psoriasis Psoriasis	A scaly condition of the skin. The keratin scales are dull and silvery; if scales are lifted, reddened, small bleeding points may be seen that affect the scalp, skin, elbows and knees.	A non-infectious condition caused by an increase in cell production, can be genetic and caused by stress. Normal hairdressing processes can be carried out, however do not use chemical applications if the psoriasis is in an active stage and the skin is broken on the scalp.	Referral to a general practitioner (GP) or dermatologist.
Eczema – Dermatitis Eczema – Dermatitis	The skin becomes dry, red and inflamed, can occur anywhere on the body.	External or internal factors can cause this complaint. It may be a physical irritant or an allergic reaction.	The stylist needs to protect their hands when using products in the salon to avoid getting dermatitis. Dry hands thoroughly and moisturize regularly. Wear gloves as a protection.

Name	Condition and symptoms	Cause	Treatment
Vitiligo Vitiligo	Complete loss of pigment in areas of the face or skin.	Loss of melanin at the site of an injury. Often the loss of pigment can be permanent. This is a cosmetic disfigurement. When melanin is no longer produced the skin becomes sensitive to ultra violet light.	Referral to a GP or dermatologist.
Keloid Keloids on ears	Overdeveloped elevated scars. Can be itchy and tender, then harden and become rubbery in texture.	Formed as a result of burns, scars, cuts or surgical wounds or irritated ear piercing.	Surgical removal tends not to be advised as scars can become unsightly. Treatment can involve steroids/ cortisone or irradiation and must be carried out under medical supervision.

Disorders that result from overproduction of the sebaceous glands

These conditions are not infectious but some of them may require medical treatment.

HEALTH & SAFETY

Always wash your hands regularly while working, then dry thoroughly and moisturize.

Name	Condition and symptoms	Cause	Treatment
Seborrhoea Seborrhea, excessive greasiness of the scalp and hair	Excessive greasiness of the scalp and hair.	Over-active sebaceous glands produce excessive amounts of sebum.	Keep the scalp, hair and skin clean. Avoid over stimulation and excessive massaging of the scalp during shampooing as this could further stimulate the sebaceous glands and produce more sebum. In extreme cases refer to a GP or registered trichologist.
Acne Acne	Overproduction of sebum which blocks the hair follicle opening, can start during puberty due to hormonal changes. Raised spots occur containing white pus and blackheads; the skin can become inflamed, irritated and sore. Scarring and disfigurement can occur in cases where the condition is prolonged.	A disorder of the hair follicle and sebaceous glands.	Referral to a GP, pharmacist, or registered trichologist.

Name	Condition and symptoms	Cause	Treatment
Sebaceous cyst Sebaceous cyst	Swelling of the sebaceous gland on the scalp or any part of the body. Forms a bump, lump or swelling that is soft to the touch, on the scalp which may be devoid of hair.	Sebum becomes trapped in the sebaceous duct, causing swelling anywhere from the size of a pea to a ping-pong ball.	Referral to a GP surgical removal.
Seborrhoea dermatitis Seborrhoeic dermatitis	A yellow greyish, greasy form of dandruff found around the hairline the nose and behind the ear or areas of excessive sebum production. The area under the scales can become red. Seborrhoeic means excessive oil and dermatitis means inflamed scalp.	An allergic reaction to over production of sebum.	Referral to a GP or trichologist.

Alopecia

Alopecia means loss of hair to the scalp. It can be found anywhere on the head, although it tends to affect the crown. The causes are not fully understood, but stress, hereditary factors, psychological pressures and hormonal changes can all play a part. Alopecia areata is one of the more common types of alopecia; the hair can grow back as soft white and downy surrounding the bald patch. The hair is later replaced by thicker strands of hair, giving a piebald appearance. Alopecia can be temporary or permanent. Traction alopecia is now one of the more common forms of hair loss seen in the salon. This is due to tightly pulled ponytails and hair extensions.

Name	Condition and symptoms	Cause	Treatment
Alopecia areata Alopecia areata	Circular or oval bald patches on the scalp; the condition can appear suddenly, sometimes overnight. The patch can be from the size of a small coin to the size of the palm of the hand. Sometimes the patches merge together. Affects both males and females.	Cause not fully known. Could be hereditary, caused by stress and/or psychological pressure.	Refer to a GP or trichologist.
Traction alopecia Traction alopecia	Hair loss due to traction or excessive tension on the hair.	Hair tightly pulled into tight plaits or a ponytail, or securing of extensions and hairpieces constantly in the same place.	Refer to a GP or registered trichologist.

Name	Condition and symptoms	Cause	Treatment
Cicatricial alopecia Cicatricial alopecia	Hair loss due to scarred tissue on the scalp.	Scarred tissue can be caused by injury or medical suturing, physical or chemical damage, burns after poor chemical or thermal application. Once damage occurs to the hair follicle it is permanent. No hair will grow between or around the scarred tissue.	Refer to a medical specialist or GP.
Alopecia totalis Alopecia totalis	Total, progressive loss of hair on the scalp, eyebrows and eyelashes.	This type of alopecia can be caused by trauma or shock.	Refer to a medical specialist or GP.
Alopecia universalis Alopecia universalis	Complete loss of body hair (a rare condition).	The hair follicle no longer replaces old hair with new hair. Once damage occurs to the hair follicle it is permanent.	Refer to a medical specialist or GP.
Post partum alopecia Post partum alopecia	Increased hair loss after pregnancy and thinning of the hair. Seen mainly on the crown.	The condition occurs due to reduced levels of hormone production after childbirth.	Refer to a medical specialist or GP.
Male pattern baldness Male pattern baldness	Loss of hair and thinning found mainly on the front hairline and crown of the head.	Can be genetic or due to hormones.	Refer to a medical specialist or GP. Micro hair transplants can be carried out under medical conditions.
Diffuse hair loss	General thinning of the hair over the vertex and top of the head. This is found in females.	Change in hormone levels – menopause, pregnancy, contraceptive pills and diabetes. Baldness may occur in old age. Also very rarely can be caused by an overactive or underactive thyroid, diabetes, fever and anaemia.	Referral to a medical specialist, GP or registered trichologist.

Other non-infectious conditions

Name	Condition and symptoms	Cause	Treatment
Canities Grey or white hair Canities – grey or white hair	Grey or white hair.	The hair lacks melanin/pigment produced by melanocytes resulting in a mix of white and coloured hair, making the hair appear grey. White hair has no coloured hair present.	No treatment apart from colouring the hair using permanent or quasi colour. Semi-permanent colour will not cover the white hair 100 per cent, but will help to blend white hair making it less obvious.
Monilethrix Monilethrix	Beaded hair along the shaft due to an uneven development of keratin. Irregular bumps along the hair shaft resembling a row of beads.	A rare hereditary condition.	None. Cutting the damaged hair can help.
Trichorrhexis Nodosa Trichorrhexis nodosa	Nodules on the hair shaft containing split hair, found on the middle of the hair length. The nodules contain split damaged hair resulting in breakage.	Found more in African type hair than other hair types. Caused by rough handling and the over use of physical heat and chemical damage.	None. Cut the hair regularly and apply a suitable programme of conditioning treatments that moisturize the hair; more careful combing and general handling.
Fragilitas crinium Split ends Fragilitas crinium: split ends	Split, dry, frayed ends.	Due to damage from physical or chemical processing and rough handling of the hair.	None. Apply a course of deep conditioning treatment and cut damaged hair.
Damaged cuticle Seborrhoeic dermatitis	Dry, dull, broken hair with a torn cuticle layer and rough to touch.	Physical or chemical damage to the cuticle surface.	Apply deep conditioning treatments and cut the hair.

Infectious conditions

Infestation by animal parasites

Parasites are insects that live off the blood of an individual and can cause irritation to the scalp. If you come across a client with an infestation, they should not be treated in the salon as these conditions are highly contagious. Recommend that they visit a pharmacy and purchase a suitable product to treat the infestation or visit their GP.

ACTIVITY

See how many of these conditions you come across in the salon on a daily basis.

Name	Condition and symptoms	Cause	Treatment
Pediculosis capitis Head lice Pediculosis capitis (Head lice)	Lice lays their eggs/nits at the root of the hair, usually in the darkest and warmest part of the head behind the ears. Lice are a parasite and feed off the blood of the person by piercing the scalp. After a period of incubation, the nits become lice. The scalp becomes very itchy due to the infestation.	An infestation of the head by lice and nits.	Referral to a pharmacist.
Scabies Scabies	The mite burrows its way between the fingers, wrists or elbows or wherever the skin folds or wrinkles and lays its eggs. Long red lines in the skin are covered with small lumps or blisters. Severe itching can be experienced.	An allergic reaction to the itch mite sarcoptes scabei.	Individuals suffering from scabies would be better using disposable towels rather than public hand towels to avoid cross infection. Refer to a GP.

If you find nits or any other contagious condition, act quickly to prevent cross infection and preserve the reputation of the salon. Dispose of any towels and/or gowns or sterilize by washing at over 100 degrees. Clean and sterilize all work surfaces and tools using a suitable chemical disinfectant and use an autoclave on tools.

Infectious factors

The human body is host to a large number of microorganisms. Some are harmless and some are harmful pathogens, i.e. they are responsible for infections and disease. Microorganisms are not visible to the naked eye, although their symptoms often are. Three types of pathogens are of great importance to the hairdresser:

◆ bacteria;

◆ fungi;

◆ viruses.

HEALTH & SAFETY

Nits are white or off-white in colour, depending on the hair colour. The colour of the nit will change (become brown) if the hair is treated with a chemical to kill lice and nits.

HEALTH & SAFETY

The egg or nit wraps itself around a single individual hair, it then cements itself on to the hair. To check for nits, gently pull the hair at the root where the nit has attached itself with the nails of the forefinger and thumb. If it becomes loose it is not a nit but if it stays secured it could be a nit.

Bacteria   These are microorganisms that inhabit the surface of the skin and hair. They reproduce rapidly when the surrounding conditions are favourable. They like the alkaline environment of body tissue and blood. Bacteria multiply by cell division (mitosis). They need seven requirements to multiply:

◆ food;

◆ moisture;

◆ time;

◆ warmth;

◆ oxygen;

◆ darkness;

◆ alkalinity.

Bacteria can be either aerobic or anaerobic. Aerobic bacteria use atmospheric oxygen, whereas anaerobic bacteria can live without oxygen. Most bacteria thrive at a temperature of 37°C. Higher temperatures usually kill bacteria but they can form spores which can survive high temperatures. Bacterial spores are the last things to be destroyed during sterilization.

Bacteria are classified according to shape:

◆ diplococci: round in pairs – pneumonia;

◆ streptococci: round in chains – sore throats, impetigo;

◆ staphylococci: round in bunches – boils, folliculitis;

◆ bacilli: rod-shaped – typhoid fever (Bacillus typhosus), diphtheria;

◆ spirochaetes: spiral-shaped – syphilis;

◆ vibrios: comma-shaped – cholera.

Name	Condition and symptoms	Cause	Treatment
Impetigo Impetigo	Blisters appear around the mouth and can spread to other areas of the face.	A bacterial infection of the skin.	Medication prescribed by a medical practitioner.
Folliculitis Folliculitis	Small raised spots around the mouth of the follicle area which can become raised and very sore.	A bacterial infection of the hair follicles. Found in hairy parts of the body.	Medication prescribed by a medical practitioner.

Name	Condition and symptoms	Cause	Treatment
Furuncles (boils) Furuncles (boils)	A red swollen painful bump or spot that is inflamed and filled with pus.	A bacterial infection of a follicle caused by the bacteria Staphylococcus or streptococcus pyogenes.	Medication prescribed by a medical practitioner.
Sycosis barbae In grown hairs in the beard area Sycosis barbae (shaving rash)	Removing curly/wavy hair against the natural growth pattern causes the hair to be pulled out of the hair follicle. The clubbed hair then springs back into its natural curl pattern and begins to grow in the follicle walls, beneath the epidermis.	The hair follicle then becomes infected by staphylococcal bacteria. This condition is found predominantly in Black males with African type hair.	Refer to a pharmacist or GP.

Fungi   Tinea is a condition caused by a fungus. It is also known as ringworm and can affect different parts of the body. Ringworm can be highly infectious and is easily passed from one client to another. It infects the skin, hair and follicle.

Name	Condition and symptoms	Cause	Treatment
Tinea capitis Ringworm of the head Tinea capitis (ringworm of the scalp)	A bald circular patch on the scalp with some broken hairs around the circle. The scalp is covered with greyish white scales.	A fungal infection of the scalp. It is most common in children and can be caught from direct contact.	Referral to a GP.
Tinea barbae Tinea barbae	A group of small circular boils with broken hairs projecting from the head and outer part of the circle.	A fungal infection of the beard. It can be spread through contact from person to person, animals, or tools.	Referral to a GP.
Tinea pedis Ringworm of the foot (Athlete's foot)	Small blisters which form between the toes.	A fungal infection of the foot.	Referral to a GP.
Tinea unguium Ringworm of the nail	The nail is yellowish grey in appearance, and becomes brittle and lifts away from the nail plate.	Fungal infection of the fingernails.	Referral to a GP.

Viral infections   These infections are airborne and can be spread from person to person. Disposable towels help avoid cross infection. Refer clients to a doctor to avoid spreading the condition.

Name	Condition and symptoms	Cause	Treatment
Herpes simplex Cold sore Herpes simplex (cold sore)	A burning prickly sensation, leading to blisters filled with pus and developing into a dry crust on the skin, lip, inside of the mouth and surrounding area.	This is a viral infection of the skin. It is believed to be triggered by ultra violet light.	Referral to a GP
Warts Warts	Warts are raised brown discoloured rough skin. They are found on the fingers, hands, face, body and the soles of feet.	A viral infection of the skin.	Referral to GP.

REVISION QUESTIONS

1 Which of the following conditions could be considered infectious?

   1   Dandruff

   2   Head lice

   3   Sebaceous cyst

   4   Seborrhea dermatitis

2 What do keloids look like?

   1   Overdeveloped elevated scars

   2   Lacking pigment

   3   Dry, red and inflamed skin

   4   Yellow flakes with seeping

3 What is hair loss in men called?

   1   Alopecia areata

   2   Bald spots

   3   Alopecia universalis

   4   Male pattern baldness

4 How would you identify dandruff?

   1   Oily scalp

   2   Dry scaling scalp

   3   Reddened scalp

   4   Itchy scalp

5 How would you protect your hands from dermatitis?

1 Drying, moisturizing and protecting the skin

2 Leave the skin to dry naturally

3 Not doing anything

4 Applying hairdressing hand serum

6 Sebum is produced by which gland?

1 Thyroid gland

2 Sebaceous gland

3 Sweat gland

4 Sudoriferous gland

7 How would you identify seborrhea dermatitis?

1 White flaky scalp

2 Grey flaky scalp

3 A yellow greasy form of dandruff

4 Abrasions on the scalp

8 Tinea capitis is a fungal infection of the head, what is it also commonly known as?

1 Ringworm

2 Impetigo

3 Herpes simplex

4 Scabies

9 Which of the following describes fragilitas crinium ?

1 Scarred tissue

2 Hair loss

3 Split ends

4 Physical damage

10 What is the resting stage of the hair growth cycle known as?

1 Anagen

2 Telogen

3 Catagen

4 Papilla

11 Which colour pigments does pheomelanin produce within the hair cortex?

1 Red and yellow

2 Yellow and brown

3 Brown and black

4 Red and brown

12 How many cuticle layers does African type hair have?

1 11 or more

2 4–7 layers

3 Less than 4

4 7–11 layers

3 Client consultation

LEARNING OBJECTIVES

This chapter covers the following:

◆ Establish client requirements

◆ Analyze the hair, skin and scalp

◆ Review options and agree on a course of action

◆ Advise clients on hair maintenance and management

KEY TERMS

Analysis

Closed questions

Consultation

Contra indications

◆ Provide client consultation

INTRODUCTION

This chapter covers the mix of technical skill, knowledge and client care you will need to carry out consultation and analysis which meets the client's requirements. Both junior and senior stylists carry out consultation and analysis. At the junior level, you need to be able to explain and identify how influencing factors will impact on the hairdressing service. You should be able to give advice on suitable products and services and make recommendations based on prior knowledge of products and techniques. You should record and update record cards in a clear and concise manner using the house style of the establishment. You also need to know when to request support from a more experienced member of staff.

It is the role of the stylist to carry out a consultation and analysis, accurately identify factors that limit or affect services, provide clear informed feedback to the client, agree a course of action, problem solve, discuss further salon visits, hair maintenance and product usage at home. You should also know when to refer upwards for specialist advice and support other salon staff. Your role also includes recording, checking and updating record cards regularly, ensuring they are written in a clear and concise manner using the house style of the establishment.

All stylists need to be aware of certain infectious and non-infectious conditions.

For details of infectious and non-infectious conditions, see CHAPTER 2, Hair characteristics.

Consultation and analysis

Before you provide any services for the client, you must undertake a **consultation** and **analysis**. This involves an examination of the client's scalp and hair and a conversation with the client about their wishes. Depending on the services the client requires, you may also need to conduct certain tests. In essence, you are looking for the answers to four questions:

1 What is the condition of the client's scalp and hair?

2 What does the client want?

3 Is the client's hair suitable for the services the client wants?

4 What services are you going to provide for the client?

The consultation and analysis process is a vital hairdressing service and must be carried out prior to any chemical hair-care treatment, cut or hairstyle.

Failure to carry out a thorough consultation and analysis could result in:

◆ damage to the scalp and hair loss;

◆ hair breakage;

◆ unsatisfactory end results for the client and a dissatisfied customer.

◆ Cross infection/infestation.

The results of the consultation can be used to develop a programme of conditioning treatments to the client, including colour or another service.

Where possible, consultation should be carried out in a quiet and calm environment. During this part of the process, the purpose is to relax the client and gather information through questioning and recorded responses. You also need to look at the client's scalp and hair and make informed decisions on a course of action, or if a service cannot be carried out. Your role is to make sure that the client is comfortable, confident and re-assured about the process and understands the service or services to be carried out and outcome to be achieved. You will find some suggestions on how to talk to clients later in this chapter.

TOP TIP

Always make sure the client knows of any problems and contra indications of why a process cannot be carried out. Make sure that the service to be carried out is reconfirmed to avoid any misunderstandings or errors taking place with the finished process or look.

TOP TIP

If you are unsure of your findings, ask for support from a senior stylist, manager or tutor.

Client consultation

What is the condition of the client's scalp and hair?

See CHAPTER 2 for details of infectious and non-infectious conditions you should look out for.

Comb the hair from the ends, working up the mid-lengths to the roots. Start at the back of the head and work up to the front hairline. The analysis process allows you look at the scalp and feel and examine the hair. During this process you should take into account the condition of the scalp and ensure there are no abrasions, alopecia, infections, infestations, or unnecessary redness. Check the hair is in good condition with no breakage occurring during the last chemical treatment or visit to the salon.

Observing the hair's texture, density, elasticity and porosity gives the stylist an understanding of:

◆ how strong the hair is;

◆ its ability to withstand a chemical and leave the hair in a good condition;

◆ the hair's suitability for the agreed cut, blow-dry or finished hairstyle.

Depending on the service that the client requires, you may have to conduct further tests to decide whether the service is compatible with the condition of their hair or scalp. These are described a little later in the chapter.

Analysis

What does the client want?

The client may have fixed ideas about the services they want, or may be looking to you for advice. Taking into consideration your client's lifestyle will help both you and your client come to a decision on the best style options. First of all you need to find out what your client's preferences are. What type of person are they? Have they got a busy lifestyle? Are they sporty and need an easy to maintain hairstyle? Do they have a family and want a fashionable, low maintenance look? Or perhaps they work as a lawyer, in business or banking and require a more corporate look. Discuss all of the options available and the likes and dislikes of your client to decide what hairdressing services might be best suited to them.

TOP TIP

When combing tangled, damaged or curly/wavy hair, hold the hair at the roots with the non-combing hand to avoid pulling hair and causing pain and discomfort to the client.

Choosing a style

Discuss your client's likes and dislikes because this will help you to tailor a style that they will like and enjoy. Find out if your client likes a low maintenance look, whether they want a fringe, what they want in terms of height and softness and whether they want their hair to cover their ears. Talk to the client about the overall cost to maintain the hairstyle and future long term costs of regular colour/lightening, cuts and relaxers to maintain the hairstyle.

Face shapes   When you create a hairstyle for a client, you need to take into account the shape of their face and head. It is said that the perfect face shape is oval because there are no irregular contours. When you style the hair you are trying to create the correct balance and shape for the face. The following table outlines six different face shapes with styling tips.

Face shapes and styling tips

Oval	Can wear any hairstyle.
Oval face	
Round	Needs height and not too much width on the sides.
Round face	Length can be left at the nape to create an illusion of length.
Square	Needs a hairstyle that creates softness against the angular lines.
Square face	Avoid creating width at the jawline.
Oblong	Requires fullness to add width.
	No height needed.
Oblong face	A fringe can be added to shorten the face.
Heart-shaped	Needs a style that will be narrow at the temples and wider at the chin. A fringe works well to narrow temples.
Heart-shaped face	
Diamond	Needs width at the temple and jaw or chin.
Diamond face	

Is the client's hair suitable for the services the client wants?

The following table gives examples of the type of questions you can ask to get the information you need, build up a history of the client's hair and identify any concerns.

Client history	Previous problems to be noted	Course of action to be discussed with the client
How was your hair and scalp since your last relaxer?	Identify any concerns with the last relaxer application, such as scalp irritation during or after the process such as abrasions, dry, itchy scalp or hair breakage.	Discuss irritation and possible causes, resolve client concerns. Discuss findings and action to be taken. Note if the client had no concerns. update the record card to reflect this.
How long is it since you last had your hair coloured? How frequently do you have colour applied?	What type of colour/lightener was used? Quasi, permanent, hi lift tint, semi or temporary colour?	Discuss the effects of using more than one chemical process on hair that has been previously coloured, lightened, highlighted, permed or relaxed.
Has lightener been used on your hair in the past?	What type of lightener (powder or gel) was used? Full head or highlights?	Discuss the effects of lightener on the hair. Discuss the current condition of the hair. Discuss how further chemical services may weaken the strength of the hair, meaning that future services cannot be carried out or the hair will need to be cut.
Have you used hair extensions in the past? How recently were your hair extensions taken out? How long were extensions in for?	Were there any problems experienced while wearing hair extensions such as itching or dry scalp? Were the extensions too tight?	Discuss the effects of extensions recently removed from the hair, prior to a relaxer, as this could cause the scalp to become irritated during the relaxer process, due to the combing to remove plaits or hair extensions which could have sensitized the scalp.
How often do you shampoo and condition your hair?	Are there any abrasions on the scalp? Does the hair feel dry or porous? Is there any evidence of breakage?	Advise on how frequent shampooing should be carried out. Discuss the type of aftercare products currently being used and if a change of product is recommended.

Natural movement and hair growth patterns

The natural movement of the client's hair may affect the decision about the style you provide. All curly hair has natural movement but this is not always seen clearly on very curly hair due to its dense appearance. Natural curl or movement is more commonly seen in curl patterns or short sculpture-cut hairstyles, worn by both men and women with straighter type hair. When we refer to natural movement we are describing any extreme changes in how the hair grows. A widow's peak is easily seen on African type hair and clearly noticeable on the front hairline; it is also noticeable on both Asian and European/white hair types. However, it is generally more difficult to identify other growth patterns on any curly or wavy hair type, regardless of ethnicity, in comparison with straight hair where growth patterns can be seen more easily.

The following table outlines hair growth patterns.

Growth pattern	Where found	How to deal with it
Widow's peak Widow's peak	Prominent point found at the front hairline.	The hair tends to work best when styled backwards; fringes are best kept long to avoid spiking.
Double crown Double crown	Two circular movements found on the crown and further back on the head on opposite sides.	Found on wavier hair; leave the hair longer in these areas to avoid spiking.
Nape whorls Nape whorls	Found in the nape; strong circular movement on either side of the head.	The hair needs to be left slightly longer so it will remain flat; alternatively cut the hair very close to the scalp to avoid spiking.
Cowlick Cowlick	Strong movement in the front hairline directing the hair to the right or left; found in straight and wavy hair.	Always cut hair in the same direction in which it naturally falls. Leave weight on fringes to avoid spiking and make the hair lie flatter.

Diagnostic tests

As part of your analysis you should carry out the following tests, prior to any chemical process, cut or hair styling. Diagnostic tests are performed in order to support and confirm previously established diagnosis. Not all tests are required for all clients. However, elasticity and porosity tests should always be performed.

Elasticity

Stretching a strand of hair to determine elasticity

Elasticity is the ability of the hair to stretch and return to its own length without breaking. Select a strand of hair and hold it between the index finger and thumb of one hand at least 12.5 mm (0.5 inches) away from the scalp. With the index finger and thumb of the other hand hold the hair near mid-length, leaving no more than 40 mm (1.5 inches) of hair between each finger. Stretching the hair between each finger and thumb will give an indication of the amount of stretch/elasticity the hair has. It will also indicate how strong or weak the hair is. If the hair snaps while stretching it has poor elasticity and is weak. If it stretches and goes back to its own length it has good elasticity and is strong.

Porosity

Porosity is the ability of the hair to take in moisture. Hold a few strands of hair between the index finger and thumb at the points. Use the index finger and thumb of the other hand to slide up and down the strands of hair. The rougher or bumpier the surface or cuticle of the hair feels, the more damaged or porous the hair is. Hair in good condition has a smooth feel as the cuticle is closed. The purpose of this test is to establish how porous the hair is (or is not), indicating how damaged the hair has become from previous chemicals or physical heat such as the use of straightening irons/wands/tongs, thermal processing and blow-drying.

Sliding the fingers along the hair to determine porosity

Hair texture

This identifies how thick or thin the diameter of a single strand of hair is. Hair texture falls into four categories:

- thick/coarse;
- medium/normal;
- fine/thin;
- very fine.

Select a few strands of hair and hold between the fingers. Look at each individual strand of hair and decide how thick or thin the hair is.

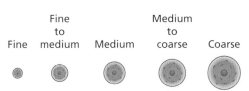

| Fine | Fine to medium | Medium | Medium to coarse | Coarse |

Hair texture

Looking at individual strands of hair

Density

Density is the number of hairs per square inch of the head. For example, you might have fine hair but if you have a lot of it, the density will be thick even though the individual hairs are fine.

Section approximately one square inch of hair on the scalp and twist the hair. This will give you an indication of how dense the hair is, e.g. thick, medium or thin (see illustration).

| Fine | Fine to medium | Medium to thick | Thick |

Hair density

Twisting the hair to determine density

Test curl

Other tests

Test curl   This is a test carried out during permanent waving to check the development of the curl during the process. The curl pattern is checked every three to five minutes after the perm solution is applied, by unwinding the rod and gently pushing the hair into an S shape. This indicates from how tight or loose the shape of the S curl is when the correct curl pattern is achieved and the perm is ready for rinsing and then normalizing/neutralizing.

Curl test/pre-perm test   This is a test carried out on the head before a full permanent wave is completed to determine the correct strength re-arranger, the roller size and development time. Apply rods with the required strength perm lotion to a section of the hair. Tests with different size rods and perm product can be applied to various sections of the hair to give an indication of:

◆ The suitability of rod size and perm product.

◆ The length of time the hair will need to be processed for.

◆ The condition the hair will be in after it has been permed.

Incompatibility test   This test is used to determine if there are any metallic salts present on the hair, which might affect any subsequent colour, lightener, relaxer or perm process. These salts are contained in colour restorers and enhancers. They react violently with hydrogen peroxide. Insert a clipping of the hair into the chemical to be used, look for discoloration, bubbling or hair breakage. Alternatively, take a hair clipping from a section of the hair where it is thickest. Apply Sellotape to one end of the hair cutting, immerse the other end into a small non-metallic bowl containing 20 parts of 20 vol/6 per cent hydrogen peroxide with one part basic perm lotion (ammonium thioglycolate). Do take care of fumes and process in a well-ventilated area.

TOP TIP

Carry out an incompatibility test on clients who have colour-treated hair with a green or brown hue as metallic salts may be present on the hair. Also on clients who may have used compound henna or progressive dyes.

Small beaker

Hair

No reaction – hair and product are compatible

Reaction (between chemicals in lotion and chemicals already on hair) – hair and product lotion are incompatible

Strand test   This test is used to check the development of a product during the colouring, lightening or relaxing process. Select a small section of hair for testing. Wipe the section with a suitably sized dampened strip of cotton wool, to see if the colour or lightener or relaxer has processed for long enough, or if the end result is even. Do remember that product companies give accurate times for colour completion. If your chosen process and colour choice is incorrect there is little you can do at this stage.

Test cutting   This test can be used for colouring, lightening or relaxing, to determine compatibility of the product to be used. Take a clipping of hair, apply the product to be tested to the unsecured section of the clipping. Leave to process according to manufacturer's instructions. Check after processing for any contra indications, such as breakage, excessive dryness, discolouration and general unsuitability of product. Any of the above contra indications identify that the process is not recommended.

Skin test/patch test/pre-disposition test   This test is used to measure the skin's reaction to permanent colouring agents. The test should be applied at least 24 to 48 hours prior to any colour application. Clean an area behind the ear or in the crook of the arm. Apply a small amount of the chosen permanent colour to the selected area with a cotton wool bud and remove any excess product. Do not use peroxide. Advise clients that if any sensitivity, redness, swelling, itching or irritation occurs they must go to the hospital immediately. Any contra indications or allergies to the product will mean that colour cannot be carried out.

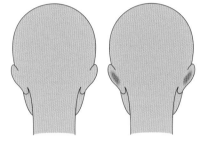

What services are you going to provide for the client?

This is the point at which you agree with the client on the services you will provide. It is important that you check that the client fully understands all the implications of these services, including cost, time and future maintenance of the style, and is happy for you to proceed.

TOP TIP

Some people suffer from severe reactions to permanent hair dye so a skin/patch test should be carried out regularly to avoid any allergic reaction, such as anaphylactic shock, due to the application of colour.

Visual prompts   Visual prompts or visual aids can be used to help clients come to decisions on the hairstyle they might like. They include hair magazines, online images and 'look books'. The use of a visual aid, coupled with questions on how long or short the client would like their hair, whether or not they want a fringe, and so on, can give you a visual picture of what your client might require in terms of hairstyle, cut, relaxer, plaits or colour/lightener. With new technology some salons are looking at creating a catalogue of images online. These images can be placed in folders in hand held devices and given to clients to inspire them. Images can also be collated into a style file to show clients while they are in the salon.

Looking at a colour chart can help a client select a colour or lightener. Colour swatches will allow you to show the client how warm, dark or cool the finished colour result will be.

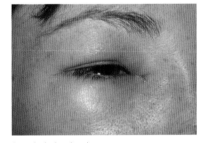

Anaphylatic shock

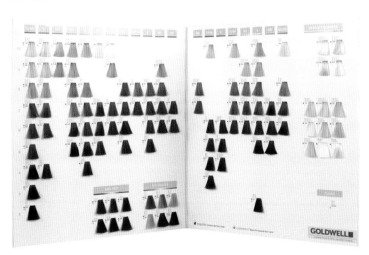

Timing Timing is important as it helps the stylist to work within time constraints and avoids clients becoming frustrated from waiting around too long. Time yourself for different applications to build up speed. Your salon and training organization will have specific times you must work within to complete a service or process. Assessments for training towards your qualification will also be time-based. Remember to break down the process and allocate timings for the following processes:

◆ consultation;

◆ shampooing and conditioning;

◆ application of treatments;

◆ chemical services;

◆ cutting;

◆ styling and finishing;

◆ aftercare advice.

Pricing Clients will often ask you about price and all stylists should know the prices of all the services provided within the salon. The information should be available in the form of a price list for services, which can be used as a reference point and given to the client. The price list should be displayed in a prominent place in the salon. If the salon has a web page, then individuals can be guided to use this resource.

Clients should be made aware of the cost of a service and also how often it will need to be delivered in order to maintain the hairstyle. Most salons have a pricing structure which means that it costs more for a senior stylist to carry out a service than it does for a junior stylist.

Talking to clients

Questioning the client, gaining feedback, identifying and confirming the client's wishes, deciding on a course of action and problem solving are all important parts of gaining the information you need to come to accurate decisions. Asking questions without appearing intrusive and insensitive is very much a skill that is acquired over time. Think about the question before asking and ensure it is relevant to the information you are trying to gain. Always remember, the purpose of asking questions is to gain a picture of the client's wishes and formulate a client history.

Open questions These are questions which cannot be answered with a simple 'yes' or 'no'. They are useful if you want to draw more information from the client. Some examples are:

◆ When was it that you last had a perm?

◆ Why do you like that particular hair style?

◆ Have you had any concerns with your scalp or hair since the last relaxer, perm, colour, lightener, cut or hairstyle?

Closed questions Closed question can be answered with 'yes' or 'no'. They do not encourage the client to give you any extra information and should generally be avoided. However, they can be useful when you are confirming information or decisions. Some examples are:

◆ Shall we go with this cut today?

◆ Would you prefer if we tried this new colour?

◆ Would you like to make another appointment to have that treatment?

Leading questions   These are questions where you lead someone towards a particular answer. They can make it difficult for clients to say what they really think and should be avoided. Some examples are:

◆ So you were quite happy with your last perm?

◆ So you haven't had any problems since I last saw you?

◆ You wouldn't want to risk that happening, would you?

TOP TIP

Why, How and When are standard ways of starting an open question. You may have to ask further questions if the initial question does not provide all the information you need.

ACTIVITY

Write down a list of open questions you can ask clients as part of the consultation and analysis process for different technical tasks you perform.

Creating a professional approach

You must present yourself in a professional manner. Always remember – first impressions count. The way you look or behave can attract or lose clients. As a junior or senior hairstylist, your personal appearance, hygiene, attitude towards clients and colleagues demonstrate your professionalism.

Your hair must be clean, well cut and styled. As a hairdresser you can help promote new looks and fashion trends. Your look could inspire clients to try a new hairstyle or colour.

Your clothes should be clean and fresh every day. It is important to avoid body odour by bathing daily and using deodorant. Brush your teeth regularly to avoid poor dental hygiene. Make sure your hands and nails are well groomed. Dry your hands thoroughly after washing and use barrier and hand creams to protect and moisturize your hands to avoid dermatitis.

As a professional hairdresser, your conduct is extremely important. You should always work in a proficient and professional manner and be respectful and loyal to your clients, colleagues and employer. All salons have their own ethos and standards they have set in codes of dress behaviour, creativity, innovation and the overall image portrayed to the public and industry at large. We call this the salon branding.

The following table lists some examples of unprofessional and professional behaviour and skills.

ACTIVITY

Look at the table and use the headings to think of some examples of unprofessional behaviour you have heard about, or observed yourself. Add them to the table, and then describe the professional way to handle these situations.

TOP TIP

Verbal communication is what we say and non-verbal communication is how we act. Both can be positive or negative.

Unprofessional behaviour	Professional behaviour
Courtesy	
Arriving late for appointments	Being on time for clients and appointments.
Failing to apologize if for reasons beyond your control you are late.	Welcoming, smiling, listening and being attentive to the client.
Chewing gum, smoking, eating or drinking when working on clients' hair.	Making the client feel comfortable.
Showing favouritism to some clients.	Treating all clients the same way.
	Taking breaks to avoid eating while working on clients.
	Refreshing your breath with mints or oral sprays or by sipping water.

Unprofessional behaviour	Professional behaviour
Communication	
Using aggressive tones. Not listening to clients. Being rude and argumentative. Grumbling and being moody. Using negative or aggressive body language. Not looking directly at clients and showing consideration.	Speaking in moderate tones and never shouting. Listening to clients when they are speaking and reconfirming requests. Smiling. Looking directly at clients. Showing empathy, patience and consideration.
Health and safety	
Not observing health and safety guidelines Cluttering work surfaces. Not cleaning work surfaces throughout the day. Not cleaning tools after each client.	Keeping the work area clean using sterilizing fluids or wipes. Cleaning and sterilizing tools after each client. Laying tools out in a professional manner. Preparing your work station and tools in advance. Cleaning up spillages immediately. Sweeping up hair cuttings regularly.

The junior stylist should understand the salon ethos, code of dress and promote the salon branding.

Stylist and staff have a duty to assist with the smooth running of the salon, ensuring clients are not waiting too long.

ACTIVITY

Develop a code of conduct booklet for the salon. Complete this task in conjunction with junior stylists and other members of staff to gain everyone's agreement. Include any relevant legislation such as health and safety, data protection etc. Also cover lunch, morning and afternoon breaks and state the time stylists should be in attendance before the start of work and procedures to be completed at the end of the working day.

As a professional hairdresser it is important that you maintain and update your skills. The following things can all help you do this:

- technical workshops/in house training;
- demonstrations;
- product company seminars;
- lectures;
- competitions;
- salon photo-shoots;
- product updates.

ACTIVITY

Use the guidance in the table to develop your own salon conduct sheet.

Stylists who do not keep in touch with changing trends could lose their clients or become bored with doing the same type of work. This could lead to a lack of motivation. As a stylist it is your responsibility to motivate both yourself and the client. If you are not aware of current fashion and trends you will not have the skills to create modern styles or be able to meet your client's requests.

Hairdressers Journal online
http://www.hji.co.uk/Home/

Client records

Recording information is all part of client care and demonstrates professional approach to your work. The record card holds a history of the services carried out for the client in the salon. Everything should be recorded, from complaints and concerns to the client being happy with the process and finished result. Client's records should be updated in a clear and concise manner on every visit to the salon or in between if a client rings or updates you of any changes.

Record cards can be kept electronically or on paper and should be updated immediately after each process. It is even better to keep them in both formats, so there will always be backup information, just in case an error takes place in any of the recording systems. Personal details such as telephone numbers and email addresses should be checked every time.

Data protection

You will be holding personal information on clients such as their address, age and profession. Clients must be assured of confidentiality throughout the process. The Data Protection Act 1998 (DPA) states:

◆ Data must not be disclosed to other parties without the consent of the individual concerned.

◆ Information can only be used for the purpose it has been collected for.

◆ The client can request in writing that data is not passed on for direct marketing by post as junk mail.

◆ Individuals have a right to access any information held about them on computer and paper records.

◆ If information held is incorrect individuals can request the information is updated and if the errors have caused distress to a client they can make a claim for compensation through the courts.

◆ Personal information may be kept for no longer than is necessary and must be kept up-to-date.

◆ Personal information may not be sent outside of Europe unless the individual whom it is about has consented or adequate protection is in place.

Record cards

Once information is gained from the client as part of the consultation and analysis process, a record card should be completed. The example here shows a basic format. There could also be a column for other information, such as allergies and medication. The design really depends on salon procedure and how detailed you or the salon feel the record card should be.

ACTIVITY

Create your own record card that would suit your client branding/image and processes carried out in the salon. Discuss with senior stylists or managers any additional areas to be included on the record card.

You can get further information on data protection online.
http://www.aimhigher.ac.uk /practitioner/resources /Data_protection_fact_sheet.pdf
http://www.bbc.co.uk /schools/gcsebitesize/ict /legal/0dataprotectionactrev1.shtml

CLIENT RECORD CARD

Name: _____   Address: _____

Telephone numbers: _____   Date first registered: _____   Age group:

Home: _____   ☐ 5–15   ☐ 16–30

Work: _____   ☐ 31–50   ☐ 50+

Stylist: _____

Hair condition: _____   Scalp condition: _____

Date: _____ Services used: _____ Remarks: _____ Stylist: _____

Client record card

Client care

Knowledge of services on offer

It is important that you are aware of every service that the salon offers. For example, you should know:

♦ the price of each treatment;

♦ what each treatment involves;

♦ the approximate time it will take;

♦ any promotional offers the salon may be launching.

Dealing with customer complaints

Always be polite and listen to any complaints or concerns clients may have. A good salon will be one which has a policy for dealing with customer complaints and resolving them to the satisfaction of the client. Salons with no such policy will eventually lose clients. Clients are the reason we exist as hair stylists.

Client complaints can be kept to a minimum by ensuring the following procedures are always carried out:

♦ Make sure that there is an efficient client booking system to avoid double booking.

♦ Confirm the process and what is to be done prior, during and when the process is completed.

♦ Let the client know the results of the consultation and analysis and diagnostic tests, confirm any actions to be taken and any contra indications (reasons why a service cannot be carried out).

♦ Confirm the client is happy with the process to be carried out and final look to be achieved.

TOP TIP

It is important that the client is involved throughout the consultation and analysis process. Signing the agreed outcomes and procedure reconfirms for the client and to you that they are agreeing with the process.

◆ Record all the information on the record card including complaints and get the client to agree and sign the record card.

◆ Do not take complaints personally or in a negative way.

It is always the stylist's duty to put right anything that the client is unhappy with.

It is the senior stylist's duty to oversee any client concerns, give second opinions and support the junior stylist if they are experiencing any difficulties.

Clients' complaints and concerns should be dealt with in a positive manner. A typical procedure for dealing with customer complaints is shown in the diagram.

Retailing and recommending products

The consultation and analysis process is an ideal time to discuss with your client the products they are using at home and how they should care for and maintain their hair. By recommending hair products to the client, you are helping to ensure that the hairstyle will be maintained in the best condition in between salon visits.

When selling retail products give clear guidelines to clients on how they should use the products purchased safely and correctly at home. Knowledge of manufacturer's guidelines and instructions are important for the safe storage and use of products. Always read instruction labels as they will vary from one manufacturer to another.

The following are examples of suitable topics for advice and discussion with your client:

◆ Discuss the type of products used to maintain the hair at home.

◆ Give advice on how often the hair should be chemically processed, for example perming, relaxing, tinting, highlights/lowlights or lightener.

◆ Give advice on how often clients should visit the salon for conditioning treatments, cuts, etc.

◆ Discuss how the hairstyle should be maintained between salon visits.

◆ Recommend a suitable shampoo, conditioner and finishing product that can be used between salon visits. Ideally these should be the same products that you have retailed to the client in the salon.

◆ Make sure that the cost of the product is made clear to clients.

Do not criticize products already used by your client. Always explain in depth why you have recommended a particular product and how the hair will benefit from its use. Advise them to purchase the recommended products once they have used their existing supply but remember that the final decision of whether or not to purchase products rests with the client.

As a retailer and promoter of products to clients you need to be aware of your rights and more so the rights of the client with regards to the selling and purchasing of products. There are various Acts you should be aware of as a retailer of goods to ensure that you are working within the remit of the law.

TOP TIP

Always encourage the client to book follow up treatments where required.

Take the client to a quiet area of the salon

Offer complementary hairdos or put right a process that has not gone well free of charge

Listen carefully to the concerns or complaint made by the client

Dealing with client's complaints and concerns

Do not allow concerns or complaints to go unnoticed

Take immediate action by correcting any faults or mistakes where possible

Do not become aggressive or rude while dealing with the complaint

Dealing with clients, complaints

Styling products/Finishing products

The Sale and Supply of Goods Act 1994

This Act provides protection for the consumer. A product that is purchased must:

◆ **Be as described on the packaging.** If the package says the product is a cream then it should not be in a liquid form.

◆ **Be fit for the purpose the product has been bought for.** The product must work properly and do the job required, as stated on the packaging. If a glued-on hair decoration that says it will work on any finishing product and hair type, under any climatic conditions and will stay on the hair for 24 hours, falls off after two hours it is not fit for purpose.

◆ **Be of satisfactory quality.** The product should not be tampered with. All instructions should be easy to read. The container and outer wrapping should be in good order and not damaged and the seal should not be broken.

The Supply of Goods and Services Act 1982

This Act states that goods and services supplied must be of a proper standard of workmanship and all work must be completed in a reasonable time for a reasonable charge. All materials or goods used or supplied must be of a satisfactory quality. This is seen as a contractual obligation and failure to meet this legislation could be deemed as a breach of contract and pursued by the client in a civil court.

The Trade Description Acts 1968 and 1972

These Acts state that you must not misrepresent a product in a misleading way by wrongfully labelling or describing the product that is for sale. The retailer cannot make false promises about a product saying it will do something that it will not. Products cannot become a sale item unless offered at full price previously for some length of time.

For more information on consumer rights, go to:
http://www.direct.gov.uk/en/Governmentcitizensandrights/Consumerrights/DG_182935

The Consumer Protection Act 1987

This Act protects the buyer under European law. It is against the law to sell any goods that do not meet standards of safety. The consumer can request to be compensated for products that are unsafe and not up to general safety requirements. Any breach of contract could result in a fine or prison sentence.

The Prices Act 1974

All goods for sale must be clearly priced to avoid giving a false impression to the customer.

REVISION QUESTIONS

Level 2

1 Which of the following is an open question?

1 What do you think about having a fringe?

2 Do you want me to give you a fringe?

3 You don't want a fringe, do you?

4 A fringe would really suit you, don't you think?

2 Why would you reconfirm a service or process to be carried out?

1 Because this is the professional thing to do

2 To confirm the process and avoid misunderstanding and errors taking place

3 To reassure the client

4 To check that the client is happy

3 A junior stylist arrives for work five minutes late and finds a client is already there waiting for her. What is the most professional way for her to behave in these circumstances?

1 Not say anything and start the consultation as quickly as possible

2 Complain about how bad the traffic is

3 Apologize for being late

4 Rush through the treatment so she will not be late for her next appointment

4 Why is it important to complete record cards?

1 So we can discuss follow up services with clients

2 So that the client can see what is written about their hair

3 So that a history of the services carried out are recorded for the client

4 So we can record retail products sold to clients

5 If a client has an oblong face, which type of style is likely to suit her best?

1 A style with fullness that will add width to the face

2 A style that will add height

3 A style that will be narrow at the temples and wider at the chin

4 A style that does not involve a fringe

6 Which of the following identifies a widow's peak?

1 Two circular movements found on the crown

2 Strong movement found in the front hairline directing the hair left or right

3 Prominent point found in the front hairline

4 Strong hair swirls found in the nape area

7 Why is it important to maintain and keep your skills up-to-date?

1 To keep abreast of current trends and meet clients' needs

2 It is a legal requirement for all hairdressers

3 To create a professional salon image

4 To be able to deliver basic hairdressing services

8 Which one of the following is not a correct procedure for dealing with client complaints?

1 Take immediate action by correcting any faults where possible

2 Becoming aggressive and rude

3 Take the client to a quiet area of the salon

4 Discuss the complaint with clients and staff

9 Which of the following refers to The Consumer Protection Act 1987?

1 It is against the law to sell any goods that do not meet standards of safety

2 All goods for sale must be clearly priced to avoid giving a false impression

3 This Act states that you must not misrepresent a product in a misleading way

4 The retailer cannot make false promises about a product

10 Which face shape is suitable for a style that is narrow at the temples and provides width at the jaw?

1 Oblong

2 Square

3 Diamond

4 Heart shaped

11 Which test is used to determine if there are any metallic salts present on the hair?

1 Relaxer development test

2 Incompatibility test

3 Patch test

4 Porosity test

4 The successful salon

LEARNING OBJECTIVES

This chapter covers the following:

◆ Contribute to the effective use and monitoring of resources

◆ Meet productivity and development targets

KEY TERMS

Demographic	Implementation	Productivity
Evaluation	Job description	Target
Gesticulation	Legislation	Viable

UNITS COVERED IN THIS CHAPTER

◆ Contribute to the financial effectiveness of the business

INTRODUCTION

Like any other business, a hair salon relies on the profit that it generates from its clientele. In order for any business to be successful it must function in an efficient manner, not only professionally but also financially. For this to be achieved, procedures must be put in place to ensure that all staff operate in a way that maximizes the salon's potential to attract and retain its clientele and make the most effective use of its human and material resources.

Most of this chapter is aimed at Level 3 stylists, to help them understand how they can contribute to the financial effectiveness of the business and enhance productivity. There is also information on reception duties which is relevant to Level 2 stylists. The chapter also examines how to promote the salon, something which is of importance when developing a sustainable business.

Managing staff

Managing staff

From the receptionist to senior management, anyone working within a business is described as a **human resource**. In order to work productively and as part of a team, all staff must have clearly defined roles that are outlined at the start of employment.

When any member of staff begins work, they should be given a **job description** which contains information about **targets** and performance reviews. These should be discussed so they have no doubt as to what will be expected of them. A written statement containing this information should be given to the member of staff no more than two months after they have started work.

In order to promote a good atmosphere within the salon environment, you and your co-workers must be considerate of each others' needs. Working neatly and safely and offering help and support where needed will go a long way towards securing clients' trust and help them feel welcome during their visit.

Reception duties

Reception duties

The reception area, whether custom built or a simple table, is central to the branding of the salon. It is the first point of contact for clients and the front of house. When clients see the reception area, they will come to conclusions about how well and efficiently the salon is run – or how disorganized it is.

The area must be kept clean and uncluttered. There must be a place for stationery where it is easily accessible. An untidy or disorganized area can make people concerned about the service they will receive. If the receptionist does not meet and greet all clients and potential clients in a welcoming manner, the salon can lose business. The receptionist also needs to be aware of certain **legislation** such as the Data Protection Act 1998 to ensure they do not contravene any laws.

The receptionist should:

There is further information on data protection and other relevant legislation in **CHAPTER 3**.

- ◆ be approachable, pleasant and friendly, with excellent communication skills;
- ◆ be presentable with clean and fashionably styled hair;
- ◆ shower and wear fresh clothes daily;
- ◆ be honest and reliable;
- ◆ make individuals feel comfortable and welcomed;
- ◆ handle clients' belongings with care and ensure that they are handed back to them safely when required;
- ◆ deal with clients' concerns in a calm and reassuring way;
- ◆ give accurate information on bookings and services;
- ◆ know approximate times taken for services on offer;
- ◆ know who to refer to about other issues;
- ◆ ensure client confidentiality is maintained;
- ◆ inform clients of any changes to bookings that are beyond the control of the salon;
- ◆ take monies and record amounts, total the day's takings and discuss any discrepancies with the manager or person in charge;

◆ understand the day-to-day running of the salon and have detailed knowledge of the prices for each and every service offered;

◆ be aware of any promotions or special events that are being offered by the salon;

◆ be able to take down accurate messages and pass them on to the relevant individuals;

◆ keep the reception area tidy, ensure that the display shelves are organized and clean taking care to rotate the stock so that older stock is at the front of the display.

The role of the receptionist is shown in this diagram

The receptionist needs to be informed about the various stylists in the salon with regard to their times of work and areas of expertise. When new clients contact the salon to book appointments, the receptionist will then be able to refer them to the most appropriate member of staff.

In order to answer enquiries, the receptionist also needs to be aware of the types of products that are retailed and stocked in the salon. However, it is usually the stylists who recommend suitable products for the clients' use. It is not usually the function of the receptionist to make recommendations unless they are a trained hairdresser. If the salon has an ecological or ethical approach to the products stocked and used in the salon, the receptionist will need to be able to discuss this with clients and then refer them to the stylist to continue the conversation.

Not all salons have a large waiting or reception area with retail products, or even a full-time receptionist. This may mean that stylists take turns to be on reception, or the salon owner may take this role. Junior members of staff are often trained to carry out the role of the receptionist in addition to their other duties. Regardless of who carries out this role, all the points discussed here must be covered by the individual who is currently acting as receptionist.

TOP TIP

A receptionist must be impartial and fair. If they book clients predominantly to their friends this could potentially cause friction and disharmony among staff.

See **CHAPTER 3** for more information on communication.

To view the NOS go to www.habia.org/c/1727/employers

Staff training

Communication

Hairdressing is a very personalized service where excellent communication skills are of paramount importance. This includes communication between one member of staff and another and also between stylist and client. Communication may be oral or written.

Oral communication happens when we speak to someone face-to-face or on the phone. It is something that we all engage in and it is often the easiest way to transfer information. Certain factors such as tone of voice, facial expression, body posture and **gesticulation** influence how the information is received. Good communication also includes being able to interpret the response to the information being passed on.

Staff should deal with each other as respectfully and courteously as possible, particularly in the presence of clients, as this can affect the ambience of the salon. Personal affairs and disagreements should never be aired in a professional environment. Staff should also be on hand to assist each other in delivering services to the client as much as possible. An effective manager will attempt to diffuse any difficult situations quickly.

Written communication provides a record of what has been communicated. It is best used in situations where lengthy instructions are given or where it is necessary to keep a record of the information, for example client records, salon procedures and stock records, or the reporting of any problems that may affect the smooth running of the salon.

In all forms of communication with clients, staff should always conduct themselves in a polite and professional manner. Particularly this includes referrals of any concerns to the relevant persons or the reporting of any problems that may affect the smooth running of the salon. An outline for the acceptable code of conduct should be included in the salon handbook.

Staff training

In order to maximize staff performance it is important that any employer invests in staff training. This ensures that professional standards are maintained and also helps motivate staff and promote team morale. These are both factors that are essential to the success of a salon. All staff members should be given the opportunity to progress and develop their role within the salon and beyond continuing professional development (CPD) or personal professional development (PPD). A good employer should ensure that all staff know who to go to for support and guidance in fulfilling their role. Junior members of staff should be allocated a senior mentor. Senior members of staff should continually be set personal development targets as this will enhance their professionalism and that of the business.

A copy of the National Occupational Standards (NOS) should be readily available to staff and trainees who should be encouraged to refer to them regularly to ensure that they are meeting their targets of learning and maintaining standards.

In the age of modern technology the discerning salon owner would do well to ensure that their staff have acquired a level of ICT skill.

Opportunities to review/appraise and update skills should be offered to all members of staff regularly.

Staff reviews/appraisals can be used as a way to give feedback on performance levels, set new targets and to assess the general welfare and satisfaction of your staff. Targets should be set using SMART criteria (**S**pecific, **M**easurable, **A**chievable,

Name	Age	Job title	Date of employment	
Jane Smith	20	Junior stylist	1/3/2011	

Date of review	Technical ability	Attitude to work	Performance target set	Training offered
16/3/2012	Outstanding	Very good	To enter colour awards next year.	Advanced and fashion colouring course

Manager: Matters arising from last review and comments	Staff member: Matters arising from last review and comments
Stylist would like the opportunity to expand knowledge of advanced colouring techniques. Arrangements to be made to attend colouring course in next 3 months	I would like to improve my colouring skills with a view to entering the colouring trophy competition

Sample performance review/appraisal card

Realistic, Time-bound). The time should be used constructively and allow for two-way interaction between staff and management. Try to resolve any negative aspects with a positive and prompt response to dealing with the issue. All staff should be aware of when they can expect a review/appraisal and be given the opportunity to prepare feedback afterwards.

Time management and target setting

Time/output = productivity Financial effectiveness is based on the **productivity** of staff and their ability to work in a cost and time effective manner. It is important to manage the flow of clients through your salon smoothly, without compromising the financial gain, while taking into account the work being done by those around you.

The first step towards achieving this is to know your staff's strengths and weaknesses as well as their professional qualifications. This makes it possible to delegate responsibility and make the most of your team, especially when you are planning some of the other tasks that must be completed aside from hairdressing. For example, a senior stylist who is not good at communicating with junior members of staff will not be ideal to supervise training but may be very organized and be happy to take charge of the recording of stock levels.

Get used to organizing your time on a day-to-day level by looking at the jobs that need to be done in the salon and decide on their priority and how often they need to be done.

The majority of the money generated in the salon will be from the services that are carried out on clients. These must be priced and time allocated in a way that makes them profitable for the salon owner.

Time/output = productivity

Time management and target setting

ACTIVITY

Get together with two other people and make a list of the non-hairdressing jobs that need to be done in the salon and which members of staff should be made responsible for them.

TOP TIP

The cost of stock and tools must be taken into account when pricing services.

TOP TIP

Some salons find it more efficient to operate a system whereby specialist technicians deal with individual areas of service offered. For example, a colourist might work in consultation with the stylists in order to produce the desired finished look.

There are costs involved in the setting up and running of the business as well as the payment of the staff. Based on these figures, the salon owner will have a target that must be met in order to keep the business **viable**.

This target can be divided among the various services offered by the salon. For example, a target can be set for the amount of money generated each week through colouring services. Most salons also set targets to be generated from retail sales. Many salons operate a commission-based wage system as a way of incentivizing and rewarding staff.

ACTIVITY

Make a list of the services offered within your salon. Give an approximate time for each service and work out how many of each service could realistically and comfortably be done by one stylist in a day. Then, using a column in an appointment book, try to build several scenarios of what a stylist could turn over in a week using a combination of services.

Retail sales

Hair retail products

Incorporating the sale of products into your salon's budget can add immensely to your turnover. The retail of salon exclusive brands can help to increase your client base through walk-in trade and can also promote customer loyalty. As a stylist, your clients will listen to you when you recommend aftercare products. Take time to inform the client of what products you are using to finish and style their hair and outline the benefits.

It is important to select the brands that you retail carefully:

◆ Look at what is being sold by other salons in your locality and try to offer something a little different.

◆ Consider what your clients can afford and do not stock lines that will prove too expensive for them.

◆ Consider the needs of your client base. Cater for all the differing hair types of your clients.

◆ If possible, offer a choice of brands.

◆ Choose brands that your staff are happy to work with and recommend.

◆ You may have a clientele who are interested in using only ecologically, environmentally and ethically sourced products.

Product display

Product display is extremely important, as it can create interest for the client and increase retail sales. Staff must be knowledgeable about the use of all retail products in the display cabinet and available for sale. Products should be displayed in a minimalistic way so that there is no distraction to the sale of goods. You can theme your display cabinet depending on the occasion, such as Christmas, Easter or summer holidays.

Retail cabinets must be stable and sturdy enough to take the weight of the goods on display. You may also want them to be lockable. Products should be displayed with the older goods to the front and newer ones behind. This will ensure you do not sell out-of-date products that are not fit for sale, use or purpose. Ideally, it is better to place retail products in a cool shaded area to keep the content or packaging from deterioration or fading. Some salons use dummy products to avoid clients opening and smelling products, which could cause cross contamination. Clients will not want to purchase products where the seal has been broken; this will, therefore, be a loss to the salon and reduce the profit margin. The products for retail can be stored separately and then brought out at the time of sale, new and fresh.

Other retail products can be sold in the salon such as electrical tools, rollers or setting/blow-dry products. These can offer the stylist the opportunity of giving the client a mini tutorial on how to safely use newly purchased products. Make-up, shower gels and nail, varnish are other areas of retail that can add to the salon's profit. Gifts for special occasions such as Mother's and Father's day or even Valentine's Day can also be displayed. When you retail products you must conform to current legislation.

Monitoring turnover

On any given day, a busy salon can be in receipt of large amounts of money, either in cash or through electronic transactions. It is important that the business owner appoints someone to monitor and be responsible for these takings.

Often this task will form part of the role of the receptionist or a senior member of the salon team. Procedures will need to be put in place to ensure that all monies are accounted for, reported and banked in the correct way.

Every stylist will need to produce a bill of sale for each service that is carried out as well as any products that are retailed. Some salons will produce a daily takings sheet for this purpose. This way it will be easy for anyone at a glance to see what the salon's takings are and how they are generated. At the end of the day, all takings should be totalled, recorded and arrangements made for their safe storage or transfer to the bank.

TOP TIP

It is important that your staff are given training on how to retail. Many manufacturers are happy to provide training for salons stocking their products. Be sure to utilize this service.

ACTIVITY

Do some research around the area local to your salon. Find out which brands are stocked in the salons closest to you and look at their cost. Can you find a brand that you think would be more competitive? State why.

See **CHAPTER 3** for more information on legislation concerning the sale of products.

TOP TIP

It is not advisable to leave large amounts of money on the salon premises overnight. Arrangements should be made for the bulk of the takings to be banked before the end of the day.

Working conditions

It is important that all members of staff are treated fairly. There are laws that the salon owner and management should be familiar with.

Working Time Regulations 1998

This outlines specific guidelines about working hours, breaks, holiday entitlement and payment for leave.

Workers over 18 are entitled to:

◆ 5.6 weeks or 28 days of paid holidays a year, based on payment for a normal working week. Bank holidays can be included in this annual allowance.

◆ Work a maximum of 48 hours a week and no more than 6 days out of every 7 or 12 out of every 14.

◆ A 20 minute break if working for more than 6 consecutive hours.

Provisions are also made for workers aged 16–17:

◆ They must work no more than 8 hours a day or 40 hours a week.

◆ They must have at least 12 hours' rest between each shift and have 2 days off per week.

◆ They must be given a 30 minute break if they work for more than 4½ hours.

◆ They must have at least 12 hours rest between working days.

Hairdressing has traditionally been a trade that attracts young workers, and many schools now offer diplomas that can be taken as young as 14.

The following criteria apply to young workers between the age of 13 and school leaving age. They cannot work:

◆ without an employment permit issued by the education department of the local council if required by local bylaws;

◆ in places such as a factory or industrial site;

◆ during school hours;

◆ before 7 am or after 7 pm;

◆ for more than one hour before school (unless local bylaws allow it);

◆ for more than four hours without taking a break of at least one hour.

During term time children can only work a maximum of 12 hours a week. This includes:

◆ a maximum of two hours on school days and Sundays;

◆ a maximum of five hours on Saturdays for 13 to 14 year-olds, or eight hours for 15 to 16 year-olds.

During school holidays 13 to 14 year-olds are only allowed to work a maximum of 25 hours a week. This includes:

◆ a maximum of five hours on weekdays and Saturdays;

◆ a maximum of two hours on Sunday.

During school holidays 15 to 16 year-olds can only work a maximum of 35 hours a week. This includes:

◆ a maximum of eight hours on weekdays and Saturdays;

◆ a maximum of two hours on Sunday.

Other legislation also protects the rights of your client. It includes:

◆ The Data Protection Act (1998);

◆ The Consumer Protection Act (1987);

◆ The Trades Description Acts (1968 and 1972);

◆ The Prices Act (1974);

◆ The Sale of Goods Act (1979);

◆ The Supply of Goods Act (1994).

When dealing with client complaints, you should always take a sympathetic approach and find out why the client is dissatisfied. Try to settle on a course of action that all parties are happy with. Take care to record the situation accurately and ensure that the matter is resolved as promptly as possible.

For further information on employment legislation visit: www.hse.gov.uk
For arbitration services visit: www.acas.org.uk

Legislation relevant to the sale of products is discussed in CHAPTER 3.

Equipment, tools, stock and utilities

All equipment and tools used in the salon must be in safe working order and conform to the health and safety standards described in Chapter 1. At Level 3 it is the stylist's responsibility to monitor and control this and ensure that good practice is maintained. Equipment should be readily accessible and treated respectfully. Many items of hairdressing equipment can be very costly to the salon owner and may not be easily replaceable. They should be stored neatly and safely when not in use, with any hazardous items being kept in a locked area. Regular checks should be carried out for things such as damage to electrical cables or plugs, with any such occurrences being reported.

Stock must be dispensed and stored in accordance with the Control of Substances Hazardous to Health Regulations (2002), as described in Chapter 1. Any stacking and storing must conform to the Manual Handling Regulations (1992).

Staff should be made aware of the need to minimize the wastage of the utilities (water, electricity and gas). You can cut down on the running costs of the salon by:

◆ turning off taps fully when not in use;

◆ switching off hood dryers once the client is dry;

◆ switching off tongs and straighteners, etc.;

◆ turning off the light in the toilet or staff room when not in use.

HEALTH & SAFETY

Staff have a duty to not place themselves at risk of injury at work.

Stock control

All hairdressers must have a certain level of stock readily available. The amount will depend on the size of the business, the range of services on offer to the client and the demand for certain products.

While it is important to have enough reserve to be able to service the demands of all clientele, it is also important not to be wasteful, as stock can often be an expensive resource. Staff should be given clear guidelines and training on the efficient use of stock, with the appropriate measuring and mixing tools provided for use if required.

In order to control stock requirements effectively, records need to be kept which will enable the person responsible for ordering to monitor the flow and use of products.

There are various methods for doing this but a good stock record should include the following:

♦ a list of all products used and sold by the salon;

♦ the current levels held by the salon;

♦ high usage items highlighted for easy identification;

♦ a record of when orders have been placed and delivered;

♦ when the next order is due to take place;

♦ the cost of each order.

These records should be kept with a list of suppliers' contact details. A time must be allocated at a regular interval (depending on salon requirements) for counting and reordering of stock.

Delivery

Delivery of stock items must be checked and verified against the invoice/delivery note with any discrepancies, including damages, being dealt with immediately. The person responsible for the stock should also be aware of the shelf life of the various products and store them so that the older products will be used first.

In large establishments product usage or ordering (known at stock rotation) may be monitored through coding systems with records of usage being stored on computer. This allows instant access to stock levels and makes ordering easier.

Choosing a supplier

When choosing a supplier, the stylist specializing in African type hair should look for a wholesaler with extensive knowledge of products that have been manufactured for use with this particular **demographic**. This way they will be able to ensure that they receive adequate training and support in the correct use of their purchases. It may be necessary to use more than one supplier, to secure a wider range of products. Orders can be placed through manufacturer's sales and marketing representatives; products are also available for purchase online. Equipment can also be purchased through wholesalers and online.

TOP TIP

At trade shows manufacturers and suppliers will often offer competitive discounts, particularly on larger orders. Use the best supplier in terms of price and deals offered and training support.

HEALTH & SAFETY

All cosmetics products are covered by the Cosmetics Products Regulations Act (1989). A guide has been written by the Cosmetics Toiletries and Perfumery Association which identifies and assesses substances that are potentially hazardous to health and provides information to employers about precautions and controls. This is available online at www.ctpa.org.uk.

Each product is identified in the following way:

◆ name;

◆ ingredients;

◆ the health hazard they pose (contact, injection, inhalation or absorption);

◆ Immediate first aid treatment;

◆ any fire risk.

Promotion of the salon

Charlotte Mensah

For any salon to remain financially viable it must be able to generate a continuous flow of clients through its doors and maximize on their spending potential. The purpose of promotional activity is to generate awareness, thereby ultimately increasing revenue. This cannot be undertaken as a one-off activity but requires continuous thought and renewal of ideas.

These ideas can be put forward and executed by any member of your staff and can often serve as a team building and motivational exercise. The important thing is that they are resource-efficient and that the goal of bringing in more salon revenue is achieved.

Planning

Promotional activities can be tailored to suit the salon budget. Not all ideas require a large financial outlay and some initiatives can be run with very little, if any, expense at all. Promotions can take many forms ranging from an effective window display to a stand at a trade fair. What is important is that they are well thought out and have the support of all staff involved.

The first step toward planning a successful promotion is to identify why a promotion needs to be run and how the salon will benefit. Then set about thinking how you will target your market using SMART objectives: **S**pecific, **M**easurable, **A**chievable, **R**ealistic, **T**ime bound to help formulate your ideas.

Here is a sample table used to plan a basic salon promotion. The idea is simple but the template can be used as a basis for planning any promotional activity.

TOP TIP

You can use a mailshot or email notification to advertise your promotion if your budget allows.

Why are you running the promotion?	What is the objective of the promotion?	What are you going to promote?	Who are you promoting this to?	How will you promote it?	When will you run the promotion?	Where will the promotion take place?	How will you review and evaluate the success of the promotion?
Because the salon is less busy during the early months of the year.	To boost turnover until business picks up in Spring	Chemical services	All clients	10% discount voucher given to all clients who come into the salon during November and December. valid for use with one chemical service during promotional dates	From January 2nd until February 28th	In-salon	In-Salon team meeting

Implementation

Once you have an outline for your promotion you will need to look more in depth at the **implementation** of your plan; what is involved and how the promotion is to be managed. This will involve consideration of the following:

◆ budget;

◆ time needed for planning;

◆ marketing;

◆ resources needed to run the promotion;

◆ the staff that will be involved;

◆ any training or coaching of staff to be involved;

◆ use of any outside resources and how they will be managed;

◆ management of the health and safety aspects of the activity.

Prior to running a promotion all staff should be properly briefed on the role that they are to play in it. Depending on the type of promotion, it may be necessary to provide some training. For example, you might need to improve your staff's presentation skills or product knowledge.

Evaluation

Once a promotional event has taken place it is important to evaluate and record the outcome, noting any particular successes or failings of the promotion. **Evaluation** will help with the planning of future activities and aid in deciding whether the promotion should be run again in exactly the same way or could be improved upon.

Use of outside agencies

Where budget permits, the use of local press may be advantageous, particularly if it is possible to secure regular advertising at reasonable rates. Larger salons may employ the use of PR and advertising agencies to promote the business on their behalf. These companies may offer the benefit of experience in promoting businesses such as yours. However such services can be extremely costly and must be weighed against the financial benefit to your salon.

REVISION QUESTIONS

Level 3

1 How many hours can someone over 18 work without a break?

1 Two hours

2 Four hours

3 Six hours

4 Eight hours

2 Why is it important to carry out regular staff appraisals?

1 To get to know your staff

2 So that you can review their salaries

3 To be able to get the best from your staff

4 To please your staff

3 Why is it best to choose a supplier who has knowledge of African type hair products?

1 They will have a larger range of products

2 To receive a discount on African Type hair products

3 To receive enhanced customer support

4 To be ahead of other salons

4 Why is retail sale important for a salon?

1 To generate extra turnover for the salon

2 To have something to offer the clients when they leave

3 Because it is usually cheaper to buy products from the salon

4 To maintain a professional salon image

5 How many hours are schoolchildren allowed to work per week?

1 Up to 12 hours

2 Up to 18 hours

3 Below 6 hours

4 Over 12 hours

6 What information should be included in a job description?

1 Targets and performance reviews

2 Staff members' names and phone numbers

3 Health and safety information

4 Client information

7 What main legislation must a salon receptionist be aware of?

1 Electricity at Work Act

2 Personal Protective Equipment at Work Act

3 Data Protection Act

4 Provision and use of Work Equipment

8 What is the main purpose of a promotional activity?

1 To create brand awareness

2 To sell new products and services

3 To increase salon profits

4 To enhance salon image

9 Why is it important to evaluate after a promotion?

1 To help with the planning of future activities

2 To inform the salon manager

3 To minimize stock wastage

4 To increase salon profit

5 Shampooing and conditioning

LEARNING OBJECTIVES

This chapter covers the following:

Level 2

◆ Maintain effective and safe methods of working when shampooing and conditioning hair

◆ Shampoo hair and scalp

◆ Apply conditioners to the hair

KEY TERMS

Effleurage	Lime scale	pH scale
Friction	Litmus paper	Rotary
Hydrophilic	Neutral product	Seborrhea
Hydrophobic	Petrissage	Surface tension

UNITS COVERED IN THIS CHAPTER

◆ Shampoo and condition hair

INTRODUCTION

As a stylist, your role is to carry out a consultation and analysis. You must be able to apply your knowledge of client care and hair characteristics to a range of hair types and select suitable products. You must identify client's needs, requests and requirements and make appropriate recommendations. You must also understand how to apply products and undertake suitable massage techniques. Your role also includes providing advice and feedback, retailing products, and keeping records. You must observe health and safety guidelines throughout the process and know when to request support.

Shampooing

Shampooing the hair is one of the most important services carried out in a salon. It is the starting point for most of the other services provided. A head of hair that is not properly cleansed during the shampooing process could spell disaster for the services that follow and a client who is aware that their hair has not been properly cleansed will be unhappy throughout their time in the salon.

Shampooing is the start of good customer care. A good shampoo will set the standard of hair care which follows. Hair that is not shampooed properly will be difficult to style, brittle, and have an odour. Once the hair is cleansed thoroughly, the optimal result can be achieved with the hairdressing services which follow.

The regular use of conditioning treatments is extremely important when working on African type hair, as well as other hair types. The application of conditioner is necessary regardless of whether the hair is in its natural state or chemically processed. It is important to condition the hair after each shampoo or chemical process, unless otherwise advised by the manufacturer. African type hair lacks moisture and needs to be conditioned on a regular basis. Regular conditioning treatments will replace moisture lost during chemical and styling processes. Natural hair also requires regular conditioning treatment and oils to keep the hair in good condition and detangled. Using the correct conditioner on all hair types will strengthen the hair and reduce breakage. The benefits of conditioning treatments will be discussed in depth in this chapter.

The purpose of shampooing hair

We shampoo hair to:

- remove sebum, grime, dirt, dead skin and sweat;
- remove product build-up;
- stimulate the scalp;
- relax the client prior to other processes.

Some of the aftercare products used on African type hair and other hair types leave a build-up on the hair which attracts particles of dust, dirt and general pollution found in the atmosphere. It is important that the hair is shampooed thoroughly to remove all natural sebum, debris and product build-up.

Shampoos are of two types:

- soap-based;
- soap-free.

Soap-based shampoos are no longer used in hairdressing. They are alkaline and in hard water they form a scum and leave a build-up on the hair. The hair will look dull, dry and feel coarse to the touch. Applying a chemical to hair that has been treated with a soap-based shampoo could result in hair breakage and an unsatisfactory result.

A rinse made with citric acid (lemon juice) or acetic acid (vinegar) in water will remove build-up caused by using a soap-based shampoo. Alternatively, use a product which will remove any alkaline deposits left on the hair. The hair will regain its shine and look healthy.

As part of the treatment the hair should be shampooed with a soap-free shampoo. These are usually slightly acidic, and cleanse as well as helping to remove any alkaline build-up.

TOP TIP

A good shampoo should cleanse the scalp and hair without stripping out all the natural oils and moisture. The hair should also be left relatively tangle-free in preparation for the conditioner.

Cleansing action of shampoo

To be able to cleanse the hair effectively, a shampoo has to act as a wetting agent. Water on its own is no good at wetting the hair. It tends to form globules on the surface of the hair or just run off. This is due to **surface tension**. To allow the hair to become wet, the surface tension has to be broken, which happens when the shampoo is added to the water.

The detergents used in shampoo are made up of special, long molecules. One end of the molecule is repelled by water and attracted to grease: it is **hydrophobic**. The other is attracted to water: it is **hydrophilic**.

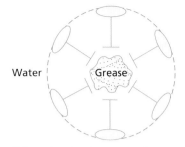

Detergent molecules surrounding grease

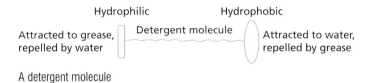

A detergent molecule

When water with detergent is put on a greasy surface such as hair, the end of the molecule which repels water attaches itself to the grease and removes it from the surface. This loosens any debris, which is also removed by the shampooing action. The grease and loosened debris can then be rinsed away.

Types of shampoos

The **pH scale** tells us how acid or alkaline products we use daily in the salon are and helps us understand the effects on the hair and the best products to use to address certain conditions and hair types. The pH scale runs from 1 to 14, with 1 being very acidic, 14 being very alkaline and 7 as a **neutral product**. **Litmus paper** is used to test how much acid or alkaline is present, blue litmus paper turns red in acidic conditions and red litmus paper turns blue under alkaline conditions. The p stands for potential and the H stands for hydrogen. Alkaline products such as relaxers will open the cuticle of the hair. Neutralizing shampoo is slightly acidic and will help to close the cuticle and bring the hair back to its natural acid mantle. The acid mantle is a protective layer on the hair formed of sebum and sweat.

Most shampoos are acidic and have a pH of 4.5–5.5, which is similar to scalp and hair and skin's acid mantle. Shampoo which is of the same acidity will have a kinder effect on the hair, leaving it tangle-free and in good condition. The softer the water conditions, the better the final result. The shampoo will also easily form a lather, which will retain the foam for a few seconds. In hard water conditions the shampoo will not lather well nor retain a foam (although we understand today that a shampoo does not need to foam excessively to function properly). A good quality shampoo will require smaller quantities to cleanse the scalp and hair effectively.

HEALTH & SAFETY

Using a shampoo with an acid mantle of 4.5–5.5 will retain the normal acid mantle of both the hair and skin and will help protect from harmful bacteria.

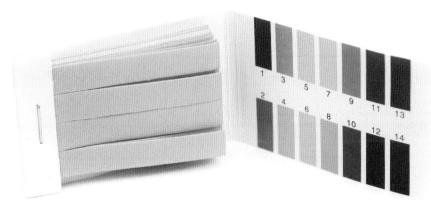

pH indicators and pH values

HEALTH & SAFETY

Remember to wear gloves before testing products to avoid sustaining burns or injury.

ACTIVITY

Wearing gloves and using litmus paper, carry out a test on different salon products to see how acid or alkaline they are, you can try testing different treatment shampoos and conditioners. Test hydrogen peroxide, acid based perm lotion, alkaline perm lotion and a variety of relaxer products at different strengths.

The active ingredients used in soap-free shampoos are *triethanolamine lauryl sulphate (TLS)* and *sodium lauryl sulphate (SLS)*. These act as a detergent. Shampoo can contain a variety of additives to correct various conditions of the scalp and hair. Some additives contained in treatment shampoos are outlined in the table on page 81.

TOP TIP

African type hair is not usually oily, this will depend on the hair type, as some more open curl/wavier textures may require minimum moisturizing. Type 2c to 4a may require more moisturizing products. Hair types 1 to 2a may require less or lighter oils. If you do come across this problem, or hair that has a build-up of products that are not easily removed by a normal shampoo, use a shampoo that will remove the oil first, followed by a moisturizing shampoo to avoid over-drying the hair.

Mineral deposits

For more information on different hair types please visit CHAPTER 2.

Mineral deposits like **lime scale** are found in hard water conditions. Rinsing with hard water will leave deposits on the hair after it is dried. These can affect the hair and interfere with further chemical processes. The hair is left dull, lifeless, brittle and with a raised cuticle. There are special shampoos or wipes on the market which can be used to cleanse the hair effectively of all deposits.

Consultation and analysis before shampooing

Before shampooing any head of hair it is important to carry out a thorough client consultation and analysis. This will give you an indication of the type of shampoo to use and any scalp or hair problems that need correcting.

It is important to discuss with your client any concerns they might have regarding their scalp and hair. Problems that would require a treatment shampoo are:

TOP TIP

Overuse of a shampoo/conditioner is wasteful – excess product is washed down the shampoo basin. Only use the manufacturer's recommended amounts of shampoo and conditioner.

- dry scalp and hair;
- damaged, dry, brittle hair;
- dandruff affected scalp;
- mineral deposits on hair;
- oily/**seborrhea** scalp conditions;
- product build-up.

HEALTH & SAFETY

Check that the client has no infestations such as lice or scabies, or contagious conditions such as impetigo or ringworm, which could cause cross infection and damage the salon's reputation. Do not shampoo or condition if any of these conditions are present.

Shampoo	Active ingredients	When to use	When not to use	Problems that can arise
Neutralizing	Ammonium lauryl sulphate/citric acid – conditioner.	After every relaxer.	Permed hair.	Could cause curl to drop due to acidity.
Dry, damaged hair	Coconut, jojoba, vegetable oil or mineral oils, hydrolyzed protein (amino acid).	On damaged, dry breaking hair or as a pre-treatment shampoo. Natural hair, relaxed hair.	Before a perm.	Could cause a barrier and prevent penetration of perm lotion.
De-tangling/ conditioning, combined shampoo and conditioning	Cationic based shampoo acts as a detergent and conditioner.	Extremely porous, damaged hair as a pre-treatment shampoo. Natural hair.	Prior to a perm.	Difficult to rinse out; clings to the hair; can cause a build-up and form a barrier to other services; will not cleanse the hair sufficiently and is not effective as a conditioner; will still need to use additional conditioner after shampooing.
Moisturizing (a good moisturizing shampoo will not form a build-up)	Hydrolyzed protein, amino acid, oil such as: coconut, jojoba, vegetable oil, mineral.	Dry, damaged hair prior to applying conditioning treatment used as a detangler. Natural hair textures.	Prior to a perm.	Can cause straight fine hair prone to being oily to become over conditioned lank and difficult to style.
Dandruff (pityriasis capitis)	Zinc pyrithione.	Dandruff infected scalp.	Prior to a perm or relaxer.	On African type hair can have an extremely drying effect on the scalp and hair; alternate with a normal conditioning shampoo; do not use before perming or relaxing as this could cause scalp irritation.
Dandruff (pityriasis capitis)	Selenium sulphide.	Prescribed by a doctor – only use on severe cases of dandruff.	As above.	Prolonged use can cause dermatitis; can make African type hair dry and brittle.
Oily hair	Lemon/citric acid.	On naturally oily or greasy hair.	Prior to any chemical process.	Can be drying on the scalp/ hair and cause some irritation if used often.

TOP TIP

Tea tree oil can be found in specialist shampoos and is a natural antiseptic which can help sooth irritated or itchy dandruff scalps. There are always new oils on the market that are used as moisturizers. Pure coconut oil is a good moisturizer for the hair, as are Moroccan and Macadamia oil.

TOP TIP

A dry scalp is not always dandruff. The scalp can become dry and the epidermis flakes in a similar way to dandruff. Flakes on the scalp tend to be drier and drop from the scalp easily in comparison to dandruff. A client with an oily scalp who has flaking may have dandruff opposed to dry scalp. Dry scalp can come from not taking enough fluid in the diet causing dehydration. Shampoo and conditioning products not being rinsed off properly can form a build-up on the scalp. Allergic reaction to products can also cause a dry scalp.

Consultation

1 Prepare the client for consultation by dressing them in a gown, towels and protective cape.

2 De-tangle the hair using a large tooth comb.

3 Make a thorough assessment of the hair as you comb through.

4 Discuss any concerns you may have about the hair and scalp with your client.

5 Establish any contra indications, allergies, lack of suitability of products.

6 Discuss any recommended changes due to a change in scalp/hair condition or based on client's concerns/requirements.

7 Discuss the type of cleansing, conditioning and aftercare products used.

8 Provide feedback to your client and recommend suitable products.

9 Fill in a record card on products used.

Analysis

1 Comb the hair and observe if any hair is coming out from the scalp or breaking during combing.

2 Look at the scalp to ensure it is healthy.

3 Look at the condition of the scalp and hair to ensure it is not dry and there is no build-up of finishing products.

4 Fill in a record card on products used based on the results of your analysis. Timing is important, discuss with your client how long the shampoo/conditioner/ treatment will take and the next step to follow.

Luster products

Preparation for shampooing

Before you can start the shampooing process you should make sure the following preparations have been completed.

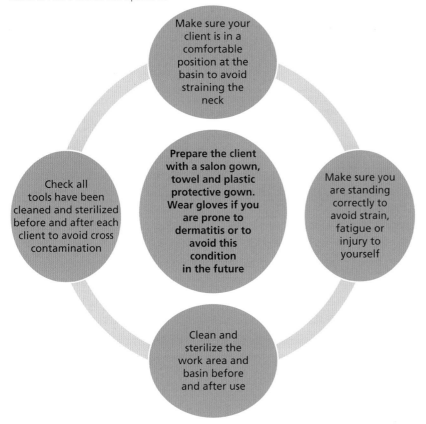

Preparation for shampooing

Shampooing process

The shampooing process is made effective by the combination of the shampoo and massage technique. The purpose of massaging the scalp during shampooing is to assist with the removal of grease, dirt and debris. It is important to make sure the technique used lifts the dirt and cleanses without being abrasive. Massaging the scalp roughly can cause breakage and damage the scalp and hair. It is rare to find naturally oily African type hair due to the curl pattern and time it takes for sebum to travel up the hair shaft. However, oily conditions can be found in straighter varieties of African type hair and in other hair types. It is important to think carefully of your shampoo choices. If you use the incorrect shampoo on European type hair it could make it oily/limp and vice versa, the incorrect product choice on African type hair can make it dry and brittle to the touch.

Always use personal protective equipment (PPE) to protect yourself before shampooing. Plastic aprons, as well as protective gloves, can be used during shampooing if you are prone to dermatitis or to protect you from this condition. Remember to dry your hands thoroughly and moisturize them after washing or shampooing.

There are two main massage movements used when shampooing the hair:

◆ **Effleurage** is a gentle, stroking movement used when applying shampoo or rinsing the hair.

◆ **Petrissage** is a circular, kneading, lifting movement used when massaging and cleansing the scalp and hair.

Two other techniques are also used:

◆ **Rotary** massage uses the pads of the fingers in a circular movement. It stimulates the scalp and can be used on all hair types.

◆ **Friction** massage uses light, fast movements to stimulate the scalp. Use the balls of the fingers when applying friction to cleanse specific areas such as the nape area and front hairline. Do not be too vigorous with this movement, as when the hair is wet it is more prone to breakage and damage. It is not suitable for long hair.

Friction hair washing

Preparing to shampoo

Before starting the shampooing process, complete your consultation and analysis. Then make sure the client is correctly gowned and protected with a towel and plastic gown. Use gloves where necessary to avoid contact dermatitis. Make sure the client's head rests comfortably in the shampoo basin.

Test the water temperature on the back of the hand to make sure the water is not too hot. Always check with the client that they are comfortable with the water temperature, which should be tepid to warm.

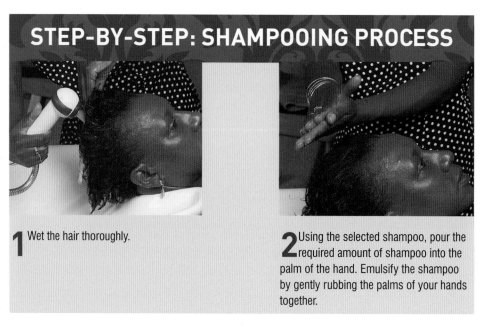

STEP-BY-STEP: SHAMPOOING PROCESS

1 Wet the hair thoroughly.

2 Using the selected shampoo, pour the required amount of shampoo into the palm of the hand. Emulsify the shampoo by gently rubbing the palms of your hands together.

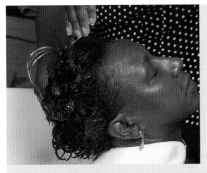

3 Distribute the shampoo throughout the hair using stroking movements (effleurage) first.

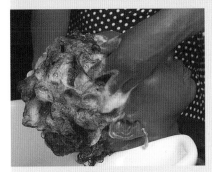
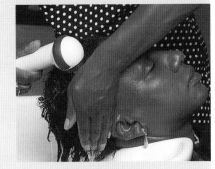

4 Then use circular movements (rotary), massaging the scalp for one to two minutes.

5 Rinse the hair thoroughly. Then apply a second portion of shampoo, using the same technique as before.

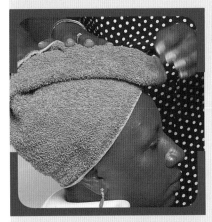

6 Once the hair has been thoroughly cleansed and all the shampoo has been rinsed out, remove the excess water from the hair by wrapping the head with a clean towel.

Water temperature

Avoid using water that is too hot as this could scald the scalp. In the case of oily-type hair it can also increase the production of sebum to the scalp. Water that is too hot can also cause the hair to tangle, especially if the hair is damaged and the cuticle has become open.

It is good to use cooler water when rinsing the hair after the last shampoo as this helps to close the pores, has a soothing effect on the scalp and helps to keep the hair from tangling. Do be aware that some clients prefer not to have water that is too cold on the scalp, so always check the temperature on the back of the wrist first and also confirm the comfort level with the client. Always recheck temperature when turning back on in between shampoos.

> **TOP TIP**
>
> Applying too many shampoo applications can cause harm by drying out the scalp and hair, which could lead to a dry scalp condition and will result in product wastage.

Supporting the client's neck and head

Make sure you support the client's neck and head as you are positioning their neck backwards into the shampoo basin to avoid any strain or damage to the back of the neck or injury. Strokes can occur from prolonged distortion to the neck. Always make sure your client is comfortable and avoid long shampoo sessions with the neck continuously in a backward position if you have several procedures or lengthy tasks to carry out. Get the client to sit upright at intervals when you are not shampooing. Avoid pulling and jerking the head during the shampoo process. Opt for gentle, but controlled movements.

www.dailyglow.com/articles/269
/hair-care/how-to-shampoo
-your-head.html

Conditioners and conditioning treatments

A good conditioner should:

- disentangle the hair and make it soft;
- close the cuticle and make the hair smooth;
- make the hair appear glossy and bulkier;
- control static electricity;
- make the hair easy to comb;
- moisturize the hair;
- strengthen the hair and help to reduce breakage (even if only temporarily);
- be easily rinsed from the hair.

Conditioners fall into three main categories:

- *Surface/external conditioners* – these work on the cuticle only and do not penetrate into the cortex to benefit damaged hair. Surface conditioners make the hair easier to comb, they act as detanglers. Surface/external conditioners tend not to act as a treatment, and have no long-term effect on the hair. These conditioners are used at the backwash, prior to a shampoo and set, wrap set or blow-dry. However there are now surface conditioners that reconstruct and add moisture designed for use at the backwash as a quick treatment.

- *Deep-penetrating conditioners* – these work on the cortex of the hair, conditioning the hair both internally and externally. They will also make the cuticle appear smoother, control breakage, disentangle the hair and add shine and moisture. Sometimes called *internal conditioners*, these conditioners help to rebuild the cortex of the hair through the addition of protein.

- *Restructurant conditioners* – sometimes called *reconstructurants*, these conditioners help to temporarily rebuild the disulphide bonds of the hair and so help to control breakage. To do this they contain proteins (amino acids) which fill gaps within the hair caused by damage to the cortex. Restructurants also moisturize the scalp and hair.

TOP TIP

Make sure that the hair is rinsed properly after the final shampoo; residual shampoo could create a dry, itchy scalp and brittle hair.

TOP TIP

Once the hair has been damaged, it cannot be repaired. In extreme cases of damage the hair should be cut off. Conditioning treatments will temporarily repair the hair and give it a better feel and appearance, but once shampooed, the hair must be re-conditioned again. Protein and restructurant treatments can delay the action of breakage, allowing the hair to grow and be cut gradually.

TOP TIP

The condition of the hair constantly changes. It is important that each time the client visits the salon a new consultation and analysis takes place to ensure the correct treatment is applied.

ACTIVITY

Carry out research into a variety of shampoo and conditioning products on the market for professional and retail use. Develop a research file on what the products do for the hair and the best use of the products to address a variety of hair conditions as discussed in the chapter. Your research should cover products that can work over a range of hair types such as natural African type hair, wavy, relaxed, permed, Asian and European hair. You can develop your research in a table format.

When working on straighter hair types, where the hair may be oilier due to natural secretion of sebum, conditioners may not always be required to be applied to the root area as it can make the hair greasy and lank. For clients with an oily scalp and hair condition, that also have dry mid lengths and ends, apply the conditioning treatment to the damaged dry parts of the hair on the mid lengths and ends only. This will avoid the scalp becoming oily as discussed earlier in the chapter. These products may contain oil which could make the oily scalp and root condition worse.

Because of the sensitive nature of African type hair and the strength of the chemical and physical heat used to process the hair, conditioning treatments are very important and must be carried out regularly. As a stylist it is your duty to make sure your client's hair is maintained in the best condition. On straighter hair types, can occur from the use of lighteners, perms, colour and physical heat; wands, tongs and electrical straighteners can also cause damage. The hair may need regular conditioning treatments. Regardless of hair type you may have to prescribe a series of corrective treatments. It is also important to recommend shampoos and conditioners to be used at home.

Mizani products

The following steps must be taken to maintain the condition of the hair:

◆ Carry out a thorough consultation and analysis.

◆ Provide feedback to your client along with a possible treatment plan.

◆ Advise your client on how to maintain the condition of their hair.

The following table identifies the ingredients found in conditioners and the effects on the

hair:

*Oil can refer to any one of the following oils: almond oil, coconut oil, jojoba oil, mineral oil, castor oil.

Conditioner	Active ingredient	When to use	Purpose
Surface conditioner	Citric acid, oil*, quaternary ammonium compound.	After a perm, relaxer or permanent colour.	Used after a chemical process to close the cuticle; will restore normal pH and act as a detangler.
Deep-penetrating conditioner	Hydrolyzed protein, *oil.	As a treatment on dry, damaged hair, relaxed or permed hair.	Adds moisture and sheen to the hair; replaces lost protein; detangles.
Restructuring conditioner	Quaternary ammonium compound, amino acids, keratin, *oil.	On extremely dry, damaged, brittle or over-processed hair.	To temporarily rebuild disulphide bonds and reduce breakage by adding amino acids and keratin to the hair; adds moisture and sheen to the hair; ideal after a relaxer or perm; also detangles hair.

Any of these can be used as an additive to shampoo or conditioning treatments.

Regularly analyze your client's hair and update your recommendations for treatment as necessary.

Consultation and analysis before conditioning

Before applying any conditioning treatment, it is important to carry out a consultation and analysis. If you are going to apply a conditioning treatment, make sure that the shampoo used is compatible with the conditioning treatment selected. Consultation and analysis is best done away from the shampoo basin and in a styling chair.

Too much protein or overuse of restructuring conditioners can cause the hair to become brittle, dry and to break. It is important that each visit to the salon by the client is treated like a new one. Make sure the client receives a new analysis and consultation prior to any treatment being prescribed.

As a result of the consultation you should obtain answers to the following questions:

◆ How often does the client shampoo and condition their hair?

◆ Does the client visit the salon for professional hair care treatments?

◆ Has the client had any previous chemical process on their hair?

◆ Were there any problems that arose after the last chemical process?

◆ If yes, what were they?

◆ Is there anything else that the client is concerned about with regard to their hair?

TOP TIP

Clients with alopecia or psoriasis should be referred to a GP or trichologist.

Analysis

1 Comb the hair starting from the ends, working up through the middle lengths towards the roots.

2 Observe how much hair comes out during combing. This could be an indication of excessive hair being lost from the roots or breakage.

3 Look at the scalp to ensure it is healthy and in a good condition.

4 During the combing process, think about the following points: Is the hair dry and lacking moisture? Has the hair been excessively exposed to physical or chemical processing? Is the hair breaking? Is the hair discoloured? Is the scalp dry? Is the scalp dandruff infected/dry? Is the scalp and hair oily? Is alopecia or psoriasis present?

Record cards

You should now be able to fill out a record card. Combining this information with your analysis will help you come to a decision on which shampoo and conditioning treatment to use. Record cards should be updated regularly to record any change of shampoo, conditioner or retail products, scalp irritation or to confirm that the products worked effectively.

TOP TIP

Avoid excessive massage when working on oily hair types. Remember massage stimulates the sebaceous gland, causing sebum to travel up the follicle, making the scalp oily, which you want to prevent. You can massage the hair to aid penetration of the product. This is a good technique to use when working with long hair.

The following table can be helpful when selecting a suitable shampoo and conditioner:

Hair care problem	Recommended treatment	Result
Dandruff	Apply shampoo for dandruff (followed by a suitable conditioner depending on hair type).	Will control flaking/dandruff and irritation to the scalp.
Dry hair	Apply shampoo for dry hair. Apply conditioning treatment for dry hair.	Will disentangle the hair and moisturize; will add sheen and moisturize the scalp and hair.
Brittle/over-processed hair	Apply moisturizing shampoo for brittle, damaged hair.	Will disentangle the hair and damaged hair and moisturize.
Brittle/damaged/over-processed hair	Apply restructurant conditioning treatment.	Will add protein (amino acids) to the cortex of the hair; will control breakage/dryness and moisturize; will help to close the cuticle and make the hair appear smoother.
Oily hair/seborrhea	Apply shampoo for oily hair. Can be applied directly to dry hair to remove oils quickly. Apply conditioner suitable for oily hair or on ends only if required.	Will help control condition.

Always keep to the same product line to achieve the maximum effect from the hair care treatment application.

Tools, equipment and products needed for a conditioning treatment

- ◆ large tooth comb;
- ◆ bowl;
- ◆ tinting brush;
- ◆ towels;
- ◆ salon gown;
- ◆ plastic cape;
- ◆ selected conditioning product.
- ◆ Sectioning clips (for long hair).

Luster's hair treatment conditioner

HEALTH & SAFETY

Make sure all tools are clean and sterilized before using them on each client. This will help to avoid cross infection from client to client.

Application and removal of conditioning treatment

1 Prepare the client for the treatment by putting on the gown and towel.

2 Make sure conditioning treatment is applied to clean hair.

3 Section the hair into four by dividing from the front of the hairline to the nape and across the head from ear to ear (1).

4 Put the selected conditioning treatment in a bowl.

5 Take 6 mm (0.25 inch) sections, working from the nape up towards the crown down to the nape. Using a tinting brush or cotton wool, start applying conditioner to the back sections first, working left to right (2). Proceed to the top sections, applying treatment to the left and then right section. If more product is required, use a clean brush/wooden spatula to avoid cross contamination.

6 Work from up or down the section, applying conditioner to the scalp and root area first depending on the scalp and hair condition. Once conditioner is applied thoroughly to this area, start applying conditioner to the middle lengths and ends. The more open the cuticle is the more damaged the hair becomes; always comb the hair gently from the ends (points) up through the midlengths to the roots to keep the hair tangle free. Avoid ruffling the cuticle upwards as it will get entangled with the open cuticle layers through the hair shaft; this can happen more on long hair (3).

7 After the application of conditioner, massage the scalp (see massage techniques).

8 Apply heat using a steamer or dryer for approximately 10 to 30 minutes. The more damaged the hair is, the longer the treatment will need to be left on. The use of additional heat will help to open the cuticle, allowing the conditioner to penetrate the cortex. Various forms of heat can be used to help the conditioning treatment to penetrate through the cuticle of the hair such as a hooded dryer, climazone or steamer. Do take care that whichever heat method is used the client is comfortable throughout the process; monitor the heat levels.

> **TOP TIP**
>
> Always follow the manufacturer's guidelines on timing for individual products, over conditioning can cause the hair to become too soft, greasy and lank especially on straighter hair types.

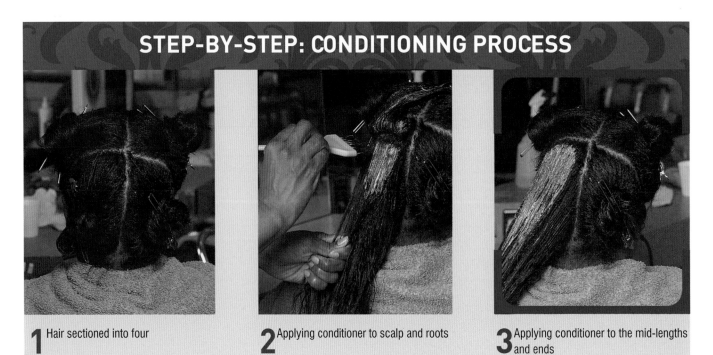

STEP-BY-STEP: CONDITIONING PROCESS

1 Hair sectioned into four

2 Applying conditioner to scalp and roots

3 Applying conditioner to the mid-lengths and ends

Removal of conditioning treatment

The amount of rinsing that is carried out will depend on the condition of the hair. On hair that is extremely damaged, it might be better to leave some conditioner in and not to rinse the entire product from the hair. However, when giving a normal treatment or working on oily hair, rinse all the conditioner thoroughly from the hair.

Massage techniques

Scalp massage:

◆ stimulates the scalp by improving blood circulation;

◆ increases oil production from the sebaceous glands;

◆ breaks up fatty adhesions caused by blocked sebaceous glands;

◆ helps stimulate hair growth;

◆ relaxes the client.

Do not give a massage if any of the following contra indications (reasons why a massage is not advisable) are present:

◆ extreme pain, e.g. headache or migraine, high blood pressure;

◆ excessive reddening, inflammation or broken skin;

◆ seborrhea/oily hair conditions;

◆ contagious diseases such as ringworm, impetigo;

◆ infestations such as lice or scabies;

As previously stated, the two main movements used in massage are effleurage and petrissage.

◆ *Effleurage* is a gentle stroking movement that produces a soothing effect on the scalp.

◆ *Petrissage* is a kneading, lifting movement which stimulates the scalp and improves circulation to the veins and lymphatics.

Friction can be used, which is a gentle rubbing up and down the scalp with the balls of the fingers in opposite directions. This can stimulate the scalp, bringing a rich supply of blood to the head and follicle, which aids growth. However over-vigorous action can increase sebum and oils to the scalp and can cause hair breakage on fragile hair.

Rotary massage uses a firmer, circular movement with the pads of the fingers. It also stimulates the scalp and is suitable for all hair types. Friction can be used to stimulate sebum production on dry scalps and hair.

A massage always starts and finishes with effleurage. All massage movement must end in the nape area where the lymph glands are positioned.

Once the conditioning treatment has been applied, comb the hair from the ends, working up the mid-lengths to the roots in preparation for the massage.

HEALTH & SAFETY

Make sure you wash your hands prior to giving a massage.

STEP-BY-STEP: EFFLEURAGE TECHNIQUE

1 Place both hands at the front hairline. Leading with the right hand and using the balls of the fingers, gently but firmly stroke the fingers downwards following the contours of the head.

2 When your right hand reaches half way down the head, start stroking with the left hand starting at the front hairline. Finish the movement at the nape in the region of the lymph glands.

3 Continue with gentle but firm stroking movements, using alternate hands throughout. Work from the middle of the head to the left ear in continual stroking movements and back to the middle. Then work from the middle of the head towards the right ear.

STEP-BY-STEP: PETRISSAGE TECHNIQUE

1 Place both hands on the front hairline. Gently but firmly apply pressure using the balls of your fingers. Lift and knead the scalp between the fingertips. Start the petrissage movement, working from the front of the head down to the nape.

2 Continue the petrissage movement, working from front hairline to the nape, and from ear to ear.

3 If required, when the massage is complete, put a plastic cap on the head and apply additional heat if necessary. Rinse the hair and finish as required. Rather than carrying out a manual massage the two following electrical massage options can be used (on dry hair only):
◆ Vibro massage
◆ High frequency massage (HF)

Vibro massage is a hand held tool with different attachment options. The required attachment is used depending on the area to be massaged, e.g. the scalp. Vibro massage can be used on dry hair or an oil or blend of oils can be used. Ensure you do not apply excessive pressure when using vibro massage. Do not use on wet hair or with wet hands.

High frequency massage, involves the use of electrodes to massage the scalp. The process can be either direct where the glass electrode is used directly on the scalp, or indirect where the client holds the electrode and the stylist massages the scalp. With this method it is important not to lose contact with the scalp. At least one hand should always remain on the scalp, while the other turns the machine of and on, to avoid the client feeling a heightened tingling sensation. The following contra indications must be observed when using HF: do not use on wet hair or with wet hands; remove jewellery from client and self; do not use if the client is pregnant; do not use if there are heart complications or the client is feeling generally unwell. Refer the client to a GP.

Never carry out a massage if the skin on the scalp is broken, or inflamed, or the client presents with a contagious condition. Always follow manufacturer's and tutors guidance prior to using any form of electrical massage.

HEALTH & SAFETY

Make sure the basin is clean before and after use to avoid the risk of cross-infection.

TOP TIP

Over use of a shampoo/conditioner is wasteful – excess product is washed down the shampoo basin. Only use the manufacturer's recommended amount.

HEALTH & SAFETY

Always follow the manufacturer's recommendations on the application, processing and removal of shampoo and conditioning products.

HEALTH & SAFETY

It is important to make sure that any massage technique is carried out gently but firmly to avoid any damage. If the client complains of any discomfort or pain during the massage, stop the massage immediately. Always check the client comfort levels throughout the process.

REVISION QUESTIONS

Level 2

1 How would you prepare a client for a shampoo and conditioning treatment?

  1 Put on a gown and towel

  2 Gowning, towels and plastic cape

  3 No need to prepare the client

  4 Gown the client and use a cutting cape

2 Why do you agree the service, process and timing with the client before proceeding?

  1 To avoid errors and confirm the process and procedure with the client

  2 To make sure the client is comfortable and happy

  3 To maintain a professional salon image

  4 To gain feedback from the client

3 Why is shampooing an important process?

  1 To cleanse the hair first

  2 To remove sebum, grime, dirt and dead skin

  3 To carry out the massage technique

  4 To prepare the hair for other services

4 What causes scum to form on the hair?

  1 Not shampooing the hair properly

  2 Using soap

  3 Using shampoo

  4 Using conditioner

5 In which way should shampoo be applied to an excessively oily scalp and hair?

  1 Directly to dry hair without wetting

  2 Wet the hair first

  3 It does not matter

  4 Ask the client what they would like

Level 3

6 Why should you avoid excessive stimulation on scalp and hair affected by seborrhea?

  1 To increase sebum production

  2 To decrease sebum production

3   To increase oil flow

4   To avoid over stimulating the sebaceous gland

7   Why should the hair be combed first prior to shampooing?

1   To relax the client

2   To observe if there is any hair loss

3   To detangle the hair and prepare for consultation and analysis

4   To remove dandruff

8   Over vigorous use of the friction massage movement can do what to the hair?

1   Cause breakage to fragile hair

2   Increase hair growth

3   Decrease blood flow

4   Improve circulation

9   What can too much protein or overuse of restructuring conditioners do to the hair?

1   Cause it to become soft and manageable

2   Cause it to become brittle, dry and to break

3   Create a barrier against other services

4   Cause nodules to appear along the hair shaft

10   Which of the following is an active ingredient in a restructuring conditioner?

1   Hydrolyzed protein

2   Citric acid

3   Keratin

4   Peroxide

PART TWO
Styling

Styling embraces a range of skills from underpinning knowledge, consultation, preparation of self and client, product awareness, that are all relevant to a variety of styling techniques on both wet and dry hair. The observation of health and safety runs throughout these chapters and is embedded within each skill area. Ultimately it is the creative aspects housed in these chapters that will excite, motivate and inspire you to develop basic as well as advanced styling techniques and skills to explore and perfect as you work through the chapters.

ROLE MODEL

JUNIOR GREEN Award winning hairstylist and salon owner

" I first became involved in the art of hairdressing after completing a taster course at Bedford College. Originally I wanted to join a photography course at the same College; unfortunately due to low uptake the course was withdrawn. Coming from a strict Caribbean background my parents insisted I got a career and my Dad said 'what about hairdressing?'. I completed an apprenticeship at Aquarius Hairdressing salon, Finsbury Park and then joined Splinters hair salon as a second year operator in 1984. After that, I worked at a variety of other salons, before joining the Errol Douglas hair salon where I worked for six years.

I always wanted to open my own hair salon in central London with my preferred location being Knightsbridge. I chose Knightsbridge because travel to the salon is easy for clients and passing trade very good, which is of the utmost importance to any business. My long term goals are to mould and develop the Junior Green brand, establish a motivated and committed team and produce my own hair care and styling product range.

6 Blow-drying

LEARNING OBJECTIVES

This chapter covers the following:

◆ Maintain effective and safe methods
  of working when styling and finishing
  natural hair

◆ Dry hair to create a style

◆ Dry hair to prepare for styling

◆ Provide aftercare service

KEY TERMS

Blow-dry products
Comb attachment
Electrically heated straightening
  irons

Electrically heated styling wands
Final finished look
Heat protector
Physical effect

Radial or spiral brush
Record cards
Straightening the hair

UNITS COVERED IN THIS CHAPTER

◆ Dry a range of hair types (type 1, 2, 3 and 4) and prepare for styling

INTRODUCTION

Blow-drying the hair allows the stylist to mould and design exciting new looks for the client. This chapter deals with the art of blow-drying and styling hair using heated electrical tools on a range of hair types. It covers everything a stylist needs to know at Level 2, whether you are studying on the Combined course or looking to specialize in African type hair.

Blow-drying

Blow-drying African type hair became fashionable in the late 1980s, due to the change in styling in this decade that heralded straighter, smoother and bouncier hair and a decrease in roller-setting the hair. The introduction of the use of the round spiral brushes to blow-dry African type hair started in the UK, with the central London salon Splinters of Mayfair which specialized in African type and curly hair. Before this African type hair was traditionally set with rollers or blow-dried straight with an attachment.

When blow-drying hair of any type, the same internal changes to the hair structure take place as when setting the hair. During the blow-drying process, the keratin of the hair is changed from alpha keratin to beta keratin, breaking hydrogen bonds and causing the hair temporarily to remain in the new shape created. Hair is hygroscopic, which means that it is able to absorb moisture from the atmosphere. Once the hair takes in moisture from the atmosphere or becomes wet, it reverts back to its natural curl.

Working safely

Health and safety is covered in **CHAPTER 1**.

The following health and safety issues are particularly relevant to blow-drying and styling.

The correct use of blow-drying equipment

Correct care of equipment is important to avoid accidents while working in the salon. Carry out the following checks before using a blow-dryer:

◆ Ensure that your hands are dry before touching the plug or switching on the dryer.

◆ Make sure the guard is securely placed so that the hair does not become entangled in the motor at the back of the hand held dryer.

◆ Ensure that the wires are not exposed and are fitted securely into the socket and the plug is in good working order.

◆ Ensure that the dryer is in good working order by switching it on prior to use.

During use:

◆ Always switch off the hand dryer from the switch on the dryer and not from the socket.

◆ If the hand dryer starts to malfunction during use, turn the dryer off from the switch on the dryer and then the socket. Unplug the dryer from the socket.

After use:

◆ When you have finished using the blow-dryer, turn it off from the switch on the dryer first, then the socket. Pull the plug out of the socket.

Tension

When blow drying African type hair it is important to keep the hair extremely smooth. Use even tension to avoid distortion during the blow-dry process. A combination of stretching and drying the hair will produce straighter looks on natural or relaxed hair. Natural hair, where there is no chemical present, may require more tension to straighten the natural curl. When working on straighter hair types; less tension but more dexterity may be required to control, stretch and mould the hair around the blow-dry tool.

HEALTH & SAFETY

Do not use excessive tension when blow-drying and styling to avoid traction alopecia.

The work area and tools

The work area should be kept clean and tidy at all times. Make sure your equipment is clean and sterilized before and after each client, using the correct chemical sterilization methods, to avoid cross contamination. Clean your work area with sterile wipes and sprays, making sure all mirrors are free from smears. Your tools should be in easy reach to avoid you overstretching and sustaining an injury by leaning over clients. Tools should be placed on your right or left depending on whether you are left or right handed. All gowns and towels should be clean and washed in a washing machine daily. Gown and protect the client in the house style of the salon. Follow and observe personal hygiene procedures.

Deportment and posture

Make sure you are standing comfortably wearing suitable shoes to avoid suffering from tired legs. Stand with your feet slightly apart, but firmly on the ground. Rotate around the client, moving the chair as you work. Try to avoid staying stationery in one place for too long to maintain circulation and blood flow to the legs. Keep upright as you work to avoid any back pains or damage to the back or neck. Move the chair up or down depending on the client's height and the task at hand.

Personal Protective Equipment (PPE)

If you are prone to sensitivity or allergies to particular products, you can use gloves while applying blow-dry and finishing products to the hair. This will help prevent irritation and possible contact dermatitis. You can wear a plastic or cotton tabard/apron to protect your clothes from any styling products or when using colour.

For further information on contact dermatitis see CHAPTER 1.

Preparation

Prior to starting the blow-drying process, you need to take the following steps:

◆ Gown the client.

◆ Carry out a consultation and analysis of the hair.

◆ Look at the face and head shape to develop a hair style that will suit the client and create the correct balance, shape and suitability.

◆ Only blow-dry hair that is in good condition.

◆ Discuss client lifestyle, style choice and hair maintenance.

◆ Think about the hair type, styling and finishing product and technique to be used.

◆ Plan the direction and shape the hair is to be blow-dried in – the hair must be blow-dried in the direction the hair is to be styled.

◆ Take into account natural hair fall and movement.

TOP TIP

Natural hair fall is the way the hair falls naturally after combing – seen easier on straighter type hair – moving naturally backwards, forwards, with a middle parting or to either side. Movement would be the natural straightness, wave or curl in the hair.

See **CHAPTER 2** Hair characteristics for more information.

- Provide the client with feedback on the style and direction the hair is to be blow-dried and the effect to be achieved.

- Shampoo and condition the hair.

- Comb the hair to remove any tangles.

- Apply blow-dry lotion, mousse or **heat protector** to protect the hair against the heat of the dryer and support the **final finished look**.

Style maintenance

It is important that you discuss with your client how to maintain their new hairstyle. You should let them know which products were used to blow-dry their hair, why those particular products were used and how often they should be applied to support and maintain the new hairstyle. Discuss any return visits to the salon and how the hair will be maintained in the maximum condition. Record and update **record cards**, to ensure that the salon has up-to-date information on the products and treatments used.

Face shapes

As part of the blow-drying and styling process the face and head shape should be considered. Looking at the client's face and head shape will help determine a suitable style – one that you will enjoy creating and your client will be happy with.

Lifestyle

Some people like to be at the forefront of fashion and would like their hairstyle to make a statement. Others prefer a more moderate look and some individuals desire a quick, easy to manage hairstyle. It is your responsibility to glean from the client during the consultation how they would like to wear their hair and to create the final look they desire.

Condition

The condition of the hair must be taken into consideration when blow-drying and styling. Hair in a poor condition that has lost elasticity and is porous may not hold a very good blow-dry; the hair may be prone to being frizzy or have split ends which may require the use of specialist products to control frizz. Observe the scalp and overall hair condition during the consultation process, looking for contagious and non-contagious conditions. This is important to avoid contamination and cross infection and safeguard the reputation of the salon.

Choice of technique

Once you have completed the consultation and analysis you will be able to decide on which blow-drying products and technique to use, and which tools you need to select to create the desired finished look.

A number of different blow-drying techniques can be used which will create movement and shape or a straight, smooth look. For example:

- A **spiral brush** will create curl and movement.

- A blow-drying attachment may be used to blow-dry the hair straight.

◆ Blow-drying the hair using a comb or brush will produce a straight effect.

◆ Blow-drying the hair after a set will loosen the curl and provide movement to the finished look.

◆ You will need to know which of the above techniques to use to achieve the required look and shape, and whether the hair will also need to be straightened with the irons or tonged to provide additional support to the finished style.

Blow-drying products and their use

Products used to blow-dry straight, wavy, curly hair, are designed to protect the hair from the heat of the dryer and moisturize the hair. Most **blow-dry products** have light conditioning properties built into them and may or may not contain alcohol. They are mainly of three types: lotions, mousses, and cream-based products. Some blow-dry lotions and mousses may contain some alcohol and fixative to create stronger hold and protect the hair from atmospheric conditions. Blow-dry and setting products create a film around the hair to control moisture from being absorbed when it rains or the atmosphere is humid, causing the hairstyle to drop and revert back to its alpha keratin state. These products therefore help the finished hairstyle to last longer.

Blow-dry lotion

Blow-dry lotion is in the form of a spray with little or no holding properties. The hair is protected from the **physical effect** of heat on the hair and remains pliable, allowing the use of blow-dry brushes or an attachment. The non-addition of alcohol will avoid the hair becoming too dry and breaking. This product is best used on the following types of hair:

◆ type 2c to type 4b hair;

◆ hair that requires a soft, flexible finish;

◆ hair that has recently been chemically processed;

◆ damaged, dry, brittle hair.

Mousse

Two types of mousse are suitable for blow-drying African type hair. The first type contains polyvinylpyrrolidone (PVP) a plastic polymer in a solvent and alcohol that creates a flexible coating on the hair to protect against atmospheric conditions. This type of mousse is best used on hair which is not dry and is in good condition. The second type of mousse contains no alcohol but adds moisture and sheen to the hair. This product is suitable for natural, permed or relaxed hair that is sensitized, damaged or in a good condition.

Blow-dry cream

Blow-dry creams coat the hair and protect it from physical heat, moisturize the hair and give it a silky appearance. They are best suited to:

◆ types 1c to 4b;

◆ short hair/long hair;

HEALTH & SAFETY

Always make sure your hands are dry prior to holding a hairdryer to avoid electric shocks.

◆ wrap setting prior to blow-drying;

◆ dry/damaged hair in need of moisture;

◆ naturally curly hair.

Depending on your clientele and your own personal interest it is worth sourcing natural ethically sourced products you can use in the salon.
http://fashion.telegraph .co.uk/beauty/news-features/ TMG9598248/The-green-guide-to-chemical-free-beauty.html

TOP TIP

Remember the above is guidance to product use and suitability. Only by testing products on the client's hair and receiving feedback from the client, can you find out what is or isn't suitable. Deciding on a product is based on the feel and look of the hair as well. It is sometimes a combination of the stylist's prior knowledge, experience, and client requirements, alongside product trial/testing that will lead you to the correct product selection.

ACTIVITY

Carry out your own research into the types of blow-dry products available in your salon, retail outlets, supermarkets and chemists. Make a table of the name of the products, features of the product (type of hair it is suitable for), how it works and its cost. Base your research on the types of blow-dry products listed above. Also include in your research a product line suitable for natural African type hair and for clients who are interested in using natural or organic products that are ethically sourced.

Tools and equipment

Tools and equipment	Use
Hand held dryer	**Hand held dryer** used to blow-dry the hair with a paddle brush, spiral blow-dry brushes or comb attachment.
Detangling comb	**Detangling comb** used to comb out tangles from the hair.
Paddle brush	**Paddle brush** used to brush out and detangle the hair prior to shampooing or using heated rollers and after setting or pin curling. Used to blow-dry the hair straight.
Pin tail comb	**Pin tail comb** used to section the hair, prior to wet/dry setting, creating pin curls or sectioning the hair when using electrical heated equipment.

Tools and equipment	Use
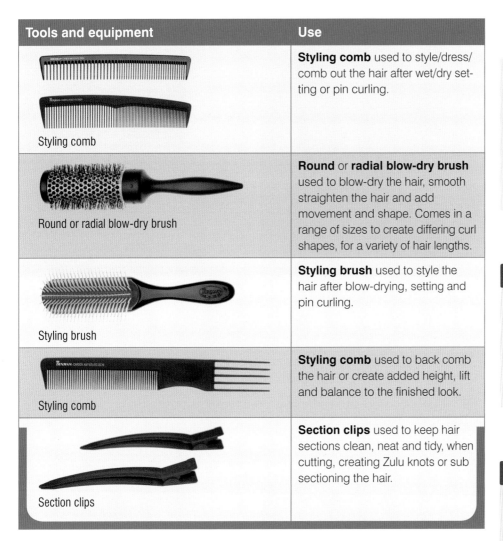Styling comb	**Styling comb** used to style/dress/comb out the hair after wet/dry setting or pin curling.
Round or radial blow-dry brush	**Round** or **radial blow-dry brush** used to blow-dry the hair, smooth straighten the hair and add movement and shape. Comes in a range of sizes to create differing curl shapes, for a variety of hair lengths.
Styling brush	**Styling brush** used to style the hair after blow-drying, setting and pin curling.
Styling comb	**Styling comb** used to back comb the hair or create added height, lift and balance to the finished look.
Section clips	**Section clips** used to keep hair sections clean, neat and tidy, when cutting, creating Zulu knots or sub sectioning the hair.

You will find it useful to do some personal research in different types of brushes and the effects they can create.

Blow-drying using a comb attachment

This technique is ideal for creating smoother, straighter looks and can be used either on hair that has been relaxed or hair that is still in its natural form and has not been chemically processed.

1 Attach the **comb attachment** to the blow-dryer.

2 Section the hair into four and apply blow-dry product/heat protector.

3 Sub-divide the hair, working from the nape section, sectioning the hair from left to right. Sub sections should not be thicker than ¼" (6 mm) to ½" (12 mm) in thickness.

4 Comb each section thoroughly.

5 Hold the blow-dryer by the handle for control.

6 Using even tension slide the comb attachment through the hair slowly, starting from the middle back section. Working from left to right, begin at the ends and work up through the middle lengths to the roots. It is important to keep dryer moving to avoid damaging the hair.

It might be a good idea to read up on naturally derived and ethically sourced products as some clients may request natural products are used on their hair.
http://lesstoxicguide.ca/?fetch=personal
www.safecosmetics.org

ACTIVITY

Level 2 If you are a junior stylist, use a tuition head and create a straight blow-dry, along with the use of electrical straightening irons.

ACTIVITY

Level 3 If you are a senior stylist, create a round **radial brush** blow-dry with movement, along with using an electrical curling wand or straightening iron to create movement and shape in the hair.

TOP TIP

When you become proficient at blow-drying you can use fewer sections or no sectioning at all.

See CHAPTER 16 on natural hair.

Blow-drying using the comb attachment on the ends of the hair

Blow-drying the middle lengths

Blow-drying the roots

7   Apply suitable finishing products, this could be sheen spray, serum, or holding spray.

8   The selection of product will be based on hair type: oily or dry hair conditions, preference and the overall condition of the hair.

9   Repeat the process until the hair in that section is completely dry and straight.

10 Continue to work up to the crown of the head until you reach the horseshoe section.

Blow-drying the crown area

Blow-drying the side section

The finished blow-dry

11 Start blow-drying the side section by sub-dividing the hair in ¼" (6 mm) sections.

12 Work up the head until you reach the horseshoe section.

13 Repeat the process on the other side of the head.

14 Start blow-drying the horseshoe section using the same technique as before, working through to the front hairline. Blow-dry the hair in the direction it is to be styled. If the hair needs to be straighter repeat the process, working up through

the nape area to the front hairline taking (¼") (6 mm) sections throughout the hair. The finished effect is smooth and straight, ideal for one-length bobs and for styles that require little or no movement. The hair can be tonged or ironed after blow-drying if more movement and direction is required.

TOP TIP

A comb can also be used in place of an attachment. Sub-divide the hair at the nape. The comb is placed at the ends of the hair with the blow-dryer following the comb. Apply gentle tension to keep the hair straight working up to the mid-lengths and then roots. Keep the heat and airflow pointing downwards to keep the hair and cuticle smooth. Follow the same technique as blow-drying using an attachment.

Blow-drying using a paddle or Denman brush

A Denman brush is used for smoothing and shaping short to medium length hair and layered hair styles. A paddle brush is best used to smooth longer length styles.

Technique

1 Remove excess water.

2 Apply blow-dry product/heat protector.

3 Section the hair into four.

4 Sub-divide the hair into ½" (12 mm) sections in the nape and blow-dry from the roots underneath the section first.

5 Continue working up the head until you reach the crown.

6 Blow-dry the sides.

7 Blow-dry the front area depending on the direction the hair is to be styled in and the finished look.

Blowdrying with Denman brush

(a) Blow-drying the front sections

(b) The finished look

Round brush placed under the section to be blow-dried

Appling root volume

Blow-drying using a radial or round brush

The purpose of using this technique is to straighten and dry the hair while adding curl and movement. It is best used on hair that has been cut in a suitable style, for example a one-length, graduated, or layered cut. Different size radial brushes can be used based on the length of the hair and curl/movement to be created.

Technique

After preparing the client and hair, select a suitable size brush depending on the length of the hair, the style to be achieved and the requirements of the client.

1 Section the hair into four.

2 Sub-divide the hair from ear to ear, starting at the nape.

3 Start blow-drying the hair from the nape area, working from the middle then the left and right sections. Take meshes no more than ¼" (6 mm) in width.

4 Place the blow-dry brush under the section to be blow-dried. Apply heat to the root area first and gently pull the brush through the hair, followed by the hairdryer. Proceed onto the mid-lengths and then the ends. Continue with this technique until the hair in this section is completely dry.

5 Continue blow-drying the crown and the fringe area of the hair into the style, direction and shape required.

6 If you require more movement and shape, when the hair is dry wind the hair around the brush and apply heat by using the blow-dryer to the curled hair. Remove the blow-dryer and let the hair cool before unwinding the brush. This process will create more curls movement in the hair and add length and durability to the blow-dry and the finished style. Tonging or ironing the hair after blow-drying will add additional curl, movement and support.

7 Apply finishing products as required.

Blow-drying the crown

The finished look

TOP TIP

Always remember to wet the hair with water from your spray bottle while you are working especially if the hair dries out during the blow-drying process. The hair needs to be wet to mould and take the shape of the blow-dry tool. It is better not to wet the hair with more styling product as this could cause a build-up on the hair; making it difficult to blow-dry. Blow-drying dry hair could tug and further damage/break the hair making it fragile.

Blow-drying after a set

The purpose of blow-drying after a set is to create a smoother, softer movement to the finished look. This technique is suitable for dry, damaged hair or for hair which has just been relaxed and needs to be treated gently but still requires a softer movement. Hair that is natural and has been set is also ideal to blow-dry after setting.

The blow-drying technique will stretch the hair and smooth the cuticle in preparation for tonging. This technique would be better suited to types 2a to 4b hair as well as relaxed hair.

HEALTH & SAFETY

Although blow-drying hair that is already dry is kinder to the hair, excessive heat can cause the scalp and hair to become dry and damaged; in extreme cases the scalp and hair can be burnt.

Technique

1 After setting and drying, remove the rollers and brush the hair out thoroughly to remove demarcation lines.

2 Apply hair dressing sparingly to the scalp and hair if necessary. Oil sheen spray can be used if preferred.

3 Start blow-drying the hair from the nape, then the middle section, working left to right as in the previous technique.

4 Continue working up the head towards the front hairline.

5 Blow-dry the roots, mid-lengths and then the ends, until the hair is completely smooth.

6 When the whole mesh of hair is smooth, roll the hair onto a brush and apply heat. Leave the hair to cool for a few seconds. This technique will produce a smooth finish, as well as a strong curl and movement within the finished style. Apply suitable finishing products as required.

TOP TIP

Over-application of hair dressing or oil spray will cause the hair to become lank and detract from the finished style.

Blow-drying after a wrap set

The purpose of blow-drying the hair after a wrap set is to encourage greater flexibility, definition, direction and movement within the finished style. The hair can be tonged if additional support and direction is required. This technique is suitable for all hair types, but should only be used when you want to achieve a straighter, softer look.

Technique

Brush the hair out thoroughly in the direction of the wrap set. Apply hair dressing oil sheen to the scalp and hair sparingly if required. Select which brush is to be used – spiral or Denman. The type of brush selected will depend on the shape, movement and style required:

◆ For styles requiring more movement and body select a spiral brush.

◆ For straighter looks use a Denman brush.

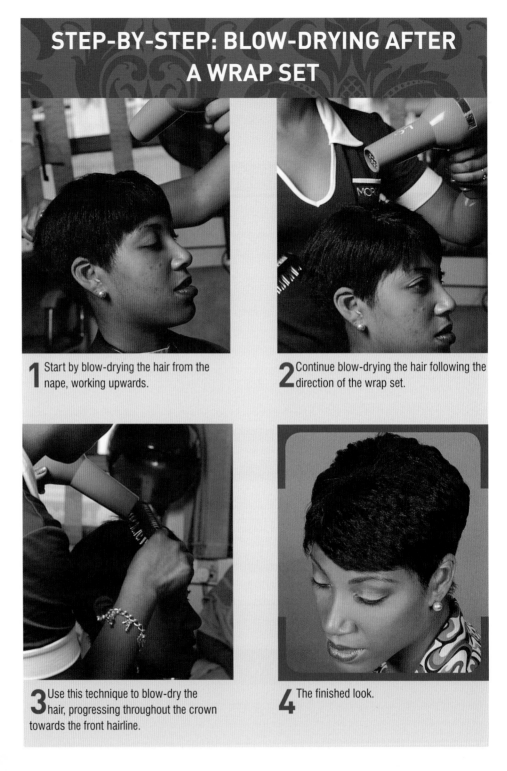

STEP-BY-STEP: BLOW-DRYING AFTER A WRAP SET

1 Start by blow-drying the hair from the nape, working upwards.

2 Continue blow-drying the hair following the direction of the wrap set.

3 Use this technique to blow-dry the hair, progressing throughout the crown towards the front hairline.

4 The finished look.

Scrunch drying

This technique can be used on all wavy and curly type hair that is naturally curly or wavy or on hair that has been permed. It is particularly suitable for hair that has been body waved. Scrunch drying will help expand the curl, giving definition and separation to the finished style.

TOP TIP

Over-drying the hair when scrunch drying could cause the hair to become frizzy. To keep curl separation, some moisture should be left within the hair. For maximum effect leave the hair semi-dry. If the hair becomes too dry, moisture with an oil sheen spray or activator. Suitable finishing products can be used such as sheen spray, hair gel, wax, serum, activator/moisturizer, de-frizzing and holding products. The choice of product(s) will depend on the finished look required; defined curls, waves, texture or hold.

Technique

Shampoo and condition the hair before blow-drying. Comb the hair out thoroughly and apply a suitable product depending on the hair type: natural, wave/curl or permed. Attach a diffuser to the blow-dryer.

STEP-BY-STEP: SCRUNCH DRYING

1 Apply medium heat and air flow to the hair. Scrunch the hair between your fingers, cupping the hair in your hand to support the curl.

2 Apply the diffuser to the hair and hold, pushing against the curl. This will help maintain the curl formation.

3 Use this technique throughout the scrunch dry, working from the nape to the crown and front hairline.

4 Apply additional mousse or oil sheen spray if the hair has become over dry. Holding spray can be added to create direction, hold and separation to the finished style.

Always remove excess water from the hair before blow-drying, by blast drying the hair first after applying styling products. This will avoid applying too much heat to the hair and over drying the hair with excessive heat. The wetter the hair is, the more heat is used, which can create long term damage to the cuticle. The hair should be damp before blow-drying and not soaking wet.

(a) Sectioning the hair prior to straightening

Straightening the hair after blow-drying using electrical straightening irons

The purpose of using **electrically heated straightening irons** after blow-drying is to smooth the cuticle and to create a straight and smooth overall finish for the client. The straightening iron can also be used for **straightening the hair** and smoothing natural hair to create a temporary straightened look for clients. The hair will revert back to its natural alpha state once moisture is absorbed. Avoid constantly straightening one section of hair repeatedly as this could permanently damage the hair and cause breakage. Avoid pulling or putting excessive strain on the hair as this could cause alopecia, particularly traction alopecia around the hairline.

Technique

(b) Straightening a section of hair with the electrical irons and protecting with the pin tail comb

1 Shampoo and condition the hair and apply suitable heat protector, blow-dry lotion or mousse as required.

2 Blow-dry the hair using the selected technique.

3 Plug the electrical tool into the socket to pre-heat to save time.

4 Section the hair and sub-divide into a square or oblong section of no more than ¼" to ½" (6 mm to 12 mm) in dimension.

5 Section the hair taking approximately ½" (12 mm) of hair. Avoid working with too much hair, so that the straightening technique will be effective (a).

6 Starting from the nape area open the plates of the iron, place the straightening iron at the root of the hair, close the iron and gently pull the iron through the section of hair ensuring the hair is straight. Use a tail comb under the section of hair being straightened for control and to avoid the straightening iron coming into contact with the scalp (b).

7 If required spray the hair with sheen then holding spray to give separation and hold the curl. Serum can also be used to further define the look.

(c) The finished look

Using the electrical irons to curl the hair

Electrical irons have become extremely fashionable not only to straighten the hair, but also to put movement and curl in the hair. The curl created can be of varying sizes and dimensions, depending on the size and heat of the straightening iron used. Some straightening irons have inbuilt control buttons to adjust the temperature depending on hair type, condition, and curl pattern, while others come pre-set and retain a consistent temperature. Electrical irons can be used to straighten and curl African, Asian and

European type hair. The irons can also be used to straighten natural African type hair that has not been chemically processed. This is a temporary and physical technique and the hair will revert once moisture is absorbed from the atmosphere. The hair is in its alpha keratin state before washing and blow-drying; once the hair is blow-dried and straightened it is in a new stretched shape due to the breaking of hydrogen bonds during the process of blow-drying and straightening. The hair will revert back to its natural alpha keratin state once moisture is absorbed. Heat protection products should always be used prior to using any electrical styling equipment.

(a) Placement of iron ¼" away from the scalp

Technique

1   Shampoo and condition the hair and apply suitable heat protector, blow-dry lotion or mousse as required.

2   Blow-dry the hair using the selected technique.

3   Plug the electrical tool into the socket to pre-heat to save time.

4   Section the hair and sub-divide into a square or oblong section of no more than ¼" to ½" (6 mm to 12 mm) in dimension.

(b) Turning the section of hair in the iron to form a curl

5   Section the hair taking approximately ½" (12 mm) of hair. Avoid working with too much hair, so that the curling technique will be effective.

6   Starting from the nape area open the plates of the iron, place the straightening iron at the root ¼" (6 mm) away from the scalp (a).

7   Close the iron and turn the curling iron gently towards you pulling the hair through the electrical iron as you turn. This will form the curl (b).

8   Continue curling the hair from the nape up through the crown up to the front hairline until the whole head is curled. If required spray the hair with sheen then holding spray to give separation and hold the curl. Serum can also be used to further define the look.

(c) The finished look

Using a styling wand to curl the hair

Electrically heated styling wands are a more recent invention. They are a similar tool to an electrical tong, in that they create a round smooth curl. Here the similarity ends, as the electrical curling tongs have two parts, a barrel and semi circular closure that holds the hair securely in place while you turn the handles of the tong. The wand has only one barrel that you wrap the hair around, once the hair comes into contact with the electrical wand hydrogen bonds are broken and change the hair from alpha keratin to beta keratin, locking the new shape into the strand of hair and creating a curl. The electrical tong was based on the original thermal marcel tong or iron which was invented by Marcel Grateau in 1872 and used to curl the hair in Victorian and Edwardian times.

TOP TIP

Styling wands, like electrical tongs, come in a variety of sizes from small to large. Selecting a suitable size will depend on the length of hair and how curly, wavy or loose the finished look is.

http://blog.myhairstylingtools.com
/blog/the-birth-of-the-flat-iron/

Technique

1   Shampoo and condition the hair and apply suitable heat protector, blow-dry lotion or mousse as required.

2   Blow-dry the hair using the selected technique.

3 Plug the electrical tool into the socket to pre-heat to save time.

4 Section the hair and sub-divide into a square or oblong section of no more than ¼" to ½" (6 mm to 12 mm) in dimension.

5 Avoid working with too much hair, so that the curling technique will be effective.

6 Place the wand a ¼" (6 mm) away from the scalp, wrap the hair from roots to points down the wand and hold for a few seconds (a) and (b).

7 Once the curl is formed pull the hair out of the wand, by holding the hair at the top with the end of the tail comb.

8 If required, spray the hair with sheen then holding spray to give separation and hold the curl. Serum can also be used to further define the look and give sheen.

9 Continue working through the head until the complete head is curled if this is required. Style the hair by separating the curls.

(a) Sectioning the hair in ½" (12 mm) sub sections. Placing the wand in the hair ¼" (6 mm) away from the scalp

(b) Curling the hair on the wand from root to points

(c) The finished look

REVISION QUESTIONS

Level 2

1 Why would you blow-dry the hair after a traditional roller set or wrap set?

1 To smooth the hair and give the hair movement

2 To make the hair curly

3 To make the hair shiny

4 Makes no difference

2 Why would you use a directional blow-dry technique?

1 To brush the hair backwards

2 To create movement in the finished style

3 To blow-dry the hair in the direction it is to be styled in

4 To set the hair into a desired shape

3 Why do we check electrical equipment and tools before using them?

1 For no particular reason

2 To check that the power is on

3 For any faults or exposed wires

4 A responsibility for the stylist

4 Why would you use the scrunch drying technique with a diffuser?

1 To dry naturally curly or permed hair

2 To make the hair frizzy

3 To make the hair thicker

4 To make the hair glossy

5 Why must tools and equipment be free of hair, washed and sterilized before and after use?

   1 Because this is the best thing to do

   2 To avoid cross infection and conform to salon policy

   3 Before putting tools in a tool bag

   4 To avoid tools becoming damaged

6 Why should you observe head and face shapes prior to blow-drying and styling the hair?

   1 To develop a hairstyle that suits the client

   2 So that the client is happy

   3 To assess the client's lifestyle

   4 To check for any contra indications

7 How would you protect the scalp while using heated equipment?

   1 Placing heated equipment ¼" (6 mm) away from the scalp and using a comb to protect

   2 To curl the hair properly getting as near to the root as possible

   3 To straighten the hair from root to tips

   4 To ensure the hair is straightened correctly

8 What is the purpose of using a blow-dry cream?

   1 To moisturize and protect from heated appliances

   2 To create volume and hold

   3 To keep the hair straighter for longer

   4 To help create curl and definition

9 Hair is hygroscopic, what does this mean?

   1 Is able to repel moisture from the atmosphere

   2 Can revert from alpha to beta keratin

   3 Has the ability to absorb atmospheric moisture

   4 Retains moisture when in its alpha state

10 Which bonds are broken during the blow-dry process?

   1 Keratin

   2 Di-sulphide

   3 Hydrogen

   4 Acid

11 Excessive tension when blow-drying can cause what to the hair and scalp?

   1 Traction alopecia

   2 Alopecia barbae

   3 Alopecia areata

   4 Alopecia universalis

7 Setting hair

LEARNING OBJECTIVES

This chapter covers the following:

◆ Maintain effective and safe methods of working when setting and dressing hair

◆ Set hair

◆ Dress hair

◆ Provide aftercare advice

KEY TERMS

Crest
Finger wave
Off-base
On-base

Pin curling
Pliable
Retro hairstyles
Reverse pin curling technique

Sub-section
Trough
Wet set
Wrap set

UNITS COVERED IN THIS CHAPTER

◆ Set and dress hair

INTRODUCTION

Setting hair is a skill that is creative, inspirational and stimulates innovative ideas. This chapter deals with the art of setting a range of whether or not the hair is straight, wavy or curly (types 1 to 4). The chapter will cover everything you need to know at Level 2, whether you are studying on the Combined course or looking to specialize in African type hair. It also serves as a foundational reminder for students studying at Level 3.

TOP TIP

Setting the hair is sometimes a kinder option to other methods of styling the hair. Setting the hair can be less stressful for damaged and breaking hair than blow-drying. However, the hair will not be as straight and smooth in the final look if it is set.

TOP TIP

You should always remind clients to protect their hair from rainy, humid environments to avoid the hairstyle becoming limp and losing movement and shape.

TOP TIP

You should always discuss choices and suitable products, client's likes and dislikes, with each client as they all have individual needs and requirements.

TOP TIP

All setting products contain moisturizers and can be used if the hair is curly, wavy or dry in texture. For straight hair, specific products should be used to avoid the hair becoming lank, oily and difficult to style.

Setting African type hair

Setting is a technique often used on African type hair to create fashionable **retro hairstyles**. The methods and techniques used are no different from setting European type hair. A cohesive set is a temporary method of creating curl or movement in all hair types. It is best carried out on hair that has been chemically relaxed, is naturally straight or wavy types 1 to 2c. African type hair (types 3a to 4b) that has not been chemically relaxed can also be set so that the natural curl can be temporarily stretched to make the hair more manageable.

A cohesive set changes the keratin in the hair from alpha keratin to beta keratin. Remember that alpha keratin exists when the hair is in its natural state, e.g. curly, wavy or straight. When the hair is set and dried on rollers or stretched during blow-drying and setting, hydrogen bonds are temporarily broken and the hair takes on a new shape – the hair is now in a beta keratin state.

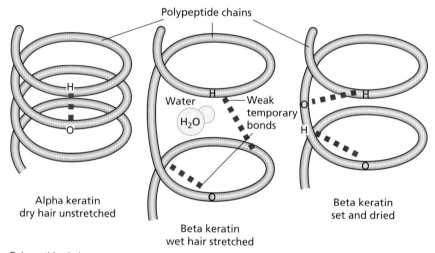

Polypeptide chains

Alpha keratin
dry hair unstretched

Beta keratin
wet hair stretched

Beta keratin
set and dried

Polypeptide chains

Once the hair has been blow-dried or set, it is in a temporarily stretched state. Being hydroscopic, the hair will gradually absorb moisture from the atmosphere and revert back to its former state.

Setting products and their use

Setting products for African type hair are designed to protect the hair from atmospheric conditions, moisture in the atmosphere, physical heat, as well as providing hold to preserve the finished look. Due to the dry nature of African type hair, these setting products contain less alcohol and more conditioning agents than those used on European type hair.

Alcohol has a drying effect when used on all hair types, especially on African type hair. It is important not to cause excessive and unnecessary drying to hair that is already naturally dry. The setting lotions, gels or mousse used should therefore be specially formulated for African type hair. Specialist products should also be used when working on Asian and European hair. On straighter hair types, products with alcohol will work well on oiler hair, as it will dry out natural oils. Remember the final decision is always with the client, who may prefer to have products which have little or no alcohol within them.

Types of setting products

The common setting products available are:

◆ *Setting lotions*. Light conditioning lotions for blow-drying or setting styles which require a soft hold; firm hold products for waves, pin curls and sculptured looks.

◆ *Mousses*. Used when a soft hold is required for setting and blow-drying the hair.

◆ *Gels*. Used for styles requiring moulding, sculpturing or **pin curling**, especially when the hair needs to be set in a style where the finished look is solid and un-movable. De-frizzer is used to remove frizz from types 2a to 3a.

Roller placement and selection

Rollers can be placed in a variety of positions to create different effects, shapes and movement. Three basic principles must be followed if you are going to produce a good result when setting:

1 Sections taken prior to roller placement must not be wider or longer than the roller.

2 Each roller can sit on its own base to create volume and root movement. When using over-directed and under-directed techniques, each roller sits on one and a half times its own base so that volume is avoided at the root area.

3 When winding shorter hair on rollers, the hair should be wound around the roller at least one and a half times to ensure a uniformed curl is achieved and the hair secured effectively.

Control mousse

Roller selection

The size of roller selected depends on the length of the hair, type of curl and the movement desired:

◆ *Large rollers* will produce open, loose curls and create a softer, looser movement in the finished style; they are normally used on hair below the shoulder.

◆ *Medium rollers* will produce a firmer, tighter look and give the style more volume; they are normally used on hair just above the shoulder and shorter.

◆ *Small rollers* will produce tight curls and lots of volume and the finished style will be more durable; they are normally used on short hair or on medium to long hair where a curlier look is required.

Sectioning of the hair

Each section of hair taken prior to placing the roller must be cleanly combed to prevent distorted roots. The points of the hair must be curled evenly under the roller to avoid fish-hook ends.

There are three basic roller placements used when setting hair:

◆ *On-base roller*. This roller sits on its own base and creates volume, height and lots of root movement. This technique is ideal for styles that require a soft, full look and is one of the most commonly used techniques when setting hair.

TOP TIP

Make sure the hair does not dry out during setting as this could cause the finished look to appear frizzy and dry instead of smooth. If the hair becomes dry while setting, keep it moist by spraying with water.

HEALTH & SAFETY

Make sure all tools are clean and sterilized prior to setting. Dropped tools must be washed (and hair removed) and sterilized before reusing. It is a good idea to have two sets of tools so one set can be sterilized while you work.

TOP TIP

Fish-hook ends will cause distorted and frizzy ends when combed out. A fish-hook end is formed when the end of the hair being rolled is not wrapped around the roller properly. The end is bent when the rest of the hair is curled. When the hair is dried and dressed out, the end will stick out straight or will remain frizzy in appearance.

◆ *Over-directed roller.* Used mainly on the front hairline to create straight, flat movement at the root, pushing the hair forward and producing volume on the ends. This technique is ideal for covering temples, particularly on styles where the hair has been designed to be styled away from the face.

◆ *Under-directed roller.* This technique tends to be used on the sides and back of the hair and keeps the hair at the roots in a flat position, avoiding the creation of any root lift or movement. When this technique of setting is used we often refer to the rollers as being **off-base**. This is ideal for bobs and creating flatter, more head-hugging hairstyles.

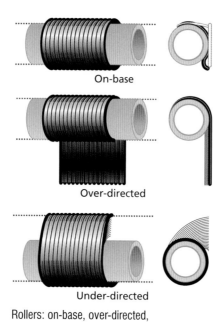

On-base

Over-directed

Under-directed

Rollers: on-base, over-directed, under-directed

Tools and equipment

Tools and equipment	Correct use
Hood dryer	**Hooded dryer** used to dry roller sets or boost the curl on pin curl sets

Tools and equipment	Correct use
Hand-held dryer	**Hand-held dryer** used to blow-dry the hair with a paddle brush, spiral blow-dry brushes or comb attachment
Heated rollers	**Heated rollers** used to create a set on previously blow-dried hair
Wet set rollers	**Wet set rollers** come in various sizes used to set the hair and create a solid curl
Plastic setting pins	**Plastic setting pins** used to secure rollers
Lady Jane clips	**Lady Jane clips** used to secure pin curls
Detangling comb	**Detangling comb** used to comb out tangles from the hair
Paddle brush	**Paddle brush** used to brush out and detangle the hair prior to shampooing or using heated rollers and after setting or pin curling. Also used to blow-dry the hair straight

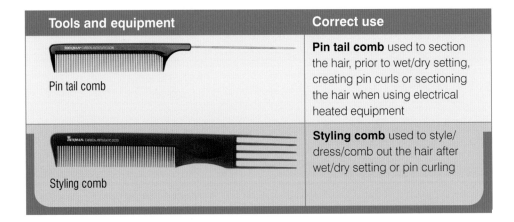

Tools and equipment	Correct use
Pin tail comb	**Pin tail comb** used to section the hair, prior to wet/dry setting, creating pin curls or sectioning the hair when using electrical heated equipment
Styling comb	**Styling comb** used to style/dress/comb out the hair after wet/dry setting or pin curling

For more information on personal hygiene procedures, deportment and posture and health and safety, see CHAPTERS 1 and 3.

Preparing for setting

The work area should be kept clean and tidy at all times, with all equipment sterilized before use. Make sure your tools are in easy reach and the client is gowned and protected in the house style of the salon.

Timing

Wet sets or pin curl sets can take some time to dry and clients can feel hot under the dryer so it is important to let them know how long their hair may take to dry. Long hair (past the shoulders) can take up to 45 minutes to over 1 hour. Mid-length hair can take 30 to 45 minutes and short hair 20 to 30 minutes. Make sure your client is comfortable and offer refreshments if this is salon policy. Keep checking with the client throughout the process that they are comfortable and adjust the heat setting on the hooded dryer if it becomes too hot.

Style maintenance

It is important that you discuss with your client how to maintain their new hairstyle. Tell them which products you used to set or pin curl the hair, why the particular products were used and how often they should be applied to support and maintain the new hairstyle. Discuss any future visits to the salon and how the hair will be maintained in the maximum condition. Record and update record cards.

Consultation and analysis

When setting hair it is important to take into account a number of factors which will help you to achieve the desired finished look. When carrying out your consultation and analysis of the hair prior to setting, you need to assess the following areas:

◆ hair condition;

◆ texture and density;

◆ degree of natural curl fall;

◆ face shape;

◆ nature of style to be achieved;

◆ client's requirements (including lifestyle);

◆ setting product to be used;

◆ any contraindications to be observed.

It is important to conduct a detailed analysis and consultation as this will influence the final result and the durability of the style. When setting African type hair it is important to keep the hair extremely smooth. Even tension must be used to avoid any distortion during the setting process. The condition of the hair must be taken into consideration when setting or pin curling. Hair in a poor condition, that has lost elasticity and is porous may not hold a very good set. Looking for contagious and non-contagious conditions during the consultation process is important to avoid contamination and cross-infection and the reputation of the salon.

Preparing the hair prior to setting

1 Analyze the hair texture, type and density to determine the correct roller placement and product selection for the look to be achieved and the durability of the hairstyle.

2 Discuss with your client the look to be created.

3 Shampoo and condition the hair in preparation for the set.

4 Comb the hair, making sure it is tangle free.

5 Apply suitable setting product to the hair depending on the hair type, length, condition, natural curl/ fall and final look to be achieved.

TOP TIP

If even tension is not used, a frizzy, unstructured curl will result.

HEALTH & SAFETY

Avoid using undue tension when setting the hair, particularly around the hairline, as this could cause traction alopecia.

ACTIVITY

Research a range of rollers that can be used to wet set the hair. Look at different designs used for heated rollers and discuss the strengths and weaknesses of using both wet and heated rollers.

Brick set

This technique of setting hair creates continual movement and allows the rollers to sit closer to each other, avoiding breaks/demarcation lines in the finished style. To create a brick pattern set, rollers are placed like tiles on a roof. Using this method to set the hair creates a much better finish and provides a continual line of movement in the dressed style. This is a much better option than channel setting, which can produce breaks/demarcation lines in the finished hairstyle.

Directional setting can also be combined with a brick set technique. This method is used when you require the hair to be styled in a particular direction. The following are examples of directional sets:

◆ middle parting;

◆ side parting;

◆ flick up;

◆ styled away from the face.

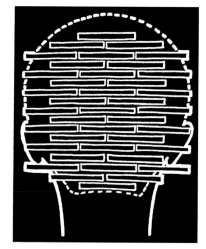

Rollers in brick pattern shape

How the hair is to be styled should be part of the discussion with the client during the consultation and analysis process. Considerations involved in selecting the direction of the set may involve lifestyle, as clients may have certain requirements for how they prefer their hair styled. Some hair, especially straighter hair types, may naturally fall towards a particular direction and this must be established prior to starting the set or blow-dry. To establish the natural direction and fall of the hair on wavier or straighter type hair comb the hair back away from the face and push forward. Blow-drying, setting or styling the hair with its natural fall/partings will mean that any hairstyle created will last longer and be more durable.

Technique

Prepare the hair for setting, as described above, applying the appropriate setting/blow-dry lotion or mousse. Comb the hair in the direction it is to be set. For this style comb the hair to the side without a side parting. This technique is an example of curling the hair points to roots, which will give an **on-base** movement.

STEP-BY-STEP: BRICK SET

1 Take your first section of hair in the front hairline above the eyebrow. Place your first roller.

2 Place rollers behind the first roller in a brick fashion, working towards the ears. Wind the hair on the sides away from the face.

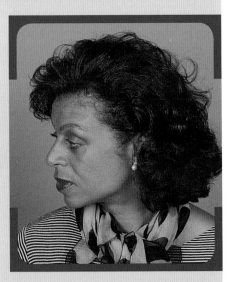

3 Take the next section of hair between each roller placed on the previous row. Continue brick setting, following the same method of placing rollers in between each previous roller until the whole head is set.

4 Place the client under the dryer until the hair is completely dry. Brush the hair thoroughly to remove demarcation lines. Apply dressing or oil sheen spray if necessary to the scalp/ends of the hair. Brush the hair into style; add height if required by back-combing the crown. Apply finishing products as necessary.

TOP TIP

Channel setting is a technique where the hair is set in rows throughout the head.

Setting the hair using Curlformers

There are a number of different setting options now available that can be used to set all hair types. Creating different looks through setting can be explored with alternative options to set the hair with. These can be pipe cleaners or placing the hair between foil then folding in a zigzag format and drying. Curlformers come in a variety of lengths and sizes to produce a range of curl formations, from tighter to wavier, in the finished look. Once the hair is set and combed out the hair can be left loose and spiral and flat, waved or expanded out to create carefree curls. The hair can be dressed in an upswept look for special occasions or red carpet events. This technique of setting is also excellent for clients who are in transition from chemically processed hair and want to go natural. The technique produces curl without the use of heat from an electrical tool, therefore causing less damage to the hair; this is a roots to ends technique.

Hook and curlformers

Wrap set

A **wrap set** can be carried out on short or long hair. This technique of setting produces a smooth look and uses the contours of the head to create shape and movement. Wrap setting provides a more natural form of setting, without the tension which can be created by blow-drying and setting, and is best used where a freer, smoother shape is required.

To add additional freedom and movement after wrap setting, the hair can be blow-dried or tonged, or a combination of both techniques may be used to produce the finished hairstyle.

Wrap setting short hair – Technique

1   Start by preparing the hair prior to setting, adding the appropriate blow-dry/wrap lotion or mousse. Comb the hair thoroughly, starting from the nape and working up towards the front of the hairline. Part the hair on the side (1).

2   Comb/brush small sections of the hair flat against the scalp, working from the nape up to the crown (2).

3   Comb the hair on the opposite side of the parting, blending the hair away from the front hairline into the hair at the back of the head (3).

4   Comb the hair on the same side of the parting, close to the scalp and just over the hairline. Blend the hair at the side behind the ears into the back of the head and nape area. Keep the hair smooth and close to the head while wrapping.

5   Cover the hair with a net and dry under a hooded dryer.

6   When dry, brush the hair in the direction of the wrap to loosen the wrap set.

7   Apply dressing or oil sheen spray to add sheen if required.

8   Finish the hair with a blow-dry. Tong the hair if additional support is required.

9   Apply finishing products (4).

Hair combed out and styled after being set using Curlformers

TOP TIP

Always keep the hair moist during wrap setting by spraying with water or lotion. This will make it more pliable and easier to mould close to the scalp.

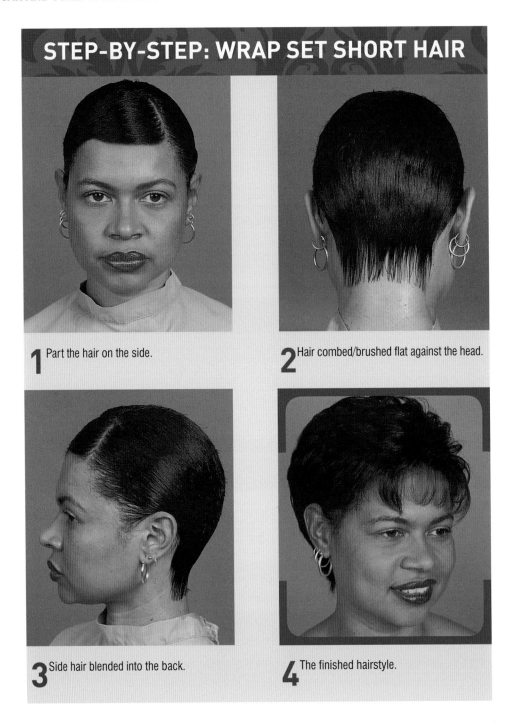

STEP-BY-STEP: WRAP SET SHORT HAIR

1 Part the hair on the side.

2 Hair combed/brushed flat against the head.

3 Side hair blended into the back.

4 The finished hairstyle.

TOP TIP	**Wrap setting medium to long hair – Technique**

TOP TIP

When wrap setting, always mould the hair in the direction of the cut and finished style.

Wrap setting medium to long hair – Technique

Start by preparing the hair prior to setting, adding the appropriate blow-dry/wrap lotion or mousse.

STEP-BY-STEP: WRAP SETTING MEDIUM TO LONG HAIR

1 Place three rollers on the crown (on-base) in a brick fashion.

2 Establish a side parting.

3 Take a small mesh of hair from the parting just under the rollers. Comb or brush the hair, keeping it close to the scalp.

4 Continue to blend the wrap by taking small meshes of hair and pivoting around the rollers in a spiral pattern.

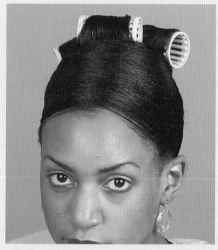

5 Continue until the whole head is wrapped.

6 The finished look

Place a net on the hair and put the client under the dryer. If the hair is long and thick, take the client out of the dryer after 20 minutes. Reverse the wrap by combing the hair in the opposite direction and dry the hair for a further 15 to 20 minutes to make sure the underneath hair is dry. Once the hair is dry, brush the hair out thoroughly. Apply dressing or oil sheen spray if required. Finish the hair with a blow-dry. Tong the hair if additional support is required. Apply finishing products.

TOP TIP

Make sure the hair is thoroughly dry before attempting to comb it out. If it is still damp the curl will drop and hair will become frizzy.

Finger waves

A **finger wave** is the moulding of the hair by the stylist to produce solid waves throughout the head. This style depends on the use of strong setting gels or lotions which are specially designed for African type hair. The products leave the hair with a solid finish once dry. Although these products have additional moisturizers built into them, continued use can have a drying effect on the scalp and hair. Because of the drying nature of these setting products, regular conditioning treatments must be recommended to the client to maintain the hairs condition.

Finger waves are made up of a **crest** and a **trough** movement. The crest is the raised part of the wave and the trough is the dip of the wave.

Technique

Prepare the hair for setting, as described above, applying the appropriate setting gel. Comb the hair, starting from the nape and working up towards the front hairline to remove all tangles from the hair. Using a styling comb, part the hair on the side.

STEP-BY-STEP: FINGER WAVES

1 Starting at the back, place the forefinger on the hair and comb the hair to the right. Push the teeth of the comb to the right and upwards. Hold in position.

2 Replace the forefinger with the second finger and apply pressure, squeezing the crest of the wave between both fingers. Remove the comb.

3 Keep the fingers in position and comb the hair to the left. Push the teeth of the comb to the left and upwards. Move the second finger down onto the section of the hair you have just moulded. Put the forefinger underneath as before and apply pressure,

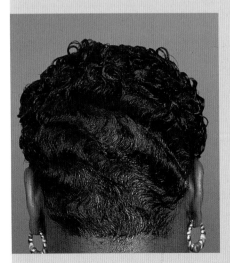

4 Continue using the same technique until the whole head is finger waved.

5 Place the client under the dryer. When the hair is completely dry take the client out and apply oil and holding spray to the hair.

Stand up barrel pin curls

Pin curls can be used as an alternative to roller setting the hair. Pin curls create a softer, less formed hairstyle, which has a more natural finished look. This technique was popular from the 1920s through to the 1960s. Pin curls are moulded by the stylist between the fingers, meaning the stylist forms the curl and shape. The curl created can vary in size from small, medium up to large pin curls. The pin curl size will produce a tighter or looser effect to the overall finished combed out hairstyle. Semi-circular, square or oblong sections can be used when pin curling.

Pin curls can be stand up barrel curls for volume or flat pin curls to create a flatter movement with less volume. This type of pin curl is ideal for shorter hairstyles and for waves and spiral curls. To control the ends or points of the hair end papers or cotton wool can be placed on the ends prior to curling the hair in a circular fashion. Using this technique can avoid fish-hook ends occurring and distorting the finished comb out and hairstyle. The hair must be kept wet at all times to help the hair become more **pliable** and easier to form the pin curl.

Pin curls can be carried out on a full head or partial head. A full head of flat reverse pin curls will create waves and is an alternative to finger waves.

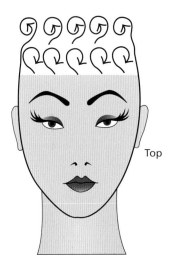

Reverse pin curling technique TOP

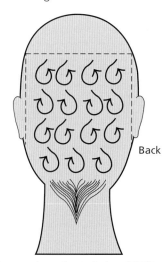

Reverse pin curling technique BACK

One row of pin curls anticlockwise and one row of pin curls clockwise is referred to as a **reverse pin curling technique**, which will create waves when the hair is pin curled, dried and styled. This technique will work well on wavy to straight hair types or relaxed hair that is fairly straight and not frizzy.

Alternatively, a mix of rollers and pin curls can be used to form a more contemporary hairstyle that combines firm curls with softer curls anywhere on the head as required and dictated by the final look or comb out. Flat pin curls can be used on the sides of the head above the ears, fringe or nape area. Barrel pin curls could also be used with rollers on the crown areas, or replace rollers to create a soft more open curl. This combination of setting was more popular in the 1950s and 1960s.

On-base barrel curl pin curl set

Discuss the direction of the final style with the client – hair combed back from the hairline, to the sides or with a fringe. Lifestyle, future maintenance and further salon visits should

Pin curling technique

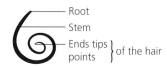

Root
Stem
Ends tips
points } of the hair

Clipping the hair from the root across the pin curl

Incorrect clipping with Lady Jane clips. Clipping from the bottom up will cause markation lines to form when the hair is dried

Flat pin curling technique and correct securing of pin curls with Lady Jane clip

also be discussed with the client. Pin curls are an ideal alternative to use when creating retro hairstyles.

Technique

1 Start by preparing the hair prior to setting, applying the appropriate blow-dry/ wrap lotion or mousse. Decide the direction and style the hair is to be pin curled in and dressed out.

2 Take a section of the hair approximately ¼″ to ½″ (6 mm to 12 mm) in diameter.

3 Comb the **sub-section** of the hair from the ends up the mid-lengths through to the roots.

4 Start by curling the ends between the fingers in a circular movement, leaving the ends open so a loop is formed; keep rolling the pin curl up to the root between the fingers into a barrel curl and secure at the root area with a Lady Jane clip.

5 Cotton wool can be placed inside the barrel curl to fill out the curl and keep the shape.

6 Place a net on the pin curl set and place the client under the dryer for 30 to 45 minutes, depending on the length of the hair. Longer, thicker hair will require more drying time.

Rolling the newly formed barrel pin curl down towards the root area

The finished barrel pin curl ready to be secured at the root with a Lady Jane clip

The finished combed out barrel pin curl set

HEALTH & SAFETY

Avoid the metal Lady Jane clip coming into contact with the scalp as this could burn the skin when heated under the dryer. To avoid burning and discomfort, strips of tissue paper can be place under the metal clip.

ACTIVITY

Carry out your own research into roller setting and pin curling techniques used throughout hairdressing history, from the 1920s to the present day, including retro hairstyles. Identify popular singers and actresses who may have set or pin curled their hair. Compile a style file of strong hair images of well-known personalities that span several decades (e.g. Josephine Baker, Betty Grable, Lena Horne, Elizabeth Taylor, Grace Kelly and Dorothy Dandridge). The file can be used as a visual look book for your clients, or to get inspiration to develop your own looks for catwalk shows, session work and special occasions.

Push waves

This style is suitable for clients who require a look that is durable and needs little or no maintenance. Push waves can be extremely drying to the scalp and hair because of the type of setting product used. When the hair is styled in this way, treatments must be applied on a regular basis to moisturize the hair. Prolonged use of this technique to style the hair can cause breakage due to the drying effect of the setting products.

Technique

1   Start with the standard consultation and preparation of the hair, as described above.

2   Comb the hair and apply a suitable dressing to the scalp.

3   Apply setting gel.

4   Comb the hair, starting from the nape and working up towards the crown and the front hair line.

5   Comb the hair and finger wave at least two rows across the front and sides.

6   Ensure the hair is combed flat against the head.

7   Start push waves on the crown of the head. You will need two tail combs – one to hold the push wave in place and the other to disentangle the hair.

TOP TIP

Keep the ends of the section of hair to be curled smooth to avoid fish-hook ends.

TOP TIP

To remove push waves from the hair, spray the hair with water until the hair is completely softened.

TOP TIP

If you are still in training, you will need to practise under supervision before working on paying clients.

STEP-BY-STEP: PUSH WAVES

1 Comb the hair and lift with the end of the first tail comb. Do not remove the tail comb.

2 Hold the push wave firmly in place with the end of the second tail comb. Do not remove the comb.

3 Comb the hair to de-tangle.

4 Use the end of the first tail comb to disentangle the hair by sliding the tail comb through the underneath section of the hair.

5 Lift the push wave with the end of the first tail comb.

6 Hold the push wave in place with the end of the second tail comb.

7 Comb the hair and free the underneath hair with the first tail comb, lift the hair with the end of the tail comb. Hold the push wave in place with the second tail comb. Repeat the procedure until complete.

8 Finger wave the hair at the back of the head. Put the client under the dryer with a net for 15 minutes to partially dry the push wave movement into the hair. Remove the client from the dryer and lift the push wave into shape using the tail comb.

9 The finished hairstyle

TOP TIP

The scalp must be kept moist by applying a suitable dressing prior to the setting product. Failure to apply dressing could result in a dry scalp and hair breakage.

The push waves must still be pliable enough to be lifted with the tail comb. If the hair is too dry, remoisten it lightly with blow-dry/wrap lotion. Replace the net on the hair and dry for another 20 minutes. When the hair is dry, spray with oil sheen spray and holding spray.

Heated roller set

Heated rollers are used as a quick way to set the hair. The technique produces soft curls and is a dry setting method, unlike the wet setting technique, which creates solid curls with lots of volume and movement. Heated rollers must be used on clean, dry hair; they are used to refresh a set or to add body and movement before styling the hair. The hair must be first washed and conditioned. Setting products such as mousse, wrap set or blow-dry lotion/heat protector must be used. Once styling products are applied then the hair is blow-dried straight and the heated rollers are applied to the hair and left in for at least 10 to 20 minutes. Heated rollers are very often used in cat walk shows, theatre, television and fashion shoots, as they work quickly to achieve the desired look.

Technique

Begin by preparing the hair prior to setting, applying the appropriate setting lotion, blow-dry/wrap lotion or mousse.

1 Blow-dry the hair straight ensuring the hair is thoroughly dried.

2 Decide on the direction the hair is to be set in.

3 Start from the front of the hair holding the heated rollers at the edge.

4 Wind the tips/ends of the hair smoothly around the roller to avoid fish-hook ends.

5 Apply heated curlers throughout the head securing with the heated roller pins or bulldog clips.

6 Leave the hair to take a set by cooling down.

The heated roller is held on the outer edge to avoid burning the fingers

The finished heated roller set
Be careful that pins are not digging into clients' scalp/skin.

Tousled soft curls that have been finger combed and styled

TOP TIP

The hair should always be allowed to cool down for a few seconds after drying, as this will help produce a longer more durable movement, prior to styling.

TOP TIP

Always make sure heated rollers are at their hottest; if the rollers have not been heated sufficiently the final set will be weak and drop out.

HEALTH & SAFETY

Hold the heated rollers on the outside edge to avoid burning the fingers on the body of the roller.

HEALTH & SAFETY

Heated rollers can be washed and then soaked in sterilizing fluid, rinsed and thoroughly dried before using again. Alternatively the rollers can be wiped with methylated spirits and allowed to thoroughly dry before placing them back on the heat rods.

TOP TIP

Holding spray can be applied after the heated rollers are placed on the whole head. This will give an added hold to the finished set; the hair will then be left for at least 10 to 20 minutes to cool down. A hooded dryer can be used for an additional 5 to 10 minutes, to produce a stronger curl result, if required. Let the hair cool sufficiently after removal from the dryer to lock in the curl and movement.

REVISION QUESTIONS

1 What will points or ends of the hair distorted during the setting and pin curling process produce?

1 Flicked up ends

2 Smooth ends

3 Fish-hook ends

4 Curly ends

2 What effect does products with alcohol in have on African type hair?

1 Gives the hair a shiny finish

2 Dries the hair out

3 Conditions the hair

4 Makes the hair pliable

3 What is a cohesive set?

1 A temporary wet set

2 A dry set

3 A heated roller set

4 A conditioning set

4 What effect do hydrogen bonds have on the hair during setting and pin curling?

1 Hydrogen bonds break when the hair is stretched and dried into its new shape

2 Hydrogen bonds reform when stretched into a new shape

3 Hydrogen bonds do not break

4 Hydrogen bonds split and then break

5 Why is it important when the hair is dry to cool the hair down after pin curling, setting and before styling?

1 So that a crisp solid curl is formed

2 To stop the hair being too hot

3 To cool the hair down

4 To create a shine on the hair

6 What effect do alpha and beta keratin have on the hair when setting?

1 Alpha is the length of the hair and beta keratin is the overall shape of the hair

2 Alpha keratin is the hair in its natural state and beta keratin is the hair after it has been stretched and dried into its new shape

3 Alpha keratin is the porosity of the hair and beta keratin is the rate the hair absorbs moisture

4 Alpha keratin and beta keratin refer to the condition of the hair

7 What happens to the hair when it absorbs moisture from the atmosphere?

1 The hair remains smooth in a beta state

2 The hair becomes shiny and smooth remaining in alpha state

3 Hair is hygroscopic so it will revert back to its alpha state

4 Nothing happens

8 What effect will setting products have on the hair during setting and pin curling?

1 Protect the hair from physical heat, atmospheric conditions and help to make the finished style durable

2 Cause the hair to become limp after dressing out the finished style

3 Make the hair greasy and lank, making it difficult to style

4 Protect the hair from moisture being absorbed

9 When would you use a wrap set?

1 To create a tight curly set

2 To create a flick up on the ends of the hair

3 To create a spiral/ringlet effect

4 To create a smoother movement in the hair

10 Why is the brick setting technique used when setting and pin curling the hair?

1 To create even curl movement

2 To produce a channel set technique

3 To avoid demarcation lines

4 To balance the shape of the curl

11 When would you recommend the use of Curlformers to your client?

1 Clients who would like a curl without the use of heated appliances

2 Clients who would like a softer more natural curl

3 Clients who would like a heated tool to create a lasting curl

4 Clients who would like curl reduced and a flatter smoother finish

12 An over-directed roller will create which type of movement?

1 Root volume with an even curl to the tips

2 Height with lots of volume at the roots

3 Flat volume at the root with curl on the ends

4 A flatter more head hugging appearance

8 Styling and finishing

LEARNING OBJECTIVES

This chapter covers the following:

◆ Maintain effective and safe methods of working when styling and dressing hair

◆ Creatively dress hair

◆ Provide aftercare advice

KEY TERMS

Above shoulders

Activator

Balance and shape

Below shoulders

Finished look

Holding spray

Moisturizers

Oil sheen spray

Serum

Session stylist

UNITS COVERED IN THIS CHAPTER

◆ Creatively style and dress hair

INTRODUCTION

Creatively styling the hair allows the stylist to create innovative and exciting hair designs for the client. This chapter deals with the art of styling the hair after blow-drying, setting and curling. It also covers hair-up looks for long hair and securing ornamentation. The chapter brings together a variety of skills used to create the finished look, on a range of hair types. It covers everything a stylist needs to know at Level 2, whether you are studying on the Combined course or looking to specialize in African Caribbean hair types, and serves as a reminder for students studying at Level 3.

Commercial

Creating the finished look

The **finished look** you create must enhance the client's features and personality. In order to achieve this, there are several points you need to take into consideration before proceeding to style the hair:

◆ the client's lifestyle;

◆ the client's face shape;

◆ any chemical process that has been applied to the hair;

◆ the style the hair was set or blow-dried in;

◆ the occasion the hair is being styled for;

◆ the **balance and shape** to be achieved;

◆ the tools needed to style the hair;

◆ maintenance and aftercare.

Different images can be created when styling the hair. Hairstyles fall into the following categories:

◆ *Commercial look*. An everyday look that is suitable for a variety of people and is easy to wear.

◆ *Fashion look*. A style that is currently in fashion and worn for a period or until it is no longer fashionable.

◆ *Classic look*. A style that never dates or goes out of fashion, for example a bob.

◆ *Avant-garde look*. A style that is ahead of its time; usually worn by the leaders of fashion before the look becomes fashionable.

◆ *Fantasy look*. Usually seen in competition hairstyling, theatre or film productions; a very dressed and exaggerated look not worn as an everyday style.

Fashion

Fantasy

Avant-garde

Hair length

This chapter will cover the hair level **above shoulders** and the hair level **below shoulders**. Shorter hairstyles such as gamin, pixie and urchin haircuts are described as styles that are above the shoulder. Other hairstyles are classified as below the shoulder. Hair extensions can also be added to the client's natural hair to extend the hair and allow the stylist to be more creative.

Hair above shoulders   Shoulder length hair   Hair below shoulders

See CHAPTER 10 for more information on hair extensions

Face shapes

When you create a hairstyle for a client, the face shape and any prominent features such as a large nose or protruding ears must also be taken into consideration. Stylists work with the concept that any style can be worn by any face shape so long as it is tailored to suit the client's features and personality.

The completed style must not draw attention to any irregularities in the face shape but should rather distract from them. For example, a client with a full face should not have width on the side of the face or a wide full heavy fringe, as these would make the face appear wider. To complement a full face, the hair could be styled forward with a feathered wispier fringe and sides. The rest of the hair could be styled to the side or away from the face with height on the crown.

The perfect face shape is supposed to be oval because there are no irregular contours. When we style the hair, we are trying to create the correct balance and shape for the face and in some respects achieve the perfect face shape.

The six different face shapes are oval, round, square, oblong, heart-shaped and diamond.

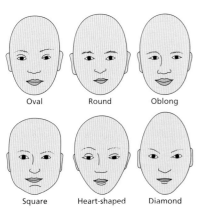

Oval   Round   Oblong

Square   Heart-shaped   Diamond

Styling tips for the six different face shapes are described in CHAPTER 3.

Prominent features on the face also need to be taken into consideration when styling the hair.

Prominent feature	Unsuitable hair style	Suitable hair style
Protruding ears	Hair combed behind the ears	Hair styled to cover the ears
High forehead	Hair swept away from the forehead	A full fringe or half fringe to soften the forehead
Receding chin	Hair swept back from the face; height on the crown	Side parting combined with fullness at the nape
Protruding chin	Hair styled away from the chin	A style that covers/softens the jaw line avoiding sharp lines; round shapes to create softness

As a stylist it is important that you do not draw your client's attention to any prominent features but mentally make a note of them and style the hair in such a way that it diverts attention away from them. Some clients are extremely conscious of their looks and will confide in you their concerns. Always try to reassure clients and build their confidence. Never openly agree with them.

Partings

Partings can create all sorts of illusions, some of which can be unflattering:

◆ A wide parting can cause the client's face to appear too wide and flat.

◆ A middle parting can make the face appear too wide, drawing attention to other features on the face.

◆ Partings which are too long could cause the crown to appear flat and the hair to lack height in this area.

◆ If you are creating a straight parting, ensure that it is straight.

The following partings can be used to create diversity in a hairstyle:

◆ Zigzag partings can create interest to the finished style. These partings work well if combined with styles that are not too fussy.

◆ Asymmetric partings can create interest and variety to a hairstyle. Balance the weight of the hair on the head (parting from temple to crown).

Middle partings are the most difficult to create as they can easily become crooked. The following technique can be used to create a balanced centre parting:

◆ Comb the hair back away from the face.

◆ Using the tip of the comb, lightly draw from the centre of the nose until you reach the hairline. Use the point of the comb to draw a line through the hair to the crown.

ACTIVITY

Carry out research into the leading hair and **session stylists**. Find out who are currently the leaders in fashion hairstyling. Look at the *Hairdressers Journal* to see who won the British Hairdressing awards. Also look at the Sensational hair awards and see who won in the various categories.

http://www.hji.co.uk/Home/

Styling tools

A variety of tools can be used to style the hair and create different effects.

Tools and equipment	Correct use
	Hand-held dryer Used to blow-dry the hair with a paddle brush, round blow-dry brushes or comb attachment.
	De-tangling comb Used to comb out tangles from the hair.
	Paddle brush Used to brush out and de-tangle the hair prior to shampooing or using heated rollers and after setting or pin curling. Used to blow-dry the hair straight.
	Pin tail comb Used to section the hair, prior to wet/dry setting, creating pin curls or sectioning the hair when using electrical heated equipment.
	Styling combs Available in a variety of sizes, some with closer set teeth and some with wider set teeth. Used to back-comb using the tighter set teeth and style/dress/comb/smooth out the hair with the wider teeth after wet/dry setting or pin curling. Also used to finger wave the hair.
	Round or radial blow-dry brush Used to blow-dry the hair, smooth straighten the hair and add movement and shape. Come in a range of sizes to create differing curl shapes, for a variety of hair lengths.
	Styling brush Used to style the hair after blow-drying, setting and pin curling and for back-brushing.
	Back-combing comb Used to back-comb the hair to create height and lift. The pick is ideal for creating lift and balance to the overall finished look.
	Section clips Used to keep hair sections clean, neat and tidy when styling the hair.
	Afro comb Used to style natural afro hairstyles or to lift hairstyle. Ideal for curly hair.
	Rake Comb Ideal for creating separation and breaking up solid styles. Also ideal for combing out natural hair.
	Vent Brush Used to create spiky, tousled looks.

TOP TIP

You can also use non-conventional items as accessories when setting hair, such as rags, chopsticks, straws and ric-racs,

ACTIVITY

Find some images of non-conventional items used as accessories when setting hair. Add some ideas of your own.

Tools for thermal styling are described in CHAPTER 9.

TOP TIP

Use a comb that feels comfortable and well balanced in your hands. Select different styling combs for different techniques, hair lengths and thickness.

Preparing for styling and finishing

As always, make sure your tools and equipment are clean and sterilized before and after each client to avoid cross-infection. Keep your work area clean and place your tools within easy reach. Think about your own deportment and posture as you work.

For more information on health and safety precautions see CHAPTER 1.

Timing

Be realistic with the length of time it will take to style long hair. It can be very time consuming so do let the client know how long it will take to create the hairstyle you are designing for them. For special occasion hairstyles, you should put aside one to two hours for the creation of the look. Take into account any adjustments you will need to make to the required final look and discussions with your client to ensure they are happy with it.

Style maintenance

It is important that you discuss with your client how to maintain their new hairstyle. Talk to them about the products used to set or pin curl the hair, why the particular products were used and how often product should be applied to support and maintain the new hairstyle. Discuss any future return visits to the salon and how the hair will be maintained in the maximum condition.

Record cards

Fill in and update record cards, to ensure that the salon has up-to-date information on treatments that have been carried out on the client.

For further information on data protection and record cards see CHAPTER 3 Client consultation and care.

Lifestyle

Lifestyle is about image and how individuals are perceived and would like to be perceived. Some individuals like to be at the forefront of fashion and like their hairstyle to make a statement. Others prefer a more moderate look, while some individuals desire a quick easy-to-manage hairstyle due to being active and busy, and some are constrained by the job they do (such as a police officer). It is your responsibility to understand your client, how they would like to wear their hair, why this is important to them and their personal commitment to their style. Based on the information given by the client, the stylist can then create the final look the client desires.

TOP TIP

Be careful how you apply dressings when dealing with very fine hair as they could cause the hair to lose body and become limp and difficult to style. Oil sheen spray can be used in place of a dressing cream if the hair is fine or you require a lighter product.

TOP TIP

On permed hair, failure to use finishing products could cause the hair to become dry, frizzy and brittle. Finishing products also need to be used on natural hair to make the hair easier to comb out and give the hair shine.

Finishing products and their use

Products help the stylist create the finished look. It is important, therefore, that you have a good knowledge of finishing products and their uses. This will help you to achieve the best results and enable you to advise your clients on aftercare. Different products will help you achieve a variety of results:

◆ *Hairdressing creams* can be heavy or light in consistency. The selection of a dressing will depend on the hair texture, for example coarse, dry textured hair will require a heavier dressing and more product; fine textured hair will need a lighter dressing and less product. Dressing should be applied sparingly to avoid flooding the scalp and hair. Only use a dressing if the scalp or ends of the hair are dry.

◆ *Oil sheen spray* can be used as an alternative to dressings. It is less oily and is absorbed easily by the hair, so is ideal for fine, limp hair. Oil sheen spray can also be used to give added shine to the hair after using a dressing. It is suitable for both relaxed and permed hair. Product should be applied sparingly, depending on the hair type, as finer textured hair will require light application to avoid product overload.

◆ *Gel* can be used on relaxed or permed hair during styling to keep the hair flat and neat on the sides and the back. It is also suitable for hair-up styles to control stray hair. Avoid using alcohol-based gels on permed hair as they can make the hair dry.

◆ *Holding spray* comes in light or strong hold formulas. Selection of the product will depend on how the hair is styled and durability required. For example, styles which need to be more mobile would be better suited to a light hold spray whereas a hairstyle that needs to be much firmer will require a stronger hold.

◆ *Spritz* is a firm hold spray used where a solid hold is required. It is ideal for upswept, scrunch or freeze styles on naturally curly or relaxed hair. It provides sheen to the hair and an immovable firm finish.

◆ *Hair moisturizer* is suitable for permed or natural hair. It comes in the form of a spray and coats the hair, making it easier to comb. It also adds sheen to the hair.

◆ *Activator* gives definition to permed or naturally curly hair. It increases the curl, adds control and stops the hair becoming frizzy. It conditions the hair and makes the hair pliable.

◆ *Moisturizer* activator is a combined product which avoids the use of two products, making application easier. It is suitable for permed and natural hair, and works well on dry hair.

◆ *Serum* is used where maximum shine is required. It has no holding properties and is ideal for use on relaxed hair. It will give definition to the finished style.

Blow-drying products are described in CHAPTER 6.

Setting products are described in CHAPTER 7.

Application of dressing

1 Comb the hair through, starting from the nape up to the hairline.

2 Part the hair down the middle and lightly apply dressing to the scalp (a).

3 Starting at the nape, section the hair using a comb (b).

4 Apply dressing to the scalp, working up to the front hairline (c) and (d).

5 Massage the dressing into the scalp.

6 Rub the dressing into the ends of the hair (e).

(a) Applying dressing to the scalp using a central parting

(b) Sectioning the hair

(c) Applying dressing to the scalp

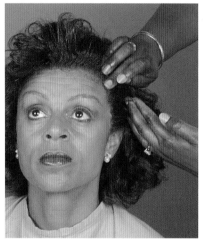

(d) Applying dressing to the front hairline

(e) Applying dressing to the ends

(f) The finished hair style after dressing has been applied.

TOP TIP

Each product has its own application technique. Check the manufacturer's instructions and make sure you know which hair types it is suitable for.

Styling techniques

As discussed at the beginning of this chapter, several factors need to be considered when creating a hairstyle. As a student of hairdressing, you need to learn basic skills which are relevant to all styles, so that when styles become fashionable again you will know how to achieve them.

Hairstyles are influenced by current fashion and social trends. As a stylist it is important to keep up-to-date with the latest fashion and trends in hair, clothes and make-up. This can be achieved by observing looks seen on the street, in clubs, at fashion shows, in fashion magazines, television pop videos and technical videos.

Back-combing/back-brushing

Creating height can play an important part in developing the finished style. This can be achieved by using one of the two following techniques:

◆ back-combing;

◆ back-brushing.

These techniques involve brushing or combing the hair through after setting/wrap-setting, blow-drying or tonging. The following method can be used for either back-combing or back-brushing.

1 Take a section of hair no wider than 6 mm (¼").

2 With one hand, hold the hair firmly in an upward position between the fingers.

3 With the other hand hold the comb between the thumb and fingers.

4 Place the teeth of the comb at the back of the section, 6 mm (¼") away from the scalp.

5 Push the teeth of the comb/brush downwards towards the scalp.

6 Place the comb/brush above the section you have just back-combed. Using the same technique as before, gently push the hair down on top of the previous section. Continue to build on the back-combing/brushing in this way until the required height and width is achieved.

7 Comb the hair on the outer side of the back-combing to create a smooth finish.

Styling the hair after a directional or brick set

1 Brush the hair thoroughly starting from the nape and working up the hair to the front hairline.

2 Brush the hair in the direction it was set to soften, blend and remove the roller marks.

3 Apply dressing or oil sheen spray to the hair as required.

4 If additional height is required add back-combing or back-brushing, dressing the hair from the nape and working upwards.

5 Look critically at the balance, shape, style and movement being created from all perspectives.

6 Adjust the height if required by lifting with a tail comb or styling pick. Ensure the hairstyle created suits the client and they are happy.

TOP TIP

Oil sheen spray can be used in place of a dressing, following the technique described here.

TOP TIP

Always back-comb the hair at the back of the section and not the front, as this could cause a ruffled appearance, making it difficult to create a smooth finish.

TOP TIP

Using the large side of the comb will produce a more textured finished look; the finer side of the comb will produce a smooth solid, immovable finish. Selecting which side of the comb to be used will depend on the look you want to achieve.

TOP TIP

To remove back-combing or back-brushing, comb or brush the hair gently from the ends, working up to the roots.

TOP TIP

Only porous, curly or hair that has a variety of different lengths will hold back-combing. Hair in good condition or all the same length will be difficult to back-comb.

TOP TIP

African-type hair may be too fragile to back-comb and does not require it, due to the natural body and pliable nature of the hair. This is particularly apparent after chemical relaxing has been carried out.

For information on a wrap set, see CHAPTER 7.

For details of the electrical straightening process, see CHAPTER 12.

Styling the hair after a wrap set

This method can be used to style the hair after wrap-setting using the round brush technique.

1   Brush out the hair thoroughly, following the direction of the wrap set.

2   Apply dressing or oil sheen spray sparingly to avoid the hair becoming limp during blow-drying.

3   Blow-dry the hair to create smoothness, movement and mobility if required.

4   The hair can be tonged if more support is needed.

5   Dress the hair in the desired style. Apply oil sheen or holding spray if required.

Styling the hair after a heated roller set

1   Brush the hair thoroughly removing roller marks and softening the curl, following the electrical straightening process.

2   Apply oil sheen spray/dressing/serum sparingly to the scalp and hair if required, to avoid the hair becoming limp and oily, this process would apply to African type hair, however on straighter hair types light sheen spray or serum can be used.

3   Style the hair in the agreed direction, looking at the balance and shape.

4   Use holding spray.

Styling the hair after blow-drying using electrical straighteners

1   Brush the hair thoroughly, following the electrical straightening process.

2   Apply oil sheen spray/dressing/serum sparingly to the scalp and hair if required, to avoid the hair becoming limp and oily, this process would apply to African type hair, however on straighter hair types light sheen spray or serum can be used.

3   Style the hair in the agreed direction, looking at the balance and shape, smoothing hair into place.

4   Use holding spray.

Styling the hair after using a styling wand

1   Finger style the hair following the use of the curling wand or for an alternative look brush or comb out the curls into waves.

2   Apply oil sheen spray/dressing/serum sparingly to the scalp and hair if required, to avoid the hair becoming limp and oily, this process would apply to African type hair, however on straighter hair types light sheen spray or serum can be used.

3   Style the hair in the agreed direction, looking at the balance and shape.

4   Use holding spray.

Finishing the hair after finger-waving or push-waving

1   Once the hair has been thoroughly dried, apply oil sheen spray; use holding spray to give additional support if required.

Styling the hair after scrunch drying

This technique can be used to finish the hair after a perm or on naturally curly/wavy hair.

1   Use an activator to promote curl and create separation.

2   Spray on moisturizer to add shine to the hair.

3   Style the hair using a pick or styling comb according to the client's requirements and the shape of the cut.

Natural styling of permed or curly hair

This method is used on permed hair and is also suitable for clients who have naturally curly or wavy hair.

1   Shampoo and condition, towel dry.

2   Pour activator or wave lotion into the palm of the hand, gently rub hands together to warm product to aid application (a).

3   Apply activator or wave lotion to the scalp by taking 6 mm (¼") sections (b).

4   Apply additional product to the mid-lengths and ends of the hair and massage the scalp (c).

5   Apply moisturizing spray (d).

6   The client can be put under a low power cool hood dryer, accelerator or climazon until the hair is semi-dry or alternatively use the diffuser to scrunch dry the hair. You should continue drying Caucasian hair until it is dry to avoid it becoming frizzy.

7   Apply activator, wave lotion or moisturizing spray to create separation and definition to the curl if required. Caucasian hair is also more likely to need hold spray rather than more moisture to avoid curl dropping.

8   Finish the hair, taking into account the client's requirements, face and head shape and haircut. Use an Afro pick or comb to style the hair.

TOP TIP

Additional oil sheen spray can be used to provide shine if the hair is dry.

Level 3

For more information see CHAPTER 5.

HEALTH & SAFETY

When using hair spray it is important to protect the client and avoid spray coming into contact with the eyes.

(a) Sectioning the hair and applying activator to the hair

(b) Applying activator to the ends

(c) Applying moisturizing spray

(d) The finished style after applying oil sheen spray

Styling techniques for long hair

The styling of long hair is a specialist area that can provide a platform for the stylist to be creative. A client with long hair has the option of a variety of styles. Any styling work on long hair should be neat and tidy with all pins and clips hidden.

The following hairstyles can be used on hair that is shoulder length and longer:

Bun

Equipment needed:

♦ paddle brush;

♦ de-tangling comb;

♦ styling comb/brush;

♦ tail comb;

♦ hair grips/hairpins.

Buns are a classic look, often worn by ballerinas and sometimes seen in catwalk fashion shows. This look can also be worn for weddings and special occasions. It is simple to create, as the hair is moulded around a bun ring which pads out the bun. This classic bun can also be achieved using back-combing to create a fuller look.

1 Shampoo and condition the hair and apply suitable setting product.

2 Dry the hair and then the hair on heated rollers; brush out.

3 Comb the hair into a ponytail with a covered band.

4 Place a bun ring over the ponytail and secure the hair around the bun ring.

5 Back-comb the hair smooth the hair over the bun ring. Secure with bent invisible pins around the edges of the bun.

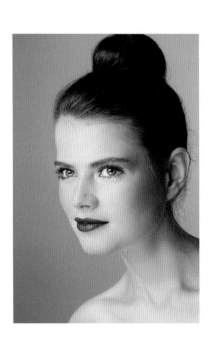

French pleat

This style can be achieved on pre-set or un-set hair. It is ideal for weddings, parties and any formal occasion. A French pleat can be styled with several options, for example with a side or middle parting, swept back away from the face. The direction in which the front of the hair is to be styled is also optional and will depend on the occasion, face shape and client's requirements.

Equipment needed:

◆ paddle brush;

◆ de-tangling comb;

◆ styling comb;

◆ tail comb;

◆ hair grips/hairpins.

Prepare the hair first by wet setting, heated roller set or blow-drying depending on the effect to be achieved.

1 Brush the hair thoroughly, starting from the ends and working up through the mid-lengths to the roots.

2 Brush or comb the hair to the centre left of the head, keeping the hair nice and flat.

3 Make sure the hair is smooth and held securely before placing the hair grips in a criss-cross position, overlapping each other up to the crown (a).

4 Place a grip in the opposite direction to stop the hair sliding out of the gripped area (b).

5 At this point back-combing can be added to the roots behind the gripped area. Handle the hair gently to avoid disturbing the hair grips. This will give support and create height to the finished French pleat (c).

6 To create a smooth finish, comb the outer back section of the hair, apply oil sheen spray and holding spray and comb the hair again gently.

TOP TIP

A pleat can be styled to the right or left of the head. If you are right-handed your plait can be coiled to the right and vice versa if you are left-handed.

TOP TIP

For a smoother, flatter pleat, do not add back-combing.

TOP TIP

Always apply oil sheen spray first rather than last. Using holding spray first will protect the hair and form a barrier to the oil sheen spray.

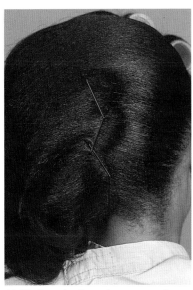
(a) Placing grips in a criss-cross pattern

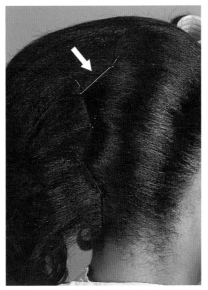
(b) Placing a grip in the opposite direction

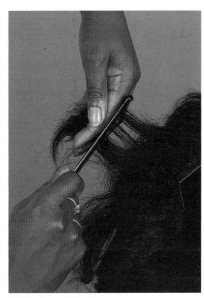
(c) Back-combing the roots

7   Hold the hair around the middle lengths and twist inwards, forming a coil (d). Secure the hair temporarily in this position with a large pin or section clip.

8   Smooth the outside of the pleat with a comb.

9   Smooth the surrounding hair, making sure all ends are secure. Apply oil sheen spray and then holding spray to the hair. Secure the pleat by using invisible pins bent at one end. This will ensure that the pleat remains in place (e) and (f).

(d) Forming a coil

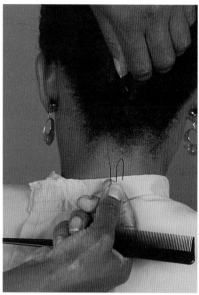

(e) A bent pin

(f) Securing the outside edge of the plait with bent pins

Horizontal roll

Level 3

Equipment needed:

◆   paddle brush;

◆   de-tangling comb;

◆   styling comb/brush;

◆   tail comb;

◆   hair grips/hairpins.

1   Shampoo and condition the hair and apply suitable setting product.

2   Dry and the hair on heated rollers.

3   Comb the hair out to the side over one ear and secure with grip. The fringe can be left out or integrated into the main body of the hairstyle.

4   Back-comb the hair then smooth the outer section.

5   Form a horizontal roll, by rolling the hair upwards and secure with pins and grips, apply sheen and then holding spray.

The finished look

Curl Cluster

Equipment needed:

◆ paddle brush;

◆ de-tangling comb;

◆ styling comb/brush;

◆ tail comb;

◆ hair grips/hairpins.

Curl cluster is a popular style that has been worn over the decades and is an excellent example of how fashion in the broad sense and hairstyles revolve and evolve. The style shows the real mastery of hairstyling and allows the stylist creative freedom to form, mould and design freely, as the style created is completely of your own ideas providing a platform to showcase your personal skills. The origin of the hairstyle dates back to the eighteenth century, hairstyles in this time consisted of stacked curls and ringlets.

Wigs and hairpieces would also be added to design and expand the hairstyle to create height, and volume wigs were powdered white. In the mid-1960s to 70s curl clusters made a re-appearance and were often styled with the client's own hair or hairpieces. Hair pieces would also be styled in clusters and placed on short cropped hair styles.

This style is suitable for medium to long hair and is ideal for special occasions. Curls can be placed anywhere on the head the nape, crown or as an asymmetric cluster. Hair pieces or hair extensions can be used, to fill out each curl or to add length. The style is created by first securing the hair in a ponytail with a protected band or placing grips in a circular fashion.

TOP TIP

The wider the circle created, the wider the finished cluster will be.

1 Wrap set or set the hair using the brick-setting technique. Comb the hair out and apply dressing or oil sheen spray to the hair. Blow-dry the hair and tong if necessary.

2 Part the hair on the side, leaving the fringe area out. Brush the hair on the sides and back upwards into a pony tail. Grip the hair in a circle and interlock the grips so that the hair is secure.

3 Take a section of hair and back-comb it. Smooth the top section of the hair.

4 Roll the hair into a curl and hold in place.

5 Fasten the formed curl with a grip or bent pin. Place curls on the outside around the perimeter near the grips first. This will build a foundation for the rest of the curls. Interlock the curls, building height in the crown.

6 Brush the fringe area into place. Spray the hair with oil sheen and holding spray.

ACTIVITY

Level 3

Carry out research looking into a variety of hairstyles to see how they have evolved over the years. Your research could look at the Afro hairstyle and how it has been used in catwalk shows. Look at Marc Jacob's catwalk show and traditional Afro hairstyles from the 1960s. This research can be done on any hairstyle that inspires you.

Back-combing a section prior to moulding
and creating a curl

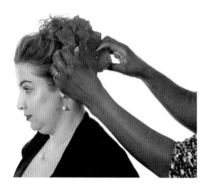

The placement of ornamentation

Ornamentation can be used to enhance any hairstyle but be careful not to overpower the whole head with ornamentation and keep a balance with the hairstyle you are creating. You might be asked to place a tiara, diamantes or flowers (natural or imitation) in the hair. When working on brides always fit veils and tiaras/ornamentation during any trial sessions, so you can agree exact placement and look to be achieved with the bride. Natural flowers are nice to work with, however you need to select flowers that will last throughout the life of the hairstyle. Remember any use of ornamentation must be aesthetically pleasing in placement, balance and style.

1 Decide where best to place ornamentation to the finished hairstyle.

2 Secure in place with grips in strategic areas.

3 Ensure the ornamentation is secure and neat.

TOP TIP

Do make sure ornamentation is securely attached, to avoid it detaching during the special occasion.

HEALTH & SAFETY

Remember when styling hair in any hair-up style not to grip or pull the hair too tightly to avoid traction alopecia and loss of hair. Do avoid placing too many grips and pins in the hairstyle as this can cause some individuals discomfort.

Client aftercare

It is important that clients use the correct techniques and products to maintain the hairstyle between salon visits. The table lists techniques and aftercare products which are suitable for a variety of hairstyles. These products can be recommended to clients for use in-between salon visits.

Hairstyle	Advice on aftercare	Finishing products
Shampoo and set; wrap set; blow-dry	Always use conditioner after shampooing the hair; conditioning treatment should be applied every two to four weeks depending on the condition of the hair and frequency of shampooing.	Oil sheen spray; holding spray; hairdressing cream; serum.
Finger waves; push waves	Do not keep the hairstyle for longer than two weeks; the hairstyle should not be worn continually – other hair styling options should be used to avoid the scalp becoming too dry and hair breakage occurring.	Regular use of oil sheen spray, holding spray or spritz.
Scrunch dry; permed hair	Shampoo and condition the hair every one to two weeks (very dry hair may require shampooing every two weeks) to allow the finishing products to penetrate the scalp and hair and the moisture balance to be built up; conditioning treatment should be applied every two to three weeks depending on the condition of the hair and frequency of shampooing.	Activator and moisturizer; oil sheen spray; hold spray.
Hair-up styles	Avoid moisture in the air (rain, cooking steam, shower) to ensure the style lasts. Reapply shine spray and hold spray when required. Return to salon for this service if unable to do this.	Shampoo and condition hair to remove product and restore natural hair condition/style.
Removal of hair-up style and ornamentation	Flowers, bun rings, tiara etc. Remove pins to loosen ornamentation, gently remove from hair.	

REVISION QUESTIONS

1 What is the perfect face shape?

  1 Round

  2 Square

  3 Oblong

  4 Oval

2 Why do we look at prominent facial features when we are styling the hair?

  1 To draw attention to a particular facial feature

  2 To create a hairstyle that enhances the features

  3 To create a round shape

  4 To reassure the client

3 What tools would you use to back-comb the hair?

  1 A de-tangling comb

  2 An Afro comb

  3 A barbering comb

  4 A comb or brush

4 Why would you use a diffuser?

  1 To diffuse colour

  2 To scrunch dry natural or permed hair

  3 To create a straight blow-dry

  4 To diffuse hairspray

9 Thermal styling

KEY TERMS

Heat protector

Hydrogen bonds

Hygroscopic

Irons

Off-base thermal curl

On-base thermal curl

Thermal

Thermal pressing comb

Thermal styling

Thermal styling stove/oven

UNITS COVERED IN THIS CHAPTER

◆ Style hair using thermal styling techniques

INTRODUCTION

This chapter is designed for senior stylists. It covers the mix of technical skill and knowledge required to be competent in the **thermal styling** of hair, working in a way which is safe, creative and meets the client's needs and requirements.

This chapter will cover all the learning outcomes at Level 3 for the senior stylist and can also be used by students studying on a combination of hair types at this level.

Thermal styling heater with equipment

ACTIVITY

Carry out your own research into Madame C J Walker and Annie Malone. Chart their contribution to the hair care industry in the 20th century and how they both developed their respective businesses within the hair care industry.

For more information on hair classification see CHAPTER 2, Hair characteristics

The history of thermal styling

The pressing comb has been used in some form or another since Egyptian times. The modern pressing comb, it is believed, was first invented in France, and patented in the USA by Annie Malone in 1900. Madam C J Walker initially worked as an agent with Annie Malone. She updated the pressing comb and like her mentor manufactured her own product line and opened schools in Cosmetology. Both women were philanthropists, giving generously to charities and organizations.

Thermal pressing and curling are only temporary processes and in the 1970s and 1980s they became less popular, due to their poor durability in moist, humid conditions which would make the hair revert back to its natural curl pattern. By the mid-1980s thermal styling had regained its popularity and was used to create a variety of different effects on the hair. Thermal styling was now being used on chemically processed hair to smooth out the cuticle and provide longevity to the finished hairstyle. Thermal styling is also suitable for the client who likes to wear their hair natural and wants the flexibility of wearing their hair straight on occasions, but does not wish to commit to long-term hair relaxers or chemical processing.

Curling **irons** can create a variety of looks and shapes, ranging from curly through to wavy and smooth. The heat from the curling irons causes curls to form and the finished style to be more durable, up until the hair absorbs moisture. Although pressing combs have remained essentially the same over the years, curling tongs have evolved and are now manufactured in a variety of shapes and sizes. This is also true of the thermal heaters, which have changed with time to come in different widths, colours and sizes to suit the needs of the individual stylist.

Thermal styling can also be a good option for the client whose hair is in a poor condition, or in need of a rest from chemical processing. When thermal styling is used on natural hair it straightens out the curl temporarily. On chemically relaxed hair, thermal styling may be used to both straighten natural regrowth and even out the hair texture, or to smooth out unevenly relaxed hair.

The science of thermal processing

The heat required to thermally style the hair should be based on the individual hair type, texture and hair condition. Some looser more resistant textures may require more heat. Some tighter curlier textures may become singed if the heat temperature of the tool is too hot. When thermally pressing hair in transition (growing out from a relaxing or perm process) only press the regrowth as this hair will be curlier than the chemically processed hair. Any heat used on the mid-lengths and ends should be minimal due to the hair being already processed and to avoid damage.

Thermal processing is a physical rather than a chemical process. When the hair is thermally processed, the heat produced by the **thermal pressing comb** or tong removes water from the hair. The more water that is removed, the straighter the hair will remain and the longer the thermal process will last.

Hydrogen bonds are broken when the hair is thermally styled. The hotter the styling tools are, the more hydrogen bonds are broken, achieving a longer lasting result. Hair is **hygroscopic**, meaning that it has the ability to absorb moisture from the environment. If the hair becomes wet/damp, during shampooing or on humid, rainy days, it will revert back to its natural state. We call this natural state alpha keratin. When we physically stretch the hair into a new shape during thermal styling, blow-drying, setting, physical straightening and tonging, we temporarily break hydrogen bonds and the hair takes on a new shape, called beta keratin. Hydrogen bonds reform when the hair becomes moist and the hair goes back to its alpha keratin state. These bonds break when the hair is stretched during setting, blow-drying and thermal styling, putting the hair into its beta keratin state.

Thermal styling products

There are many products on the market which are suitable for use when thermal styling. These products are of two types:

◆ pre-thermal styling **heat protectors**, sprays/lotions/dressings;

◆ post-thermal styling sprays.

Pre-thermal styling sprays

These are used *before* thermal styling takes place. These products are applied to wet or dry hair and protect the hair from the heat of the dryer or thermal styling tools. They are sometimes called heat protectors. They contain conditioners and polymers which coat and protect the hair during processing. The hair is then blow-dried. Thermal processing can then take place.

Post-thermal styling sprays

These are hair styling sprays that sometimes consist of a synthetic, adhesive polymer dissolved in alcohol to give hold. They may also contain small amounts of conditioning agents to create a soft hold. They are sprayed onto the finished style to create a solid, firm finish and protect the hair against atmospheric conditions. Post-thermal styling sprays can be used on the hair *prior* to tonging to protect it from the heat of the tongs and create a crisp, smoothly defined curl.

Spraying heat protector on the hair

Preparation of self and client

Make sure your client is sitting comfortably in the chair and at the correct height and position during the thermal styling process. Check that the client's feet are firmly on the foot rest. Advise that the equipment is hot and can damage the skin, especially if the client should make any rapid or sudden movements. Explain the technique to be used and the precautions you will take, such as keeping thermal irons away from the scalp, hairline and ears to avoid damage to the skin. It is important to let clients know that the tools are hot and that they should not make direct contact with thermal ovens/heaters/tools or place personal possessions near equipment.

Stand correctly with your feet slightly apart and rotate around the client as you are working. Adjust the chair's position to avoid overstretching or stooping over clients, which could cause shoulder/back injury or neck strain. Always remember to check for any infestation and infectious and non-infectious conditions prior to starting the process.

Checking of electrical equipment prior to use

Make sure that all electrical equipment is safe for use and fit for purpose, by checking that electrical cords are intact and not broken on **thermal styling stoves/ovens** and electrical pressing combs and tongs. If stray strands of hair are left in the oven they will burn and could cause clients to become concerned their hair is becoming damaged or burnt. If this situation occurs, let your client know what is happening to avoid them becoming alarmed. Hair is constantly being shed as we comb it and can easily become trapped in tools, so check that any hair has been removed before placing tools back in electrical stoves/ovens.

Cleaning and preparation of the work area

Make sure your work area is kept clean at all times with sterile wipes or sprays and remove any hair; clean and sterilize all tools after each client. Lay your tools out in advance of your client, so they are in easy reach and in a tidy accessible manner. Avoid over usage of products on the hair to stop the hair being over burdened with products and becoming lank and limp during the thermal process. Any product taken out from containers to be used on the client must not be put back in containers as this could cause cross contamination. Excess product will need to be disposed of in a suitable manner, only use the specific amounts of product required for the client's hair to avoid wastage.

Aftercare advice

Once you have carried out the thermal styling process, discuss with your client how they must maintain and care for their hair, and how often they need to return to the salon for shampooing, conditioning treatments and re-do the thermal process. Introduce a range of products that would be good for their hair texture and curl pattern, depending on whether the client's hair has been chemically processed or if the hair is natural and free from chemicals. Products designed for chemically styled hair may not always be suitable for natural hair. The client with natural hair may like to use products that have been naturally sourced, which they may feel is in keeping with their philosophy and approach to hair care and product usage.

TOP TIP

A thin silk scarf could be used to protect the hair during sleeping as it will incur less friction on the hair. However, it should be noted that scarfs or stocking caps may be uncomfortable during sleeping as they could keep the head hot and cause the thermal pressing to revert. Friction can also occur when covering the hair around the hairline, causing breakage or traction alopecia. We do lose heat from our head when we sleep and it would be best to allow the natural evaporation and cooling of the scalp to take place uninhibited.

TOP TIP

Exercise will cause perspiration in most people. This may cause thermally processed hair to revert back to its natural curl due to humid conditions. Clients who exercise regularly should be advised to wear a hairstyle that is easily maintained, such as natural hair, plaits or short cropped hair. Hair that has perspiration on it becomes brittle, dry and difficult to manage. When this happens the hair should be shampooed and then freshly thermal processed. An anti-reversion wax can be used around the hairline, which can protect the area from humid damp conditions. These products are made of a thick heavy wax and can cause product build-up and attract debris and dirt to the hair. Regular shampooing and conditioning can avoid this happening.

Preparation of the hair prior to thermal styling

Prior to any thermal styling being carried out, the client must be properly gowned and protected. This will give added protection against thermal equipment coming into contact with the body, or sections of hair that are still warm from the use of thermal appliances resting on the neck or shoulders. A thorough consultation and analysis should be carried out to assess the client's needs and the hair's ability to be styled in the selected look. The hair must be shampooed and conditioned. Failure to cleanse the hair properly can result in unpleasant odours and a mist of smoke during thermal processing caused by the burning of residue oils and debris on the hair.

For further information go to CHAPTER 6.

Consultation

1 Examine the client's scalp and hair.

2 Discuss with your client the result to be achieved.

3 Discuss any concerns they may have about the process to be carried out.

Analysis

1 Assess the natural curl pattern, texture, condition and density. This will help you and your client decide and agree on the degree of straightness required.

2 Decide which shampoo and conditioning treatment should be used.

3 Select the thermal styling products to be used.

4 Select the thermal styling technique to be used.

TOP TIP

Never thermally process dirty hair as this could cause unhealthy fumes, due to the debris in the hair, which could cause the hair to become damaged and break.

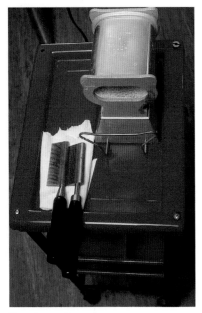

Pressing equipment

Use of thermal combs

Thermal combs come in a variety of shapes and sizes. Some have a curved back for added smoothness. Some have widely spread teeth for thicker, coarser hair; others have closer set teeth for finer hair. As with the choice of a pair of cutting scissors, the selection of thermal styling tools is decided on the ability of the tool to do the job at hand and the personal choice of the stylist.

Thermal combs are of two types, electrical and non-electrical:

◆ *Non-electrical combs* tend to be hotter than electrical pressing combs. These combs are heated to a high temperature in a special electrical heater or oven. Before using the comb on the hair, its temperature must be checked and if necessary it must be first cooled on a thermal cooling pad or tissue.

◆ *Electrical combs* are plugged into the mains and the temperature is controlled by a thermostat gauge built into the comb. The disadvantage of using electrical pressing combs is that the element can burn out, also the temperature tends to be lower and may not be sufficient to straighten the hair effectively.

Equipment needed for thermal pressing

◆ Pressing comb;

◆ Thermal heating stove or oven (if using a non-electrical pressing comb);

◆ De-tangling comb;

◆ Water spray;

◆ Thermal cooling pad (to control the heat of the pressing comb);

◆ Tissue paper (to test the temperature of the thermal tool prior to use).

HEALTH & SAFETY

If a non-electrical pressing comb is excessively hot, place it on the cooling pad and spray with water. A water spray can be used as an alternative to cooling non-electrical equipment.

HEALTH & SAFETY

Thermal tools must be cleaned with special thermal cleansers to avoid unsightly build-up and keep equipment hygienic and in good working condition. Thermal cleansing spray or wipes can be used to remove residue on tools.

For more information on shampooing and conditioning see CHAPTER 5.

HEALTH & SAFETY

Be extra careful when working with white hair. If the thermal comb or iron is too hot, it can discolour white hair, making the hair yellow or even singeing the hair. Always check the heat temperature on tissue paper first, prior to use, to avoid damage occurring to the scalp and hair.

Safe use of thermal pressing combs

1   Select a suitable pressing comb depending on the thickness of the hair.

2   Check the temperature of the pressing comb before attempting to press the hair. To test the temperature of the comb, place it on a tissue. If the tissue becomes scorched or burns, the comb is too hot.

3   If the pressing comb is too hot, cool electrical pressing combs by reducing the temperature – never spray water on them. When working with non-electrical pressing combs, cool the comb by placing it on a cooling pad. If necessary spray with water.

4   Place the thermal pressing comb 12.5 mm (½") away from the scalp to avoid burning.

5 Always hold the hair at a 45° angle to avoid burning the scalp with the pressing comb.

6 Use the back of the pressing comb to straighten the hair.

Pressing technique

1 Gown and protect the client.

2 Carry out a thorough consultation and analysis.

3 Prepare the hair by applying the correct shampoo and conditioning treatment.

4 Select a suitable drying technique for the hair.

5 De-tangle the hair and divide into four sections.

6 Sub-divide the hair into a 6 mm (¼") section starting at the nape.

7 After testing the temperature, first on tissue paper and then on the ends of the hair, to gauge the temperature is correct, place the teeth of the pressing comb 12.5 mm (½") away from the scalp in a upwards position, pressing the underneath of the hair first.

8 Place the comb on the top section of the hair, place the pressing comb in the root of the hair and glide the comb through the roots, mid-lengths and ends of the hair (c), (d) and (e).

9 Turn the wrist outwards, away from you. Use the back of the comb to straighten the hair. Feed the hair slowly through the comb as you work down towards the ends of the hair (f).

10 Continue the straightening process throughout the hair using the same technique.

11 Stand in front of the client to gently press around the front hairline.

(a) Before application

(b) Back view of natural hair prior to pressing

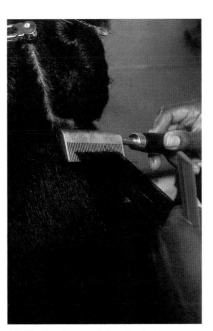

(c) Placing the comb into the hair 12.5 mm (½") away from the scalp

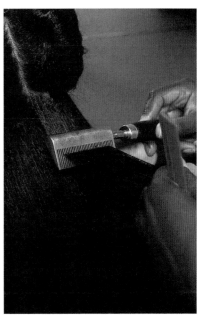

(d) Taking the comb through the hair

(e) Continuing to press the section of hair

(f) Using the back of the comb to press and smooth the section of hair

(g) The finished style

12 Process the hair according to the hair texture and the kind of look you would like to achieve. For example, when working on natural hair, repeat the above process so that the hair is pressed twice. This will give a straighter look. When chemically relaxed hair is being pressed to smooth out the cuticle, the process should be carried out only once or lightly, to avoid over processing the hair.

> ### TOP TIP
> When pressing the regrowth area on a client who is transitioning (going natural and growing out a chemical process), only press the regrowth area. If the chemical processed hair is frizzy a cooler thermal processing can be used on the ends, to avoid over processing or damaging the chemically processed hair. Alternatively if the hair is being tonged, the chemically processed hair will become straighter.

> ### TOP TIP
> Prior to thermal pressing it is better to blow-dry the hair using the blow-dry attachment or paddle brush technique. This will smooth the natural curl in preparation for thermal pressing.

> ### TOP TIP
> To avoid burning the scalp, always make sure the hair is completely dry before attempting any thermal processing, as heat on damp hair will produce a steam that could burn the scalp.

Use of thermal tongs

Thermal tongs, like thermal combs, are available in a variety of shapes and sizes. The size of tong selected is dependent on the length of the hair and the style to be achieved. A variety of curl shapes can be produced by tonging:

◆ waves;

◆ barrel curls;

◆ spiral curls;

◆ root curls;

◆ off-base/dragged curls.

Using professional tongs proficiently and correctly comes only with practice and experience. Before attempting to use tongs, particularly those with swivel handles sometimes known as marcel tongs, it is important to learn to control and use them correctly.

The correct way to hold electrical tongs

There are two basic movements used to control the tongs:

- opening and closing the barrel;
- turning the tongs.

Opening and closing the barrel

1 Hold the tong upright with the thicker end of the barrel at the bottom.

2 Place the first three fingers on the outside of the handle.

3 Place the thumb on the inside of the handle nearest to you.

4 Place the tip of the little finger on the lower handle so that it is pointing in towards you.

5 Open and close the fingers using the little finger to control the movement.

This action will produce a clicking sound with the tongs and enables the hair to move smoothly through the barrel. Once you have mastered this, move on to the next stage.

Turning the tongs Try rotating the tongs, turning the handles inwards and towards you. This action enables a curl to be formed. Practise this movement until you are comfortable with it. The correct use of the tongs involves a combination of these two movements.

Curling tongs can be electrical or non-electrical.

- *Electrical tongs* have a thermostat built into them which controls the temperature. They are kinder to the hair as they do not become as hot as non-electrical tongs. However, because of this, styles that can be achieved are limited. The disadvantage of using this type of tong is that the end result is not as durable as with non-electrical tongs. Electrical tongs do not come in such a wide variety of shapes and sizes as non-electrical tongs.

- *Non-electrical tongs* can get much hotter, allowing the stylist to achieve a greater variety of effects. The hotter the tongs, the greater will be the durability of the finished style. For this reason they must be used with additional care, observing the correct safety precautions as outlined earlier in this chapter for non-electrical pressing combs. Non-electrical tongs are available in a wide variety of shapes and sizes.

Equipment needed for thermal tonging

- Tongs;
- Thermal heating stove (if non-electrical tongs used);
- De-tangling comb;
- Tail comb;
- Water spray;
- Thermal cooling pad (to control the heat of the tongs).
- Tissue.

HEALTH & SAFETY

It is best to apply dressing to the scalp after the hair has been thermally pressed, rather than during the pressing process, otherwise the heat of the comb combined with the dressing could scald the scalp.

TOP TIP

Before using the pressing comb, test the temperature on tissue or a cooling pad. Make sure the temperature is correct by testing on the ends of the hair first.

TOP TIP

Opening and closing the tongs will allow the hair to move freely while tonging; turning the tongs allows a curl to be achieved.

Safe use of thermal, non-electrical tongs

1. Select the size of tongs to be used according to the length of the hair and the style to be achieved.

2. Check the temperature of the tongs before attempting to tong the hair. Test the temperature by placing them on a tissue. If the tissue becomes scorched or burns, the tongs are too hot. Place extremely hot tongs on a cooling pad and spray with water or leave to cool naturally.

3. Always smooth the root area of the hair first by placing the tongs at the roots. Grip the hair and gently pull the tong down the hair shaft a few times, then place the tongs in the desired position for tonging. This will do two things – smooth the cuticle and establish a firm grip on the hair with the tongs.

4. When creating root curls or barrel curls, hold the hair at a 90° angle when tonging.

5. When creating dragged curls, hold the hair at a 45° angle when tonging.

6. For added protection and if you are unsure, place a comb under the tongs to protect the scalp, especially when working on short hair. This will allow you to get closer to the scalp.

TOP TIP

Place a comb under the tongs when working near the root area to avoid burning the scalp.

Tonging techniques

Barrel curl

Barrel curls produce a soft, open-ended curl ideal for styles which require a softer, freer look, or support after wrap-setting or blow-drying.

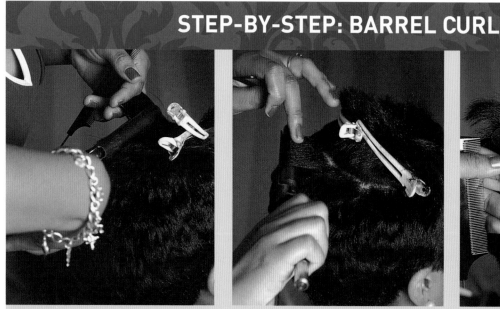

STEP-BY-STEP: BARREL CURL

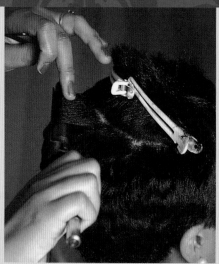

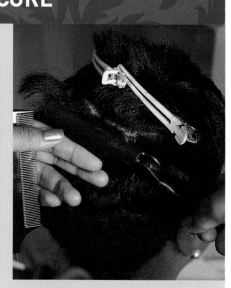

1 Take a section of hair and smooth the roots between the two barrels of the tongs. Pull the tongs to the ends of the hair, maintaining an even tension.

2 When you reach the ends of the hair, wind the tongs up to the roots.

3 Maintain tension to avoid the ends slipping out of the tongs.

 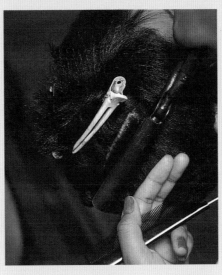 

4 At the root area, open and close the tongs to free the ends of the hair. Hold the tongs in place for a few seconds to develop a firm, smooth, even curl.

5 Rotate the tongs within the newly formed curl to free the points of the hair.

6 Gently remove the tongs.

Spiral tonging

This technique is suitable for shoulder-length and longer hair. It produces vertical curls that cascade downwards, forming a spiral/ringlet effect.

1 Section the hair in nine sections (as for perming). Take a vertical section 25 mm (1") in length, starting at the nape of the neck.

2 Work from left to right.

3 Place the tongs 12 mm (½") away from the scalp. Smooth the roots of the hair with the tongs.

4 Turn the strand of hair to be tonged inwards towards the left.

5 Open and close the barrel to feed the hair through.

6 Continue to wind the hair down the barrel of the tong, opening and closing the barrel to release the hair through.

7 When you reach the ends of the hair, rotate the barrel to ensure the ends of the hair are curled.

Off-base tonging

This technique is ideal when movement is required on the ends of the hair. The hair is tonged at a 45° angle throughout the head and produces dragged curls with no root movement. The hair can be tonged in an upwards or downwards position.

Off-base tonging long, layered hair

This technique is ideal for creating styles where the ends of the hair will be flipped upwards.

STEP-BY-STEP: OFF-BASE TONGING LONG, LAYERED HAIR

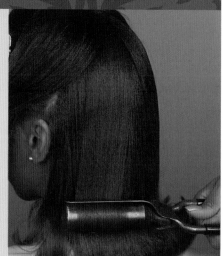

1 Smooth the hair along the roots between the two barrels of the tong.

2 Pull the tongs to the ends of the hair, maintaining an even tension. When you reach the ends of the hair, start winding the hair upwards, turning the ends under.

3 Hold the tong in position and allow the curl to be formed. Rotate the tong inside the hair to free the ends. Remove the tongs gently.

4 The hair after tonging

5 The finished hairstyle

Off-base tonging a short, graduated hairstyle

This technique is ideal for styles where the ends of the hair need to be curled under. For this technique a C-shaped tong is used. The C tong is comprised of two half sized barrels, designed to curl the end/perimeter of the hair only.

STEP-BY-STEP: OFF-BASE TONGING A SHORT, GRADUATED HAIRSTYLE

1 Start tonging the hair from the back, smoothing the hair along the roots between the two barrels of the tong.

2 Curl the ends of the hair under.

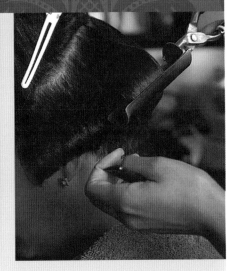

3 Follow the same procedure as in step 3 for long, layered hair.

4 Proceed onto the sides, then work up to the crown of the head and tong the front of the hair.

5 The finished style after tonging.

Flat irons

Flat Irons will smooth the hair and bevel (bend) the ends of the hair, creating smoothness and movement on the perimeter of the hair only. This technique is ideal for bobs or straighter hairstyles and creates an off-base look with no internal movement and movement on the ends only.

Technique

1   Test the flat iron on the tissue paper first to test the temperature (a)

(a) Testing the temperature of the thermal irons on tissue paper.

2   Section the hair at the nape area.

3   Test the temperature also on the ends of the hair first to ensure the iron is at the correct temperature.

4   Smooth the hair throughout the section first to smooth and straighten the cuticle.

5   Straighten the hair at the root section first with the flat irons, then mid-lengths and bevel the ends by turning the wrist towards the client.

6   Protect the scalp and hair by placing the comb underneath as you work through the section of hair (b).

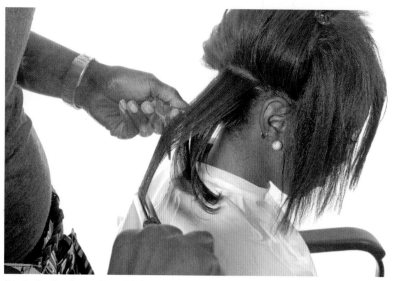

(b) Protecting the scalp and hair by placing the comb under the flat irons as the hair is smoothed and styled.

7 Replace the flat iron on the thermal heater to warm, take another subsection smooth through the hair and bevel the ends.

8 Continue taking sections throughout the head until the whole head is straightened and styled (c).

Thermal styling tools

(c) The finished look after using the flat iron.

Thermal styling tools	Correct use of thermal tool	Styling products
Pressing comb (electrical and non-electrical)	To straighten out the hair using physical heat and the teeth and back of the comb with moderate pressure to temporarily press and straighten the hair.	Thermal hair sprays, pressing creams, thermal seal sprays and serum reversion wax used around the hairline if required.
Thermal irons/tongs	Will smooth out the cuticle and create **on-base thermal curls**, **off-base thermal curls**, ringlets and differing degrees of curl movement in the hair based on the size of the thermal iron.	Thermal hair sprays to protect the hair as you curl it, sheen spray and serum to add moisture. Holding sprays used to improve longevity of the hair style and create a durable curl, reversion wax used around the hairline if required.
C iron/tong	Used to smooth the cuticle, straighten the hair and bevel ends under to create movement on the perimeter of the hair only. Only suitable for straighter styles.	Thermal hair spray used to protect, sheen sprays and serum used after thermal styling. Holding spray used to create a firmer, crisper look, reversion wax used around the hairline if required.
Thermal flat Iron	Used to smooth the cuticle, straighten the hair and bevel ends under to create movement on the perimeter of the hair only. Only suitable for straighter styles and where more movement is required in the finished hairstyle.	Thermal hair sprays, sheen sprays and serum used after thermal styling. Holding spray used to create a firmer crisper look if required, reversion wax used around the hairline if required.

REVISION QUESTIONS

Level 2

1 Which products are used to protect the hair during thermal styling?

1 Conditioner

2 Re-arranger

3 Heat protector

4 Dressing

2 What type of method do we use to describe thermal styling?

1 A chemical and physical process

2 Addition of water

3 Removal of water

4 A physical process

3 What could happen to white hair during thermal styling?

1 The hair can become discoloured

2 The hair will singe

3 The hair will lose its elasticity

4 The hair will become dry and break

4 Which thermal styling tools get the hottest?

1 Thermal pressing tools

2 Electrical tongs

3 Gas heated tools

4 Electrical pressing combs

5 If the hair is not shampooed or not cleaned properly prior to thermal styling what could happen?

1 The hair could become, lank, limp and easy to style

2 The hair will become dry and brittle after pressing

3 The hair will be limp, smoke and have an unpleasant odour

4 The hair will be easy to style

6 What shapes can curling tongs/irons create?

1 Straight

2 Ringlets

3 A variety of curl patterns

4 Bevelled ends

7 Which bonds are broken when the hair is pressed?

1 Sulphur bonds

2 Disulphide bonds

3 Hydrogen bonds

4 Salt bonds

Level 3

8 If the hair has been chemically processed and has a re-growth what heat setting should be used?

1 Varying heat settings

2 Consistent heat settings

3 Low heat settings

4 High heat settings

9 How should you test the temperature of a thermal styling tool?

1 Touch with your hand

2 Test it on the client's hair

3 Use tissue paper

4 Test on your own hair

10 What is a post thermal styling product used for?

1 To add moisture prior to styling

2 To give hold and protect from humidity

3 To condition the hair before setting

4 To mould the hair into a finished style

11 At what angle should the straightening comb be held?

1 90°

2 180°

3 0°

4 45°

12 What is the purpose of a thermal cooling pad?

1   Control the heat of the tool

2   Heat the tool to hotter temperature

3   Rapidly cool the tool down

4   Acts only as a resting mat

13 What style does a C-shaped tong produce?

1   Root volume and even curls

2   Smoother straighter hair styles

3   Spiral tong effect

4   Curls the ends/perimeter of the hair only

10 Hair extensions

LEARNING OBJECTIVES

This chapter covers the following:

◆ Maintain effective and safe methods of working when attaching and removing hair extensions

◆ Plan and prepare to attach hair

◆ Attach and blend hair extensions

◆ Remove hair extensions

◆ Provide aftercare advice

KEY TERMS

Bonding
Bonding glue
Cap weave

Clip-on extensions
Curved needle
Mesh weave

Micro bonding
Weft

UNITS COVERED IN THIS CHAPTER

◆ Provide hair extension services using temporary and longer lasting attaching techniques

INTRODUCTION Level 3

Specializing in hair extensions can open an exciting new world for both the stylist and client alike. There is no end to the variations and styling options, technical designs and looks that can be created. This chapter covers hair extensions on a range of hair types although the main emphasis is on the application of hair extensions to African type hair. The techniques of stitched weaving, bonding, self-adhesive bonds and clip-on extensions work across all hair types.

At Level 3, adding hair extensions requires more planning, dexterity and technical know how. At this level, it is time to build on the skills gained earlier and become creative. You may well be developing your own clientele, and it is important to work efficiently and effectively.

The history of hair extensions

The use of hair extensions and wigs goes back to early Egyptian times when wigs were widely worn by royalty and officials. The wigs made in ancient Egypt were of a superior quality and not dissimilar from those used today. Adding extensions to the hair on the other hand, has been practised for centuries throughout the African diaspora, with both men and women wearing extensions in a variety of materials, with some styles taking days to complete due to their elaborate design.

In the 1960s women in the UK started using hair **wefts** made out of yak hair after experiencing damage from the early hair relaxers which were very caustic and caused severe breakage and harmed the scalp. The use of hair wefts originated from theatrical productions where an actor required long hair. Wefts were used because they looked more natural than wigs and would be worn for the duration of the production. Yak hair, which was also used to make false beards, was thought at the time to look similar to African type hair, but it was not a good blend and had a coarse, wiry appearance and was not representative of the range of curl patterns and hair textures found in African type hair.

In the UK, the hair extension market has exploded over the last 15 years, with hair extensions being used across all cultures. The choice ranges from the more outrageous coloured extensions for fun, to subtle pieces giving the appearance of thickness or length, or providing a completely new look. The products and techniques are varied. Hair extensions are available from bulk hair for plaiting/cane-rowing/fusing or weft hair for weaving **bonding**. They can either be human hair, synthetic hair which is made out of nylon or a blend of both and can vary in types from straight to curly, crimped or waved.

Some types of human hair are chemically treated to produce more varied styles and colours while others are not put through harsh treatments so have a softer, natural feel. This latter type of hair, known as *Brazilian hair*, has been cut from the donor with the cuticle aligned, gently shampooed then stitched on to a weft. You should always use the hair that is best suited to your client's hair type, whether it is straight, curly or wavy. On African type hair, extensions can be carried out on natural, chemically processed hair, or hair which has been treated with a keratin treatment.

Working safely

As with all services, make sure you follow all salon rules about health and safety, ensuring that your tools are sterilized before use to avoid cross-infection and infestation. Ensure that your work area and mirror are clean and tidy and that you use clean protective clothing (gown and towel) for your client and that you are well presented. Remember to position yourself and client in such a way as to minimize fatigue to yourself and to ensure comfort to your client especially as extension work can take several hours to complete. Where possible use a stool.

See CHAPTER 1 for more information on health and safety.

Make sure that your tools and equipment are fit for purpose. When carrying out extension work involving the use of **bonding glue**, it is advisable to test your client beforehand for any allergic reaction to the glue. You should also pay particular attention when attaching hair for weaving using the sewing method. If you are not experienced then it is best to use a **curved needle** so as to avoid injuring the client's scalp.

Consultation and analysis

Consultation must take place before any kind of extension work is carried out. Gather as much information as possible from the client about the history of their hair and their lifestyle. Pay particular attention to hair texture, length, whether the hair is natural/virgin or chemically processed, the client's face shape, hair growth patterns, the desired style to be achieved (whether it is plaiting, cane-rowing or weaving), the type of extension to be used and any contra indications relating to the client's scalp/hair. In addition it is important to find out whether the client would like temporary extensions or something which will last longer. All information gathered will help you to determine how long the service will take to complete and the price which should be charged for the service.

The client's lifestyle is very important as it will help to determine what type of extensions should be used. If the person does a lot of sports and will therefore be shampooing the hair regularly, then bonded extensions will not be the best choice as the extensions will loosen quickly. If, of course, the client only requires the extension as a temporary measure then that problem will not exist.

Do not forget to complete a record card with all the relevant information so as to have a record for future purposes. This information will help you to guide your client as to the procedure, style and choice of hair to use.

Hair texture

As with all hair types, African type hair is either fine, medium or coarse, with variations in-between such as fine to medium texture and medium to coarse texture. When working on fine hair, take precautions so that any extension work does not put too much strain on the client's natural hair thereby causing stress points and, in some cases, alopecia areata. Use small amounts of hair for cane-rowing/plaiting and split wefts when weaving/bonding.

Hair length

The length of the client's hair is important as it determines the style that the client could have and it could affect the longevity of the extended hairstyle. This is discussed in more detail later in this chapter.

Natural/virgin or chemically processed hair

Any type of extension service can be carried out on chemically processed hair, but with natural hair there are some restrictions:

◆ *Cane-rowing/plaiting*. On natural hair, any type of extension hair can be used. However, for durability and longevity of style, a slightly coarse grade of synthetic hair is generally preferred, commercially known as 'yaki hair'. Any other type of extension could look untidy after a few weeks if the natural hair starts to revert. This will be particularly unsightly if human hair has been used for the extension work.

◆ *Weaving*. Any type of weft hair can be used as long as none of the client's hair is to be left out, otherwise it could revert. To avoid this, the hair which is left out can either be thermal styled, treated with a keratin treatment or chemically relaxed so that it blends in with the texture of the extension hair. This often defeats the object of having natural hair as part will be chemically processed.

◆ *Bonding*. This can be carried out on natural hair but only as a temporary style because the natural hair will revert after a while.

Face shape

Extensions can add bulk to the hair so whatever style is chosen, it should complement the client's face shape. If necessary, think about thinning out some of the extension to avoid swamping the client's face with an abundance of hair. See cutting techniques discussed later in this chapter.

The desired style

Most clients know what style they would like but you can help your client to decide by using visual aids such as style books, posters, the Internet or even someone else in the salon with a style which you think might suit the client.

TOP TIP

Clients with long hair who would like a change to short hair can only opt for a stitched weave, where all their hair has been cane-rowed and the weave attached, or a cap weave. If any hair is to be left out at all, whether they are having cane-rows, braids, a stitched weave or bonding, the extension should be cut to the same length as the client's hair or longer. The desired style will determine what type of extensions is used and the placement of the extension, especially when using clip-ons, sewn or bonded extensions.

HEALTH & SAFETY

Excessive tension should not be used when attaching extensions so as to avoid traction alopecia.

HEALTH & SAFETY

Research different types of extension hair for braiding and weaving and list the manufacturer's instructions on aftercare.

Contra indications

Contra indications are anything relating to the hair, skin or scalp which would prevent the desired service from being carried out. They include a sensitive scalp, previous history of irritation to the scalp due to the use of bonding glues, hair breakage/loss or skin disorders or medical treatments such as radio or chemotherapy.

Resources

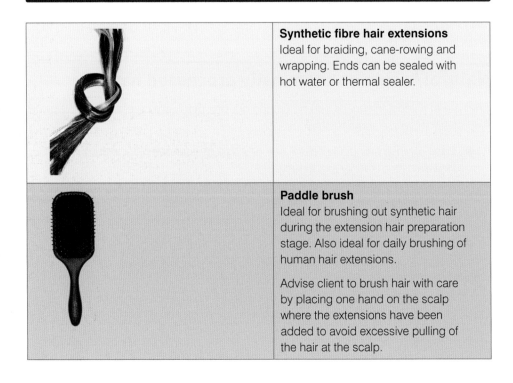

	Synthetic fibre hair extensions Ideal for braiding, cane-rowing and wrapping. Ends can be sealed with hot water or thermal sealer.
	Paddle brush Ideal for brushing out synthetic hair during the extension hair preparation stage. Also ideal for daily brushing of human hair extensions. Advise client to brush hair with care by placing one hand on the scalp where the extensions have been added to avoid excessive pulling of the hair at the scalp.

Weaving needles
Curved and straight needles used for weaving. If you are new to weaving it may be advisable to weave with a curved needle as this helps to minimize the risk of injuring the client's scalp with the point of the needle.

Human hair weave – body wave
Ideal for stitched weaving or bonding. This type of hair has a natural wave so you will not need to use additional heat to obtain movement. It also minimizes the amount of time a client may need to spend on maintaining their new style.

Human hair silky weave and dip dyed extensions
Ideal for stitched weaving or bonding. This type of hair can be razor cut for a more natural finish.

Extension clips
These can be sewn on to wefts of hair to add volume length and/or texture to client's own hair. They are a quick and easy way of adding interest to an old style or giving the client a temporary new look. Clip-ons work well on medium to coarse textured hair but may not hold so well on fine hair.

Clip-on extensions
Pre-done clip-on extensions cut to different lengths. They can be bought as a set and are designed for use on different parts of the head.

Single pre-sewn clip-on extension
Can be used as fashion pieces to add interest to a style or to create a block highlight effect.

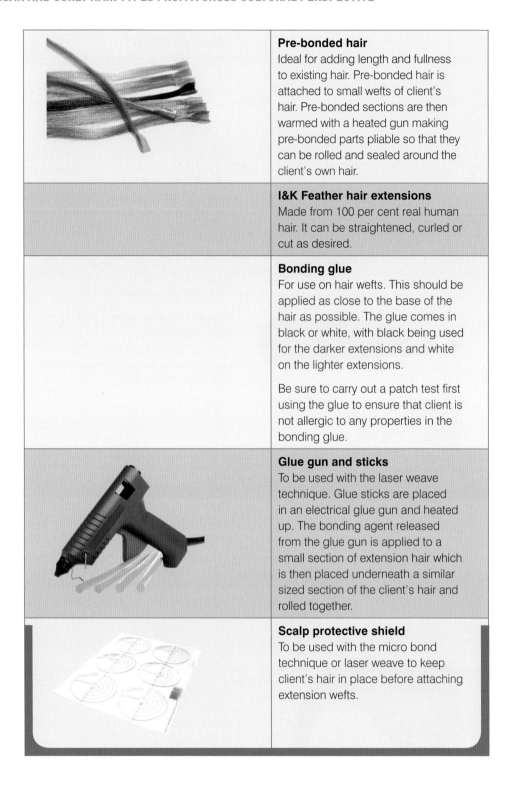

Pre-bonded hair

Ideal for adding length and fullness to existing hair. Pre-bonded hair is attached to small wefts of client's hair. Pre-bonded sections are then warmed with a heated gun making pre-bonded parts pliable so that they can be rolled and sealed around the client's own hair.

I&K Feather hair extensions

Made from 100 per cent real human hair. It can be straightened, curled or cut as desired.

Bonding glue

For use on hair wefts. This should be applied as close to the base of the hair as possible. The glue comes in black or white, with black being used for the darker extensions and white on the lighter extensions.

Be sure to carry out a patch test first using the glue to ensure that client is not allergic to any properties in the bonding glue.

Glue gun and sticks

To be used with the laser weave technique. Glue sticks are placed in an electrical glue gun and heated up. The bonding agent released from the glue gun is applied to a small section of extension hair which is then placed underneath a similar sized section of the client's hair and rolled together.

Scalp protective shield

To be used with the micro bond technique or laser weave to keep client's hair in place before attaching extension wefts.

Preparing for extension work

Hair preparation

Prior to all extension work the client's hair should be shampooed, conditioned (preferably with a deep penetrating, moisturizing treatment), a leave-in conditioner should be applied and then the hair blow-dried. A light moisturizing oil/hairdressing can be applied to the scalp at this stage or at the end of putting in the extensions. When carrying out bonding extensions do not apply any oil to the hair or scalp before or after blow-drying as this will make the base too slippery to work with and the bonding glue will not be as effective.

> For more information on shampooing and conditioning see CHAPTER 5.

Preparing the extension hair

Prepare all tools, equipment and materials beforehand so that the process runs smoothly and effectively. If weaving, ensure you have more than one needle so that someone else can assist you by threading the needles for you. If you are going to be braiding/cane-rowing and using yaki hair, prepare hair in advance by separating and lengthening the strands of hair so that the extension hair is not blunt at the ends, allowing it to fall more naturally. This will also help to minimize wastage and free the hair from tangles.

Cane-row/Ghana braids

Cane-row, sometimes called corn row, originated in Africa where the technique has been used to create a number of intricate styles. Cane-rowing is designed by working along channels of hair and is carried out using three subsections of hair. It can be woven under or over. There are different techniques for starting off the cane-row, however the simplest and most effective way is to divide the extension hair into three sections, and place them section for section with the client's own natural hair, which also should be subdivided into three sections at the start of the cane-row. The technique carried out below is known as *Ghana braids* which uses the cane-rowing technique with synthetic hair. While carrying out this technique, the stylist may require some assistance from another work colleague whose job it will be to pass up prepared small sections of extension hair to be added incrementally as the stylist works along the cane-row channel.

Sectioning cane-row channel

HEALTH & SAFETY

While cane-rowing, care must be taken not to use too much tension, especially around the hairline, as for some clients their scalp may be very tender and tight cane-rows may cause them pain. Apart from this, excessively tight cane-rowing/braiding can cause traction alopecia.

Technique

1 Prepare extension hair in advance.

2 Shampoo, condition and blow-dry hair.

3 Section the client's hair bearing in mind the desired style to be achieved (a).

4 Use section clips to hold the rest of the hair out of the way.

5 At this point, the cane-rows can either be started off with just the client's own hair or with a small amount of extension hair. If starting off with extension hair, take two small sections of extension hair, according to how thick or thin the cane-rows are to be, loop one section over the middle of the other section so that there are three sections (b).

6 Subdivide the client's hair into three sections and line up extension hair, section for section, with client's own hair.

TOP TIP

For equipment needed, aftercare, shampooing/conditioning and removal for all techniques see the equipment and maintenance tables at the end of this chapter.

7 Hold the right sections of hair in the right hand between the middle and third fingers while holding the middle strands in the right hand between the index finger and third finger. Then hold the left strands between the third and fourth fingers, looping the ends over the thumbs.

8 Place the left index finger under the right index finger and middle strands.

9 Pick up the right strands along with some of the client's hair with the left index finger, drawing it across under the middle strand into the left hand and holding it between the left index finger and third finger. The middle strands are now transferred to the right hand between the third and fourth fingers, leaving the right index finger to cross under the left index finger and what has now become the middle strands.

10 Continue crossing under, adding more extension hair as you proceed along the channel of cane-row, pick up more of the client's hair along the channel as each section is taken up. Continue this until the end of the cane-row is reached. (c)

11 Finish the cane-rowed channel with a three stemmed plait.

12 When all is completed, the plaits can be styled as desired which could be either the hair being left to fall free, sealed with a thermal sealer or hot water sealed. Read the manufacturer's instructions for sealing.

(a) Sectioning hair for cane-rowing

(b) Beginning the cane-row

(c) Adding more hair along the channel

Finished style

Single plaits

Plaiting can be carried out on natural or chemically processed hair using synthetic or human hair extensions.

TOP TIP

When plaiting hair which has been treated with a curly perm or body wave product, the curl pattern can become distorted once blow-dried and may loosen significantly. Ideally, one should avoid plaiting this type of hair. However, if it is the client's wish, then inform them that if any liquid product is applied to the hair or if the hair is shampooed, the permed hair will begin to revert and will no longer sit straight inside the extension. This could make the appearance very untidy.

Technique

1   Shampoo, condition and blow-dry hair.

2   Starting at the nape, section hair horizontally and secure the rest of the hair out of the way.

3   Divide this horizontal section into smaller square or triangular sections and attach extension hair to each of the square/triangular sections of the client's hair using the same technique as described above for cane-row extensions – the only difference being that once the extension hair is attached, the hair is plaited as a three stemmed plait rather than worked along a channel as in the cane-rows described above.

4   Continue working up the head horizontally, adding extensions until the whole head is completed. For continuity, ensure that each horizontal section is the same size and that each square section of hair is the same size.

5   Place each square/triangular section of plaits in a brick formation so as not to reveal too much of the scalp and to give the hair a fuller appearance.

6   Continue adding extensions until the whole head is completed.

7   Finish off by letting the ends fall free or sealing according to manufacturer's instructions.

Single plaits

HEALTH & SAFETY

When working around the hairline, make sure that plaits are not too tight otherwise this could cause traction alopecia. Also ensure that the sections of hair are not too small because if the weight of the extension hair is too heavy for the section of hair this can create hair loss around the hairline.

Extension hair being added

Three stemmed plait

Finished look

Senegalese twists

Senegalese/double strand twists

As the name suggests, this style has its origins in the West African state of Senegal. It can be done with and without extensions and the method is the same for attaching single plaits except that the plaiting technique is carried out only to the root area, then the rest of the hair is split into two and twisted to the end of the extension hair. This technique is also called rope twists.

Flat twists

Flat twists can be carried out with or without extensions and can be done in different designs. For the look to be effective, the extension hair should not be too coarse in texture but pliable enough to be twisted onto the scalp and sit snugly on the scalp.

Technique

1   Prepare client's hair by shampooing and blow-drying.

2   Make partings according to the desired style.

3   Separate client's hair into two and extension hair into two. Add extension hair to client's hair with a twisting action along the channel.

4   At the end of the channel, a covered elastic band can be attached to keep hair in place.

5   Once all the channels have been completed, the rest of the hair can be styled as desired – plaited, twisted, double strand twisted or left to fall free. Depending on the type of hair that is used, the ends of the hair can be flat ironed or curled for added styling.

Flat twists with extensions

ACTIVITY

Research various styles which can be carried out with extensions and decide which type of hair would be suitable for the different styles.

Weaving

The idea for weaving originated from the technique used in the production of wigs. Wefts of hair (human, synthetic or mixed fibres) are woven onto a nylon strip. It is usual to find two strips woven together to create what is known as a weft. The weft has a right and a wrong side and this can easily be detected by looking closely at where it is stitched to the nylon strip. This weft is then used to sew onto the client's own hair to create a variety of hair styles. It can be done for fullness or for length.

When using the sewing technique, the client's hair is generally cane-rowed using either a circular, horizontal or vertical base. If the client's hair is fine, split the weft to avoid weighing the client's hair down and putting strain on the root of the hair.

Circular base   If the client's natural hair is short, use a small amount of synthetic extension to attach to the client's own hair while doing the cane-rowed base. The method for attaching synthetic extensions to the client's hair to form the cane-rowed base is described earlier in the chapter.

Vertical base   This can be done with one circular row around the hairline and the rest of the hair cane-rowed vertically. This method is sometimes preferred as it allows the weave to lie flatter than on a circular base.

Horizontal base   This is similar in appearance to the circular base except that instead of a continuous circular pattern, the hair is cane-rowed horizontally with ends being cane-rowed into the next subsection. Alternatively, two cane-rows can be placed along each horizontal channel, one from the left side of the head to the middle and one from the right side of the head to the middle. Where the hair meets in the middle, the ends are crossed over and sewn to secure them from unravelling, leaving the rest of the hair to fall free. This section of the hair should not be plaited all the way through to the ends and can then be used to blend into the client's hair especially if some of the client's own hair is being left out and not weaved in.

Full head sewn/stitched weave

If the client requires a full head sewn weave with none of their own hair left out, then the whole head must be cane-rowed. Alternatively, most of the client's own hair can be cane-rowed leaving sufficient hair around the hairline free in order to cover the weave if styled upwards or backwards. If this is preferred then the extension hair has to be as close a match as possible to the client's hair, both in colour and texture.

Technique

Circular base

STEP-BY-STEP: FULL HEAD SEWN/STITCHED WEAVE

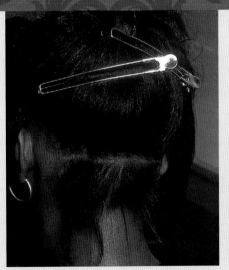

1 Shampoo, condition and blow-dry hair.

2 Starting at the nape, section client's hair for cane-rowing.

3 Cane-row hair using the technique shown earlier in this chapter, bearing in mind the desired finished look. If cane-rowing in a circular fashion, ensure that the cane-row finishes at the crown of the head. If not, when the weave is sewn on, it will look out of line with the natural contour of the head.

4 Thread the needle. Measure lengths of weft to hair sections and cut weft.

5 Using the blanket stitching described below, apply weft extension to cane-rowed base ensuring that weft is stitched on the right side and not the wrong side.

6 Continue working up the head until entire head is covered.

7 Cut and style weave to achieve finished look. (Cutting and styling is described later on in this chapter.)

Blanket stitch

TOP TIP

To blanket stitch, first feed needle through cane-rowed base and weft, looping needle with each stitch. This ensures that stitching is secure and will not unravel easily.

Natural weave parting

The natural weave parting was created so as to give the appearance of a parting in the hair, when in reality all of the client's hair has been cane-rowed. The natural weave parting is hair attached to a rubber/latex base, which is dyed to give the appearance of the natural tones of the scalp. It is similar to a *postiche*.

Technique

1 Sew wefts of extension hair to cane-rowed base working up to the crown area.

2 Attach natural weave parting to cane-rowed base at front of head using sewing technique. It is important that the cane-rowed hair underneath is not too bulky or the natural weave parting will not sit close to the scalp (a).

3 Cut and style weave (b). (See cutting and styling later on in this chapter.)

(a) Natural hair parting being sewn in

(b) Finished style with natural hair parting

Bonding

Bonded extensions can be applied to the whole head or partial head. They are attached directly to the root of the client's hair and therefore lie flatter on the head than a sewn weave. This gives a more natural appearance to the weave.

The disadvantages are that the bonding technique tends not to last as long as the sewn weave and, if not removed properly, can strip away some of the client's hair during the removal process. Bonded extensions are ideal for the client who wants a temporary change in hairstyle, perhaps for a special occasion. The amount of bonding glue used and the attachment method will also determine how long the bonded extensions will last.

Bonding can be carried out on hair which has been chemically processed with a relaxer or hair which has been treated with a keratin/amino acid treatment. If neither of these processes have been carried out and the hair is either blow-dried or thermal styled, then reversion will take place to the client's own hair and this will eventually be visible through the extension hair as the textures would be different.

Technique for partial head

Shampoo, condition and blow-dry hair. Do not apply any oil-based product at this stage as it will make the surface of the scalp too slippery: wefts will not adhere well to the root area or they will come away quickly. Ensure that placement of the extension is in keeping with the overall style to be achieved and that the client's own hair blends well into the extension so as to give the appearance of it being the client's own hair.

STEP-BY-STEP: BONDING FOR PARTIAL HEAD

1 Section hair according to where bonded wefts need to be placed. Measure lengths of weft to hair sections and cut weft.

2 Apply bonding glue to weft strips. For additional hold, the glue can also be applied to root of hair close to the scalp.

3 Press weft strips to section of hair where bonding glue has been applied. For added hold, use medium heat from a hand held blow-dryer to seal glue. Take care to keep the airflow moving to avoid burning clients scalp.

4 Continue adding weft strips until desired look is achieved. Cut and style to achieve finished look. (See cutting and styling later in this chapter.)

Clip-on extensions

This technique has become popular in recent times and is the least permanent of all the hair extension techniques. It is easy to apply and to remove, so much so that clients tend to buy the products and put them in themselves. However, if you are creative enough, you can make your own to suit your client's hair type and colour and cut it to blend in with your client's hair, thereby giving you an edge over your competitors.

Clip-ons are wefts of hair which have small clips sewn onto them and can be made up of synthetic or human hair. They come in different widths and the clips can be purchased separately and sewn onto hair wefts as desired.

Technique

1 Open clip-on.

2 Section hair where clip-on is to be attached.

3 (Optional) Take a small section of hair the same width as the clip-on weft and cane-row loosely. If the hair is long, it is best to carry out two cane-rows which meet in the middle and allow the ends of each cane-row to fall free so that the cane-row is not too bulky.

4 Slide comb near the root of client's hair/behind the cane-rowed base.

5 Snap the clip-on closed.

6 Cover the clip-on extensions with client's hair.

7 Cut and style as desired.

Because there is no base for the clip-ons to be secured onto, they can slide out easily on fine hair. Some stylists favour cane-rowing the area where the clip-ons are to be attached then placing the comb of the clip-ons behind the cane-row thereby making it more secure.

ACTIVITY

Using clip-ons, work in pairs and carry out an analysis on your partner's hair. Look at face shape and the current style and think how it can be enhanced with clip-ons. Attach clip-ons with or without a cane-rowed base. If the hair is long, let your cane-rows join in the middle and let the ends fall free otherwise it may look bulky.

TOP TIP

Always check the manufacturer's instructions for the type of hair you are about to use. Check whether the hair should be styled without the use of any styling aids such as straightening irons, whether lower heat settings should be used, or whether there are other constraints.

Extensions using mesh/net base

This type of extension is carried out using a hair net. It can be used for a full head of extensions or to act as a base for adding volume to a client's hair if the hair is sparse in particular areas. In the latter case, the hair is cane-rowed in the area where it is sparse and the net is measured and cut and sewn to the cane-row. The extension hair is then sewn to the net. One disadvantage of using the net method is that shampooing is more difficult as it will not be easy to massage the scalp because of the net. The client's hair can either be cane-rowed, wrap set or gel wrapped before application of the net and the weft extensions can either be stitched or bonded to the net.

Technique

Shampoo, condition and blow-dry client's hair. Wrap set, cane-row or gel wrap the hair using method described earlier in this chapter or other sections of this book. The hair can be cane-rowed in any fashion, whether it is circular, horizontal or diagonal, or can simply be cane-rowed into one. The method is not important as the net will be covering the hair.

STEP-BY-STEP: EXTENSIONS USING A MESH/NET BASE

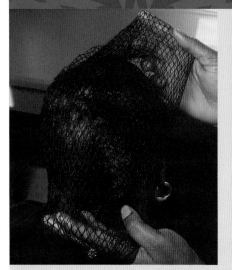

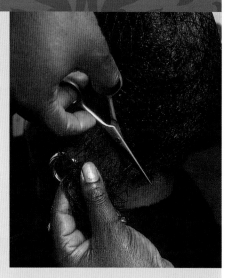

1 Place net over entire head.

2 Spray holding spray/spritz over entire head and use a blow-dryer to seal the net in place.

3 Once dried, cut the outer perimeter of the net, following the shape of the client's head.

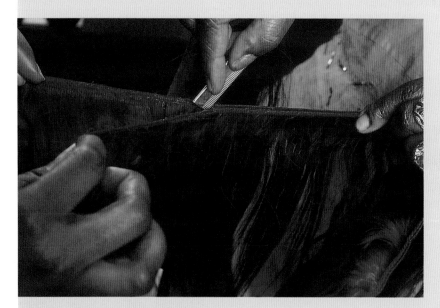

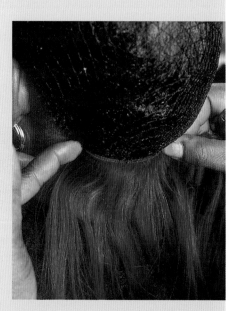

4 Using a razor, separate extension hair where it is sewn together to produce two weft strips.

5 Measure weft extensions horizontally to area of the head where the extensions are to be placed.

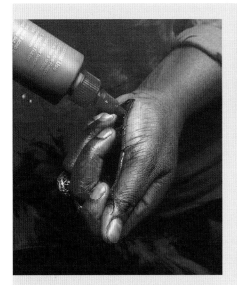

6 Apply bonding glue to weft strip or sew weft extensions to cane-rowed base and net. Again, bear in mind the desired style to be achieved. If the hair is sparse in areas, sew weft to net only and continue until it is possible to sew weft to net and cane-rowed base again.

7 Continue sewing/bonding, placing weft at measured spaces apart from each other. Do not place them too far apart otherwise the final look will be lacking in body. Once the crown is reached, begin to place wefts in a circular fashion, working towards the centre of the head.

8 Once finished, cut a small bit of weft and use the end of a tail comb to push this bit of weft in the centre so that no gaps are showing in the head.

9 Apply wrapping lotion to entire head, wrap set and dry hair.

10 Once dried, cut and style as desired to achieve the finished style.

Extensions using the cap technique

Level 3

In the cap technique, weft extensions are bonded to a soft mesh-like material which fits snugly to the head like a cap. Because the cap fits the contour of the head, the whole appearance is more natural. In addition, the cap can be removed and replaced as and when the client likes, in the same way as a wig. This technique allows the user flexibility as well as a tailored look which is custom built for the individual. A further advantage is that if a client has long hair and would like a short look without having to cut her hair, the cap technique allows her the best of both worlds.

ACTIVITY

Look at magazines or on the Internet and choose three weaved styles which you think could have been carried out using a weaving net. Recreate one of them using your tuition head. Think about weft placement and centre closure.

Wig cap

One of the disadvantages of using the cap technique is that after a while the cap can shrink and become too small to fit the head as it should. This means that the durability of this technique can be short and it can be expensive to keep repeating this process on an on-going basis.

When carrying out the cap technique, the client's hair is normally wrap set so that it lies flat on the head. Cling film is then placed over the entire head followed by the cap. The cling film prevents the bonding glue from seeping through the mesh cap onto the client's hair.

Technique

1   Shampoo, condition and wrap set or cane-row the client's hair.

2   Place cling film over the entire head, keeping it as flat and as close to the head as possible (a).

3   Place cap over cling film and stretch it so that it fits snugly to the head.

4   Take the weft extension hair and, as for the mesh technique described above, use a razor or a pair of scissors to separate the two wefts which have been sewn together to produce one weft strip.

5   Using bonding glue, start bonding single wefts to the cap, cutting weft strips to fit across the head in accordance with the desired style to be achieved. Single wefts can be placed closer together so that it gives a more natural appearance (b).

6   Work upwards, placing wefts in line with the contour of the head (c).

7   Follow steps 7–9 of the instructions for extensions on a net/mesh base, ensuring that your centre closure is neat, flat and does not appear bulky on the head (d).

8   Take off cap, remove cling film, replace cap and cut and style weave.

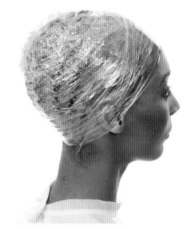

(a) Cling film covering head

(b) Cling film and cap on client's head for bonding

ACTIVITY

Look at magazines or the Internet and choose two hairstyles which you think have been carried out using the cap technique. Recreate one of these using two different colour wefts to produce a highlighted or block colour effect.

(c) weft being bonded on following contour of the head

(d) Centre closure

(e) Finished look

Laser weave

The laser method of using hair extensions consists of small quantities of extension hair bonded to small sections of the client's hair; these sections are repeated in a pattern to achieve the desired effect. One of the advantages of wearing a laser weave is that providing due care is taken, it can be shampooed, combed and styled almost in the same way as the client's own hair.

The laser method should only be used on certain textures/types of hair, especially African type hair, and should only be carried out by a professional who is fully qualified and trained in this technique. Failure to recognize the different hair types can result in damage/breakage to the hair and even long term damage to the hair follicles.

(Level 3)

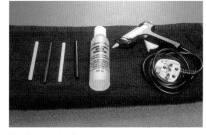

Equipment for laser weave

Technique

1   Shampoo, condition and blow-dry the hair into the direction of the style to be achieved. Do not use any oils in the hair or scalp as this can hinder application and cause the hair to slip or adhere insufficiently.

2   Starting just below the occipital bone, section hair horizontally into neat rows, using section clips to keep the rest of the hair out of the way (a).

3   Subdivide the first section into smaller triangular sections (about 1/8th in area) and without gaps between, thus maximizing bulk but minimizing bond thickness. Do not apply to the nape area as it is too weak and the scalp more tender. In addition, this nape area will cover over any extensions when hair is worn in a ponytail or in an upswept style.

4   Leave sufficient hair all around the hairline – about 50–75 mm (2"–3") – to cover over all extensions. It is important at this stage to ensure that any extension hair to be used is a close match to the existing colour and texture of the client's own hair, otherwise it would look false.

5   Taking extension hair, cut the top to leave the top ends neat. Place glue sticks in electrical glue gun and allow to heat. Apply the hot bonding agent to the extension hair, which is then placed beneath the receiving section of the client's own hair. Care should be taken to avoid overloading the section – the thickness of the extension should never exceed that of the receiving section (b).

6   The extension hair should be applied close to but slightly away from the scalp, thereby avoiding root lift which can cause uneven tension and risk of breakage during brushing (c).

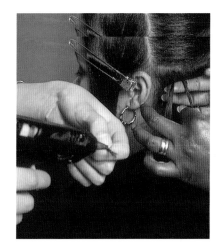

(a) Parting below occipital bone

7   Using the fingertips, roll the glue and the extension hair around the receiving section of the client's own hair (d).

8   As each row is completed, check the extensions for mobility in all directions, making sure that any cross hairs which may have inadvertently strayed during the application process are removed. Continue to work up the head in a brick formation so as to minimize gaps.

9   Once all extensions have been completed, carefully brush hair, starting at the ends and working towards the root with an appropriate brush. The hair can then be cut and styled as desired (e).

The client now has fuller, longer hair which can be shampooed, conditioned, brushed and styled as if it were her own. The client must then be advised to return to the salon every two weeks for maintenance.

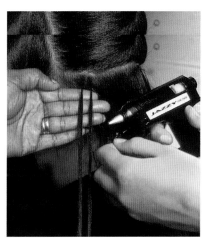

(b) Glue gun for bonding

(c) Extension hair added to client's hair

(d) Rolling glue, extension hair and client's hair together

(e) The finished style

Micro bond extensions

Level 3

The micro bond technique is an alternative to the laser technique. The principles of attaching the extensions are the same. The main difference between this technique and the laser technique is in the removal process. Both techniques use a liquid solvent to soften the seal where extensions have been fused to the client's hair. With the micro bond technique, the solvent is made up of a plastic resin which helps to break down the seal to a powdery substance. To assist with the removal, a pair of pincers is used to crack the seal once the solvent has been placed on the hair. This then releases the client's hair from the extension hair.

Separated strands for micro bonding

Extension hair being micro bonded

Completed section

The finished look

Self-adhesive hair extensions

These usually come in a pack of 24 pre-taped strips and last for up to about three weeks. The strips are reusable and easy to apply. They are ideal for wedding hairstyles or formal occasions. They can be synthetic or human hair.

Technique

1 Section client's hair to where the self adhesive extensions are to be applied.

2 Take a section of client's hair the same width as the self adhesive extensions.

3 Peel off self adhesive strip from extension and place under sectioned strip of the client's hair as close as possible to the root.

4 Take another self adhesive strip and place on top of the client's hair.

5 Press together so that client's hair is sandwiched between the two self adhesive extensions.

6 Continue placing extensions in a brick formation.

7 Cover extensions with client's hair for a natural look.

8 Cut and style as desired. If using synthetic hair, take care not to use heat on the extensions as they will melt.

TOP TIP

When fixing self adhesive strips ensure that they are placed close to the root otherwise the extensions will not be evenly placed which could look unsightly, especially if client's hair is short, or it could impact the longevity of the style. When cutting extensions remember to use razoring technique so that there are no blunt solid lines.

Giving advice

With the exception of clip-ons, most clients tend to leave extensions in their hair longer than they should. It is your duty to advise your client as to the length of time they should keep their extensions in. This very much depends on whether it is natural or chemically processed, such as with a relaxer. Clients will also need advice on how to care for their extensions (brushing/combing, shampooing/conditioning, whether to use heat or not, how long to keep extensions in for, when to revisit the salon and the type of products they can use on the hair). Remember to use the manufacturer's instructions on caring for extensions as a guide when advising clients.

This table contains information on how to care for more advanced hair extensions on natural or chemically processed hair.

Hair Type	Extension	Duration	Notes
Natural hair	Sewn weave	8–12 weeks	Natural hair may revert if the client attends the gym or work out so may need to be taken out sooner.
	Bonding	Short life span possibly 2–4 days but may last longer if the client's hair has been treated with a keratin treatment.	If the hair has been treated with a keratin treatment the natural hair will not revert until shampooed and, although the client's hair can be blow-dried straight again, shampooing the hair will have loosened the bonding so it may need to be taken out.

Hair Type	Extension	Duration	Notes
	Laser	N/A	Natural hair may revert and will look unsightly as it will be a different texture to the extension hair used.
	Micro bonding	N/A	As for laser technique above.
	Mesh	2–4 weeks	It is advisable not to keep this hairstyle too long (2 weeks) as the use of spritz to hold the net in place may make the client's hair and scalp dry.
	Self adhesive extensions	N/A	Service not advisable as some of client's hair will be left out and hair in its natural state may revert.
Relaxed hair	Sewn weave	4–8 weeks	Hair should only be weaved if in good condition and about 4 weeks after a relaxer service as some new growth will be coming through. Once the weave is taken out, the hair should be shampooed, deep conditioned and left for 1 or 2 weeks before relaxing again.
	Bonding	2–3 weeks	Bonding is not as long lasting as a sewn weave. Its life span will be shortened with the use of hair oils or when shampooed/conditioned, this can loosen the bonding glue.
	Laser and Micro bonding	8–12 weeks	Hair removing solvent can sometimes be a bit harsh for some hair types so should be used with care.
	Mesh	2–4 weeks	This is suitable for shorter hair styles as the hair can be wrapped before the mesh is added. One disadvantage is that the hair cannot be shampooed for the duration of the style and the scalp can become quite dry.
	Cap	It depends on how often it is used. If it is used every day then 2 weeks. 2–4 weeks	If this has been carried out using cling film to protect the client's hair, then the **cap weave** can be treated like a wig as it is taken off and put back on as and when the client wants to. If however, the edges of the cap has been bonded to the client's hair then it will perform as the mesh technique described above.
	Self adhesive extensions	8–12 weeks	While this can last up to 12 weeks, it depends on the length of the client's hair as the shorter the hair is, the adhesive strip will become visible as the hair grows.
Permed hair	Sewn weave	4–8 weeks	Hair should only be weaved if in good condition and about 4 weeks after a perming service. This will allow some new growth to come through and not put too much strain on the permed hair. It would be best to use hair for weaving which has a curl pattern similar to the client's permed hair or carry out a full head weave. The permed hair however will be lacking in moisture and may become dry and break. Once the weave is taken out, the hair should be shampooed, deep conditioned and left for 1 or 2 weeks before perming again. It is worth noting that if permed hair is blow-dried often, then it loses some of it curl pattern.

Hair Type	Extension	Duration	Notes
	Bonding	N/A	Bonding is not advisable on this hair type due to the fact that some of the client's hair will be left out which will have to be moisturized as often as required. The moisturizer may seep onto the bonded area and affect the longevity of the bonded extensions.
	Laser and Micro bonding	8–12 weeks	This procedure can be carried out on permed hair as long as the hair is in good condition and curly hair is going to be used. Hair should be blow-dried first before application of extensions. Once the procedure completed, the hair can be dampened and client's hair moisturized to revive curl pattern. Best to use a curl mousse so that the extension hair is not compromised. Hair removing solvent can sometimes be a bit harsh for some hair types so should be used with care.
	Mesh	N/A	Not advisable to carry out this technique on permed hair as the client will be unable to access the hair to keep it moisturized. This will result in the permed hair becoming dry and breaking.
	Cap	It depends on how often it is used. If it is used every day then 2 weeks. 2–4 weeks	If this has been carried out using cling film to protect the client's hair, then the cap weave can be treated like a wig as it is taken off and put back on as and when the client wants to. The client can carry out the normal routine of moisturizing the hair as and when it is required. If however, the client does not want to be able to remove the cap at night (for instance), but requires the edges of the cap to be bonded to the hairline then it would be best to advise the client against this procedure for the same reason as in the **mesh weave** above.
	Self adhesive extensions	N/A	Not advisable for the same reasons as in bonding above.
Keratin treated hair	Sewn weave	4–8 weeks	This process can be carried out as long as the client's hair is going to be worn straight. If the hair is porous, you will need to inform client that the keratin treated hair may revert with humidity. This would involve them having to blow-dry and straighten their hair more often which long term will not be good for the hair.
	Bonding	1–2 weeks	Bonding as a temporary process will be possible especially if it is for a short period such as one day for a special occasion. Longevity of wearing a bonded style would again depend on how porous the client's hair is.
	Laser and Micro bonding		While it is possible, it is not advisable due to the fact that when the hair is shampooed, the keratin treated hair will become curly – this includes the hair where the micro bond has been applied. More pressure will have to be applied to the micro bonded sections to straighten out the curly hair which could compromise the micro bonded sections and ultimately the client's hair.
	Mesh	N/A	Not advisable in case there is any reversion of client's hair underneath the mesh which will then make the mesh weave appear too bulky.

Hair Type	Extension	Duration	Notes
	Cap	If removable, as and when cap weave needs replacing. If not removable, hair must be cane-rowed for it to last. (2–3 weeks).	If hair has been straightened, then cap weave can be worn. If hair has not been straightened then it would be best to cane-row hair before wearing cap weave as style could look bulky otherwise. If client desires the cap weave not to be removable, then client's hair will need to be cane-rowed beforehand as above.
	Self adhesive extensions	N/A	While it may be possible with looser curl structures, the self adhesive extensions may be compromised when the hair is shampooed and blow-dried, especially with tighter curl structures as more stress will have to be placed on the self adhesive sections to get the client's hair straight. This will both compromise the extensions and the client's own hair and could result in breakage.

Cutting and styling

Level 3

HEALTH & SAFETY

Dispose of all sharps in the correct manner and in accordance with your salon's health and safety procedures.

On the whole, the principles for cutting and styling extensions are the same as for cutting and styling the client's own hair. Various cutting techniques can be used such as freehand, club cutting, texturizing and thinning. Because extensions add bulk to the hair, it is often necessary to thin out some of the hair. This can be achieved using a pair of thinning scissors or a razor.

If using synthetic hair for cane-rowing or plaiting, it is advisable to choose a length which does not require cutting once completed. There may be some evening up of the ends to do, but a full hair cut should be avoided as it may distort the natural pattern in the hair and create an unnatural appearance.

Hair extensions equipment and maintenance: Cane-row

Equpment	Aftercare	Shampoo	Conditioner	Removal
Tail comb Section clips Hair for extensions	The scalp may become dry. Advise client to use oil sheen or braid spray as and when necessary. Hair should be combed/brushed from points to root.	If necessary, hair can be shampooed during the wearing of cane-rows. Use cleansing shampoo first, then a moisturizing shampoo to replace moisture. Use only gentle movements.	Liquid leave-in conditioner should be used as a cream conditioner may not rinse out fully.	Use a tail comb to separate the plaits at the end of the cane-rows. Unpick cane-rows and use a wide toothed comb to comb hair free. Shampoo and condition hair, preferably giving a deep penetrating treatment at this stage.

Hair extensions equipment and maintenance: Single plaits

Equipment	Aftercare	Shampoo	Conditioner	Removal
Tail comb Section clips Hair for extensions	A light scalp dress, oil sheen or braid spray can be applied as and when necessary.	Shampoo with care, concentrating on scalp area. If curly extensions have been used do not use vigorous movements during shampooing as this may cause the hair to tangle.	A cream or liquid moisturizing conditioner can be used, but liquid conditioner will penetrate better. A cream conditioner may cause hair plaited with human hair to loosen.	Same as above. Note however, that after extensions have been removed and the client's hair is being combed, care must be taken because during the time of wearing the extensions there will be a build-up of dirt and oils which would have collected at the base of the plait. This sometimes forms a knot and, if not combed out with care, can bring about excessive shedding.

Hair extensions equipment and maintenance: Sewn weave

Equipment	Aftercare	Shampoo	Conditioner	Removal
Tail comb Denman brush Section clips Thread Thread cutter Weave needle (preferably curved) Razor/thinning scissors	Use oil sheen or a light hair oil applied directly to the scalp. Avoid the use of braid spray as this may affect the styling of the extension hair if it becomes too saturated with braid spray. Hair should be combed free of tangles daily and hair can be thermal styled as often as client desires depending on whether synthetic or human hair was used.	Hair should be combed free of tangles before shampooing. Section hair into four and plait each section. Follow manufacturer's instructions for shampooing.	Follow manufacturer's instructions. Alternatively use a light conditioner to assist the combing out of any tangles.	Starting from the nape comb hair free of tangles, then using a thread cutter or a pair of scissors, carefully cut thread used for sewing. Care must be taken not to cut the client's own hair during this process. Undo cane-rowed base, comb hair with a wide toothed comb then shampoo and condition with a deep penetrating conditioner.

Hair extensions equipment and maintenance: Bonding

Equipment	Aftercare	Shampoo	Conditioner	Removal
Tail comb Section clips Denman brush Razor if necessary Weft hair Bonding glue Glue solvent Razor/thinning scissors	Avoid applying too much force during combing/brushing as this could put too much stress on the client's natural hair. Avoid using a lot of hair oil as this could loosen the bonding. Hair can be thermal styled as often as client desires.	Comb hair with a wide toothed comb or brush hair to remove tangles. Shampoo with care as this could loosen bonding. Use cleansing shampoo. Where bonding has become detached, re-apply bonding glue after shampooing.	Avoid using cream conditioners as this could loosen bonding. A liquid conditioner is suitable.	Comb/brush hair free of tangles. Apply bonding remover/glue solvent to root area of each section. Do this to the entire head so as to allow the areas applied first to soften. Starting at one end of the weft, lift it away from the client's hair. This should peel away easily. If not, apply more remover or, alternatively, apply a heavy cream conditioner to the root area and place client under a warm dryer. Once removed, comb hair carefully as some of the glue may still be left on the hair. If care is not taken, hair breakage may occur.

Hair extensions equipment and maintenance: Laser weave

Equipment	Aftercare	Shampoo	Conditioner	Removal
Tail comb Section clips Hair for extensions Laser gun Glue sticks Glue solvent Denman brush Razor/thinning scissors	Hair can be treated as client's own hair. Oil sheen, hair sprays, scalp dress can all be used. However, care must be taken when combing/ brushing — start from the ends of the hair and work towards the root.	Comb/brush hair to ensure it is tangle free before shampooing. Use a gentle cleansing shampoo to remove product build up (if any) followed by a moisturizing shampoo. A deep penetrating conditioning treatment would also be beneficial to the hair at this stage. Towel dry hair then roller set or blow-dry with a round/paddle brush taking care not to put too much stress on the root area.	A liquid leave in conditioner should be used. This will help to keep hair tangle free.	Thoroughly dissolve glue using a hair-friendly solvent. Client's hair should come away freely from glue without damage to hair. Read manufacturer's instructions for solvent to ensure that solvent is applied correctly and safely and required time is allowed for the softening of the glue before removing extensions from the hair.

Hair extensions equipment and maintenance: Mesh technique

Equipment	Aftercare	Shampoo	Conditioner	Removal
Tail comb Section clips Holding spray Denman brush Hair net Weft hair Depending on technique, thread	Use oil sheen. Avoid using too much holding spray as this will filter through net to the hair underneath and cause build-up.	Although it is possible to shampoo this type of weave, it is advisable not to as it will be impossible to shampoo the scalp area properly due to the fact that the net is placed between the client's hair and the weft hair. If the stitched method is used then shampooing is easier. If the	If the hair has been shampooed, use either a liquid leave-in conditioner or a light cream conditioner to de-tangle	Depending on whether the stitched or bonding method has been used, follow the appropriate removal technique as described above.

Equipment	Aftercare	Shampoo	Conditioner	Removal
and curved needle for stitching or glue for bonding. Razor/thinning scissors		bonding method is used, advise client not to shampoo but remove weave after 2–3 weeks. If shampooing is absolutely necessary, then shampoo with care using a cleansing and a moisturizing shampoo.		

Hair extensions equipment and maintenance: Cap technique 'The Wig'

Equipment	Aftercare	Shampoo	Conditioner	Removal
Tail comb Section clips Hair spray Wrapping lotion/ oil moisturizer for wrapping hair prior to cutting. Denman brush Razor/thinning scissors Cling film Weave cap Bonding glue Weft hair	As this technique is similar to a 'wig' effect, it can be removed and replaced as and when the client desires. Once removed, it can be placed on a wig stand to maintain shape. It can be thermal styled as often as the client desires.	Do not apply vigorous movements while shampooing, use gentle squeezing actions. Use cleansing shampoo.	Light conditioner to be used. After shampooing and conditioning, check hair for any loosening of bonding and reapply if necessary or remove weft strip and apply a new strip.	The cap weave simply needs to be discarded after use.

Hair extensions equipment and maintenance: Self-adhesive strips

Equipment	Aftercare	Shampoo	Conditioner	Removal
Tail comb Section clips Self-adhesive extension Denman brush Razor	Comb hair from nape area upwards ensuring that not too much tension is placed in the root area. Use sheen spray sparingly – it is better to spray sheen onto palm of hands and then run through hair. Avoid using oils on the scalp as this can loosen the strips.	Shampooing is possible, however avoid brisk manipulation of the scalp as this could dislodge extension quicker.	Use a light conditioner to de-tangle hair as a heavy conditioner will loosen the self adhesive strip.	Apply removal pad beneath each self adhesive strip and using surgical spirit, gently peel away the extensions.

REVISION QUESTIONS

1 If hair is braided too tightly, it may cause:

1 Headaches

2 Traction alopecia

3 Psoriasis

4 The client to faint

2 Extensions should not be carried out on:

1 Bleached hair

2 Short hair

3 Damaged scalp

4 Relaxed hair

3 When using bonding glue you should:

1 Carry out a patch test beforehand

2 Make sure you have sufficient glue to carry out the job

3 Wear gloves

4 Advise your client not to comb the hair

4 Sewn in extensions should be added:

1 To the root of the client's hair

2 Half way down the length of the client's hair

3 To the ends of the client's hair

4 To a corn-rowed base

5 Which statement below is true?

1 Extensions can only be worn on hair in good condition

2 Only human hair can be added to relaxed hair

3 Extensions can be worn to add length and thickness to the hair

4 Bonding can make the hair look and feel bulky

6 What can cause traction alopecia?

1 Excessive use of blow-dryer

2 Continuous pulling on the hair shaft

3 Incorrect brushing technique

4 Vigorous manipulation of the scalp during shampooing

7 Why is it important to condition the hair after extension services?

1 To replace lost moisture

2 To avoid hair tangling

3 To keep the hair shiny

4 To increase circulation to the scalp

8 Which of these hair types are not suitable for bonded hair extensions?

1 Natural hair

2 Short hair

3 Relaxed hair

4 Coloured hair

9 A skin test is required when carrying out:

1 Sewn weave

2 Cap weave

3 All extension techniques

4 Bonded extensions

10 Which one of these would you record on a record card following an extension service?

1 Client's name, stylist, service, amount of extension used

2 Stylist, client's address, cost of service, technique used

3 Client's name, cost of service, service carried out, date

4 Client's name, service carried out, date, email address

11 Why is it important to carry out a thorough consultation prior to extension services?

1 To ascertain if there are any contra indications to the service being carried out

2 To know when to book your next client

3 To know what products to sell to the client

4 So clients cannot blame you if they do not like their new look

12 How is alopecia best described?

1 Split ends

2 Circular bald patches

3 Damaged cuticle

4 Hair loss from part or all of the head

13 Which of these is a contra indication to hair extensions?

1 Relaxed hair

2 Permed hair

3 Hair in good condition

4 Hair which is shedding excessively

PART THREE
Chemically Processing Hair

Chemically processing the hair is a technique that should only be carried out by those individuals who have honed their skills and understand the science of chemical processing and how these chemicals work on the hair. Part Three gives you guidance on how to work safely and correctly understanding contra indications (reasons why you would not carry out a chemical process) and how to implement the required tests to avoid unfavourable results caused by poor application and processing when colouring, perming and relaxing clients' hair.

ROLE MODEL

DIONNE SMITH Hair artist and session stylist

❝ My hairdressing career started when my dad assigned me the weekly chore of shampooing and plaiting both my sisters' hair. Then I started doing their friends and then neighbours and it went on from there. I was working as a freelance hair stylist and one of my clients assisted me in setting up my own hair salon and I've never looked back. I believe in high standards of hairdressing particularly when it comes to chemically processing the hair. These include client care, following manufacturer's instructions, product knowledge and observing health and safety procedures throughout.

I am involved with editorial shoots and have my own bi-monthly page in *BlackHair* magazine where I demonstrate how to create various step-by-step hairstyles. Contributing to the magazine on a regular basis has also made me grow as a hairstylist and this has been an amazing experience. It has powered me up, given me a lot of exposure, helped me to develop my career as well as allowing me opportunities to build great relations with hair product companies. My inspiration when creating hairstyles comes from life itself, the catwalk, faces, shapes and magazines. I love creating hair that makes a woman feel beautiful and gives her confidence. 'They say your hair is your beauty and I truly believe in that'.

11 Perming

LEARNING OBJECTIVES

This chapter covers the following:

◆ Maintain effective and safe methods of working when perming and neutralizing hair

◆ Prepare for perming and neutralizing

◆ Perm and neutralize hair

◆ Provide aftercare advice

◆ Maintain effective and safe methods of working when perming hair

◆ Prepare for perming

◆ Create a variety of permed effects

◆ Provide aftercare service

KEY TERMS

Basic perm winding

Creative advanced perm
   winding technique

Dual action perms

Incompatibility test

Perm burns

Perming

Pre-perm test curl

Product selection

Pull burns

UNITS COVERED IN THIS CHAPTER

Level 2

◆ Perm and neutralize hair using basic
techniques

Level 3

◆ Create a variety of permed effects

INTRODUCTION

Perming hair allows the stylist to permanently reconfigure movement in the hair to create tighter, medium or softer, wavier movements on all hair types. This chapter deals with the art of perming African hair types and will also look at perming hair of European and Asian hair types. The chapter will cover everything you need to know at Level 2, whether you are studying on the Combined course or looking to specialize in African type hair. It also serves as a foundational reminder for students studying at Level 3. Towards the end of the chapter, advanced perming techniques are described for the benefit of senior stylists. Perming of the hair started in Egyptian times, when hair would be wound on sticks and baked by the sun to create curl in the hair.

The history of perming

Perming African hair type is a technique that was created in the mid 1970s. The process was developed by Jheri Redding and early perms were called a *Jheri curl* after their inventor. Other names applied to perms include *wet look* and *Californian curl*. Some names were linked to the finishing products used at the time, which gave definition and moisture to the curl and produced a highly glossed, oily finish to the permed hair. As this look became unfashionable the more generic term *curly perm* was used.

This look is now commonly described and understood within the African type hair industry as a 'perm'. Perms are currently not as popular as in the 1980s and 1990s, however it is important that stylists still develop the skills required to perm hair successfully.

Permanent waving is a term used to describe all types of waving systems which create an artificial curl or wave in the hair which remains there permanently until it is cut off, or grows out. If the hair is not cut the perm will grow further away from the scalp until eventually the hair reaches the end of its growing period and falls out. In the 1930s the perms we know of today as cold waves, were created by Karl Nessler. These machine perm systems were only used on straighter hair types 1 to 2a Asian and European hair.

When perming African type hair, we are rearranging the curl pattern of the naturally curled hair so that we get a larger curl diameter and a more structured curl pattern. This allows the client to have greater manageability and freedom of style. It is important to remember that among African–Caribbean people, there are over 40 different curl types. When we refer to hair types, we are looking at the variety of curl patterns, which can vary from tight curly to wavy in texture. It is also not uncommon to find more than one curl pattern on one head, for example tighter curls towards the nape of the head and a looser curl pattern towards the crown or vice versa. Because of this variety, a thorough consultation and analysis is important before perming the hair. Remember curl pattern is different and individual to each client.

TOP TIP

The pH of perms used on African type hair is 9.5 and above.

HEALTH & SAFETY

Care must be taken when working with hair that has perm product on it. The hair is now in a fragile state as the disulphide bonds have been broken and these are fundamental to the strength of the hair. Irreparable damage can occur at this stage if the hair is handled roughly.

The science of perming

The active chemical found in most perms used on African type hair is *ammonium thioglycolate*. There are two types of perms used on African type hair:

◆ one step perms (single action perms);

◆ two step perms (**dual action perms**).

Most perms used on African type hair are dual action perms, which tend to be kinder to the hair.

◆ The single action perm remains on the hair throughout the chemical process, first to smooth and straighten the hair. The hair is then wound onto rods or formers and the desired curl pattern is produced.

◆ In dual action perms, the first application of ammonium thioglycolate is usually in the form of a cream. This is step one and is called a *rearranger*. The first step straightens and smoothes the hair in preparation for winding. In the second step the hair is wound with a weaker solution of ammonium thioglycolate which produces the curl pattern in the hair.

Perms used for straighter European and Asian hair types are varied and come in different strengths from mild, normal, colour treated, highlighted and resistant hair. There are two methods of applying perm lotion:

◆ Pre damping technique.

◆ Post damping technique.

Types of perm product available to use on Asian and European hair are:

◆ Alkaline perm

◆ Acid perm

◆ Exothermic perm

Further information on perming Asian and European hair is discussed later in this chapter.

All hair types have the same structure and are made up of a Cuticle, Cortex and Medulla. All hair is made up of keratin, an amino acid that is also a protein. The differences found in each hair type are the following:

◆ More layers of keratin build-up in Asian hair, making it the strongest hair type, particularly oriental hair.

◆ In African–Caribbean hair varying degrees of thickness and keratin build-up can be found throughout a strand of hair making the hair weaker where the keratin is less and therefore prone to breakage.

◆ European or individuals who are of white heritage as a rule have thinner/finer hair, that is average to normal in tensile strength.

◆ All hair is held together by Polypeptide chains, found in the cortex. These polypeptide chains run parallel on both sides. Between each chain are links of hydrogen bonds, disulphide bonds and salt bonds.

By a chemical process known as *reduction* the hair structure is gradually softened, allowing it to straighten out the hair's natural curl. The ammonium thioglycolate breaks both disulphide bonds, donating hydrogen atoms to prevent them reforming, Cystine now changes to Cysteine.

The concentrated cream rearranger is then thoroughly rinsed from the hair. The hair in its now pre-softened state is wound onto the perming rods or rollers. Prior to winding, a second application of ammonium thioglycolate, in the form of the winding lotion, is used. This is a weaker lotion and therefore less damaging to the hair. Disulphide bonds continue to be broken while the hair takes on its new shape, which is dictated by the diameter of the rods or rollers. Always remember that a cold environment will slow the process down: the development of the S curl, which will indicate if the wave or curl is to the desired movement required. The warmer the environment, the quicker the perm will process. If stated by the manufacturer, you can use additional heat to speed up the perm processing time. Do check the perm development regularly as prescribed by the manufacturer to avoid over-processing the hair.

Once the hair has been processed with the rods or curlers in place and the S curl developed, it is then rinsed thoroughly. *Neutralizer* is then applied to the hair. The chemical action of the neutralizer is oxidation, which is the chemical opposite of reduction. Oxygen provided by the neutralizer removes the hydrogen from the broken disulphide bonds. The disulphide bonds can then reform in new positions to fix the hair into its new curl. Within the hair, cysteine once again becomes cystine.

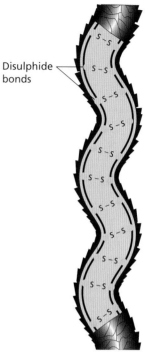

The hair before perming

Disulphide bonds

Hair before perming

See **CHAPTER 2** for further information on hair structure.

TOP TIP

The same process happens to straighter hair types during perming, regardless of the product used. Of course only one application of perm product is applied, opposed to the two steps sometimes used on African type hair. See process later on in this chapter.

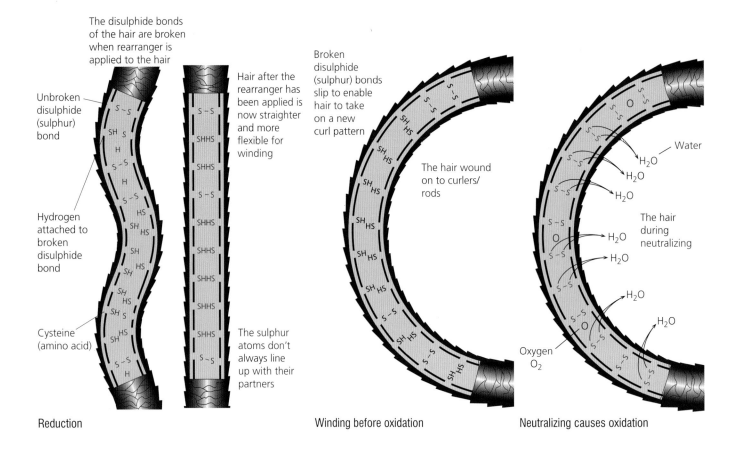

The disulphide bonds of the hair are broken when rearranger is applied to the hair

Unbroken disulphide (sulphur) bond

Hydrogen attached to broken disulphide bond

Cysteine (amino acid)

Hair after the rearranger has been applied is now straighter and more flexible for winding

The sulphur atoms don't always line up with their partners

Broken disulphide (sulphur) bonds slip to enable hair to take on a new curl pattern

The hair wound on to curlers/rods

Water

The hair during neutralizing

Oxygen O_2

Reduction

Winding before oxidation

Neutralizing causes oxidation

The pH scale

Representative pH Values	
Substance	**pH**
Battery acid	0.5
Gastric acid	1.5–2.0
Lemon juice	2.4
Cola	2.5
Vinegar	2.9
Orange or apple juice	3.5
Beer	4.5
Acid rain	< 5.0
Coffee	5.0
Tea or healthy skin	5.5
Milk	6.5
Pure water/neutral	7.0
Healthy human saliva	6.5–7.4
Blood	7.34–7.45
Sea water	8.0
Hand soap	9.0–10.0
Household ammonia	11.5
Bleach	12.5
Household lye	13.5

pH stands for the 'potential for hydrogen' and is an indicator of how acid or alkaline a substance or product is. The pH scale runs from 0 to 14. 0 is the strongest acid, 7 is neutral and anything from above 7 to 14 is alkaline, 14 being the strongest alkaline.

The normal pH of the skin and scalp is about 4.5 to 5.5. Looking at the pH scale and how acid and alkaline products we use daily in the salon, helps us understand why the scalp and hair must be restored back to its natural acid mantle.

We refer to the pH of the skin and scalp as the skin's 'acid mantle'. This is a film that coats the scalp and skin and protects against bacteria, viruses and reduces body odour. To maintain this protection, any shampoos or conditioners we use must restore the scalp, skin and hair to its normal acid mantle. The acid mantle is produced by substances found in perspiration, such as amino acids, lactic acid, sebum, hormones and fatty acids. As hairdressers we need to be aware of the pH scale and the acidity and alkalinity found in products we may use in the salon. This will help us to select and use products wisely and carefully in the salon and ensure that we give clients advice based on the correct information to preserve the condition of the scalp and hair. Universal indicator or litmus paper will identify if a product is acid, neutral or alkaline. Blue litmus paper turns red under acidic conditions and red litmus paper turns blue under alkaline conditions. Litmus paper can be used to identify how acid or alkaline individual products we use in the salon are. PH balancing conditioner is slightly acidic and therefore closes the cuticle, restores the hair back to its normal pH of 4.5 to 5.5 and will neutralize any alkaline present in the hair from an alkaline process.

It is for this reason that soap is not good to shampoo the hair with, as it forms a scum on both the scalp/skin and hair, making the scalp dry and prone to bacterial infection, the hair brittle and prone to breakage.

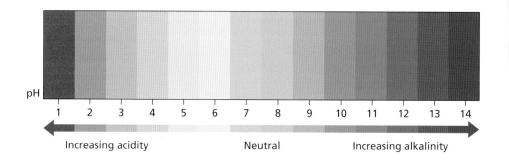

pH

1 2 3 4 5 6 7 8 9 10 11 12 13 14

Increasing acidity   Neutral   Increasing alkalinity

Working safely

As with any process, you should make sure the work area is clean and tidy and your equipment is clean and properly sterilized before and after each client. Use sterile wipes and sprays to clean your work area and make sure your tools are in easy reach so you do not have to lean over the client. All gowns and towels should be clean and washed in a washing machine daily and used in accordance with the house style of the salon. Remember to follow personal hygiene procedures. Stand comfortably and rotate around the chair as you work. Follow general guidance on posture, trying to avoid staying stationary for too long and keeping upright as you work to prevent damage to your neck and back.

See CHAPTER 1 for more information on health and safety.

Timing

The perming process can be extremely time consuming. The average perm can take up to three hours, or even longer, depending on the length, thickness and density of the hair. More intricate curling techniques may take longer to complete. Let the client know how long it will take to perm and style their hair. Of course once the perm is finished, you will need to cut and style the hair. Practise speed winding prior to starting work with clients so that you can wind the hair in approximately 20 minutes or less.

Style maintenance

It is important that you discuss with your client how to maintain their new perm. They will need to know how often they should have regular conditioning treatments. Inform clients they may need to have regular haircuts to maintain the condition of the hair. Also tell them about products to be used to maintain the new permed look and keep the hair in the best condition and how often the hair has to be re-permed.

Record cards

Update record cards to ensure that the salon has up-to-date information on the last perm the client had and make sure that any concerns are noted. Check for other chemicals used on the hair that may still be present and not compatible with a perm (**incompatibility test**). Note any previous problems recorded such as breakage or scalp irritation and scalp infection.

Lifestyle

When carrying out any chemical process it is extremely important to find out if the client has ever worn a perm before and try to link the finished hairstyle to their lifestyle choices or preferences. Make sure the client understands that once hair is permed it is difficult to change the hair back because it may have become sensitized and to apply another chemical may compromise the hair too much. Once the hair is permed the hair needs to be treated gently for at least 48 hours, allowing the hair bonds to be properly restructured in the new curl configuration. Do not pull back the hair in elastic bands and ponytails, as this could stretch and distort the newly formed curl. If the client is sporty or swims a lot it is important to let them know that constant shampooing may dry the hair out, and introduce a product line that will help to provide moisture to the permed hair, which will now be drier than before. How tightly or loosely the hair is permed should be decided on in conjunction with the client prior to carrying out a perm as it can be damaging to reverse the process.

Finishing products and their use

Products go a long way towards helping the stylist create the finished look. It is important therefore, that you have a good knowledge of finishing products and their uses. These could include curl activators, defrizzing lotion and holding sprays designed to repel atmospheric moisture and sheen sprays designed to moisturize and lock in curls. This will help you to achieve the best results and enable you to advise your clients on the correct aftercare. Carry out research into a variety of finishing products to be used on various hair types that have been permed.

Tools and equipment

Tools and equipment used when perming the hair

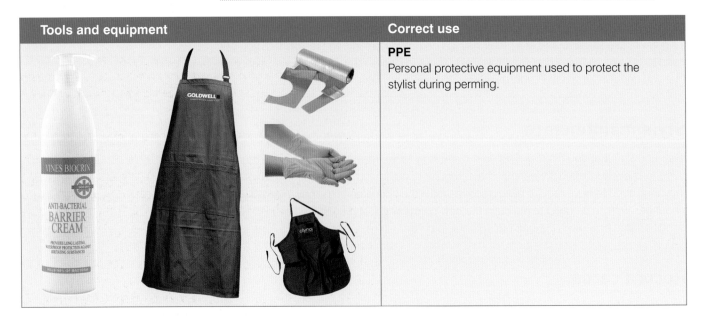

Tools and equipment	Correct use
	PPE Personal protective equipment used to protect the stylist during perming.

Tools and equipment	Correct use
	**Gowning and protecting the client** Use the salon style for protecting clients. The usual process is: ◆ gown ◆ towel ◆ plastic cape.
Ellisons: Beauty Essentials neck wool 1.81kg 4lb	**Cotton wool** Place under each rod to absorb excess perm lotion.
	Bowl and brush Product should be dispensed from the container into the bowl. Do not pour excess product back into the original container. This could cause cross contamination and the oxygenation of product, which would diminish its strength and make it unsuitable for further use. The brush is used to apply perm product to the hair.
	Heat accelerators Heat accelerators such as climazones or roller balls can be used if recommended by perm lotion manufacturers. They will speed up the process by half of the normal processing time.

Tools and equipment	Correct use
	Perming sticks Used to protect the perm rods from causing indentations on the hair, which can lead to breakage during the perming process.
	De-tangling comb Used to comb out tangles from the hair.
	Pin tail comb Used to section the hair, prior to perm winding. The metal tipped comb is good when requiring precise sectioning.
	Comb for winding
	Styling comb Used to style/dress/comb out the hair after perming.
	Section clip Used to section the hair during perm and when using the nine section winding technique.
	Double pronged section clips Used to section nape areas or on thinner hair or sub-sections when perming.
	Standard perm rods Used for basic perming techniques and to create spiral perm winds. Available in a variety of sizes.
	Julius perm rods Used for a looser, softer perm result and to create fashion techniques. Available in a variety of sizes.

Tools and equipment	Correct use
	**Bendy perm rollers** Used to create fashion techniques and spiral perms. Create a softer, less structured perm result. Available in a variety of sizes.
	Perm paper Used to protect the ends of the hair while winding.
	Neutralizer Used to return the hair to its natural pH and to lock in the newly changed restructured curl.
	Products used to maintain the curl Lotions, mousses and mists to add moisture and lock in curl.

Consultation and analysis

Consultation

Consultation prior to a permanent wave is very important. Correct consultation and analysis will avoid long-term damage to the hair after a chemical process.

The following consultation sheet contains questions you should ask your client prior to perming the hair. This information, coupled with your analysis will tell you the condition of your client's hair and whether or not the hair can be chemically processed.

Permanent waving consultation sheet			
Client's name:		Stylist's name:	
Address:		Date:	
When was your hair last permed?			
Which product was used?			
Were there any problems during or after your last perm? (e.g. scalp irritation, hair breakage/hair loss, other)		yes/no	
When did you last shampoo your hair?			
When was your last conditioning treatment?			
Do you know which product was used?		yes/no	
If yes, please state name of product.			
Have you recently had braids, extensions, hair weave removed from your hair?		yes/no	
If yes, how long ago?			
Have you had permanent colour/bleach on your hair?		yes/no	
If yes how long ago?			
Has your hair been relaxed?		yes/no	
If yes, how long ago?			
Have you experienced any hair breakage?		yes/no	
Has your hair been thermally processed with a thermal comb or tong?		yes/no	
If yes, how long ago?			
Does your scalp ever become sensitive during the perming process?		yes/no	
If yes, is it in isolated areas or the complete scalp?			
State type of perm to be carried out:		full head	☐
		regrowth	☐
State the technique to be used:		general perming technique	☐
		creative advanced perm winding technique	☐
State the hair type:		straight	☐
		wavy	☐
		curly	☐
		very curly	☐

Contra indications

Contra indications are reasons why a perm cannot be carried out. It is important to ascertain any contra indications that may exist prior to perming. They should emerge during:

◆ the consultation process and questions asked via the consultation sheet;

◆ the visual checks carried out during the analysis;

◆ any tests carried out prior to deciding if the hair can be permed.

The following table outlines when a perm should or should not be given by listing problems you may come across when perming and suitable action to be taken to solve them.

Contra indications Table

Problem	Course of action	Solution
Braids, extension, hair weave removed within the last week.	Do not perm	Give a course of conditioning treatment. If the hair is in a good condition, perm after two weeks to one month; hair in poor condition will need a prolonged course of conditioning treatments.
Hair thermally processed within the last week.	Do not perm	Give a course of conditioning treatments; perm hair after four weeks to two months, providing no thermal processing remains in the hair and the hair is in a good condition.
Hair permanently coloured or lightened within the last month.	Do not perm	Give a course of conditioning treatments; perm within two to three months of permanent colour providing the hair is in a good condition; keep perm to regrowth only; protect ends; do not process colour-treated ends.
Hair breaking and weak.	Do not perm	Give a course of conditioning treatment; cut damaged hair if necessary to avoid further breakage; do not perm until hair condition improves.
Hair permanently coloured two to three months ago.	A perm can be carried out once the hair is in a good condition.	Protect the ends; keep perm product on the regrowth only.
Hair previously relaxed.	Do not perm	Give regular conditioning treatments; the hair should not be permed until there is at least six months' regrowth. All previously relaxed hair must be cut off.
Active psoriasis or breaks in the skin.	Do not perm	Refer to doctor. Proceed once the skin is healed and no visible broken skin can be seen. This will avoid any secondary effects of perm lotion entering the bloodstream.

Analysis

When analyzing the scalp and hair prior to perming, you need to consider the following factors:

◆ condition of scalp and hair;

◆ natural curl pattern (how curly or wavy the hair is);

◆ areas identified during the consultation process;

◆ strength of product required;

◆ processing time.

As part of your analysis you must carry out the following tests:

◆ porosity test elasticity test;

◆ hair texture test (thick, normal, fine);

◆ perm test (depending on the condition of the hair).

Discuss with your client the type of curl/style required. If all the above incompatability tests are positive, you can carry out a perm.

Product selection

The client's responses to the questions asked during the consultation should tell you whether or not their hair may safely be permed and which product should be selected.

If there is any doubt, a **pre-perm test curl** should be carried out. This test will also help if you are not sure whether the hair is strong enough to be permed or which strength of product to use. It will also help you decide which size of rod or roller to use, and give an indication of processing time and curl result. Use the contra indication table as a guide when making your decision on whether or not to carry out a perm test.

Pre-perm test

You will need the following items and products in order to complete a perm test:

◆ tint brush;

◆ tail comb;

◆ perm rod or curlers;

◆ rearranger.

Procedure

◆ Do not pre-shampoo the hair.

◆ Select the size of rod or curler you intend to use.

◆ Take sections of hair the width and depth of a perm rod.

◆ Place one rod at the nape, one at the crown and one at the side of the head.

If you intend to carry out a regrowth application when perming your client's hair, apply cream rearranger to the regrowth area only. If it is a virgin application, apply the rearranger to the whole length of the hair.

Wind the hair on the selected rod/roller. Leave the hair to process for five to ten minutes only. Test the 'S' curl (shape developed). This will give you an indication of the following:

◆ which strength of rearranger to use;

◆ which size rods or rollers to use;

◆ the finished result that will be achieved;

TOP TIP

When carrying out a perm test do not place rods too near the front hairline as this is the more sensitive area of the head and more prone to damage as the hair will process more quickly.

TOP TIP

If in doubt of the strength of rearranger to use, you could carry out your perm test with two different strengths of perm, depending on the strength of the hair and natural curl pattern.

HEALTH & SAFETY

Keep the application of different strength rearrangers on separate rods.

◆ the processing time;

◆ the condition the hair will be left in after perming.

Types of perm

Perms come in different strengths:

◆ extra super/maximum;

◆ super;

◆ regular;

◆ mild.

Two main types of perm are used on African type hair – *curly perm* and *body perm* (also known as *body wave*). They produce quite different end results:

◆ A *curly perm* produces a tighter, firmer look with solid curls. This perm is used on clients who prefer a more traditional 'permed' style in which the curls form the basis of the hairstyle.

◆ A *body perm* or body wave produces a softer, freer look and is for the client who enjoys the flexibility of wearing the hair in a soft curl or wave. Hair with a body perm can also be set to produce a straighter look.

Pre-perm treatments

A pre-perm treatment should be used on hair which is porous from previous perm treatments. Pre-perm treatments coat the hair with a protective polymer film. This evens out the porosity of the cuticle and acts as a buffer against the chemical action of the perm product. Pre-perm treatments slow down the action of the chemical product but cannot prevent the hair from becoming over-processed.

Perm winding techniques

A variety of **basic perm winding** techniques can be used on African type hair:

◆ nine section winding;

◆ brick winding;

◆ directional winding;

◆ spiral winding.

Nine section winding

The hair is divided into nine sections, which allows the hair to be wound neatly within each section. The nine section technique is ideal for students who are beginning hairdressing. The hair is wound horizontally in each subsection.

Brick winding

This technique is ideal for African or Asian or European type hair or where the hair is worn in a curly/wavy hairstyle. It allows the perm rods or rollers to sit closer to each other and avoids gaps and demarcation lines developing in the finished style. The hair is wound by placing rods or rollers in a brick pattern, similar to tiles on a roof.

TOP TIP

The time spent in carrying out a perm test will ensure the best end results with the minimum damage to the hair, meaning a happier client.

TOP TIP

Not every company produces extra super strength perms.

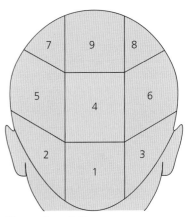

Nine section winding

Nine section method

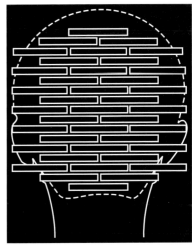

Brick winding

Directional winding

Spiral winding

Directional winding

This technique is used to wind the hair in the direction it is to be styled after perming. For example, if the hair is worn with a side parting, establish the parting and then wind the hair to the side. If the hair is styled away from the face, wind the rods/rollers away from the face.

Winding the hair directionally will increase the durability of the finished hairstyle.

Spiral winding

This technique is used to produce spiral curls on hair which is shoulder length and longer. The hair is wound by taking vertical sections and winding the hair from ends to roots, spiralling up and down the roller or rod as you wind the hair. The hair is divided into nine sections prior to spiral winding to allow all sections to be wound neatly. The brick winding technique can also be used when spiral winding.

Rod or roller size

The size of the rod or roller selected is dependent on several things:

◆ the type of curl desired;

◆ the length of the hair;

◆ the style in which the hair has been cut;

◆ client requirements.

The larger the curl or rod selected, the softer and looser the end result will be; the smaller the rod or roller the tighter the end result. Variety, texture and support can be achieved by winding the hair with alternate large and small rods or rollers. This will produce a soft more natural look with texture and support in the finished style.

General winding techniques

When winding the hair, it is important to avoid fish-hook ends developing, by ensuring the tips of the hair are wound smoothly around the rod or roller. A fish-hook end will produce a bent end on completion of the perm which will have to be cut off. **Pull burns** can be caused when sections of the hair at the root are pulled during the winding process, once perm lotion has been applied. Damage can occur on the scalp and result in hair loss in the specific area of the pull burn.

Perm rod or roller placement

The following points should be observed when winding the hair:

◆ The section taken must be no wider or deeper than the perm rod or roller. This will allow the rod or roller to sit on its own base and avoid root drag and straight roots in the finished perm.

◆ The section taken when perm winding long hair must be slightly narrower than the perm rod or roller to avoid the hair spreading over the edges.

◆ Avoid fracture marks by making sure rubber bands on the perm rods are not placed too close to the hairline, as this could cause the hair to break at this point.

TOP TIP

Always check the tension at the root area once the hair has been wound to avoid any pulling of individual hairs. Adjust rollers, rods or formers to remove any unnecessary tension at the roots prior to applying perm lotion.

TOP TIP

When securing rollers with plastic pins, make sure that the pin is passed through the side of the roller where there is no hair and not through the middle of the roller, which could cause irreparable damage as the hair has a chemical solution on it. On longer, thicker hair you can secure with pins on both sides of the roller to give support and balance.

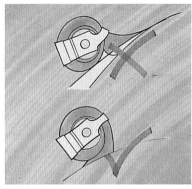

Width of section

Depth of section

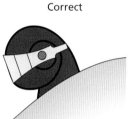

Correct

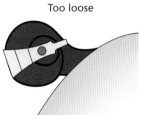

Too loose

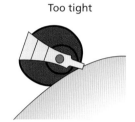

Too tight

Winding

Sectioning

Application of end paper

End paper folded in over the ends of the hair

◆ Make sure the hair is combed smoothly and the end papers are placed on the ends of the hair and held securely to avoid frizzy ends in the finished perm. The illustrations show the correct sectioning of the hair and application of end papers prior to winding the hair on rods or rollers.

Regrowth perm application

Technique

Begin by gowning your client and protecting them with towels and a plastic cape. Check the condition of the scalp and carry out elasticity, porosity and density tests.

Porosity test

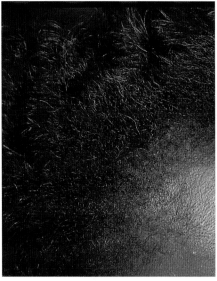

Regrowth area to be permed – front hairline

Regrowth area to be permed

STEP-BY-STEP REGROWTH PERM APPLICATION

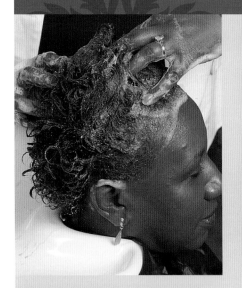

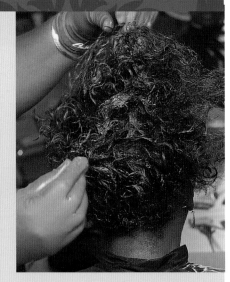

1 Shampoo the hair gently once, using the shampoo recommended by the manufacturer.

2 Apply protective base to the skin just below the hairline, being careful not to get it onto the hair as this could create a barrier to the perming process.

3 Protect your hands with rubber gloves. Apply pre-perm treatment to the hair which is not to be chemically processed.

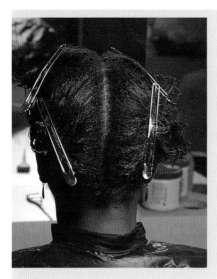

4 Divide the hair into four sections.

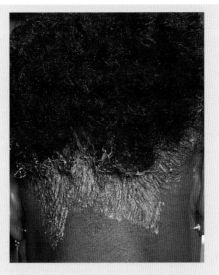

5 Using a tinting brush, start by applying rearranger to the most resistant part of the hair. This is usually at the back of the head between the ears and nape area.

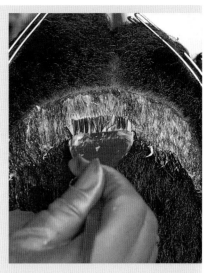

6 Take sub-sections no bigger than 6 mm (¼") from ear to ear and apply rearranger 6 mm (¼") away from the scalp to allow for expansion. It is better to apply the product to sections of the hair working from ear to ear, rather than working on one quarter section of the head at a time, as otherwise the quarter section treated first will have product on it for longer than the other sections. The last section treated could be under-processed as the product may not be left on for long enough. This could lead to an unevenly processed head of hair. Working from ear to ear will ensure that the perm process is methodical and consistent.

7 Once you have applied rearranger to all of the hair, cross check the application to make sure that the whole head is evenly covered with product. Put on a plastic cap and allow the hair to process. If the salon is cold, wrap a towel around the head to give additional warmth.

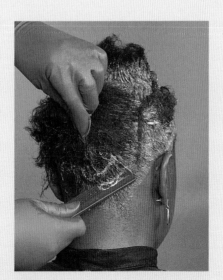

8 Process the hair for 10–20 minutes, check to see how the hair is processing every 5–10 minutes depending on manufacturer's instructions. Once the hair shows signs of the natural curl becoming straight, start combing the hair.

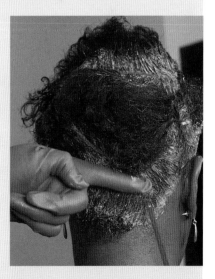

9 Comb the hair gently at the regrowth only and smooth with the fingers.

▶

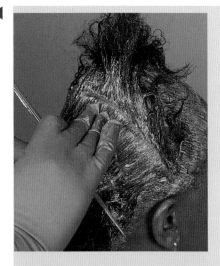

10 Work from the nape area to the front hairline. Repeat the process once again if the hair needs to be straighter.

11 To check whether the hair is straight enough, remove some of the rearranger with a piece of cotton wool.

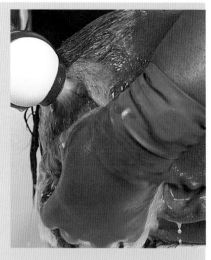

12 Once the hair is straight enough, rinse thoroughly.

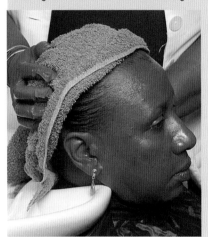

13 Towel dry.

14 Use a tinting bowl and brush to dispense some winding lotion, or use directly from the bottle if it has an applicator nozzle.

15 Apply winding lotion to the regrowth only. An 'S' curl will develop very quickly on African type hair as the cuticle has already been opened by the rearranger.

16 After applying winding lotion, comb regrowth area only, starting from the nape and working up to the crown.

17 Start winding the hair from the back of the crown or from the front hairline, depending on where the most resistant part of the hair is. Continue winding the hair down to the nape.

18 Continue winding the hair from the front hairline to the top of the crown and sides until the whole head is wound.

19 Leave the hair to process, follow the manufacturer's directions for timing. Processing time for most perms used on African type hair is between 10 and 20 minutes.

20 After 10 minutes check for an 'S' curl by unwinding the rod or roller one and a half times. Gently push the hair upwards and look for an 'S' shape. Once this shape has developed, look at a variety of perm rods throughout the head to ensure the required curl pattern has been achieved.

21 Once you are certain the hair has processed sufficiently rinse thoroughly for 10 minutes or follow manufacturer's instructions.

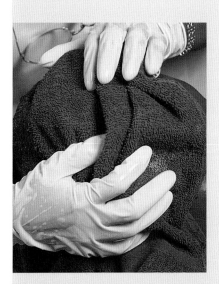

22 Towel dry the hair.

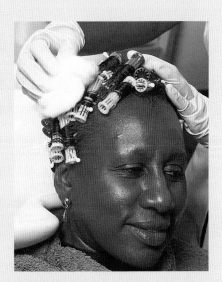

23 Blot with cotton wool to remove excess water and avoid diluting the neutralizer.

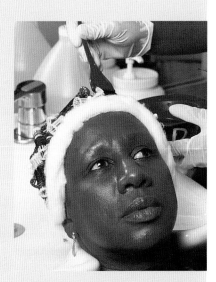

24 Apply neutralizer recommended by the manufacturer. Leave the neutralizer on with the rods in for the time instructed, which is usually 10 minutes. Make sure the neutralizer is left on for long enough, allowing the chemical bonds in the hair to be reformed. This will also allow any perm lotion that might have been left in the hair to be neutralized.

▶

25 Once the neutralizing process has been completed, gently remove all rods. Rinse the hair thoroughly and apply a conditioner as recommended by the manufacturer.

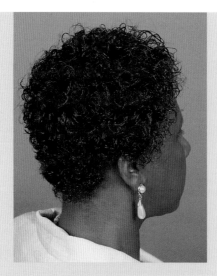

The finished style – back

The finished style – side

Apply aftercare spray moisturizer and activator or the aftercare recommended by the perm product manufacturer – this will prevent the hair becoming dry and frizzy, so that curls are more defined. The chemical process is now complete. It is recommended that the hair is now cut into style. Once African type hair has been permed it tends to be worn in its newly formed shape. If required, the hair can be set or blow-dried on a following visit to the salon.

TOP TIP

It is recommended that the hair is not set or blow-dried immediately after a perm, even if a perm product has been used which can be set or blow-dried. The hair should be naturally dried in its newly formed curl; it can be set on a follow-up visit to the salon. Setting and blow-drying of permed hair should be done rarely to avoid the hair becoming dry, damaged and breaking.

HEALTH & SAFETY

Follow manufacturer's timings as these will vary according to the product. Do not leave the hair too long without checking as it could easily become over-processed.

TOP TIP

Some neutralizers used on African type hair contains sodium bromate. This has a more gentle action on the hair than peroxide-based neutralizer, but it takes longer to lock the new curl pattern into the hair. This is the reason why the rods remain in the hair throughout the neutralizing process. Hydrogen peroxide-based neutralizers are used on European hair and in recent times in some neutralizers for African type hair.

Virgin hair application

Technique

Complete the preliminary procedures as outlined for regrowth perm application.

1 Shampoo the hair gently, taking care not to sensitize your client's scalp. Use the shampoo recommended by the product manufacturer. Remove excess moisture with a towel.

2 Apply a protective barrier around the hairline.

3 Apply pre-perm protective treatment to the ends if the mid-lengths and ends of the hair are porous and dry.

4 Apply rearranger to mid-lengths and ends first, as the ends will take longer to process. Start from the nape of the head working towards the front of the head.

5 Once you have applied rearranger throughout the mid-lengths and ends, begin applying rearranger to the root area, starting from the most resistant part. Cross check application for even coverage.

6 Put on a plastic cap and leave to process for 10–20 minutes, following manufacturer's instructions on timing.

7 Comb the hair gently, starting from the ends and working up through mid-lengths to roots, smoothing with the fingers. Repeat the process if necessary.

8 When the hair is straight enough, rinse thoroughly.

9 Starting at the nape and working up towards the front hairline, apply winding lotion to mid-lengths and ends then roots using a tinting brush or dispensing bottle. Comb the winding lotion through the hair.

10 Start winding from the middle of the crown, working backwards to the nape but leaving the crown and hairline until last.

11 Leave the hair to process with a plastic cap on. Follow manufacturer's directions for timing. The processing time for most perms used on African type hair is between 10 and 20 minutes.

12 After the hair has been processed for 5–10 minutes or according to manufacturer's instructions, check for how the 'S' curl has developed, by looking at a variety of perm rods throughout the head. If the curl pattern is not sufficient, check again every 3–5 minutes until the desired curl pattern is achieved. Rinse thoroughly for 10 minutes.

> **HEALTH & SAFETY**
>
> Make sure all product is rinsed from the hair as perm left in the hair could cause irreparable damage to scalp and hair.

> **TOP TIP**
>
> Always use conditioner on the hair after a perm as this will neutralize any traces of perm that may remain in the hair. Using a conditioner will restore the hair to its normal pH.

> **HEALTH & SAFETY**
>
> Do not over-process the hair as this could weaken it and cause breakage.

> **TOP TIP**
>
> When applying a chemical product to a virgin head of hair, always apply to the mid-lengths and ends first, working towards the root area. The hair nearer the scalp is warmer due to the heat from the head and this causes the hair to process more quickly. The further the hair is away from the scalp the longer it will take to process.

Follow steps 22 through to 25 in the step-by-step sequence above for regrowth perm application.

Problems can develop during or after the perming process. The table outlines some problems and their causes and solutions.

> **HEALTH & SAFETY**
>
> Never use heat during the perming process unless stated by the manufacturer. Additional heat can cause severe damage to the scalp and hair.

Level 3

Problem	Cause	Solution
Hair frizzy after the perm.	Hair not processed enough during the rearranging/straightening stage; incorrect strength perm used (product not strong enough)	Give a course of conditioning treatments if the hair cannot immediately take another perm. If the hair is in good condition, re-perm after two weeks; give a conditioning treatment in-between perms.

Problem	Cause	Solution
Roots/regrowth frizzy, ends curly and smooth.	Incorrect strength perm used; rearranger not left on long enough.	Apply perm to regrowth only after giving the hair a course of conditioning treatment.
Curl drops after the perm.	Rearranger product selected too strong or left on too long; hair has become over-processed.	Do not re-perm. Treat the hair until new regrowth appears and the hair is strong enough to perm. Cut the hair if necessary.
Curl drops after the perm.	Hair not neutralized properly. S curl not firm enough. Rods should have been left in longer and the hair processed longer.	Re-perm using winding lotion only; neutralize for the recommended time; do not rearrange the hair if it is straight enough.
Hair breaking after a perm.	Hair damaged during the perming process (over-processed); chemical not rinsed out properly during the perming process.	Give the hair a course of conditioning treatment; cut the hair if necessary.

Creative advanced perming techniques

Creative perming can provide an exciting and creative experience for the stylist. It is important for the senior stylist to be aware of some advanced techniques because the more conventional basic techniques will not give the required texture or variation in curl pattern that is required. There are some advanced perming techniques which are not suitable for African type hair, such as stack winding techniques. African type hair needs a more structured approach where all of the strands of hair are supported with movement. This does not mean that techniques which use larger rollers or create variety in movement (such as a piggy back perm winds or double decker perm winds) are not suitable.

As a rule, creative perming techniques are carried out on straighter hair types. The winding technique varies, depending on the effect to be created. Experiment by using different curling tools, such as chopsticks, perm rods, formers or bendy rollers that will create a variety of effects for both the client and stylist. It is the use of the different rollers, rods or formers used, winding technique, along with the perm lotion, that creates a fashion technique known as advanced or creative perming. Of course the cut will only enhance the final look.

The following table covers a variety of perm techniques that can be used to create fashion or creative perming techniques.

TOP TIP

Some creative/advanced perming techniques where natural hair is left out in-between rods do work on African type hair. However, in the main, all of the hair will need to be wound as the finished style worn on African type hair is the hair in its new permed curled shape. Straighter hair sections combined with curled hair could be unmanageable for the client and stylist, unless an avant-garde effect is required for the final look.

Perming technique	Use	Suitable for the following hair types	Method
Bendy rollers – spiral wind	To create spiral perms, take a vertical section, wind from points/ends to roots. Best on hair below the shoulder (at least mid of the back).	European, Asian and African type hair.	Wind the hair from points to roots up to ½ of the length of the bendy roller and bend the top of the roller to secure. Start winding from the nape using a nine section technique. Wind up and down the bendy roller to avoid hair layering and building up on the section of the roller. This technique will give an even curl and will allow the perm product to penetrate evenly.
Perm rods – spiral wind technique	To create spiral perms. Best on hair below the shoulder.	European, Asian and African type hair.	Using a nine section technique, start winding vertically at the nape working from the ends/points winding up and down the rod finishing the section at the root area to get an even spiral effect over the rod and avoid hair building up in one area.
Double decker wind	To create variations in curl pattern throughout the length of the hair using two different size rods or stylers/formers. Best suited to hair above or below the shoulders.	European, Asian and African type hair.	This technique involves winding the hair with two different size rods/ rollers. Section the hair, start winding horizontally. Use smaller shapers at ends, up to where the loose movement is required, then place the other shaper under the first shaper and wind both together to the root area and secure both shapers in place.
Root wind	To expand on the curl shape by increasing movement at the root to control, expand or change curl direction at the roots while the mid-lengths and ends will remain straight. Best suited on hair above or just below shoulder length.	Asian and European type hair.	Wind the hair at the roots around a rod or styler at least once, or for one and a half turns, and secure the rod or roller at the root leaving the rest of the hair free.
Weave wind/piggy back	To create texture, movement and varied curl dimensions in the finished look. Suited to below and above shoulder lengths. Best suited to hair that is not dead straight, but has some natural movement. Not suitable for curly or African Hair types but could work on wavy type 2 hair.	Asian and European type hair or wavy hair type 2.	From a nine section, sub-divide the hair and take a section as wide as the rod or styler, weave hair out with a tall comb and wind one section with a larger or smaller roller/former, then wind the woven section with a different size roller. Alternatively, the woven section can be left unwound to create texture, volume and movement.

Perming technique	Use	Suitable for the following hair types	Method
Stack wind	Movement on the mid-lengths and ends. Best suited for bobs and graduated hair styles to create volume on the mid-lengths and ends and no movement on the mid-lengths.	European and Asian hair types.	Working from nine section technique start winding at the nape section as you work up the head start stacking the rods/rollers. Leave the mid-lengths straight, so that only the ends are permed. Use plastic sticks to support the stack wind.
Hopscotch technique	Creates root lift from straighter woven subsections and variation in degree of curl pattern.	Above and below shoulders Asian and European hair types	Working from a nine section technique, take a subsection one and half to two sizes of the curler selected. Sub-divide the hair. Wind one section with the selected curler horizontally and leave the other section out. Winding across the placed rollers, vertically wind the hair left out forming a hopscotch effect.

HEALTH & SAFETY

Remember to avoid excessive tension as the hair is wound to the roots to avoid pull burns and traction alopecia. Be especially cautious not to pull strands of hair when perming using the spiral wind technique.

TOP TIP

During neutralizing, when removing the perm rods on a spiral wind, unwind the hair vertically from the roller to make sure the spiral formation is kept and supported.

Perm lotions used on European and Asian hair types

Perm lotions used for perms on straighter hair types are made up of a range of active ingredients. All the examples in the chart are suited to Asian/European hair types. Always follow the manufacturer's instructions and guidelines on timing. All of these perm lotions come in various strengths for resistant, normal, bleached and colour treated hair.

Perm lotion	Active ingredient	PH of products
Alkaline perms Stronger crisper curl.	Ammonia thioglycolate.	9.5
Acid perms Softer curl/wave.	Glycerol monothioglycollate.	Lower pH 6.7
Exothermic perms Medium curl results. Has its own built-in heat when activator mixed with perm lotion. No additional heat required. Dispose of unused product.	Can be a mix of acid and alkaline.	pH variable

ACTIVITY

Level 3

Carry out research into suitable products for your salon brand that can be used for creative advanced perming techniques on all hair types. Research the following products suitable for African, Asian and European type hair with the following active ingredients:

◆ ammonium thioglycolate;

◆ acid perm;

◆ exothermic perm.

Research the different types of rollers and formers available on the market for perming. Draw up a table giving the strengths of the specific perming brands, their suitability to specific hair types and hair condition, and the type of curl result to be achieved by using different rollers and formers. Your research must also include perming on highlighted and colour treated hair.

Regardless of the hair type, all the following points need to be taken into consideration before carrying out advance/creative perming techniques:

◆ condition of the hair;

◆ consultation and analysis;

◆ the required curl pattern and effect to be created;

◆ any previous chemicals present on the hair;

◆ known contra indications;

◆ the results of the tests carried out;

◆ **product selection**.

Applying perm lotion on European and Asian hair

The hair is usually shampooed prior to perming, following manufacturer's guidance. Apply a pre-perm treatment if the hair is colour treated, or sensitized from a previous perm, or porous.

◆ *Pre-damping technique.* The perm lotion is applied to all the hair prior to winding, once the hair is in good condition or resistant. Use this method only if you can wind quickly and avoid the product being left on the hair for too long and causing over processing and damage and breakage occurring as a result.

◆ *Post-damping technique.* The perm product is applied after the hair is wound. Apply product carefully, placing cotton wool under each roller to avoid any perm lotion flooding the scalp and causing **perm burns**.

Monitor the perming process, as with African type hair. Check the 'S' curl development every three to five minutes once perm lotion has been applied. Unwind the hair at least one or one and a half turns and push the curl upwards to see the 'S' curl development. When the desired 'S' shape is achieved, rinse the hair thoroughly and towel dry in preparation for neutralizing.

Take care not to allow stray perm lotion to rest on the skin or between the skin and gown/towel/protective cape, as this can cause perm burns. If perm lotion does spill onto the skin, remove it immediately with cold water, using a saturated cotton wool swab, until all perm lotion is removed from the skin. Re-gown the client using clean protective clothing.

Perm lotion will deteriorate fabric if it comes into contact with material, so be careful as you apply lotion and ensure the client is adequately protected. Wipe any fabric that has perm lotion on immediately with water to limit the damage.

Neutralizing products

Follow the manufacturer's instructions on neutralizing the hair after the perm; each product may vary in timing. A perm could be unsuccessful if neutralizer instructions are not followed to the letter. Most neutralizers used on straighter hair types contain hydrogen peroxide.

Applying neutralizer to the hair

Prepare neutralizer as instructed and apply to thoroughly rinsed hair. Leave for the required time, remove the rods/formers gently and apply neutralizer to the mid-lengths and ends of the hair, if stated in the manufacturer's instructions. Leave for the prescribed time.

The same process of reduction and oxidation that takes place on African type hair also takes place when perming and neutralizing European and Asian hair types.

Applying conditioner and advising the client on aftercare procedures

Soft textured waves on European type hair

Apply the recommended conditioner, following the manufacturer's guidance on timing. Rinse well and prepare the hair for styling. Update record cards and guide clients on the use of aftercare products, style maintenance do's and don'ts, and how often the hair should be cut. Recommend future follow up visits to the salon.

Straightening hair using perm lotion

In previous years perm lotion was used to straighten curlier/wavier European or Asian hair. Talcum powder would be added to the perm lotion so that the weight of the product would help straighten the hair as it was combed through. More recently ammonia thioglycolate-based hair straighteners have been developed for use on straighter hair types. These products are not suitable to be used to straighten African type hair as they can dry out both the scalp and hair, causing irreparable damage resulting in breakage.

Keratin straightening products

See **CHAPTER 12** for more information on keratin straightening treatments and how to process the hair.

In more recent times specialist products known as *keratin straighteners* have been developed to be used on people of Asian, European and Latin American descent. These products are now also used on wavier, curlier African type hair. Some of the original products contained a chemical called formalin. Due to the potential of the product to give off fumes from the formalin formaldehyde, it has been legislated that only 3 per cent strength formalin can be used in such straightening products.

REVISION QUESTIONS

Level 2

1 The term permanent waving refers to?

1 Curling the hair

2 Marcel waving

3 An artificial curl or wave

4 Tonging

2 What is a Jheri Curl hairstyle?

1 A perm

2 A relaxer

3 A conditioner

4 A straightener

3 Why would you use a rearranger on the hair prior to perming?

1 To wind the hair and develop a curl

2 To smooth the hair prior to using rods, rollers or formers

3 To test the strength of the hair

4 To test the curl pattern

4 On what type of hair would you use a dual action perm?

1 Asian type hair

2 European type hair

3 Straight hair

4 African type hair

5 What is the active ingredient used in perms for African type hair?

1 Ammonia thioglycolate

2 Sodium hydroxide

3 Hydrogen peroxide

4 Sodium bromated

Level 3

6 Why is it important to identify any contra indications prior to perming?

1 To avoid causing irreparable damage to the scalp or hair

2 To decide on a suitable hairstyle

3 To confirm it is okay to proceed with the perm

4 To decide whether or not to use a pre-perm treatment

7 Which one of the following techniques is a basic perm wind?

1 Nine section wind

2 Piggy back wind

3 Root wind

4 Weave wind

8 What should we look for to see if the perm has taken sufficiently?

1 A marcel wave

2 A movement

3 The development of an 'S' curl shape

4 It is not important to check for curl development

9 On what type of hair would you use an acid perm?

1 Asian and European hair

2 Naturally straight hair

3 African type hair

4 All hair types

10 During a perm the hair structure is gradually softened, what is this chemical process known as?

1 Expansion

2 Reformation

3 Reduction

4 Aligning

11 Re-arranger should first be applied to the most resistant part of the head, which area is this?

1 At the back of the nape area, but can vary

2 Along the perimeter of the head

3 The front hairline

4 From the crown forward

12 Relaxing hair

LEARNING OBJECTIVES

This chapter covers the following:

◆ Maintain effective and safe methods of working when assisting with relaxing services

◆ Remove chemical relaxers

◆ Normalize relaxed hair

◆ Maintain effective and safe methods of working when relaxing hair

◆ Analyze the hair and scalp

◆ Relax hair

◆ Provide aftercare advice

KEY TERMS

Case study	Disulphide/sulphur bonds	Pre-relaxer treatment	Relaxer application
Corrective relaxer	Lanthionine bond	Protective base	Virgin relaxer
Damaged brittle hair	Ortho-cortex	Regrowth relaxer	
Diagnostic tests	Paracortex	Relaxer	

UNITS COVERED IN THIS CHAPTER

◆ Assist with relaxing services for
African type hair

◆ Relax hair

INTRODUCTION

Relaxing the hair allows the stylist to change the natural curl pattern of the hair. This chapter deals with the art of relaxing African type hair and will also look at straightening hair of other types. The chapter covers everything you need to know at Level 2, whether you are studying on the Combined course or looking to specialize in African type hair. It will also serve as a foundational reminder for students studying at Level 3.

The history of relaxing hair

Early hair straighteners used in the 1940s in America were a homemade concoction, for example, lye, a strong alkali created from wood ash, potato and eggs, which was prepared by the individual and applied to the hair. Vaseline was used to protect the scalp. However, the product was extremely caustic, would burn the scalp and could damage the hair. This early formula was used in the main by young men who wanted to achieve a 'conked' hairstyle, a forerunner to the quiff which became fashionable in the 1950s. The look was achieved by straightening the hair and styling it with gel to produce a wavy/straight look, which was the height of fashion and obviously worth the initial discomfort.

Chemical relaxing, also known as *straightening*, first became popular when Garrett Augustus Morgan Senior invented the first manufactured and patented product in the early nineteenth century. He is named 'as one of the most prolific inventors of the nineteenth century'. In the 1960s the product had evolved, however they were not as sophisticated as present day **relaxers**. The straightening products of the 1960s were not very successful, often resulting in very **damaged brittle hair** and scalp damage.

The 1970s saw the rebirth of the straightener in a more sophisticated form, now called *relaxer*. Companies currently carry out a lot of research to ensure that their products are much kinder to the hair than previous ones. Today's relaxers are packed with buffers, protein and oil, with the result that the hair retains more moisture and is left in a better condition.

Chemical relaxers are used on the hair to increase manageability, flexibility and durability when styling. The process involves relaxing or straightening the natural curl or wave in the hair. The chemical relaxing process is permanent – as the hair grows, the new growth will be naturally curly in contrast to the area that has been relaxed. The only way to get rid of previously relaxed hair is to let it grow out and cut it off, as once the hair is relaxed sufficiently it will not revert back to its natural curl pattern.

Product development for chemical relaxers has, in the main, been initiated by American companies. There has been increased research into the development of chemical relaxers in the UK, Europe and Africa but America remains the leader in this type of research.

TOP TIP

If the hair reverts after the relaxer process, not enough disulphide bonds have been broken. If the hair is in a good condition it can be relaxed after one to two weeks or a conditioning treatment if required.

For more information about the structure of the hair see CHAPTER 2.

The science of relaxing

Hair is made up of keratin – a protein also found in nails and skin. Keratin gives the hair its tensile strength and elasticity, allowing the hair to be stretched. Each strand of hair is made up of three parts: *cuticle*, *cortex* and *medulla*.

There are three bonds that we are mainly concerned with when chemically processing, blow-drying, setting or thermally styling hair. These are *disulphide, salt* and *hydrogen bonds*. **Disulphide or sulphur bonds** are the strongest. These bonds are broken when the hair is relaxed or permed. If too many of these bonds are broken during the chemical process, the hair will become weak and break. Salt bonds are weak and break when the hair is shampooed. blow-dried or set, reforming as the hair dries. Hydrogen bonds are broken when the hair is set, blow dried or thermally processed; they reform once the hair becomes wet or moist.

If you look at an individual strand of African type hair, some parts appear thicker than others. This uneven keratinization causes the hair to become curly, with the cortex consisting of two types – **paracortex** and **ortho-cortex**.

When a chemical relaxer is applied to the hair, the product causes the cuticle to swell, allowing it to penetrate the cortex. The disulphide bonds in the cortex are broken and one sulphur atom is removed from the broken bond. They then re-join with a new partner – **lanthionine bond**. The hair now has one sulphur bond and one lanthionine bond. Relaxed hair cannot be permed because in order for a perm to be effective both disulphide bonds must be intact. After the relaxing process, one bond is permanently straight and cannot be altered.

Once the hair is relaxed sufficiently, the chemical relaxer is rinsed from the hair to halt the process. The hair is then shampooed using a neutralizing shampoo which is acidic and removes any traces of alkaline which may still remain in the hair. The shampoo closes the cuticle and brings the hair back to its normal pH of 4.5.

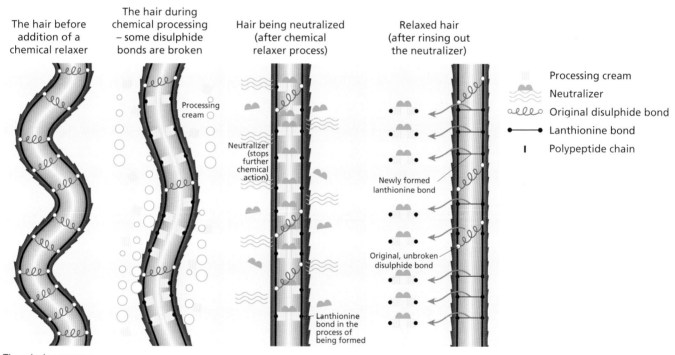

The relaxing process

Relaxed hair should not be permed under any circumstances as this would result in:

◆ no curl pattern;

◆ excessive damage and dryness, causing hair breakage;

◆ long-term damage to already processed hair.

In other words it would be a complete waste of time.

For more information on cutting natural hair see CHAPTER 16.

Contra indications

Contra indications are reasons why a relaxer cannot be carried out, such as abrasions on the scalp due to psoriasis or eczema, damaged hair during previous relaxers, perm, lightened or colour-treated hair. These factors must be taken into consideration prior to carrying out a relaxer treatment. In cases where a relaxer cannot be given, suggest a course of treatments or a haircut to remove damaged hair. A relaxer can then be applied once the scalp and hair are healthy. Clients also have the option of resting their hair from chemical processing by going natural.

Consultation and analysis

Chemical relaxers can be applied in different situations:

◆ to virgin hair (**a virgin relaxer**);

◆ to regrowth on hair that has been relaxed previously (regrowth relaxer);

◆ to correct a previous uneven relaxer treatment (a corrective relaxer).

These situations will be treated separately after a discussion of the safety precautions that need to be observed and the methods and techniques to be used when relaxing the hair. If the necessary care is taken during the consultation, analysis and application of any chemical process, this will minimize any damage to the scalp and hair.

Consultation and recording client information

An in-depth client consultation carried out prior to the application of any chemical process can avoid complications occurring during the application of products and after the chemical process has been completed. A properly structured consultation will help you construct your client history and prepare client records for present and future use.

A record card must be completed for each relaxer process carried out. Record cards should be updated before, during and after each salon visit and should provide a history of the service carried out. They should cover:

◆ condition of the hair;

◆ name, strength and type of relaxer product used;

◆ length of time processed;

◆ previous colour/lightening or highlighting processes

◆ condition of the hair after relaxing;

◆ if the hair was cut or a cut recommended;

◆ any future styling and salon visits advised;

◆ any problems that occurred during the process.

The consultation sheet lists questions that should be asked by a stylist when carrying out a consultation with the client prior to relaxing. The results of the consultation will provide

TOP TIP

Extreme caution must be used when applying a relaxer because the products used can cause irreparable damage.

you with the necessary information to enable you to decide whether or not the client's hair is suitable for relaxing. Record the information gained from the consultation on the record card.

Client consultation sheet			
Client's name:		Stylist's name:	
Address:		Date:	
When did you last shampoo your hair?			
When was your hair last relaxed?			
Which product was used?			
Were any problems experienced during the chemical relaxing process such as:			
◆ scalp irritation		yes/no	
◆ insufficient processing		yes/no	
◆ hair breakage?		yes/no	
Have you recently had braids, extensions or hair weave removed from your hair?		yes/no	
If yes, how long ago?			
Have you had permanent colour on your hair?		yes/no	
If yes, how long ago?			
Has your hair been permed?		yes/no	
If yes, how long ago?			
When was your last conditioning treatment?			
Do you know which product was used?		yes/no	
If yes, please state name of conditioner.			
Has your hair been thermally processed with a thermal comb or tong?		yes/no	
If yes, how long ago?			
Does your scalp ever become sensitive during the relaxing process?		yes/no	
If yes, is it in an isolated areas or the complete scalp?		yes/no	
What was the name of the relaxer used previously?			
What type of relaxer was used previously?	Lye ☐	No lye ☐	
Type of relaxer to be carried out:	regrowth ☐	full head ☐	
	corrective ☐	texturizer ☐	
	hair straightener ☐		
Are there any signs of:	alopecia ☐	traction alopecia ☐	

For more information about contagious and non-contagious conditions see CHAPTER 2.

The table lists conditions under which a relaxer should *not* be applied, together with corrective procedures.

Problem	Causes/effects	Solution
Psoriasis/abrasions on the scalp	Psoriasis: scratching the scalp prior to a chemical relaxer can cause abrasions on the scalp.	Apply conditioning treatment to the scalp and hair; do not apply relaxer until the scalp has healed. (A client experiencing a bad outbreak of psoriasis should seek medical advice.) If the psoriasis is dormant and there are no abrasions a relaxer can be applied. As a precaution the scalp must be protected prior to processing.
Damaged, brittle hair	Too many chemical processes; overlapping of chemical relaxer; not enough conditioning treatments.	Apply reconstructive conditioning treatment; cut off the over-processed hair; recommend a course of conditioning treatments.
Hair extensions	Removal of hair extensions three to seven days prior to applying a relaxer could cause it to irritate the scalp.	Apply a course of conditioning treatment to the hair (any hair that has just had extensions removed should have a course of conditioning treatment); relax hair after two to four weeks provided the scalp and hair is in a good condition.
Hair has been shampooed within the last three days	Scalp could have become sensitized and cause the relaxer to irritate.	Apply conditioning treatment; relax hair within one week once the hair is in a good condition.
Permanent colour/ bleach/highlights	Could cause the hair to become over-processed and brittle.	Relax the hair two to three months after colouring; recommend a course of conditioning treatments. Use a milder strength relaxer.

TOP TIP

You can chemically relax hair where you have identified your client as having a naturally sensitive scalp by first applying a protective base (see later in this chapter).

Analysis and consultation

When analyzing the scalp and hair before relaxing, you need to consider the following:

◆ condition of scalp and hair;

◆ natural curl pattern (how curly or wavy the hair is);

◆ areas identified during the consultation process;

◆ strength of product required;

◆ processing time.

As part of your analysis you must carry out the following tests:

◆ elasticity test;

◆ porosity test;

◆ density test;

◆ hair texture;

◆ Pre-relaxer strand test (optional).

For more information about the consultation and analysis process see CHAPTER 3.

Elasticity test

If the hair is in a good condition, it will stretch and return to its normal length without breaking when you carry out this test. If the hair breaks, recommend a course of treatments to strengthen the hair. In extreme cases you may need to cut off the damaged hair. If breakage is not extreme, you can chemically relax the hair and then give a course of treatments afterwards. Always protect relaxed or colour-treated hair first, with pre-perm protection prior to relaxing the hair.

Porosity test

If you find the hair to be extremely porous, recommend a course of conditioning treatment prior to relaxing. With normal or average porosity apply a pre-perm product to coat and protect the cuticle prior to relaxing. Avoid the relaxer coming into contact with previously processed hair. Further information on pre-perm products is given later in this chapter.

Scalp condition

Examine the scalp for abrasions and question the client on any sensitivity experienced during previous relaxing processes. If abrasions are present, do not chemically process the hair.

Hair condition/natural curl pattern

Observe the natural curl pattern and hair texture, which will help you to establish the extent of the relaxation required and the correct strength of relaxer to use. Check the hair condition for signs of breakage.

Hair texture

Assessing the client's hair prior to chemically relaxing it is important, as it helps to decide which strength product should be used. Hair which has a thick texture may be resistant and require a super relaxer. Medium texture hair will need a regular relaxer, while fine texture hair requires a mild relaxer.

Scalp sensitivity

If your client has a sensitive scalp, you can protect the scalp by applying a **protective base**. Avoid using a heavy oil-based scalp protector as excessive application could leave a barrier on the hair and prevent the relaxer from penetrating the cuticle, resulting in insufficient processing.

Relaxer strand test

This test is optional. If you are in any doubt about the strength of relaxer you need to use, or whether your client's hair is in a good enough condition to be relaxed, you can carry out a pre-relaxer test by isolating and treating a small section of hair. The section taken should be in the nape area or where the hair is more resistant and should not be wider than 12 mm (½").

◆ Use non metal or plastic-coated section clips to clip surrounding hair away from the area to be relaxed.

◆ Cover clipped hair with a wad of cotton wool to prevent chemical relaxer from coming into contact with it.

TOP TIP

If in doubt about any previous products that might be present on the hair, see Chapter 3 on how and when to carry out an incompatibility test.

HEALTH & SAFETY

Never apply relaxer to wet hair as this could cause breakage.

Relaxing products

TOP TIP

There is no such thing as a no lye relaxer. Lye describes hydroxide, so once the product contains any form of hydroxide it contains lye.

◆ Apply the selected strength to the test section.

◆ Smooth and check strand every three minutes; observe the hair continuously.

◆ When the hair is relaxed sufficiently, rinse off the chemical thoroughly and apply neutralizing shampoo.

If you decide to proceed with the relaxer on completion of the test, do not do this on the same day but apply a conditioning treatment to the hair. If the hair is in good condition you can apply the relaxer within four to seven days. (Remember to omit the strand that has been previously tested when you carry out the chemical relaxer process.)

The results of the test will give you an indication of:

◆ whether the hair is in a good enough condition to be relaxed;

◆ the strength of product to use;

◆ the processing time;

◆ the condition the hair would be in after the chemical relaxer has been applied.

Types of relaxer

There are five types of chemical relaxers:

◆ sodium hydroxide;

◆ calcium hydroxide

◆ potassium hydroxide;

◆ guanidine hydroxide;

◆ lithium hydroxide.

Some new relaxers on the market are a combination of hydroxides. Always read the back of the relaxer container to see what the active ingredients are.

All relaxers contain hydroxide. They all process the hair in the same way, by opening the cuticle and penetrating the cortex where they break the disulphide bonds and cause the hair to become relaxed (straight/straighter). All relaxers are strongly alkaline, i.e. they have a high pH.

Product companies have divided relaxers into two types: *lye* and *no-lye* products. Sodium hydroxide relaxers are classified as lye products, while calcium, potassium, guanidine and lithium hydroxide relaxers are classified as no-lye.

Lye relaxers have a tendency to:

◆ be irritating to the scalp;

◆ cause less drying of the hair;

◆ leave the hair with more sheen;

◆ penetrate the cuticle more quickly.

No-lye relaxers have a tendency to:

◆ be less irritating to the scalp;

◆ be more drying on the hair and scalp – the hair will need to be moisturized more often to avoid dryness and breakage;

- leave the hair in need of frequent conditioning treatments;
- penetrate the cuticle more slowly.

There are exceptions: potassium hydroxide penetrates the cuticle rapidly and is no longer used often in relaxers; guanidine hydroxide does not have as drying an effect on the hair as other no-lye relaxers; lithium hydroxide is less drying on the hair and produces a similar result to a sodium hydroxide relaxer but is kinder to the scalp.

Sodium hydroxide relaxers are available in three strengths, with a pH range of 12 to 13:

- *Super relaxer* for resistant hair.
- *Regular relaxer* for normal hair.
- Mild relaxer for thin or colour-treated hair.

Calcium hydroxide relaxers are available in one strength only, with a pH range of 12 to 13. They can be used on all hair types. More recently some product companies have produced a stronger 'resistant' strength for coarse, resistant hair.

Associated products

Pre-relaxer protective treatments   These are used on porous hair before application of the relaxer. They coat the cuticle with a polymer film, which acts as a buffer to slow the action of the chemical product. They will not prevent the hair from becoming over-processed but they make it easier to control by slowing down the process.

Protective base   A protective base is used to coat the scalp prior to applying a chemical relaxer. It usually has a petroleum base and is light to the touch, spreads easily on the scalp and is easily removed when the hair is shampooed after the relaxing process. It is usual to apply a protective base when working with sodium hydroxide relaxers. It is not usually necessary to use a protective base when using calcium hydroxide relaxers as these tend not to sensitize the scalp. Always follow manufacturers instructions.

Post-perm treatments   A post-perm treatment is applied after the relaxer has been rinsed from the hair. These products are acidic and will help bring the hair back to its normal pH level and moisturize the hair after the chemical relaxing process.

Neutralizing shampoo   A neutralizing shampoo is used after the hair has been relaxed sufficiently and all the product thoroughly rinsed out. It will cleanse the hair of any remaining relaxer and neutralize any alkalinity still present, bringing the hair back to its normal pH of around 4.5 and close the cuticle.

> **TOP TIP**
>
> When working on clients with a sensitive scalp, and providing no abrasions are present, use a protective base before applying a relaxer.

> **TOP TIP**
>
> Not all product manufacturers produce a post-perm treatment. Some manufacturers produce a product that can be used across a range of relaxing products.

Working in a professional manner

The salon work area, trolleys, floor and equipment must be kept clean, sterilized and tidy at all times. Tools must always be clean and sterilized after each client. Particular attention should be paid to ensuring relaxer is removed and cleaned from all shampoo basins, when used to rinse, shampoo and neutralize a relaxer. Effective cleaning will avoid harming the skin or clothes of any other client. You should always present yourself in a clean manner – remember you represent the salon. Any relaxer that has been taken out of the container it is housed in must not be returned to that container once used. Replacing used relaxer product in the relaxer tub can cause cross contamination and also lessen the strength of the product so it becomes less effective.

Lifestyle

You must consider your client's lifestyle. Consult with the client continuously throughout the relaxing process and make clear the cost, commitment and time involved in relaxing the hair. This process can be high maintenance with regular conditioning treatments required. Regular cutting, follow up relaxers every two to three months will be necessary. The use of several products is involved in maintaining the hair in a good condition. Find out if your client swims, as a swimming cap should be worn if swimming in chlorine pools. Some pools now do not use chlorine as a sterilizer within pools and use less aggressive purification systems instead; chlorine (bleach) can further sensitize relaxed and fragile hair, causing the hair to become damaged and break. Regular exercise routines can make African type hair a bit brittle, frizzy and dry, due to perspiration. However, this state is reversed when the hair is shampooed and conditioned. Follow-up salon treatments should be recommended to such clients, along with a suitable shampoo and conditioner to be used at home.

Face shapes

Look at your client's face shape to decide on the look to be created once the hair is relaxed. Is fullness, length, height, layers or a short look required in the finished hairstyle? Discuss the options available with your client during the consultation process and after the hair has been relaxed as your client could change their mind on what they want. This will help ensure your client is happy with the final look.

Tools and equipment

Tools and equipment	Correct use
	PPE Personal protective equipment is used to protect the stylist during the relaxing process. Gloves must be used to avoid damage to the skin or dermatitis due to exposure to harsh relaxing chemicals. A tabard or apron can be worn to protect the clothes during relaxing as the chemical could damage fabric. If relaxer comes into contact with fabric remove with a wet cloth or cotton wool with neutralizing shampoo on it.
	Gowning and protecting the client Use the salon style for protecting clients. The usual process is: ◆ gown ◆ towel ◆ plastic cape

Tools and equipment	Correct use
Ellisons: Beauty Essentials neck wool 1.81 kg 4lb	**Cotton wool** Used to test relaxer result.
	Bowl and brush Relaxer product should be dispensed from the container into the bowl. Do not pour excess product back into the original container. This could cause cross contamination and the oxygenation of product, which would diminish its strength and make it unsuitable for further use. Do not work from large tubs of relaxer for the same reason.
	De-tangling comb Used to comb out tangles from the hair and for creating a texturized relaxer look.
	Pin tail comb Used to section the hair and used to apply relaxer.
	Styling comb Used to style/dress/comb out the hair after relaxing.
	Section clip Used to section the hair during the relaxer process.
	Relaxers These come in different strengths (mild, regular and super). They fall into two categories (lye and no-lye).
	Products used to maintain relaxed hair

Application of a regrowth relaxer

If the consultation, analysis and tests are positive you can now proceed with the chemical relaxer process. You will need the products and equipment shown in the chart, plus any other products recommended by the product company.

TOP TIP

It is important to take great care before and during application of a chemical relaxer. If your consultation and analysis have been thorough, you will avoid damage to the hair and scalp.

Procedure for chemical relaxer application to regrowth

1 Gown and protect your client with towels and plastic cape. Wear an apron to protect your own clothing.

2 Apply a protective base to the scalp if required. Apply protective base to the skin just below the hairline, being careful not to apply protective base onto the hair as this could cause a barrier to the chemical relaxing treatment (a). If your client is sensitive to the relaxer apply protective base to the scalp also.

3 Apply a **pre-relaxer treatment** to the hair mid-lengths and ends of the hair which will not be chemically processed (b).

4 Divide the hair into four sections and protect your hands with rubber gloves. Dispense the product into a bowl.

5 Using the back of a comb or clean tint brush start applying the relaxer to the most resistant part of the head. This tends to be in the nape area (c).

6 Take sub-sections no bigger than 6 mm (¼"). Apply relaxer 6 mm away from the scalp. It is necessary to apply the relaxer 6 mm away from the scalp because the chemical product expands after it is applied due to natural body heat and the reaction of the product on the hair. If the relaxer is applied too close to the scalp there will be no room for it to expand without coming into contact with the scalp, which could cause irritation and the rinsing and neutralizing of the hair before the relaxer is processed sufficiently.

Regrowth area to be chemically relaxed

(a) Applying protector around the hairline

(b) Applying pre-relaxer to the mid-lengths and ends

(c) Applying relaxer to the most resistant part of the hair, in the nape area

7 Apply the product to the hair working from ear to ear, rather than working on one quarter section of the head and then another (d). This will ensure a more consistent end result.

8 Hold the ends of the hair for control, while you apply the relaxer so that the regrowth area can be clearly seen (e).

9 Continue to apply relaxer to the crown regrowth area, working up towards the front of the hairline. Just lay the product onto the hair – make sure you do not comb the relaxer into the rest of the hair at this stage as this could damage the hair (f) and (g).

10 Once you have applied relaxer to the whole of the regrowth area, go back to the area where you first started your application. Start by combing the regrowth area only and smoothing it with your fingers (h), (i), (j), (k) and (l).

(d) Working from ear to ear

(e) Holding ends of the hair so that regrowth area can be seen clearly

(f) Applying relaxer to the crown regrowth area

(g) The finished application

(h) Starting the relaxing process by gently combing the regrowth area

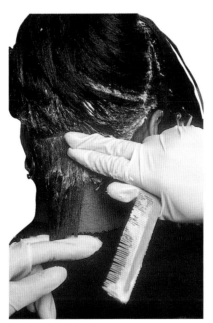

(i) Smoothing the section after combing

TOP TIP

Hold the hair gently; do not pull the hair as this could cause the scalp to become irritated.

HEALTH & SAFETY

Do not flood the hair with too much relaxer as this could cause over-processing.

(j) Combing and smoothing the sides

(k) Smoothing the side section after combing

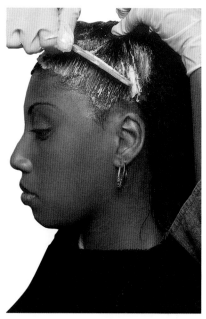

(l) Relaxing the front hairline

TOP TIP

Hair can be relaxed to remove some of the natural curl. This technique is called texturizing and is ideal on short hairstyles or styles that require minimum straightening.

Do not comb beyond the regrowth area as this could cause overlapping. Take care not to scrape the scalp as you work with the hair as this could sensitize the scalp. It is kinder to the hair and less damaging to use your fingers to smooth the hair. Methods and techniques of processing the hair when chemically relaxing can vary depending on how you were taught, product company's instructions, practical experience and personal preferences. Some stylists will prefer to use a comb, some a tint brush and some their fingers. There are well known trainers who have promoted using the fingers only (of course wearing gloves), as this method transfers heat and is gentle. Whatever your preferred method ensure you are skilled and take the utmost care not to scrape the scalp or pull the hair, overlap or over-process the hair when using tools such as tint brushes and combs as these could sensitize and irritate the scalp, meaning the relaxer product will have to be removed immediately.

As you work the relaxer through the hair, apply more product to those areas where coverage is not sufficient and even. You will be doing two things at this stage – cross checking your application and continuing to chemically relax the hair. Using this method of application will mean that you can work through the hair more quickly and efficiently. It will result in a more accurate application and at the same time be more effective.

Once you have worked completely through the hair, if the hair still needs to be straighter start processing the hair again from the area where you first started your application, combing and smoothing the relaxer only up to the regrowth area. Once this has been completed the hair should now be relaxed. To check if the hair is relaxed sufficiently, take a strand of hair and remove the relaxer with cotton wool. Once the hair does not revert to its original curl and keeps the newly formed relaxed formation, the product can be removed.

HEALTH & SAFETY

Always follow manufacturer's recommendations on application and removal procedures.

TOP TIP

Some product companies advise once the product is applied and cross checked to leave the hair to process without any manipulation. As with any relaxing process caution should be taken when processing, check the hair at intervals to avoid scalp burns, over-processing, loss of hair and breakage. Check your client's comfort throughout the process.

Rinsing

11 If the hair is relaxed sufficiently, start rinsing the hair thoroughly, using tepid water. Allow the force of the water spray to flush the chemical relaxer out from roots to points. While rinsing, use your fingers gently to assist removal of the relaxer from the scalp and hair; this will help to prevent the scalp being sensitized. When rinsing off relaxer use medium spray force to avoid sensitizing the scalp. Always check your client's comfort throughout the process. Always follow individual manufacturer's instructions.

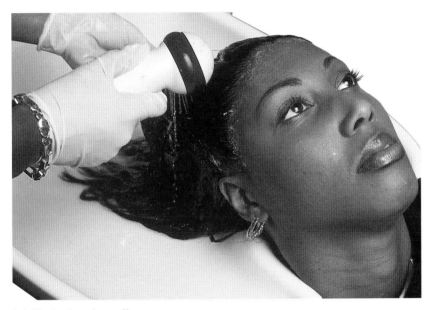

(m) Rinsing the relaxer off

12 Once you have finished rinsing, check to make sure all traces of the relaxing chemical have been removed from the scalp and hair and apply post-perm treatment.

Neutralizing

13 Apply a neutralizing shampoo to the hair. Shampoo gently but thoroughly taking care to make sure all areas of the scalp are massaged. Rinse thoroughly.

14 Re-apply shampoo and rinse thoroughly. The hair should be shampooed at least twice to ensure that all the chemical relaxer has been removed. It is important that you rinse the hair thoroughly after shampooing.

15 Towel-dry the hair.

16 Comb the hair to ensure it is tangle free. Apply styling lotion of your choice.

17 Style as desired.

18 Fill in a record card.

HEALTH & SAFETY

Never use hot water to rinse the hair as this could cause scalp irritation and burn the scalp. If the scalp has become sensitive during the relaxing process, rinse with cold water.

HEALTH & SAFETY

Do not massage or rub the scalp vigorously as this could cause it to become irritated and sensitized.

TOP TIP

For hair that is in poor condition it is better to set the hair after relaxing rather than blow-drying as this can put undue stress on the hair.

HEALTH & SAFETY

Particles of relaxer left in the hair will continue to process, damage the scalp and hair causing breakage.

The finished style

HEALTH & SAFETY

If the scalp is sensitive apply a protective base, take care not to over-saturate the hair as it could act as a barrier.

Procedure for chemical relaxer application to virgin hair

Complete all the tests as described in **regrowth relaxer** application. Select your products and equipment as before.

1   Apply pre-relaxer treatment if the hair is dry and porous. Pre-protection can be added to the ends to maintain the hair in good condition.

2   Apply a protective base around the hairline. Apply protection to the scalp if required.

3   Divide the hair into four sections.

4   Protect hands with rubber gloves and clothes with an apron. Apply relaxer to the mid-lengths and ends first. Starting from the most resistant part of the head or nape area, work upwards towards the crown and forward towards the front hairline.

5   Once you have applied relaxer to mid-length and ends throughout the head, start applying relaxer to the root area, taking care to apply relaxer 6 mm (¼") away from the scalp. Work from the nape area up to the front hairline as before.

6   Start combing and smoothing the hair with the fingers, taking 6 mm (¼") sub-sections of hair. Work from ear to ear, applying more relaxer where necessary. Once this has been completed, comb through the hair from roots to ends and smooth with the fingers. Work with your fingers or tools of choice until the desired degree of relaxing is achieved as in regrowth **relaxer application**.

7   Rinse the hair thoroughly, following steps 11–14 as in regrowth relaxer application. Style as desired.

8   Fill in a record card.

TOP TIP

Sodium hydroxide and calcium hydroxide relaxers are not compatible. Once the hair has been processed with a calcium hydroxide relaxer, if it is not straight enough you should not try to relax the hair with sodium hydroxide relaxer, as it will not have any effect.

Applying a corrective chemical relaxer treatment

This process should be carried out by an experienced practitioner, who has a greater understanding of curl patterns and knowledge of **corrective relaxer** application techniques.

A corrective chemical relaxer will need to be applied to any head of hair where the relaxing process is uneven. The table illustrates some problems that can occur during chemical relaxing and procedures that can be used to correct them.

Problem	Causes/effects	Solution
Ends of the hair under-processed.	Relaxer not left on the ends of the hair for long enough. Calcium hydroxide relaxer used on the ends, sodium hydroxide relaxer used on the roots.	Apply relaxer to the ends and process until the desired result is achieved. Do not apply sodium hydroxide relaxer to the ends, as the hair will not become straighter and more damage will be caused; treat the hair on a regular basis with a reconstructive conditioner; cut regularly.
Mid-section of the hair is under-processed; roots and ends processed evenly.	Relaxer has not been left on for long enough in this section; incorrect strength of relaxer used.	Apply relaxer to mid-section and process until evenly matched with the roots and ends of the hair. Do *not* process if calcium hydroxide relaxer has been used previously.
Roots of the hair under-processed; ends straight.	Relaxer has not been left on the roots for long enough; incorrect strength relaxer used.	Apply relaxer to the root area only; process until evenly matched.

Corrective chemical relaxer application

Technique

Carry out **diagnostic tests** for elasticity, porosity and density as previously described. Apply protector around the front hairline and pre-protector to mid-lengths and ends.

Before application

Elasticity test

Porosity test

Density test

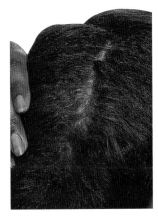
Regrowth area to be relaxed

Mid-length area where the chemical corrective relaxer will be applied

STEP-BY-STEP: APPLICATION OF CORRECTIVE CHEMICAL RELAXER

1 Start application at the nape area (the most resistant part of the head on this client).

2 Lay the relaxer on with a comb.

3 Work up the head towards the crown.

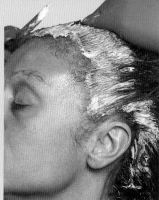

4 Apply relaxer to the front hairline.

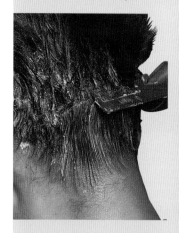

5 Go back to the nape area and start combing and smoothing with the fingers.

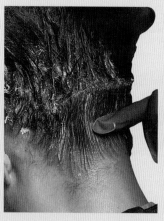

6 Smoothing regrowth with the fingers.

7 Continue processing the hair using the same technique.

8 Continue until you get to the front hairline.

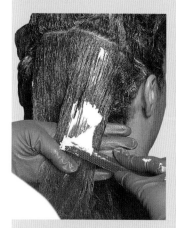

9 Go back to the nape area and apply more relaxer to the under-processed mid-length area.

10 Comb the hair from the regrowth to the mid-length.

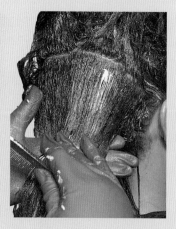

11 Smooth the hair with the fingers.

12 Continue the process until you reach the front hairline.

13 Remove relaxer from a small strand of hair with a piece of cotton wool to ensure the hair is sufficiently relaxed.

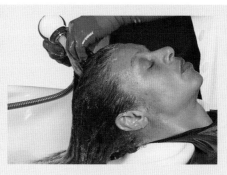

14 Rinse the chemical relaxer thoroughly from the hair.

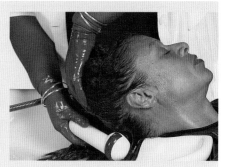

15 Make sure all product is removed from the nape area.

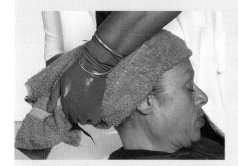

16 Towel dry the hair.

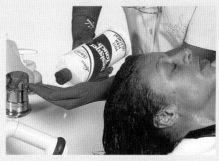

17 Apply post-perm treatment if recommended by the product company.

18 Comb post-perm treatment through the hair. (Follow the manufacturer's instructions on the use of the post-perm treatment.)

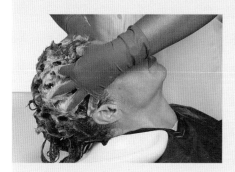

19 Apply neutralizing shampoo. Shampoo the hair twice to ensure all chemical relaxer is removed. Rinse the hair thoroughly.

20 Towel dry the hair; apply styling lotion.

21 Style as desired. Remember to fill in a record card.

ACTIVITY

Level 3

Write a guide designed to help and support individuals who are assisting with the removal and neutralizing/normalizing of relaxer services in the salon. The guide should identify, how, when and why. Write a to-do list for a junior stylist. Cover the following points:

◆ how to prepare for a relaxer process;

◆ how to successfully neutralize the hair after a relaxer;

◆ the importance of gowning and protecting the client;

TOP TIP

When rinsing the hair, do not rub the scalp as there may still be relaxer present which could cause the scalp to become irritated. Lift the hair when rinsing chemical relaxer and allow the power of the water to remove the product.

HEALTH & SAFETY

On permanently coloured and lightened/highlighted hair, only relax the regrowth to avoid over-processing and hair breakage.

TOP TIP

Discuss how clients should protect and care for their hair, particularly when sleeping, such as wrapping the hair, or using breathable nets. This can minimize the repeated use of electrical equipment, which could damage the hair.

◆ preparation of the salon;

◆ the use of PPE by the stylist/practitioner;

◆ use of open questions for consultation/analysis and the completion of record cards in the house style;

◆ who the to do list is for, and who they should refer to for guidance;

◆ health and safety precautions to be followed throughout the process;

◆ any risk assessment to be observed when using relaxer products or from fumes given off by keratin straightening products;

◆ how to dispose of waste relaxer.

Texturizing relaxer

Hair texturizers are used for removing frizz or expanding the natural curl pattern. Curl texturizers work best when used on hair that shows a distinct natural curl pattern, as opposed to hair with a very tight curl pattern, which may become straighter rather than wavy. This technique is also well suited to hair that is sculpture cut. The hair is then texturized with relaxer to create a curl or wave movement; gel, serum and finishing products are applied and the hair is then styled. The same relaxer products are used when texturizing. The relaxer is combed through using tools such as a wide tooth comb to expand the curl.

Technique

Use the products and equipment listed under regrowth relaxer. Complete all the tests as described in regrowth relaxer application and select your products based on your consultation and analysis.

1 Apply pre-relaxer treatment if the hair is dry and porous. If the hair is in good condition, there is no need to apply any pre-relaxer treatment, unless you wish to preserve the condition of the pre-relaxed hair. If the hair is longer it would be good practice to protect the ends.

2 Apply a protective base around the hairline. Apply protection to the scalp if required.

3 Comb the hair through from the nape up to the crown and hairline area.

4 Using a tint brush, de-tangling or large tooth comb, lay the relaxer on the hair first starting from the nape up through the mid-lengths and front hairline covering the whole head with relaxer.

5 Start combing the hair from the nape using a large tooth comb working up to the front hairline to keep the hair separate and create texture and a wave/curl.

6 When the hair is processed sufficiently rinse the hair thoroughly.

7 Apply neutralizing shampoo and rinse thoroughly until all relaxer is removed, following manufacturer's instructions throughout the process.

8 Apply conditioner, rinse.

9 Cut and style the hair as desired and according to the client's requirements.

10 Recommend follow-up salon visits and aftercare, advise on products to use for style maintenance.

Keratin straightening products

Keratin straightening products smooth out the frizz from the hair, allowing the hair to keep straighter for longer. Keratin straighteners describe a new generation of straighteners which are not chemical hair relaxers and are not hydroxide based. After the keratin treatment, the hair is processed with an electrical straightening iron at a fairly high temperature. This seals and straightens the hair after the process.

Keratin straighteners have been developed to be used on people of Asian, European and Latin American descent. Some of the original products contained a chemical called formalin. These products had the potential to give off fumes in the form of formaldehyde (a gas) that could potentially affect the stylist and possibly the client. Legislation has been brought in so that only 3 per cent strength formalin can be used in such straightening products. Most of the new generation of keratin products do not contain any chemicals and are therefore considered to be a chemical-free way of styling the hair, as the keratin conditions the hair. Some keratin products are acidic, allowing the product to enter the cuticle and soften the curl. The hair is made up of (keratin which is a protein built from amino acids). A keratin straightening treatment could last from 6–10 weeks and is considered to be a temporary method of processing the hair which is milder and kinder to the hair than a relaxer. It is, therefore, a very good option for clients who do not want to use strong chemicals to process their hair but want to expand their natural curl and control frizzy hair.

The heat from the straightening iron must be monitored carefully as excessive heat could cause damage and breakage to the hair. In most cases straightening irons must be used in conjunction with the straightening product to be effective. It should be noted that excessive heat can discolour white hair, so test heat levels and monitor the use of heat styling irons to avoid this happening.

Keratin straightening procedure

Always follow manufacturer's instructions throughout the process and only use products listed in the product line. Prior to using keratin products, carry out a thorough consultation and analysis.

◆ Carry out diagnostic tests for elasticity, porosity, density and strand test as previously described.

◆ Perform a strand test with keratin product to be used on bleached, colour-treated and relaxed hair, or any hair you feel the need to establish and identify any previous treatment/s present on the hair.

You should apply protection to the hair as described by the manufacturer and wear gloves, again as advised by the manufacturer. Start application at the nape area (the most resistant part of the head on the client) and do not use on scalps with abrasions or irritation present.

Permanent hair colour may become faded when using straightening products. As with perm lotion, apply any colouring products after the keratin straightening process. Do not apply colour or lightening products immediately after the keratin straightening process, as this could damage the hair. Only apply these products if the hair is in a good condition and if recommended by the manufacturer, otherwise recommend a course of conditioning treatments.

Technique

Please note that the steps for this process may vary depending on the manufacturer's guidelines and recommendations.

1 Cleanse the hair with the prescribed shampoo.

2 Section the hair into four and apply product from the nape upwards, from roots to points (a).

3 Comb the keratin product through to distribute it evenly.

4 Process the hair for the prescribed time listed by the product manufacturer.

5 Keep the hair moist during blow-drying by spraying with water spray. Blow-dry the hair until it is thoroughly dry.

6 Flat iron the hair taking small sections and letting the hair sit for the required time.

7 Shampoo the hair thoroughly if required.

8 Apply moisturizing conditioner as prescribed by the manufacturer.

9 Apply thermal protection product to the hair.

10 Blow-dry, flat iron, set or style as required.

TOP TIP

Using a keratin hair straightener on tight curly hair may result in opening up the curl pattern, not making the hair straight, but acting as a texturizer.

(a) Applying keratin product to the nape area of the head

(b) Straightening the hair with electrical irons after blow-drying the hair

(c) The finished keratin process

REVISION QUESTIONS

Level 2

1 Why is it important to monitor the client's comfort levels during the relaxing process?

1 To avoid damaging the scalp

2 To ensure the hair is sufficiently relaxed

3 To check that the hair is straight enough

4 To check the client is not experiencing sensitivity/burning

2 Why would you section the hair prior to applying a relaxer?

1 To apply the relaxer neatly and accurately

2 To test the length of the hair

3 To apply pre protection to the scalp

4 To carry out an elasticity test

3 What do contra indications give us a guide to?

1 How often to condition the hair

2 The elasticity of the hair

3 Reasons why a relaxer cannot be given

4 How often the hair should be shampooed

4 Why do you have to identify if the scalp is sensitive prior to applying a relaxer?

1 To see if the scalp is smooth

2 To protect the scalp and avoid irritation, burning and scalp damage

3 To see how quickly the hair will process

4 To decide on the condition of the hair

5 Why would you not apply relaxer to broken skin on the scalp?

1 To avoid breakage on the ends

2 To avoid discolouration of the hair

3 To prevent an uneven result

4 To prevent scalp irritation and long-term hair loss

6 Why would you carry out a relaxer strand test?

1 When in doubt of the strength of the relaxer to be used and the condition of the hair

2 To test how much the hair will stretch and which product to use

3 To test for hair shrinkage and condition of the hair

4 To see the true length of the hair

7 What does a pre-relaxer treatment do?

1 Evens out the porosity of the hair and coats the cuticle

2 Gives the hair elasticity

3 Makes the hair oily

4 Stretches the hair

8 Why is relaxer applied 6 mm (¼") from the scalp?

1 To allow the scalp to breathe

2 To keep the scalp clean

3 To be tidy and thorough in application

4 To allow the relaxer space to expand when affected by natural body heat

9 Why is virgin relaxer applied first to the mid-lengths, ends then roots?

1 The scalp is warm and therefore processes slower

2 No particular reason

3 The application technique selected can vary and is up to the stylist

4 Best way to apply any relaxer

10 What effect does a keratin straightener have on the hair?

1 Creates curl within the hair strands

2 Controls frizz when used in conjunction with a straightening iron

3 Curls the ends of the hair

4 Creates ringlets

11 After the removal of hair extensions when is a safe time to recommend a relaxer process?

1 two to four weeks

2 two days

3 one week

4 six months

12 When texturizing the hair which tool should be used during the smoothing process?

1 Hand

2 Fine tooth comb

3 Tint brush

4 Wide tooth comb

Notes

PART FOUR
Cutting and Colouring

The cutting and colouring chapters will provide you with a range of creative tools at a variety of levels. Your creative and visual awareness will be enhanced by following the step-by-step guidance that will support the acquisition of your cutting, colouring and problem solving skills, which support technical competencies and vocational ability at both basic and advanced levels. You will learn and understand how to use and adapt your newly learnt skills to enhance a client's individual look and overall hairstyle, providing the hairstylist with the self-satisfaction of catering to the client's needs, taking into account aesthetics, design, balance and shape.

ROLE MODEL

KORELL WILLIAMS Award winning stylist

> For as long as I can remember I have loved styling hair. I learnt to braid hair at an early age and developed a natural talent over the years. Having initially taken up performing arts, I decided to follow my passion and enrolled on a hairdressing course at Cornell College, Tottenham and have never looked back. My tutors were very encouraging and entered me for the 'Junior Stylist' category of the Wahl awards in 2008 where I walked away with the trophy.

When cutting in the salon, I am inspired by shapes and the texture of the hair. I believe in creating definition through a good cut; that way a style can always look good with minimum fuss. I use traditional styling and cutting methods, incorporating my own brand of creativity, to produce something that I consider to be current and edgy.

I would advise any aspiring hairdresser to master all the basic hairdressing skills, and research in the past and present to gain inspiration for new looks. Keep pushing your personal boundaries in order to evolve with your own style and do not be afraid to let your own personality show through your work, as this is what will make you stand out from the crowd.

13 Cutting hair using basic techniques

LEARNING OBJECTIVES

This chapter covers the following:

◆ Maintain effective and safe methods of working when cutting hair

◆ Cut hair to achieve a variety of looks

◆ Provide aftercare advice

KEY TERMS

45° angle	Client requirements	Lifestyle
90° angle	Cutting cape	Stray ends
180° angle	Cutting terminology	Template
Angle	Enhance the shape	Thinning scissors
Classic cut	Hair growth patterns	

UNITS COVERED IN THIS CHAPTER

Level 2

◆ Cut natural African, Curly, European and Asian type hair using basic techniques

INTRODUCTION

Cutting hair using basic techniques allows the stylist to create new and different haircuts for the client. This chapter deals with the art of the basics of cutting all types of hair. It covers everything a stylist needs to know at Level 2, and serves as a foundational reminder for students studying at Level 3. More advanced creative cutting techniques are described in Chapter 14.

Cutting techniques

A good haircut is the basis for achieving any hairstyle. Cutting the hair into style allows the hairdresser to show his or her creativity – when we cut hair we are using it as a medium to design and create an overall look for the client.

As hairdressers, it is important that our cutting skills are as good as all the other services we carry out within the salon. A good haircut can totally transform a head of hair. To be able to create the right effect and be technically correct you need to be able to execute a number of different haircutting techniques. You must also have a knowledge of face and head shapes, hair texture, natural movement, **hair growth patterns** and curl patterns, all of which must be taken into consideration prior to carrying out any haircut.

It is essential to have knowledge of basic cutting techniques before attempting to cut anyone's hair. Knowledge and experience can be gained through watching demonstrations and videos, and practising on tuition heads and models. Practise will help you develop technically along with developing the art of dexterity, hair control and cutting design.

Over the years hairdressers and large salon groups have developed their own terminology for describing various cutting techniques. These techniques have not changed throughout the history of hairdressing and regardless of terminology used they create the same effect. There are three basic cutting techniques that can be achieved when cutting hair:

- layering;
- graduation;
- one-length shapes.

All three techniques can be executed at differing lengths, thereby creating varied and individual looks for the client and allowing the stylist to pursue several cutting and styling options.

Basic cuts and shapes can be totally changed by texturizing, tailoring or personalizing a cut to suit the client's **lifestyle**, requirements, face shape and hair texture. Fashion is constantly revolving and evolving. Each time a style becomes fashionable again the basic style remains but is updated to reflect current trends.

There are many reasons for cutting hair:

- to design a new shape;
- to **enhance the shape**;
- to make the hair manageable;
- to remove damaged hair.

Regardless of the hair type, the basic techniques of cutting hair are the same. When working with curly hair, allowances must be made for natural movement within the hair. Always use even tension when cutting naturally curly hair; this will help you to stretch and control the hair during cutting. Always cut the hair slightly longer than the intended length as the hair will appear shorter when dry.

Cutting tools

Tools and equipment	Correct use
	PPE Personal protective equipment used to protect the male and female stylist during the cutting process.
	Gowning and protecting the client Use the salon style for protecting clients. The usual process is: ◆ gown ◆ towel ◆ plastic cape
	Cutting scissors Used for cutting hair only.
	Thinning scissors Used to remove weight from the hair, to thin a hairstyle out or create spiky hair.
	Powder puff Used to gently remove hair cuttings to clean the face and neck.
	Traditional Afro comb Used to de-tangle and comb out Afros and African type hair. Also used in conjunction with scissors or clippers when cutting Afro hairstyles or sculpture cuts.
	De-tangling comb Used to comb out tangles from the hair and for texturized relaxer techniques.
	Pin tail comb Used to section the hair and to apply relaxer.
	Cutting comb Used to style/dress/comb out the hair after relaxing.

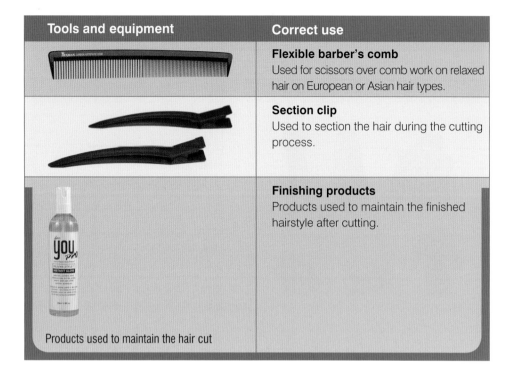

Tools and equipment	Correct use
	Flexible barber's comb Used for scissors over comb work on relaxed hair on European or Asian hair types.
	Section clip Used to section the hair during the cutting process.
	Finishing products Products used to maintain the finished hairstyle after cutting.

Products used to maintain the hair cut

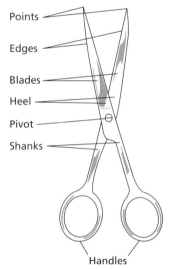

Points
Edges
Blades
Heel
Pivot
Shanks

Handles

Cutting scissors

Hairdressing scissors are made up of two blades fastened with a screw which acts as a pivot. The diagram details the parts of a pair of cutting scissors.

Before even attempting to cut a head of hair, the correct tools must be selected. When choosing scissors you should take into account their weight, length and most importantly how comfortable they feel in your hands and the cutting edge. Scissors can range from the fairly cheap to the very expensive. The more you pay for scissors, the better the quality and more accurate the cut.

The correct way to hold a pair of cutting scissors is between the thumb and third finger. Holding the scissors in this way will give the best control and balance. The action used when cutting is the opening and closing of the scissors using the thumb only. When cutting the hair, use the points to the middle of your blades. Work through the hair in small precise bites for control.

Thinning scissors

Thinning scissors are used to remove bulk and weight from the hair. They are of two types:

◆ *Scissors with notched teeth on the cutting edge of both blades*. These will remove maximum bulk or weight from the hair.

◆ *Scissors with notched teeth on the cutting edge of one blade only*. The other blade has a straight cutting edge. These scissors will remove minimum bulk and weight from the hair.

Cutting combs

Cutting combs vary in size and the choice very much depends on the stylist selecting the comb with which they are most comfortable. Sometimes a larger tooth comb is better, for example when working on a thicker head of hair. For barbering and scissors over comb technique a flexible barbering comb can be used on the nape and sides of the head.

A more flexible comb is better for scissors over comb work when cutting very short hair in the nape area. For sculpture cutting natural African type hair, an Afro comb is best for controlling the hair lengths and following the contours of the head.

Natural movement and hair growth patterns

All curly hair has natural movement but this is not always seen clearly on very curly hair due to its dense appearance. Natural curl or movement is more commonly seen in relaxed, natural soft curled or natural wavy hair textures. When we refer to natural movement we are describing any extreme changes in how the hair grows. The following table outlines hair growth patterns.

Growth pattern	Where found	How to deal with it
Widow's peak	Prominent point found at the front hairline.	The hair tends to work best when styled backwards; fringes are best kept long to avoid spiking.
Double crown	Two circular movements found on the crown and further back on the head on opposite sides.	Found on wavier hair; leave the hair longer in these areas to avoid spiking.
Nape whirls	Found in the nape; strong circular movement on either side of the head.	The hair needs to be left slightly longer so it will remain flat; alternatively cut the hair very close to the scalp to avoid spiking.
Cow lick	Strong movement in the front hairline directing the hair to the right or left; found in straight and wavy hair.	Always cut hair in the same direction in which it naturally falls. Leave weight on fringes to avoid spiking and make the hair lie flatter.

Cutting terminology and techniques

Before attempting to cut a head of hair, it is important to have a knowledge of **cutting terminology**. The words used vary within the hairdressing industry but the techniques remain the same.

Terminology

◆ **analysis** stylist looks at natural growth pattern, movement and decides on techniques to be used and the look to be achieved.

◆ **angle** the way hair is held when cutting to determine the shape. Also the degree of lift/elevation.

◆ **area** a specific section of the head that is being cut.

◆ **asymmetric** one side of the hair is cut longer than the other.

◆ Avant Garde is a hairstyle worn by the leaders of fashion. Is before its time, experimental, edgy and pushes boundaries.

◆ **basic cut** covers basic techniques of cutting that do not include texturizing and intricate cutting/technique.

◆ **blending** technique that describes the continuation or blending of one section of the haircut into another.

◆ **blunt cut** a solid one-length cut or geometric line.

◆ **channel cutting** working in lines throughout the haircut.

◆ **classic cut** a cut that is timeless and always in fashion.

◆ **concave shape** creates an inversion or A-line shape, with the hair shorter in the middle and longer on the sides like an A-line bob shape.

◆ **consultation** discussion between client and stylist on look to be achieved, manageability and aftercare.

◆ **convex shape** creates a round curved outline shape this could be u-shaped, round or v-shaped.

◆ **crown** top middle section of the head.

◆ **disconnected haircut** a haircut that goes from short to longer, with shorter hair under longer hair or vice a versa; a short line next to a longer line shape where no marrying or blending of the haircut is present or visible.

◆ **elevation** degree of lift or angle the hair is cut at within a haircut, 0° to 180° angle.

◆ **external shape** the perimeter of the haircut.

◆ **fashion cutting** using a combination of cutting techniques to create a fashion look.

◆ **freehand cutting** cutting the hair without tension – not holding the hair during the cutting process.

◆ **guideline** first section of hair cut to establish length and shape to be achieved.

◆ **hairline** hair growth framing the outside of the head nearest the face and neck.

◆ **horseshoe section** hair sectioned from the crown to the front hairline between the temples in a horseshoe shape.

◆ **internal guideline** the first section of hair cut to determine the internal shape.

◆ **internal shape** the internal/inner shape of the haircut.

◆ **mesh** sub-division or smaller piece of hair taken from the main section.

◆ **nape** back section of the head at the hairline near the neck.

◆ **occipital bone** the bone that sits between each ear, sometimes identified by a prominent bump.

◆ **running out of hair** where the subsequent hair lengths are shorter than parts of the hair that have already been cut.

◆ **sculpture cut** cut following the contours of the head.

◆ **sectioning** dividing the hair into manageable sections prior to cutting.

◆ **sub-division/subsection** a smaller section of hair taken from the original section.

◆ **symmetric** both sides of the haircut are the same length.

◆ **tension** the amount of stretch placed on the hair during cutting.

◆ **weight** length and bulk of the hair.

Cutting techniques

◆ **club cutting** produces a solid blunt line – this can make the hair appear thicker.

◆ **graduated cut** the hair is held away from the scalp at a 45° angle and cut – this creates layers on the perimeter of the hair.

◆ **layer cut** hair cut at various angles to create layers and movement within a haircut.

◆ **one-length cut** hair cut on the perimeter only.

◆ **over-directed** technique used to create length and weight on the perimeter of the hair with shorter layers internally, or create length on the sides. This is done by over directing the hair to it's longest point and cutting.

◆ **scissors over comb** cutting the hair close to the scalp using scissors or clippers over a comb.

Texturizing techniques

◆ **point cutting technique** the points of the scissors are used to snip into the hair at intervals along the hair strands to break up solid lines and create texture/ disconnect the cut.

◆ **serrating** the blunt edges of the hair are broken up by chipping into it with the points of the scissors.

◆ **slice/slither cutting** the scissors are glided through meshes of hair, taking away length and bulk.

◆ **texturizing** the removal of weight from the hair using a variety of techniques described below; the points of the hair are left thinner; this technique is ideal for breaking up solid lines.

◆ **twist-texturizing** sections of the hair are twisted and the scissors run up and down the hair, removing length and bulk.

◆ **under-directed** technique creates length in the area the hair is being under-directed by pulling the hair back to the furthest point.

Outline shapes

A variety of shapes can be created on the perimeter of a cut, regardless of the length of the hair. Different shapes and angles can create hard or soft lines. For example, a solid straight line can create a hard finish. Softer lines can be created by texturizing, layering or graduating the hair.

Short shape outlines

Before changing the outline shape on the perimeter of the hair, the shape of the client's head, neck and hairline must be taken into consideration. Cutting the hair following the client's natural growth pattern can create a softer finish, particularly when creating short looks on female clients.

Designing perimeter shapes

Different outlines can be created on the perimeter by using the techniques described below. Always remember that the angle and direction at which you hold the hair will determine the effect and shape created. For example, the lower the fingers are held (a), the less graduation will be achieved; the higher the fingers and hand are held (b) the more graduation will be achieved.

If the fingers are sloped or angled in a downward position, the hair will be cut shorter at one point and longer at another. This will encourage the hair to move forwards and create weight where the length has built up. For example an inverted bob (c).

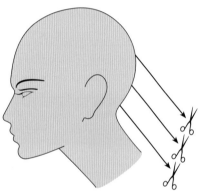

(a) Hair held at a lower angle to create longer internal graduation and weight on the perimeter lengths

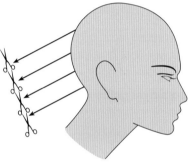

(b) Hair held at a higher angle to create shorter internal graduation and perimeter shape, leaving length internally

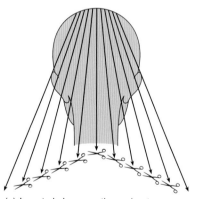

(c) Inverted shape on the perimeter

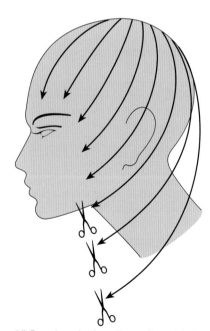

(d) Page boy: feathered/over directed hair cut on the perimeter

When the fingers are sloped or angled in an upward position, the opposite will take place. The hair will be shorter at one point and longer at another. This technique will push the weight away from the front to the back of the hair where it is longer, as in a page boy style (d) or feathered cut.

Cutting angles

The cutting angle is the angle the fingers are held at to determine the shape of the guideline and overall shape of the haircut, e.g. inverted, asymmetric or straight. The cutting angle can also refer to the degree of lift or elevation the hair is cut at, for example **45° angle**, **90° angle** or **180° angle**. Sometimes combinations of the different angles are used when creating the desired finished haircut.

Cutting a fringe

A fringe can add variety and interest to a hairstyle but will not suit all clients. It can vary in length, thickness and texture. The choice of the type of fringe to be worn will depend on the hairstyle, **client requirements**, hair texture and creativity of the stylist.

A fringe can be cut using a variety of shapes such as:

◆ *Curved.* Ideal for clients who like the hair to frame the forehead and sides of the hairline. This will produce softer lines.

◆ *Square.* Will produce a straight, hard, geometric, solid line.

◆ *Triangular.* Ideal for creating a thicker, fuller fringe. This type of fringe can be one length or layered to give more volume and softness layered to give more volume and softness.

When cutting a fringe, cut the hair without using too much tension or cut it freehand, allowing the hair to fall naturally while cutting. Using this technique will stop the hair from springing up and sticking out. Once you have decided on the shape of fringe you want to create, proceed as follows.

1 Sub-divide the hair, starting at the front hairline.

2 Bring down sections of hair, cutting to the guideline.

3 Cut to the thickness required (If fullness is required, layer-cut the hair once all the hair has been cut to a solid length).

4 Cross-check the fringe to ensure it is even.

Consultation and analysis

Before a cut is carried out, the following details concerning the client need to be taken into account:

◆ lifestyle;

◆ head and face shape;

◆ hair texture and movement;

◆ requirements;

◆ the look to be achieved.

TOP TIP

Fringes can be layered to create fullness and softness or cut to one length to create a solid, straight line.

TOP TIP

Discuss with your client the length they would like their fringe to be.

http://www.hairfinder.com/ techniques/long-graduated-cut.htm

For more information on consultation and analysis see CHAPTER 3.

Lifestyle

You must consider your client's job, interests and hobbies. It is important to find out how active a lifestyle your client leads as this will help you to plan a suitable haircut. For example, if your client is involved with sports on a regular basis, a style which needs minimum maintenance would be best.

Head and face shape

It is important to take into consideration the client's head and face shape prior to cutting the hair. Your observations will help you to decide on a suitable style, overall design and shape for the client.

Hair texture

Prior to cutting, you must look at the client's hair texture as certain cuts will be more suitable for particular textures. For example, fine hair cut in a one-length style will appear thicker.

In African type hair, tighter curled textures show little or no movement. However, when the hair has been relaxed or sculpture cut, natural movement is more apparent. In wavy textured African type hair, natural partings and texture are more prevalent and more easily defined than in curly hair. On Asian and European hair types, growth patterns are easily defined. A variety of hair growth patterns can be seen such as nape whirls, widow's peak, double crown and cow lick. All these growth patterns must be taken into consideration prior to cutting.

Client requirements

Discuss in depth with your client the style you are going to create. Make sure the client agrees and is happy with the changes you are going to make to their hair. It is also important that the client will be able to manage the finished look. Give advice on how the cut and shape is to be maintained and make sure of your client's ability to look after the new look. There is no point in giving a client a new style which they will not be able to maintain at home.

The look to be achieved

Once you have reached agreement with your client on the cut to be achieved, you can proceed. The finished style should suit the client and work in harmony with the hair texture, face shape, natural movement and lifestyle. Give the client the approximate time the haircut will take, try to organize yourself so that you work quickly and efficiently and within the allocated time.

TOP TIP

Nothing looks worse than hair cut short in the nape which does not complement the client's hair growth pattern or neck.

Working safely

For more information on health and safety see CHAPTER 1.

Personal hygiene and readiness for work

Always make sure you pay attention to personal hygiene. You should be freshly bathed or showered and your teeth, nails and hands should be clean. Well manicured nails will not snag the hair or scalp as you work. Your clothes must be clean and suitable for work.

Wear comfortable shoes that allow your feet to breathe and support both your feet and legs during the long days of standing; support tights might also assist.

Keep a clean work area, tools and equipment

The work area must be clean and tidy at all times. The work surfaces and surrounding areas should be cleaned every morning and during the working day. All hair cuttings must be removed after each client using sterile wipes to clean the chairs and work surfaces. All mirrors must be wiped, including hand held mirrors. Remember these are passed from client to client and should be kept as clean from hair and bacteria as possible. All tools and equipment should also be washed and sterilized after each client. Floors must be swept up constantly to avoid hair that has been cut becoming a hazard and causing a client or stylist to slip, resulting in injury.

Dealing with cuts and injuries to the client

Always try to work safely when cutting client's hair. Unfortunately, accidents do occur sometimes when working around the ears or cleaning up **stray ends**, that is stray soft hairs in the nape area. If the skin is cut, wear gloves and provide the client with clean tissues or cotton wool and get them to put pressure in the area until the flow of blood stops. You should not apply pressure especially if you are not a first aider as the pressure you apply may be excessive and cause further damage. Inform the salon first aider, tutor or senior stylist as soon as the accident has happened. If the injury is serious refer to a medic. All injuries must be recorded immediately in the accident book.

Correct position when cutting

When cutting hair continually adjust the height of the chair depending on the section/area of the head you are working on. People's heights vary, so with each new client adjust the height of the chair so that the client is in comfortable reach. Overstretching to reach your client could cause you back, arm and neck strain. You should be in line with the hair and head when you are cutting. Get your client to sit up in the chair with legs uncrossed. Crossed legs will cause your client's head and shoulders to be at an angle, which could make the finished cut lopsided. Always check your client's head and body position prior to cutting their hair and adjust their head as you work through the haircut. Rotate around the client as you cut the various sections. On longer hair you can use a cutting stool, so that your eyes are in line with the hair that is being cut. Remove all hair cuttings from the client's neck and clothes once the cut is finished and sweep up cuttings from the floor.

Contra indications

At the start of every hairdressing process, contra indications need to be checked to avoid cross contamination and passing on infectious conditions/diseases or infestations such as head lice. If you are ever in doubt as to whether a client has an infectious condition, ask for a second opinion from a more experienced member of staff. It is not worth the salon's reputation to treat a client with any contagious condition as you could put other clients at risk.

Client preparation

A **cutting cape** can be used over the gown for added protection; this will fit snugly around the neck avoiding hair coming into contact with the skin. This also gives a cleaner line to the shoulders and neck improving visibility.

One-length hair cut (below the shoulder)

A one-length hair cut is the same length all over the hair, with weight on the perimeter/ ends of the hair. A one-length haircut can be cut just above or below the shoulders. This haircut is often referred to as being *blunt* or *club cut*, meaning the hair is cut in a solid line. The technique is usually used when cutting one-length shapes or to remove length without layers and is cut at a 0° to 45° angle. When cross-checking a one-length cut that is below the shoulders it is a good idea to get the client to stand up. You can then see how the hair will fall naturally and any ends that need to be removed to balance the haircut.

TOP TIP

When cutting subsequent sections of uncut hair, comb the section to be cut together with the previously cut section. Flip the uncut section up to reveal the cut guideline. This will help ensure that the following sections will be cut to the guideline which is used as the **template** for the cut on the perimeter.

Technique

1 Gown and protect the client.

2 Carry out a consultation and analysis with the client.

3 Shampoo and condition the client's hair.

4 Divide the hair into four sections and sub-divide the two nape sections. This should be no thicker than 6 mm (¼"). Use a cutting cape to help keep the area uncluttered if required.

5 Sub-divide the hair from the third and fourth back section.

6 Using an even tension to stretch curly hair, start cutting the hair from the middle nape area first (a). Then using the middle as a guide, cut and blend from the middle to the left side and then cut from the middle to the right side. Check the guideline is straight before taking down the next subsection to be cut.

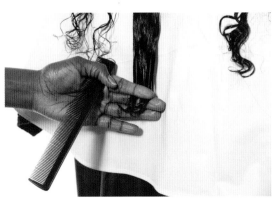

(a) Starting to cut the guideline

(b) The two completed back sections

7 Take subsections down on both sides till you reach the crown and both the back third and fourth sections are cut. (b)

8 Sub-divide the first left side section and cut the guideline by under directing the hair to the back section and cut to the side guideline to match the hair that has already been cut. Continue taking down subsections until you reach the top of the crown.

9 Sub-divide and cut the right side, using the same technique as used to cut the left side.

10 Cross-check the haircut for accuracy, starting from the middle of the cut working from left to right using the same technique that the hair was cut with. Cut off any hair that is uneven, so that the hair is cut at one-length.

11 The finished look (c).

(c) The finished look

One-length cut with a triangle section fringe

Forward graduated haircut (below the shoulders)

A forward graduated haircut creates a solid length at the back perimeter of the haircut and shorter graduated lengths that frame around the front of the face. The hairstyle combines both a one-length shape and graduated/layering together, to give movement and shape at the front of the hair. The decision on how short or long the graduation and feathering around the face will be depends on how short or long the hair is cut along with client's requirements. Use the eyes, eyebrows, ears, nose, mouth, jaw or chin to decide where the shorter lengths will start or finish. This will then be your guideline for how long or short the graduated layers will be. The hair is over-directed at the sides to create length and cut at a 45° angle to create the graduation, from shorter in the fringe mid-length sections to longer at the perimeter.

Technique

1 Gown and protect the client. Use a cutting cape to assist keeping the area uncluttered if required.

2 Carry out a consultation and analysis with the client.

3 Shampoo and condition the client's hair.

4 Divide the hair into four sections and sub-divide the two nape sections. This should be no thicker than 6mm (¼") (a).

5 Sub-divide the hair from the third and fourth back section.

(a) Dividing the hair into sections

(b) Cutting a section diagonally

(c) Blending the fringe

(d) The finished forward graduation haircut

6   Using even tension on curly hair and slightly less on straighter hair, start cutting the hair in the back nape area, at a 0 to 45° angle from the middle back section to start the guideline, cutting from middle left and then middle right. Bring all subsections down until the hair is cut to a one-length guideline (see previous section on the one-length haircut).

7   Starting on the left side, taking a diagonal section, over-direct the hair and decide on the length the hair is to be cut at. Use the features of the face to determine how long or short the graduation to be created will be. Cut the left side diagonally following the angle of the section elevating the hair to a 45° angle. Continue bringing subsections from the side over-direct and cut until all the hair on the side is cut (b).

8   Follow the same procedure as used to cut the first side. Run your hands down both sides of the hair. This will give a clear idea of how much hair to remove on the uncut side.

9   Marry or blend the fringe to the previously cut sides (c). Again, check the balance of the fringe and forward graduation on the sides by running the fingers down both sides. Where the fingers stops first, indicates the shorter side. Balance the longer side to match the shorter. Another method of cross-checking the hair for length is to twist both sections of the hair to stretch the hair out. Do not forget to look in the mirror as you cut, checking for balance and symmetry. Stand away from the client to look at the balance, shape, length and suitability of the overall haircut or to look at a specific area. Cross-check the haircut, following the original technique used to cut the hair and remove any stray or uneven ends.

Basic inverted A-line cut/bob (above the shoulder)

A basic classic inverted bob haircut creates weight on the perimeter with shorter internal lengths in the middle nape area of the head. It is important that all meshes of hair are cut using even tension to create an even and balanced finish. If you cut the hair close against the skin you will create a 0° angle. Cutting the hair between the fingers will produce a 45° angle. A classic bob is a good example of a one-length haircut. The inversion works against the curvature of the head, to create an illusion of a square effect, producing solid perimeter lines all cut to a blunt/club cut solid length ideal for making thinner hair look thicker.

TOP TIP

When cutting a one-length bob, the guideline on the perimeter of the hair in the nape area can be cut straight or with an inverted shape (sometimes called an A-shape). If the hair is cut straight, when the head is held in an upright position a curved outline will be produced on the perimeter. The reverse happens if the hair is cut with an inversion – the outline on the perimeter is straight when the head is held upright.

Technique

Begin by gowning and protecting the client. Carry out a consultation and analysis and shampoo and condition the client's hair.

STEP-BY-STEP: BASIC INVERTED A-LINE CUT/BOB

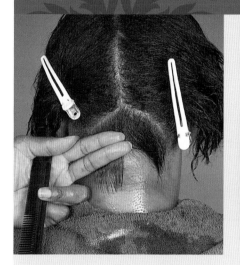

1 Divide the hair into four sections and sub-divide the two nape sections. This should be no thicker than 6 mm (¼"). Start cutting the guideline on the left side first, holding the fingers in a downwards sloping position.

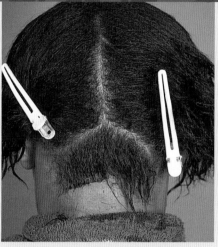

2 The first section of the guideline after cutting.

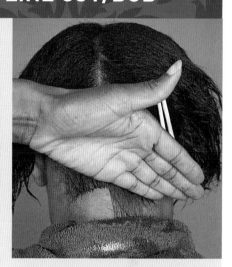

3 Proceed towards the right side of the head, sloping or angling the fingers in the opposite direction.

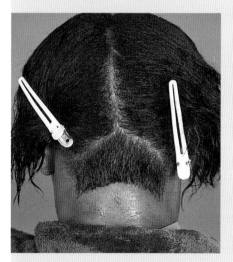

4 This will create an inverted shape shorter in the middle and longer on the ends.

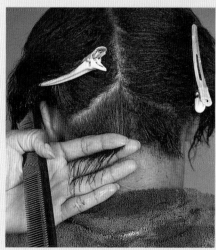

5 Continue cutting the hair to the initial guideline, holding the hair at a 45° angle.

6 As you work up the hair, gradually straighten the section.

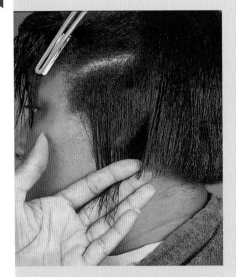

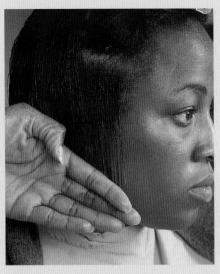

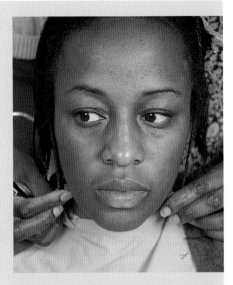

7 Continue to proceed up the head, taking 6 mm (¼") sections and working left to right until you reach the crown. Proceed to the left side of the head. Sub-divide the hair taking 6 mm (¼") sections. Blend the back section to the side, angling the fingers downwards to create a sloped effect on the sides. This will establish your side guideline.

8 Follow the same procedure on the right side of the head.

9 Check that both sides of the haircut are equal.

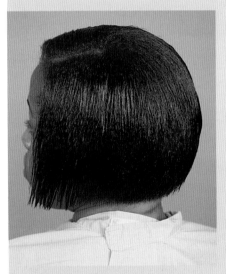

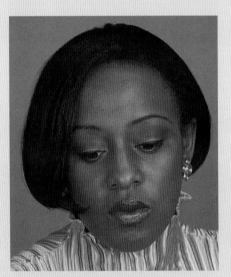

The finished cut.

The finished style after blow-drying and tonging.

One-length bob with a fringe, a variation on the classic bob haircut.

TOP TIP

Do not use too much tension, as too much tension could cause the hair in this area to spring up because the ears can protrude at varying degrees, resulting in shorter hair over the ear where it is essential for the hair to be longer for this haircut.

Graduated cut

This cut creates gradual layers and weight on the perimeter of the hair. The layers can be high or low depending on the result to be achieved. However, never cut basic graduated layers higher than a 45° angle. Elevating the hair higher than this would create layers and not graduation.

Technique

Begin by gowning and protecting the client. Carry out a consultation and analysis and shampoo and condition the client's hair.

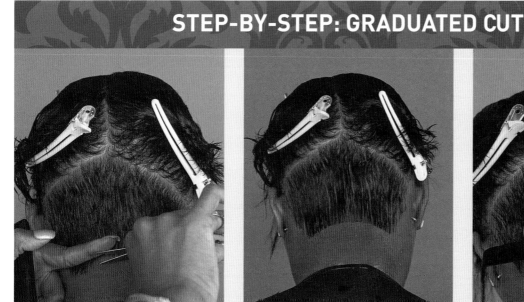

STEP-BY-STEP: GRADUATED CUT

1 Divide the hair into four sections. Sub-divide the hair in 6 mm (¼") sections at the nape. Cut the guideline close to the neck at a 0° angle.

2 Take three sub-divisions of hair down until a solid line is formed in the nape area.

3 Blend the hair in the nape area by layering at a 90° angle.

4 Take a horizontal subsection of hair and create the internal guideline by cutting the hair at a 45° angle. Do not lift the hair higher than the ears when graduating at this angle.

5 Make sure the hair is combed from roots to ends to ensure that the hair is cut evenly. When the back of the hair is completely cut, proceed to the sides. Establish the side guideline and blend to the back guideline. Once a solid line has been developed, start lifting the hair using the same technique as before so that graduation is developed throughout the perimeter.

6 Repeat the process on the opposite side of the head. Cut the fringe area starting in the middle and blend to both sides.

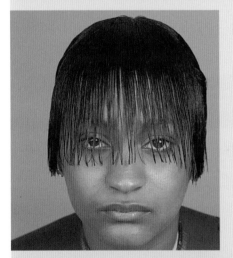

7 The fringe after cutting using a curved guideline.

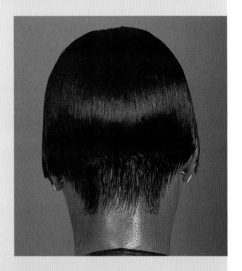

8 Cross-check the cut.

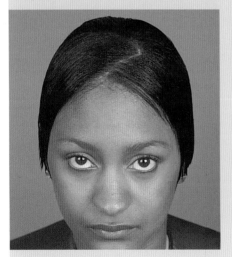

The finished wet cut – wet.

The finished style after blow-drying and tonging.

Short layered cut

A uniform layer is cut at a 90° angle. Length is removed internally throughout the cut. All sections of hair are cut to the same length, following the contours of the head.

Technique

Begin by gowning and protecting the client. Carry out a consultation and analysis and shampoo and condition the client's hair.

ACTIVITY

Start to collate images of one-length, layered, over-directed, short and long graduation haircuts for a visual portfolio. Describe briefly (in no more than 150/200 words) how each hair cut was achieved and the effect that has been created. Scan images from magazines or download from the Internet and compile them in categories in a word document. You can then place your research into a folder of visual images to show clients.

STEP-BY-STEP: SHORT LAYERED CUT

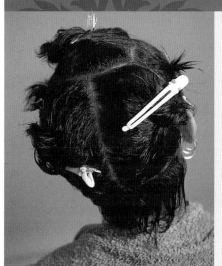

1 Divide the hair into six sections.

2 Starting at the nape, sub-divide the hair taking 6 mm (¼") sections.

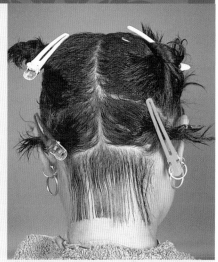

3 Cut the guideline at a 0° angle.

4 Continue to take subsections down, cutting the hair to the original guideline until a solid line is formed.

5 Take a vertical section from the nape to the occipital bone or just below the ears.

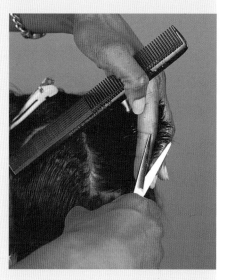

6 Hold the hair at a 90° angle and cut. Work from left to right, holding the hair at the same angle until you reach the crown.

7 Proceed to the sides. Cut the perimeter guideline at a 45° angle.

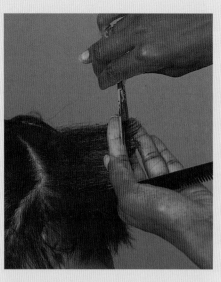

8 Continue cutting the hair at a 90° angle throughout the sides. Cut the other side of the hair using the same technique.

9 Start cutting the horseshoe section horizontally until you reach the front hairline. Finish by cross-checking the whole cut, checking in the opposite direction to the direction in which the hair was cut. For example, if the hair was cut by taking horizontal sections, cross-check with vertical sections and vice versa.

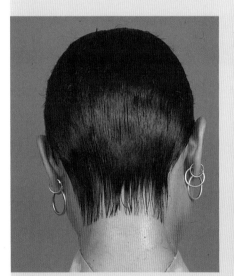

The finished wet cut – back.

The finished wet cut – side.

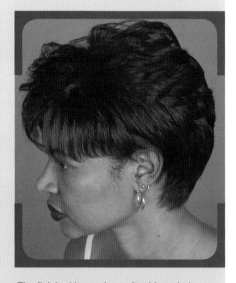

The finished layered cut after blow-drying and tonging.

Long graduated/over-directed cut (below the shoulders)

This cut produces long layers with weight maintained on the perimeter of the hair, graduating to shorter lengths internally. It is ideal for clients who want to keep length but would like movement in a hairstyle or a shorter crown and fringe area. The internal layers are cut at a 180° angle.

Technique

Begin by gowning and protecting the client. Carry out a consultation and analysis and shampoo and condition the client's hair.

STEP-BY-STEP: LONG GRADUATED/OVER-DIRECTED CUT

1 Divide the hair into four sections and sub-divide into 6 mm (¼") subsections. Cut the hair horizontally on the perimeter at a 45° angle.

2 Once the guideline has been established, continue to bring sections down until you reach the crown.

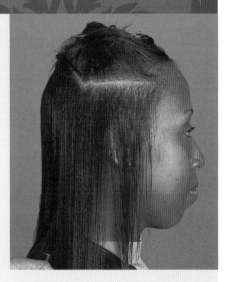

3 Continue the same technique on the sides, blending in the back section.

4 The right side after cutting.

5 Take a horizontal section on the crown and establish the internal guideline. Use this technique to cut the whole horseshoe section until you reach the front hairline.

6 Cut the fringe area so it blends with the sides .

7 The fringe after cutting.

8 Starting at the back, blend the internal sections to the crown by taking pie-shaped sections from the crown to the nape. Over-direct the hair at a 180° angle and blend the two sections together. Pivot around the head using pie-shaped sections until the crown area is cut.

Finished look.

TOP TIP

To avoid gaps developing in the cut during the scissors-over-comb technique, the scissors must move over the comb simultaneously.

Please note that the hair on the perimeter will not be cut when you use this technique as it will be too short to over-direct to the crown. Finish by cross-checking the finished cut in the opposite direction. For example, if the hair was cut by taking horizontal sections, cross-check with vertical sections and vice versa.

REVISION QUESTIONS

Level 2

1 How would you decide on the size of comb to use when cutting hair?

1 Based on individual stylist choice and technique

2 Based on the look of the comb and technique

3 The colour and thickness of the teeth

4 Thinness of teeth and design

2 What is the correct way to hold the scissors when cutting hair?

1 Thumb and little finger

2 Any fingers you choose

3 Thumb and second finger

4 Between the thumb and third finger

3 When creating a haircut it is a good idea to have knowledge of:

1 Face shapes, hair texture, movement and hair growth patterns

2 A one-length cut

3 Basic cuts

4 How to trim the hair

4 Why do we cut the hair?

1 To enhance/update/create a new look and remove damaged hair

2 To make the hair grow quicker

3 To strengthen the hair

4 To give the hair elasticity

5 Why is it important to use even tension when working on curly or wavy hair?

1 So that the hair is shorter when it is cut

2 To straighten the lengths of the hair

3 To stretch the hair and make sure that all the hair is cut evenly

4 Makes it easier to see the natural curl or wave in the hair

6 What is club cutting?

1 An asymmetric cut

2 A graduated shape

3 A solid blunt straight line

4 A zigzag line

7 Where is the occipital bone?

1 The front of the head

2 The sides of the head

3 In the wrist

4 The bone with a curvature that sits between each ear

8 Why would you point cut a client's hair?

1 To create an effect on the ends

2 To change the overall shape of the haircut

3 To remove blunt ends and soften the haircut

4 To remove bulk

9 What is a classic haircut?

1 A cut that is timeless and always in fashion

2 A classic shape

3 A classic 1920s bob

4 A round layered shape

10 How is the guideline used when cutting the hair?

1 To cut the first length

2 To create the initial overall shape and design of the cut

3 To create a shape that the client likes

4 To create graduation

11 What are thinning scissors used for?

1 Cutting in guidelines

2 To create solid lines in sculptured styles

3 To remove length and bulk from the hair

4 To remove weight from the hair, to thin a hairstyle out

12 What angle should be used to create a short graduated cut?

1 45°

2 180°

3 90°

4 0°

13 What should you do if you accidently cut your client?

1 Apologize and continue with the hair cut

2 Wearing gloves, give them a clean damp tissue, instructing them to apply pressure

3 Get the first aid box and treat them accordingly

4 Pretend you haven't noticed and continue with the haircut

14 Colouring hair using basic techniques

LEARNING OBJECTIVES

This chapter covers the following:

◆ Maintain effective and safe methods of working when colouring and lightening hair

◆ Prepare for colouring and lightening

◆ Colour and lighten hair

◆ Maintain effective and safe methods of working when correcting hair colour

◆ Determine the problem

◆ Plan and agree a course of action to correct colour

◆ Correct colour

◆ Provide aftercare advice

KEY TERMS

Albinism

Ammonia

Base shade

Colour correction

Colour swatches

Complementary colours

Compound dyes

Eumelanin

Hydrogen peroxide

ICC (International Colour Chart)

Incompatibility test

Melanin

Melanocytes

Metallic salts

Neutralize

Oxidation

Para dyes

Permanent hair colours

Pheomelanin

Pigment

Pigment granules

Primary colours

Quasi permanent colours

Secondary colours

Semi permanent colours

Shade charts

Skin test

Strand test

Target colour

Tertiary colours

Tints

Tone

Trichosiderin

UNITS COVERED IN THIS CHAPTER

◆ Colour and lighten hair

◆ Colour correction

INTRODUCTION

Colouring hair is an exciting and creative aspect of hairdressing. It allows the client freedom of expression and maintains individuality. For the stylist, it provides opportunities for imagination and creative ability. It can also add a new dimension to an old hairstyle or allow an additional service to be offered to the client.

To be able to carry out colouring services successfully takes skill, knowledge and creativity. This chapter deals with the art of colouring African type hair and will cover everything you need to know at Level 2. It will also serve as a foundational reminder for students studying at Level 3. More advanced creative colouring techniques are described in Chapter 15.

Why colour?

As long as 2000 years ago, Africans and Egyptians coloured their hair with the aid of the henna plant. Today, although henna is still favoured by some, hair colouring has become more intricate with the use of one or several pigments in the form of synthetic dyes or by the removal of the natural **pigment** from the hair.

The science of colouring

For more information on the structure of hair see CHAPTER 2.

Colour is the reflection of light falling onto an object in view. In hair, the outer layer (the cuticle) is translucent and reflects light. The cortex, on the other hand, is the storehouse for colour **pigment granules** and it is these pigmented granules shining through the translucent cuticle which results in the colour that is seen on the hair. Colour pigment (**melanin**) is produced by the cells **melanocytes** in the germinal matrix and its composition is determined by genetic influences.

The colour we see on the hair can be affected by the light in which it is seen. It is best, therefore, to carry out the consultation in a well lit room and with plenty of daylight coming in. Daylight and white light from halogen bulbs will give a true reading of the client's natural hair colour, whereas light from a fluorescent bulb gives off a bluish green tinge and can make the hair look dull. Light from an ordinary electric light bulb, on the other hand, emits a yellowish tinge and can add warmth to the hair colour.

Hair shaft
Sebaceous gland
Arrector pili muscle
Bulge
Hair bulb

Hair shaft
Cuticle   Cortex   Medulla

Matrix
Dermal pipilla
Melanocytes
Connective tissue sheath
Capillary
External root sheath
Internal root sheath
Follicle wall

Hair follicle with melanin granules

Colour composition

Synthetic colour is made up from the three primary pigment colours: red, yellow and blue. When two primary colours are mixed together, they produce secondary colours: orange, green and violet, and these form the basis for synthetic hair-colouring products.

Natural hair colour

Natural hair consists of varying proportions of black, brown, red and yellow pigments. Black and brown hair contain mostly the dark pigment **eumelanin** while blonde hair contains very little pigment, predominantly the yellow-red pigment called **pheomelanin**. White hair has very little or no melanin. This loss of pigment occurs naturally as part of the ageing process but it can sometimes come about due to extreme stress or a shock. There is a condition known as **albinism** where the hair has very little or no pigment, with pigment also lacking from the eyes and skin.

Grey hair tends to be a mixture of white and coloured hairs. Depending on the **tone** of the hair, it is possible to identify which pigments are present. For example if the hair is reddish brown then there will also be some red pigments, notably **trichosiderin**.

Primary and secondary colours mixing together

The difference in African type hair

Pigment is mainly found in the cortex of the hair. However, some Oriental and African hair types also have pigment distributed in the cuticle. In African type hair, the pigment granules are larger than in other hair types and they appear less frequently. This allows them to be broken down quickly when using **oxidation tints**. When certain colouring services are carried out, such as tinting and lightening, the arrangement of the natural pigments is altered to embrace the introduction of the new colour pigments.

How is colour made up?

When colouring hair, pigments are used in a similar way to paints. They can either be used separately or mixed together to achieve different colours. There are four main sets of colours: primary, secondary, tertiary and complementary.

Primary colours: red, yellow and blue   These colours cannot be created by mixing pigments together. However, when all three primary colours are mixed together in the same quantity then a neutral colour is achieved which is brown. When mixed in varying quantities, shades ranging from black to very light brown can be obtained.

Secondary colours: orange, green and violet   These are obtained when two primary colours are mixed together:

- ◆ red + yellow = orange;
- ◆ yellow + blue = green;
- ◆ blue + red = violet.

Tertiary colours   These are obtained when equal proportions of adjacent primary and secondary colours are mixed together (see illustration of colour circle). These give the more vibrant fashion shades and can also be used for corrective colouring. **Tertiary colours** include:

- ◆ red + orange = copper red (chestnut);
- ◆ orange + yellow = gold;
- ◆ yellow + green = lime green (seen in fashion colours);
- ◆ green + blue – ash;
- ◆ blue + violet = pearl;
- ◆ violet + red = mahogany.

Red, orange and yellow are known as warm colours; green, blue and violet are known as cool colours.

Complementary colours   **Complementary colours** are made up of a **primary colour** and a **secondary colour** which are opposite each other on the colour circle. They can be used to **neutralize** unwanted hair colour and, when mixed together, produce a shade of brown.

Neutralizing unwanted hair colour

'Neutralizing' colour is a way of getting rid of unwanted colour which has emerged during the tinting process. Any colour can be neutralized by the addition of its opposite colour in the colour circle.

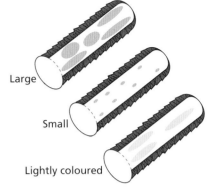
Types of pigment granules

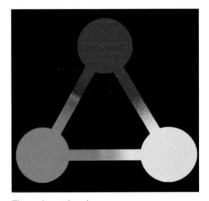
The colour triangle

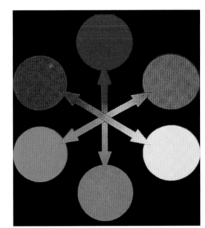
The colour circle

Unwanted hair colour	Corrective colour
Too much yellow	Cool violet (mauve)
Too much orange	Cool blue (ash)
Green	Red
Violet	Yellow (golds)
Blue	Orange (coppers)

Depth and tone

Depth refers to how dark or light a colour is, depending on the proportion of pigments in the hair. With artificial colours, if more black is used then the colour will be darker and if more white is used, then the colour will be lighter. *Tone* is the colour we actually see, meaning that brown will be the depth of the colour whereas reddish brown would indicate a red tone.

Health and safety

As with all services, you need to ensure that you take responsibility for the health and safety of yourself and your clients. You will find more in-depth information about health and safety procedures in the salon in Chapter 1 but as a reminder you must ensure that you:-

◆ Use clean resources to minimize the risk of cross-infection and infestation.

◆ Keep your work area clean and tidy.

◆ Wear PPE (gloves to minimize the risk of contact dermatitis and salon apron to protect clothing).

◆ Protect client's clothing.

◆ Monitor your posture and position so as to avoid fatigue and injury.

◆ Position client to ensure comfort throughout service.

◆ Use the correct tools, products and equipment in accordance with the results of your findings from consultation and analysis and only use tools and equipment that are fit for purpose.

◆ Conduct all necessary tests to achieve desired results.

◆ Inform senior staff or the relevant person if results from tests cause doubt as to the suitability of the service for the client.

◆ Mix products in a well ventilated room in accordance with COSHH policy.

◆ Use products in accordance with manufacturer's instructions.

◆ Only use additional heat if absolutely necessary.

◆ Dispose of waste adequately and in accordance with salon policy.

◆ Pay particular attention to personal health and hygiene so as to avoid risk of cross-infection and not to cause offence to others.

◆ Work efficiently and effectively so that service is carried out in a timely fashion.

◆ Restore the pH balance of the hair at the end of the colouring/lightening service.

The COSHH policy is the policy contained in the Control of Substances Hazardous to Health Regulations 2002 which can be found on the government's website at: http://www.legislation.gov.uk

Consultation and analysis

Communication

It is important to gain accurate information from the client when carrying out consultations as this will determine, along with your analysis, how you proceed with the service requested. In addition, it will let you know whether there are any contraindications to the service being carried out. Other information such as the client's age and lifestyle will be relevant in helping you and the client to decide what is the right service to carry out. Necessary information gleaned should be recorded on a record card. Remember to ask open ended questions and not closed questions to gather as much information as possible.

Conduct all necessary tests in particular **skin test**, **incompatibility test**, porosity and elasticity tests as these are very important to the colouring process. In addition, analyzing the hair characteristics of your client and deciding on the hair classification that your client's hair comes under will be vital in helping you to come to a decision about the correct procedure to carry out. For more information on hair characteristics and hair classification please see Chapter 2.

When working on all hair types hair, it is important to check your client's scalp for visible irritation. This might have been caused by relaxers, texturizers or perms which might have left the scalp irritated. If this is the case, do not proceed with colouring service but allow scalp to heal first.

There is a EU Directive regarding permanent colours on minors. For more information on *Guidance on Use of Hair Colour on and by People Under 16 Years Old* visit www. habia.org.uk

Shade charts

To simplify the colouring process, manufacturers produce **shade charts** using synthetic hair swatches in order to show their colour range. All shade charts have to conform to the **ICC (International Colour Chart)** system, showing a numbering system to differentiate between the different colours. These are numbered from 1–10 or, for some companies, from 1–11 (some companies have tints numbered 12). Some companies also employ a number and letter system along with the colour identification name. The numbers and letters will tell you, the hairdresser, what depth and tone the colour is. However, not all manufacturers apply the same numbering system to the various colours.

Most shade charts will include a selection of concentrated colours which can be used with other colours in the range to produce more vibrant tones. Therefore, if a client would like a red-brown colour but wants the red to be vibrant, a measured amount of concentrated red can be added to achieve more vibrancy.

Ascertain the client's natural depth by holding the hair swatch as close to the root of the client's hair as possible. You may find it useful to use both the 'N' (natural) and 'NA' (natural ash) swatches to try and get as close a match as possible.

TOP TIP

If the client has recently removed braids or weaves out of the hair it would be best to carry out of a course of conditioning treatments before embarking on colouring processes such as tinting and hair lightening as braids/weaves can make the hair feel and look dry.

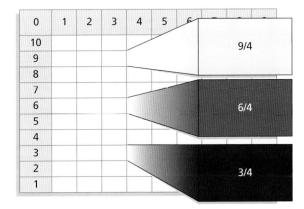

Depth and tones

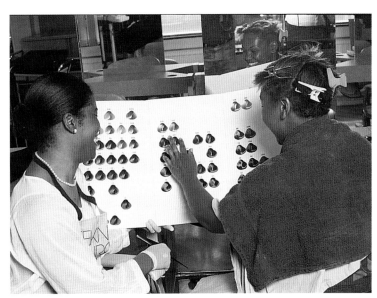

Stylist and client selecting a suitable colour

Due to the fact that African type hair is usually dark in colour, it is often impossible to achieve some of the lighter colours without pre-lightening the hair. Shade charts can be used very effectively to show the client the colour that is achievable with and without pre-lightening. However, you must bear in mind the number of lifts required to achieve the desired colour, the volume of hydrogen peroxide to be used, the chemicals already on the hair and the information gathered from an analysis of the hair before making a final decision as to the **target colour**.

ACTIVITY

Using your salon shade chart and **colour swatches**, work in pairs and find out what your partner's natural **base shade** is. If your partner's hair is already colour treated, then you will need to record the base shade and the colour on the remaining parts of the hair. Write down your findings. Remember when checking for base shades, only use the 'N' (natural) or 'NA' (natural ash) swatches.

TOP TIP

All information gathered must be recorded on a client record card and all stylists must adhere to the Data Protection Act.

Recording information

It is important to have a separate colour record card for each client, giving a brief outline of your findings from your tests and analysis of the hair. This will enable another stylist to carry out subsequent colouring services if you are unavailable.

Analysis

Colour record card								
Client's name				Tel no:				
				Mobile:				
Address:								
Email:								
Natural hair colour:				Percentage of white hair:				
Incompatibility test carried out Yes/No Date of test?				Results of tests:				
Date	Stylist	Type of colour	Full head regrowth	Target colour	Preparation method	Hydrogen peroxide	Comment	

Colour analysis sheet	
Name:	Address:
Tel:	Date:
What type of colouring process does the client require?	temporary ☐ semi-permanent ☐ quasi-permanent ☐ permanent ☐ lightening ☐

Colour analysis sheet	
Has the client had a skin test? Date of test:	Yes ☐ No ☐
Does the scalp reveal any conditions which will prohibit the colouring process (abrasions, cuts, infections)?	Yes ☐ No ☐
Texture:	Fine ☐ Medium ☐ Coarse ☐
Porosity	Porous ☐ Normal ☐ Resistant ☐
Has the client had any other chemical services?	Yes ☐ No ☐ Relaxer ☐ Permanent wave ☐
Incompatibility test:	Another colouring service ☐ If another colouring service, what?
Elasticity test:	Good ☐ Average ☐ Poor ☐
What type of application does the client require?	Full head ☐ Regrowth application ☐
Has a test cutting been carried out?	Yes ☐ No ☐
If yes, what was used and what was the result achieved?	
Strand test (see notes below)	
What is the client's natural base shade?	
What is the client's target colour?	
What was the client's shade of previous colour (if any)?	
What is the percentage and distribution of white hair?	
If the client has white hair, is it resistant white hair?	Yes ☐ No ☐
What is the colour developer/peroxide strength to be used?	
What is the required processing time allowed on the roots/ends?	
State the result achieved and comment on the procedure.	

Notes on carrying out analysis

Description	Points to note
Hair texture	This will affect the development time as coarse hair may be more resistant than fine hair. It is important to remember however, that all hair textures, whether coarse, medium or fine, will absorb colour more quickly once relaxed, texturized or permanent-waved.
Porosity	This will affect development time as porous hair will absorb colour quickly.
Elasticity test	This checks the condition of the hair to see whether it is strong enough to accept a chemical.
The client's natural base shade	This will give an indication of the underlying predominant pigment and whether you will need to use a complementary colour instead of the target colour to neutralize any unwanted colour which may emerge.
Target colour	Is it lighter or darker than the natural base shade? This will determine the strength of peroxide to use (if necessary).
Shade of previous colour (if any)	This will be seen on the mid-lengths to ends of hair. If this is the case, check for colour fade and whether colour on the ends need to be refreshed.
Full head or regrowth application	This will determine your method of application, either roots first or mid-lengths, ends and then roots.
Other chemicals on the hair	This will automatically make the hair slightly porous and will determine the type of colouring process the client can have.

TOP TIP

There may be occasions where a colour/lightener has been applied and the client is unhappy with the colour and wishes for it to be altered. In such a case, the colour will appear throughout the entire lengths of the hair. It is advisable to carry out a thorough consultation and analysis to check if the hair is suitable for colour correction. The hair may need to be pre-pigmented or the unwanted colour neutralized. Before deciding to carry out more in-depth colour correction work, please consult with a senior stylist for guidance.

Skin tests

HEALTH & SAFETY

Retesting must take place every time the client has a colouring service as a reaction can develop at any time.

Some clients may be allergic to certain colouring processes. It is necessary to carry out a skin test 24 to 48 hours before using colouring products which contain para-phenylenediamine or para-toluenediamine, otherwise known as **para dyes**. Para can be contained in either permanent, quasi permanent or semi permanent dyes. Always read manufacturer's instructions for guidance.

HEALTH & SAFETY

Do not apply tint to a client who has had a positive reaction to a skin test. Other colouring services should be offered, such as highlights (preferably cap highlights), temporary colours, vegetable colours and some semi-permanents, making sure that the latter do not contain 'para' dyes. It is also important to stress to clients the gravity of the consequences should they then decide to shop around for another hairdresser who will carry out a colouring service using 'para' dyes as the body can go into an anphylactic shock should there be an extreme reaction to the para dye.

Incompatibility test (20:20 test) This tests for the presence of **metallic salts** on the hair. Metallic salts are generally found in hair colour restorers, some coloured hairsprays and **compound vegetable dyes**. They are incompatible with any product requiring the use of hydrogen peroxide which can lead to hair breakage. If during your consultation you have reason to believe that metallic salts may be present on the hair, then an incompatibility test would be advisable. For information on how to carry out an incompatibility test see Chapter 2.

Test cutting

The next stage is to carry out a test cutting to ensure that the chosen colour is achievable and to ascertain the approximate length of time it will take for the colour to develop.

Procedure

1 Cut a small amount of hair, preferably from the back of the head where the hair is thickest, and secure it with thread or sellotape.

2 Mix the chosen colour with the appropriate strength peroxide and apply to a hair sample.

3 Leave to develop, allowing extra time for development due to lack of body heat.

4 Check the result and compare it with the target colour.

5 If the target colour has not been achieved, check that the correct peroxide strength has been used, ensure that there are no other colouring products on the hair (even if you cannot see an obvious colour), ensure that there is no build-up of other products on the hair such as gels, waxes or pomades. Retest if necessary.

HEALTH & SAFETY

Do not apply products which require the use of hydrogen peroxide to hair which has shown a positive incompatibility reading as this could result in breakage and chemical burns to the skin. Again, stress to the client the consequences of not taking note of the result of the test. If necessary show them the test and advise them not to try to get the service carried out elsewhere.

TOP TIP

Do not make the mistake of assuming that the colour on the client's hair is her own natural colour even if you cannot see any obvious regrowth. This can sometimes happen if the client has a colouring product on the hair which is the same colour as her natural colour.

TOP TIP

If there is tint on the hair, and the client wishes to go lighter in colour, then a pre-lightener may need to be applied first as a tint cannot lighten another tint. A thorough consultation should reveal what is not immediately obvious to the naked eye and guidance should be taken from a senior stylist.

Strand test

This is carried out *during* the colour service and checks the colour development from the roots to the ends.

Procedure

1   Follow the manufacturer's instructions regarding processing time.

2   Using a damp piece of cotton wool, remove tint from a strand of hair so as to assess the colour.

3   Make sure that it is an even colour from roots to ends.

4   Remove the tint if the colour is even. If it is not even, leave to process for a further length of time or apply more tint if necessary.

Hydrogen peroxide

Hydrogen peroxide is the active ingredient which is used as a catalyst to activate tints and lighteners by providing oxygen. In its chemical structure it is similar to that of water, except that hydrogen peroxide has an extra oxygen atom attached to it.

◆ water = H_2O

◆ hydrogen peroxide = H_2O_2

During the chemical process of tinting or lightening, oxygen is given off due to the interaction of hydrogen peroxide and **ammonia**/monoethanolamine which can be found in tints and lighteners. Hydrogen peroxide is therefore called an *oxidizing* agent.

Hydrogen peroxide comes in different strengths which can be measured in percentage strength (per cent) or volume strength (volume). Percentage strength tells us how many parts of pure hydrogen peroxide are found in 100 parts of pure solution. Therefore a 6 per cent solution would contain 6 grams of pure hydrogen peroxide in 100 grams of solution.

Volume strength is the number of parts of free oxygen that one part of hydrogen peroxide would give off during the oxidation process. Therefore 1 ml of 20 volume hydrogen peroxide gives 20 ml free oxygen.

The stronger the hydrogen peroxide, the more oxygen is given off. Therefore 1 litre of 20 volume would give off 20 litres of oxygen, while 1 litre of 40 volume would give off 40 litres of oxygen. Due to the fact that it is the oxygen which is given off from the hydrogen peroxide that brings about the oxidation process, the higher the level of hydrogen peroxide, the more intense the result.

When working with hydrogen peroxide it is wise to note that the product is at its most effective immediately after mixing. This is particularly important when working with full head applications of tints/lightener or woven highlights/lowlights. If mixed tint or lightener is still in use after half an hour of mixing, the product will work more slowly as it will have oxidized too much. It is better to mix fresh product for a more even result.

HEALTH & SAFETY

The darker the base shade of the client, the higher the strength of hydrogen peroxide needed to achieve lighter colours. While it is possible to use the full range of hydrogen peroxide strengths on African type hair, care must be taken especially when another chemical is already on the hair, or (in the case of virgin hair) if the client intends to have an additional chemical service to the hair at some stage. It is advisable to carry out an incompatibility test along with a strand test.

Different strengths of hydrogen peroxide are used as follows:

◆ *10 volume or 3 per cent* is used for toning, e.g. lightener toners or going darker.

◆ *20 volume or 6 per cent* is used to deposit colour when tinting, i.e. white coverage, or can be used to lighten base shade by up to 2 lifts.

◆ *30 volume or 9 per cent* is used to lighten base shade by up to 3 lifts.

◆ *40 volume or 12 per cent* is used mainly for highlighting and will lighten base shade by 4 lifts.

White hair coverage

White hair is an optical illusion. It is the mixture of both white hair and the client's natural colour which gives the appearance of grey hair. When colouring white hair, it can either be covered completely or 'blended'. To cover white hair, you will first need to work out what percentage of the hair is white on the client's head and you will need to add the right proportion of the natural (N) shade on the same level as the target colour you are aiming to achieve. For example, if your client is a base shade of 4N with 50% of white hair and aiming for a target colour of 6RB, you will need to add 20 mls of 6N along with your target colour in order to achieve 100% coverage of the white hair. If you were to use the target colour without any of the natural base shade, the white hair will be 'blended' (giving about 75% coverage of the white hair). This will give the hair a translucent appearance and may appear bright which may be unacceptable to your client.

Use the table below to help you to decide how much of the natural shade to include.

Percentage of white hair	Natural shade required	Target shade required
10–30%	15 ml	25 ml
40–60%	20 ml	20 ml
70–100%	25 ml	15 ml

TOP TIP

If the hair has been styled with heavy oils or gels it will be resistant to tint because the oils/gels act as a barrier. It will therefore be necessary to gently shampoo the hair first before proceeding with the tinting process ensuring that the scalp is not vigorously palpitated. Dry hair under a cool dryer to avoid sensitizing the scalp.

Most manufacturers recommend that tints be mixed equal part hydrogen peroxide to equal part tint. Therefore, for a full head application, depending on length, a mixture of 40 ml of hydrogen peroxide of the desired strength and 40 ml of the target shade should be mixed together. However, if white hair is present, the mixture is different as some natural base shade needs to be added. Using the table above, if the client is a base of 4N with 40 per cent white hair and requires a target shade of 6B (brown) then it is necessary to add 20 ml of natural tone which is 6N, plus 20 ml of the target tone which is 6B. Together this makes a total of 40 ml of tint which should be added to 40 ml of 30 volume (2 levels of lift) for a full head application. Read manufacturer's instructions to ascertain mixing ratios.

Resistant hair

You will come across hair which is resistant to tint. This is generally hair which is coated with products or hair which has a tightly packed cuticle so that penetration of chemicals does not take place easily. White hair sometimes falls into this category. However, it is important to note that white hair can 'grab' certain colours such as reds more easily than others. Colour any identified resistant areas first before proceeding to colour the remaining hair. If the client is known to have a resistant patch of white hair, pre-soften the white hair first before tinting (see method for pre softening later in this chapter).

ACTIVITY

A client comes in to have a colouring service. She is a base of 3 and would like a 5R permanent colour. She has had no previous colour on her hair. She has 50 per cent greys and would like them to be covered not blended in. What strength peroxide would you use? Give the quantity of peroxide and colour that you would use.

Choosing a colour

We are now ready to start our colouring service. There are many colours to choose from. It is wise, before you show the client the shade chart, to discuss what colour they have in mind. This will help you to pick out about three or four colours from which the client can choose. It is better to look at these colours in natural daylight by the window or even outside as salon lighting may distort colour.

At this stage, the client's age, job, mode of dress, lifestyle, skin tone and the results from your analysis of the hair, can be taken into consideration to help you to narrow your options down to one or two colours. Remember that your colour options may be reduced by the presence of other chemicals such as other colouring products, a relaxer, texturizer or permanent wave.

Very often a client may try to persuade you to carry out a colouring service which you think may endanger the hair. Remember always to rely on the results of your tests and analysis. Be gentle but firm if you believe that the result could be problematic – your reputation is at stake.

Colouring options

Different colouring options are available to your client. These can be classified under four headings: temporary, semi-permanent, quasi-permanent and permanent. They are identified by their lifespan on the hair.

- *Temporary* colourants last for one shampoo.

- **Semi-permanent colours** last from 6 to 8 shampoos.

- **Quasi-permanent colours** last from 8 to 12 shampoos and may contain 'para'. They can last longer on porous hair and may even produce a line of regrowth.

- **Permanent colours** do not shampoo out but grow out as new hair emerges. They contain 'para'.

Colourants are derived from a variety of sources such as vegetable, vegetable and mineral, and mineral.

Vegetable colourants

Vegetable colourants have been in use for centuries, mainly in the Middle East and Northern Africa. In the 1980s vegetable colourants were very popular with African–Caribbean clients as this was a means of colouring the hair with minimum damage. However, these colourants were very limiting in the choice of colours which were achievable, as most African type hair tends to have darker base shades which means that not many vegetable colours will show on the hair, especially after one application. Often, more than one application has to applied for the colour to be seen. The main vegetable colourants are camomile and henna.

Camomile

This is usually added to shampoos and conditioners and is used to achieve yellow/gold tones. Due to the fact that African type hair is dark in colour, camomile-based products are only of benefit if the hair has been pre-lightened. Even then it would only serve to enhance pre-lightened areas.

Henna

This is probably the most widely known vegetable colourant. It is derived from the henna bush (Lawsonia alba) and is especially known for its conditioning properties. Although henna can lose some of its colour on shampooing, it can be classified as a permanent colour because it results in the need for regrowth application. This is due to the fact that henna is a natural oxidation dye – the colour develops gradually as the dye molecules are slowly oxidized by the oxygen in the air. Over several applications the properties in henna can attach to the protein (keratin) in hair and therefore create a build-up.

Henna is able to deposit in both the cuticle and the cortex layers but, unlike permanent colour, it does not cover grey hair and cannot lighten hair. There is no need to carry out a skin test prior to application. It does, however, have the benefit of sealing the cuticle which gives the hair a high sheen. Henna is naturally red in colour. However, additional powdered substances are often added to henna to make up other shades. For example, the addition of indigo leaves results in a blue-black colour.

Application method

1. Choose a henna shade and put the required amount into a large enough bowl for mixing (see manufacturer's instructions).

2. Add sufficient boiling water from a boiled kettle to mix the henna into a smooth paste.

3. Leave the paste to cool.

4. Gown and towel the client.

5. Apply a barrier cream to the client's hairline and section the hair into four.

6. Check the henna mix to ensure that it has cooled down sufficiently to be applied to the hair.

7. Put on gloves and using a brush, apply henna from roots to ends, starting at the nape area first. Take larger sections than you would for applying a tint.

8. Put a strip of cotton wool around the hairline and cover the head with a plastic cap.

HEALTH & SAFETY

Henna should not be confused with compound henna, which is henna combined with minerals or metallic salts. This was used to widen the range of colours from henna. Such compound hennas react violently with hydrogen peroxide – an incompatibility test will reveal whether metallic salts are present.

TOP TIP

When using henna that contains an additional substance such as metallic salts, a skin test should be carried out prior to use, as this type of product can cause an allergic reaction.

9 Place the client under a pre-heated dryer for about 15–30 minutes or more depending on the depth of colour you require (one hour is usually more than adequate).

10 Once processing time is over, rinse the hair thoroughly using warm water until all the mixture is out of the hair. Shampoo the hair, preferably with an acid balanced shampoo. Towel dry and style accordingly.

Vegetable and mineral colourants

These are a combination of vegetable and mineral substances, such as the compound henna mentioned above.

Mineral colourants can be divided into two categories:

◆ *Metallic dyes* are mainly found in hair restorers and only coat the surface of the hair.

◆ *Aniline derivatives* are synthetic dyes made from substances found in crude oil.

While aniline derivatives fall under the category of mineral colourants, they operate very differently from the inorganic metallic dyes. Aniline derivatives are used in semi-permanent, quasi-permanent and permanent colourants and are commonly known as 'para' dyes. They can be used simply to tint the hair or to lighten the natural hair colour and deposit a tint simultaneously.

Temporary colourants

As the name suggests, temporary colourants only colour the hair temporarily. This is because the colour molecules in temporary colourants are so large that they cannot penetrate the hair shaft unless the hair is excessively porous. The colour molecules only coat the surface of the hair and last only one shampoo. Temporary colourants can be applied without a skin test.

Types of temporary colours

◆ *Setting lotions* are coloured plastic setting lotions and blow-dry lotions.

◆ *Gels or foams* are coloured mousses and gels.

◆ *Water rinses* are concentrated colour drops added to very hot water.

◆ *Coloured hairsprays/glitter dust* may contain metallic particles of gold and silver which in the past were often dyed aluminium particles.

◆ *Crayons/hair mascaras* are mainly used around the hairline or in small areas where colour is required. The crayon is lightly stroked against the area to be coloured.

Temporary colours can be used:

◆ to enhance dull looking hair – temporary colour will not lighten hair but will revitalize natural colour;

◆ to blend white hair;

◆ to get rid of a yellowish tinge in grey hair;

◆ to add colour to hair which has been pre-lightened.

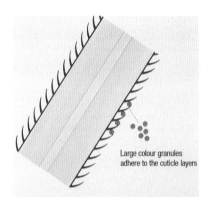

Large colour granules adhere to the cuticle layers

Temporary hair colouring

HEALTH & SAFETY

Hairsprays containing metallic particles may cause breakage or interference with chemical processes.

TOP TIP

The use of coloured setting lotions and mousses which are not specifically designed for African type hair could temporarily make the hair dry due to their alcohol content. Also, if temporary colours are applied to porous hair then an uneven result may occur.

Unless the hair has been pre-lightened, only certain temporary colours will be effective on African type hair. Colours such as blue-black, brown, red, burgundy and copper will add more depth/warmth to the client's natural colour.

Application method   Most temporary colour products do not require mixing and can therefore be used straight from the container.

1   Gown and protect the client with a suitable towel for colouring.

2   Make sure client is comfortably seated in styling chair.

3   Wear rubber gloves as staining of the hands may occur.

4   Avoid the colour touching the scalp and hairline as staining will occur.

5   Care must be taken to apply colour evenly.

◆   *Water rinses*. Hair must be shampooed prior to applying coloured water rinse. The water rinse will be the final rinse. Hair is then towel dried and styled as required.

◆   *Coloured setting lotions and mousses*. Hair must be shampooed and towel dried before applying. Too much water left in the hair will dilute the effect of the setting lotion/mousse. They can be applied by hand or using a comb to run through the hair thereby giving even coverage.

◆   *Coloured hairsprays*. These are applied to dry hair. Care must be taken to protect clothes, skin and areas of the hair which do not require colouring. If too much hairspray is applied to the hair, it will have to be shampooed out and the hair restyled.

Remember to check coloured hairsprays to see if they contain metallic particles. If they do, it is wise not to use on hair which is already chemically processed with a relaxer, texturizer or permanent wave product as there will be incompatibility of products.

Semi-permanent colourants

Semi-permanent colourants are different from temporary colourants in that the colour molecules are smaller and are therefore able to partly penetrate to the outer cortex of the hair. It takes about six to eight shampoos before a semi-permanent colourant is washed out of the hair completely. Retouching is not necessary because the colour fades away naturally without leaving a line of regrowth. Should the client wish to retain the same colour then it will be necessary to carry out a full head application again.

Types of semi-permanent colourants

Semi-permanent colourants consist of mixtures of nitro-phenylenediamine (red and yellow colours) and anthraquinones (blue colours). However, some also contain paraphenylene-diamine (more commonly known as 'para') found in tints. They come in the form of creams and lotions.

Semi-permanent colourants can be used:

◆   to enhance dull looking hair;

◆   to add colour to pre-lightened hair;

◆   to blend grey hair.

Large/small colour granules penetrate the cuticle layers

Semi-permanent hair colouring

Application method   Some semi-permanent colourants can be used straight from the container. Others, which may need to be mixed, should be applied using a tint bowl and tint brush.

1   Gown and protect client using a dark towel and tinting gown.

2   Shampoo the hair prior to application of semi-permanent colourants. This cleanses the hair and opens the cuticle to allow penetration. Do not use conditioning shampoos or conditioners at this stage as these will coat the hair and act as a barrier.

3   Towel dry the hair to remove excess water which could dilute the product.

4   Wear rubber gloves to avoid staining of the nails and hands.

5   Ensure that there is sufficient product. One bottle may not be sufficient, especially if the hair is long.

6   Using tools and equipment which have been cleaned and sterilized, apply product, starting from the nape area where the hair is more resistant, using an applicator bottle, sponge or tinting brush. If grey hair is present around the hairline, then apply to these areas first.

HEALTH & SAFETY

Semi-permanent colourants do not alter the chemical balance of the hair. However, if the hair is excessively porous, colour will grab more easily and uneven colouring may occur in areas which are more porous than others.

HEALTH & SAFETY

A skin test should be carried out with semi-permanent colourants as a precautionary method because some clients are allergic to 'para' which the colourant may contain.

ACTIVITY

Make a list of the temporary and semi-permanent colours in your dispensary at college or workplace. Make a note of the form they come in (gel, mousse, setting lotions etc.). What does the manufacturer say about the way the products should be handled?

TOP TIP

Due to the fact that African type hair tends to be dark in colour it is not possible to achieve light hair colours with semi-permanents as they do not lighten the hair. Semi-permanents are mainly used on African type hair to enhance the natural colour, to add red and golden highlights, to tone pre-lightened hair and to blend grey hair.

7   Take neat, even partings and work up towards the hairline. Care must be taken to apply colour evenly, working from roots to ends.

8   Avoid the colour touching the scalp and hairline as staining will occur.

9   Cross-check application to ensure all the hair is covered. It is always wise to cross-check in the opposite direction to which the product was applied.

10   Use a wide-toothed comb to ensure that the colour is applied evenly and to sufficiently loosen the hair to allow air to circulate freely, especially if additional heat is required.

11   Apply cotton strip around the hairline to ensure the colour does not come into contact with any other areas such as the eyes, face, neck and ears.

12   Check the manufacturer's instructions to see if the addition of a plastic cap or drier is required.

13   Allow the colour to develop, following the manufacturer's directions. It can take between 5 and 30 minutes for semi-permanent colourant to develop.

14   Check development and confirm results by carrying out a strand test, removing some product from the hair with a damp piece of cotton wool and placing the hair over a fresh piece of cotton wool to get a better reading of the colour achieved.

15   Once development has taken place, rinse the hair thoroughly at the basin until the water runs clear. Do not shampoo the hair at this stage as colour fade will begin to take place.

16   Remove any stains on the skin or scalp with cotton wool and stain remover. Rinse thoroughly and style as desired.

Quasi-permanent colourants

These colourants are not permanent but they are mixed with a very low volume developer which allows them to enter the cortex where they enlarge and cannot easily be shampooed out of the hair. Most manufacturers have more than one strength of developer to use with their quasi- permanent colourants. The varying strengths allows for greater depth of colour and less colour fade. They last between 8–12 shampoos and, depending on the developer used, can last up to 24 shampoos, which is longer than the other non-permanent hair colourants. Quasi-permanent colourants do not lighten natural hair colour because they use only 'low strength' developers, but they can leave a regrowth especially if the hair is porous.

Quasi-permanent colourants can be used:

◆ to add colour to pre-lightened hair;

◆ to tone hair which has been coloured/highlighted;

◆ to refresh old highlights;

◆ to refresh ends of permanently coloured hair when carrying out a regrowth application;

◆ to add gloss to natural hair;

◆ to blend grey hair;

◆ to neutralize unwanted tone;

◆ to introduce new colours to clients without the commitment of a permanent colourant.

Model, Colaura® by Design Essentials®

Hair courtesy of: Design Essentials® HydraStrength® Relaxer System

> **TOP TIP**
>
> Some quasi-permanent colours will produce a regrowth on very porous hair, e.g. relaxed, texturized or permed hair.

> **HEALTH & SAFETY**
>
> Always carry out a skin test before using 'para' dyes. Quasi-permanent colourants contain a small amount of 'para', therefore a skin test is necessary.

> **TOP TIP**
>
> Due to the depth of colour of African type hair, only certain colours in the quasi-permanent range can be effectively used for colour change. Colours such as reds and blue-black are the most effective, but dark brown can be used in hair which is mid to light brown in colour.

Permanent hair colouring/oxidation tints

Permanent hair colouring is a process whereby the natural pigment in the hair is changed by means of a chemical oxidation process, as described earlier in the chapter. There is quite a wide range of colours to choose from. However, not all of these colours are achievable on African type hair due to the depth of the natural hair colour. To achieve the lighter hair colours, lightening will first have to be carried out.

Although the word *permanent* is used, the process is only permanent in the hair which has been tinted and does not refer to any subsequent regrowth.

Types of permanent colours

Permanent tints come in the form of creams, gels or cream/gel mixtures. They are synthetic in make-up and have to be mixed with hydrogen peroxide for the product to become active. The chemical reaction between the tints and the hydrogen peroxide brings about an oxidation reaction of the hair's natural pigment, thereby removing the natural colour from the hair, while depositing the new colour from the tint into the hair.

Model, Colaura® by Design Essentials®

Hair courtesy of: Colaura® by Design Essentials®

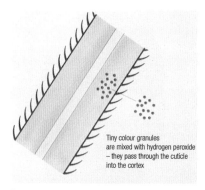

Tiny colour granules are mixed with hydrogen peroxide – they pass through the cuticle into the cortex

Permanent hair colouring

When it is freshly mixed, the 'para', which is found in all permanent tints, is colourless and its molecules are small enough to penetrate the cortex of the hair. As it oxidizes, the small molecules combine to form larger molecules which are then too large to be shampooed out of the hair.

Permanent colourants can be used:

◆ to darken or to lighten existing hair using either full head application method or regrowth application method;

◆ to add colour tone to existing hair;

◆ to cover white hair;

◆ to neutralize unwanted colour tones;

◆ to highlight, apply low lights or for fashion colouring.

◆ to carry out high lift colouring when working on a natural base shade of 6 or above.

Preparation of tints for application

Once the incompatibility test, strand test and test cutting have been carried out successfully indicating that the hair is suitable for the intended colouring service, you may now continue with the colouring process. Where, on European type hair, it may be possible to achieve two lifts with 30 volume or 9 per cent peroxide, on African type hair you may not achieve the true target colour with the same strength of peroxide because of the natural depth of the base shade. It may be necessary to go one strength up. This is only advisable for natural hair and should not be carried out on hair which has already been chemically treated, as this type of hair will tend to be more porous and therefore any new product applied will enter the cortex quicker. Always remember to follow the manufacturer's instructions accurately.

Preparing the tint

Tints come in tubes or cans. If using tubes, half a tube is usually sufficient for a regrowth application. A full tube may be necessary for a full head application or if the hair is very thick. Be sure to mix the tint with the correct strength hydrogen peroxide, following the manufacturer's instructions. Blend the two together using a tint brush. Tints should only be mixed prior to application.

> **TOP TIP**
>
> Manufacturers tend to produce a large range of shades of tints. However, they can be intermixed, within the range, to suit individual needs.

Virgin hair application

1 Ensure the client is adequately covered with a tinting gown and appropriate towel.

2 It is advisable not to shampoo hair prior to tinting as the natural oils produced on the scalp will act as a protective barrier against possible sensitization. However, if the hair is saturated with heavy oils one shampoo can be administered, taking care to avoid over-stimulating the scalp.

3 Divide the hair into four sections.

4 Wearing PPE, mix the tint for application. At this stage only mix half the desired amount.

5 Taking 6 mm (¼") partings horizontally, work around the head, applying to mid-lengths to ends first (a).

6 Check manufacturer's instructions to see if heat is required and leave to develop for half the processing time.

Permanent hair colour

7 Prepare the other half of your tint mixture.

8   Apply to the root area and leave to develop for the second half of the processing time.

9   If darkening hair, the colour can be applied to the full length of hair in one application.

10   Check the progress of the service by wiping off some tint with damp cotton wool 10 minutes before the processing time is up. If colour is progressing well, make sure that the area which has been wiped off is recovered with tint, and leave to develop for the remainder of the processing time. If there is any doubt as to whether the colour will be achieved, it may be that the colour needs some heat to speed up the process, in which case the client can be placed under a Climazone for the remainder of the time.

11   Once the desired result has been achieved, take the client to the shampoo basin and damp the hair with a little tepid water. Tint removes tint so massage the tint at the hairline in order to avoid colour settling on the skin.

12   Shampoo the hair twice, using an acid balanced shampoo in order to close the cuticle and to ensure that hair and scalp are free of any product residue. Rinse with an antioxidant rinse to prevent the tint from oxidizing any further and to seal the colour.

13   The hair is now ready for styling. Remember to fill out a record card.

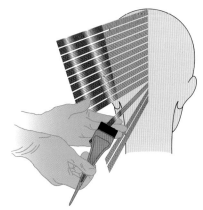

Tint being applied from mid-lengths to ends

HEALTH & SAFETY

If another chemical service is evident on the hair or if the client intends to wear a relaxer, texturizer or permanent wave in the near future, ensure that the hair is relaxed, texturized or permanent waved first and that there is no regrowth showing. If permanent colour is applied to hair which has a regrowth area then breakage may occur when carrying out subsequent relaxing/texturizing/permanent wave processes, as this will overlap the previous colouring service.

TOP TIP

The client should be advised to use an aftercare shampoo specifically designed for colour-treated hair in order to avoid colour fade.

Regrowth application

1   Gown the client and section the hair as for a virgin head application. Ensure you have your PPE, gloves and apron.

2   Check the client's record card if the tint was carried out at your salon to ensure exact colour as used previously.

3   If the tint was not carried out at your salon, use hair swatches from the manufacturer's colour chart to guide you in making a decision about the previous colour applied to the hair.

4   Proceed with the regrowth application in the same manner as a virgin head application except that tint is applied to the roots only where the client's natural base colour can be seen.

5   Check the manufacturer's instructions for development time.

6   Once the roots are developed, check the colour at the roots and compare with the rest of the hair to see if you need to blend through to the rest of the hair. Use damp cotton wool to wipe a few strands of hair clean at the root area.

7   If necessary, comb through to ends of hair and leave for ten minutes.

8   If colour fade on the mid-lengths and ends of the hair is obvious, then add an equal amount of tepid water to any remaining tint in the bowl and apply to the rest of the hair. The water dilutes the mixture so that there is no colour lift, but the mixture acts more as a semi/quasi-permanent. Alternatively, prepare semi/quasi-permanent mixture and apply to mid-lengths and ends.

9 Depending on the degree of the colour fade, leave on the hair for 10–15 minutes.

10 If colour fade is excessive, fresh tint should be mixed with equal parts of 6 per cent hydrogen peroxide and applied to the previously colour-treated hair. Leave to process for 10 minutes.

11 Rinse the hair with tepid water and proceed with the shampooing process as for full head application.

12 Fill out a client record card.

Matching ends to a colour swatch

Regrowth colour application

ACTIVITY

Make a list of the quasi-permanent and permanent colours in your dispensary at college or workplace. Make a note of the form they come in (liquids, creams, etc.) What does the manufacturer say about the way the products should be stored?

Complete coverage of regrowth area

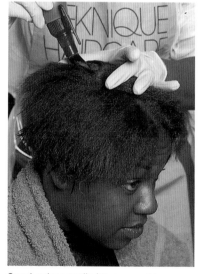

Quasi-colour applied to even out tone

Problems encountered during permanent hair colouring

The table outlines some of the problems associated with permanent hair colouring, together with causes and recommended treatment.

Problem	Cause	Treatment
Skin/scalp irritation	Peroxide strength too high; tint still present in hair; hair not shampooed properly; allergic reaction to tint.	Shampoo hair thoroughly and advise client to seek medical advice.
Not enough coverage of white hair	Resistant white hair.	Apply more product and leave to develop for longer on resistant areas. Pre-soften grey hairs prior to tinting.
Too dark	Incorrect volume of peroxide used; over-processing when going from light to dark; extremely porous hair.	Use colour reducer if necessary; carry out another tinting application using the correct volume peroxide but only after the hair has been treated.
Too light	Porous hair; peroxide strength too high.	Use a darker shade or colour rinse between shampoos.
Too light on ends	Not enough time on comb through.	Leave to develop for a further period.
Too much red tone	Too dark a natural base.	Use a matt or a natural ash colour in the same target colour range to get rid of unwanted red tones.

TOP TIP

High lift colours are used to lighten the hair. They are mixed with either 9% or 12% peroxide. They are often used instead of bleach because they produce similar results to bleach but without the drying effect that bleach can sometimes have on the hair. They work better on natural base shades of 6 and above if you are aiming for target shades of 10 upwards. Nonetheless, they can also be used on darker natural bases such as African type hair to achieve results you would normally want to achieve with the use of bleach.

Remember that African type hair which is already chemically processed may be compromised by the usage of higher strengths hydrogen peroxide.

Dealing with resistant grey hair

HEALTH & SAFETY

Pre-softening should only be carried out on hair which has not been treated previously with another chemical as the health of the hair could be compromised.

As hair loses its pigment and become grey, its texture also changes and become more wiry and coarse. As a result of this, some grey hair can be difficult to colour. If this is the case, then pre-softening the grey hair will allow it to accept the colour more readily.

Method

1 Prepare client for colouring service.

2 Wearing PPE, pour enough 6 per cent (20 volume) hydrogen into a colour developer bottle with applicator brush to cover the grey hairs you are working with.

3 Apply cotton wool around the hairline to protect the client.

4 Apply hydrogen peroxide directly to grey hairs while rubbing the hair to encourage swelling of the cuticle.

5 Leave for 5–10 mins then rinse.

6 Air dry hair then apply desired colour mixture.

7 Continue process as above for permanent colouring.

Lightening

The term 'lightening' means the removal of natural pigments (eumelanin/pheomelanin) from the hair. Lightening is carried out for two reasons:

1 To lighten hair to a shade which cannot be achieved by using a tint.

2 To pre-lighten hair in preparation for another colour which could be a temporary colour, a semi-permanent colour, a quasi-colour or a permanent colour.

Chemistry

Lightener is achieved with a mixture of hydrogen peroxide (the oxidizing agent) and ammonium hydroxide or ammonium carbonate (an alkaline substance). Lightening African type hair is a very delicate process, especially when working with hair which is already chemically processed. It is advisable to use lightening products mainly for highlighting purposes or only on short hair when carrying out a full head application.

Lightener, when mixed, is alkaline in composition. The alkaline lightener enters the cortex of the hair, changing the natural darker pigments (eumelanin) to colourless compounds. This takes place by the addition of oxygen to the pigment from the hydrogen peroxide, bringing about an oxidation process.

In African type hair, due to the fact that the eumelanin granules are large and widely spaced, it is easier for the lightener to have an effect. However, the lighter pigments (pheomelanin) are small in molecular structure and therefore more resistant to lightener. These pigments are also found in African type hair but in smaller quantities than in other hair types.

TOP TIP

Lightening African type hair to a white stage is virtually impossible and is stressful to the hair. It is important to note that because of the predominant red pigment found in African type hair, when the hair is lightened it may appear 'brassy yellow' or 'orange yellow'. If the hair is already chemically processed, it is not wise to carry out more than one application of lightener. However, if it is virgin hair, the effect of white hair can be achieved by lightening the hair to a level 6 and thereafter using a high lift tint with an ash or violet base.

The chemical reaction of lightener and hydrogen peroxide can be shown thus:

Melanin (black/brown)	+	oxygen (from hydrogen peroxide)	=	oxymelanin (colourless)
pheomelanin (red/yellow)	+	oxygen (from hydrogen peroxide)	=	oxypheomelanin (colourless)

As mentioned above, black and brown pigments are more easily oxidized and oxidation therefore takes place in three stages:

black/brown ➔ red/yellow ➔ yellow

African type hair, when lightened, will lighten in this order:

black ➔ brown ➔ red ➔ red-gold ➔ gold ➔ yellow ➔ pale yellow ➔ (white)

If lightening is necessary, it is more advisable to carry it out on virgin African type hair. If the hair is already chemically treated, then it is likely to be more porous than virgin hair. The effect of lightener on this type of hair will cause the hair to become even more porous, thereby causing damage to the internal structure of the hair. Some lightening processes may require the hair to have more than one application of lightener to lift the hair up to the desired colour. This can cause disintegration of the disulphide bonds to such an extent that permanent damage may occur.

During lightening of African type hair, almost 50 per cent of the disulphide bonds may be degraded. This weakens the hair considerably and it is therefore unwise to carry out any other chemical services such as a relaxer or curly perm on a client with a high percentage of lightened hair.

Full head application

1   Gown and protect the client with a suitable towel.

2   Protect yourself with apron and gloves.

3   Do not shampoo the hair before lightening as natural oils on hair and scalp will protect the scalp from sensitization, especially if more than one application of lightener is necessary. However, in cases where there is heavy usage of moisturizing gels, the client must be advised to shampoo her hair at least two days prior to lightening and not to use any more gels until after the lightening service.

4   Divide hair into four sections, from ear to ear and forehead to nape.

5   Apply barrier cream to the hairline and over the ears.

6   Mix the lightener following the manufacturer's instructions and ensure that the room is well ventilated. The lightener should not be allowed to stand but should be used immediately following mixing.

7   Apply lightener to the nape area first which tends to be the most resistant part of the head.

8   A full head of lightener application to virgin hair is carried out in the same manner as that for tinting, i.e. apply mid-lengths to ends then roots.

9   Always use an adequate amount of lightener and take smaller sections than when tinting because the smallest area left uncovered will show up.

10   Cross-check application thoroughly.

11   Leave to develop until half way through the desired time then apply to the root area and leave to develop for the second half of the time. The body heat from the client should speed up the lightening process on the root area.

12   Once the correct colour has been achieved, rinse with tepid water and shampoo with an acidic shampoo.

13   Follow through with an antioxidant rinse to neutralize the alkalinity of the lightener and to prevent further oxidation. This would prevent any traces of lightener left in the cortex from causing creeping oxidation – the antioxidant rinse gives off hydrogen which will connect with any oxygen from the lightener to form water (H_2O).

14   The hair is now ready for toning if necessary Toning will get rid of any unwanted hair colour. Remember, yellow is one of the hardest pigments to get rid off so if there are unwanted yellow tones in the lightened hair, they can be neutralized with violet.

HEALTH & SAFETY

A strand test should always be carried out beforehand to ascertain whether the hair can withstand the lightening process.

HEALTH & SAFETY

Remember to conduct all necessary tests before deciding to carry out any lightening techniques to the hair. If the hair is over 50 mm (2″) long and already chemically processed with a relaxer, texturizer or permanent wave, it is not advisable to carry out a full head lightening application.

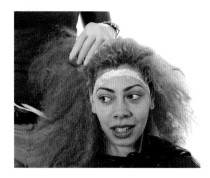

Regrowth application

1 Follow safety procedures as with a full head application.

2 Apply lightener to regrowth only.

3 Make sure that the colour on the root matches the colour on the rest of the hair.

4 Remove lightener as for full head application and apply toner if necessary. Style as desired.

Development time

Consult the manufacturer's instructions about timing the lightening process. However, do bear in mind that extreme salon temperature conditions can affect the timing, as can hair which is porous. Do not leave your client during the lightening process and constantly check development by removing lightener from a few strands of hair using cotton wool and warm water. Some lightening products are blue in colour and may give an incorrect reading in certain lighting conditions.

Fashion techniques

Once you have mastered the art of lightening, there are many exciting ways to enhance a hairstyle with the addition of lightener. Always envisage the finished hairstyle then decide where lightening would be most effective.

1 Wearing gloves, apply lightener with the fingertips to the ends of the hair.

2 Once the processing time is over, shampoo the hair and proceed with styling or applying other colour products if necessary.

Highlighting and lowlighting

The term *lowlights* is used to describe the addition of darker tone or the darkening of the hair using tint. Highlighting using lightener or tint and lowlighting are both effective ways of colouring African type hair. They allow you to control the amount of hair which will be colour-treated and can be a good introduction to a client considering full head colour. Highlighting and lowlighting can be carried out by using one of two methods, cap or foil/meche.

Hair can also be highlighted using lightener or high lift tint. Lightening products will produce rapid lift, allowing the hair to be lightened to a platinum blonde shade if necessary, depending on the hair type. As mentioned before, lightener can damage the hair and must be used carefully and only on hair in very good condition. Alternatively, high lift tint can be used on hair of a base 5 and lighter for the best results. High lift tint can produce a variety of blonde shades with differing tones. It should be noted that this type of product is less damaging on the hair than lightener and is possibly better suited to chemically processed hair, particularly when trying to achieve blonde shades.

Lightening the hair using tint will lift the hair up to three shades lighter and add tones such as copper, burgundy and mahogany. Ultimately the use of tint on African type hair to lighten and add tone is kinder and less damaging, than high lift tint or lightening products.

Cap method

When cap highlighting or lowlighting, always ensure that the holes in the cap have not become too large with previous use, otherwise seepage may take place. If the hair is coated with gel or heavy oils, it is advisable to use a gentle cleansing shampoo to cleanse the hair before beginning the process, but otherwise it is not necessary to shampoo the hair.

Procedure

1   Gown and protect the client with a towel.

2   Shampoo the hair if necessary and dry it entirely before starting.

3   Comb all the hair back to allow the cap to be fitted with ease.

4   Check the hairline first to ensure that there is no previous history of breakage. If there is, do not pull any strands of hair through from the hairline.

5   Using a crochet hook, start at the outer edge of the cap and pull strands of hair through holes in the cap until you have pulled through sufficient hair for highlighting.

6   Once you are satisfied that enough hair has been pulled through, mix the lightener or tint. Do not mix beforehand otherwise the mixture will oxidize and therefore lose some of its strength.

7   Apply the tint.

8   Use PPE, gloves and apron. Monitor the development of the colour by doing a strand test and remove as soon as the desired colour is achieved.

9   Rinse the hair thoroughly until all excess colour is removed.

10   Apply conditioner to colour treated hair before removing the cap. This will make removing the cap easier and avoid pulling on the hair or scalp.

11   Remove the cap holding the roots of the hair to avoid pulling the scalp.

TOP TIP

To make fitting of the highlighting cap easier, sprinkle a little talcum powder inside the cap.

TOP TIP

Pulling through more strands of hair will result in stronger highlights. Fewer strands will give a more subtle effect.

Placing hair cap on the model

Correctly fitted cap

Hair pulled through

Product application

Foil method

This method of highlighting or lowlighting is time-consuming but there are added benefits in that you are able to work closer to the scalp than with the cap method. Also, you are able to see exactly where the highlights are being placed on the head. Foil or self-adhesive strips (meche) are used to keep hair for highlighting in place. Hair is separated using a pintail comb with a weaving technique.

A systematic approach is necessary when working with foil/meche highlights. It is best to use the nine section method.

Procedure

1   Apply foil strips to the hair, shiny side down and fold along the top edge to create a lip 6 mm (¼") wide. This allows you to place the pintail end of the comb inside the lip of foil and gives a more secure edge to work with.

2   Prepare the lightener/colourant according to the manufacturer's instructions. Do not mix too much product at this stage because it is a lengthy process and the product may oxidize. Ensure you are using PPE, gloves and apron for this.

3   Weave the hair with the pintail comb and place a weaved section on the foil. Place the folded edge of the foil as close as possible to the scalp with the dull side facing up.

4   Apply the colour mixture with a tinting brush to approximately 6 mm (¼") of the folded edge. Do not apply too much product as it will expand during processing and may cause seepage.

5   Seal the foil by folding in half diagonally so that the top and bottom edges meet. Fold the side edges in towards the middle. Then, using the pointed end of the tail comb, press the top edge of the foil packet across the root section to seal it and prevent the packet from slipping off.

6   Continue working up the head until the application is completed. As this is a long process, some of the packets closer to the nape area may have developed before you have finished your application.

7   Constantly check development. Once some of the packets have developed sufficiently, take the client to the shampoo basin, remove the packets and rinse the lightener from the hair, making sure to secure out of the way any packets which are still developing.

8   Alternatively, open the packets, spray each section with water and remove the lightener with cotton wool. Apply conditioner (anti-oxidant) to ensure the action of any lightener residue is stopped. If tint is being used there is no need to remove the product, as tint will stop processing once it reaches its developing time.

9   Remember not to mix too much lightener at once – you may need to remix, apply and remove when processed.

10   Remove the remaining foil packets once the hair in them has developed and shampoo the hair.

11   Toner can be added at this stage if required.

Hair sectioned and mapped out before application of foils and lightener

Section to be highlighted being woven out

Hair placed on foil strips and lightener applied

Working through the sides

Finished look

Tipping

This is similar to highlighting and can be done using either a highlighting cap or foil. In both cases, use thicker sections of hair than for highlighting. Tipping is sometimes preferred to highlighting as it is only the ends of the hair which are treated with the lightener mixture.

Procedure

1   Gown and protect the client with a towel.

2   Put on protective gloves.

3   Mix the colourant and apply to the tips with the fingers. If the hair is long, wrap individual sections in foil to avoid seepage.

4   Check development and remove when processed.

Toning

If the client requires a lightener toner, choose a suitable colour with them. Remember, on darker skins a pale yellow depth will look too brassy so apply an ash toner for a more matt effect.

1   If applying toner to cap highlights, do not remove the cap.

2   Using PPE, gloves and apron, apply the toner but remember that the hair is very porous at this stage so use a 10 volume/3 per cent peroxide to mix with the toner as the hair will grab the toning product quickly.

3   Continually monitor the development of a lightener toner. Once it is ready, rinse off immediately as it will be difficult to remove colour which has grabbed too much.

4   Lay the section you are checking over a fresh piece of cotton wool and check the degree of lightness obtained. If the hair is not light enough, reapply lightener and leave to develop.

HEALTH & SAFETY

It is advisable to carry out a tensile strength test while checking the degree of lightness, as this will indicate the amount of elasticity in the hair and whether the process should be continued.

Block colouring

When block colouring, it is best to look at the finished style and decide where colour should be applied to maximize the effect:

◆   On layered hair, a section around the front hairline can be coloured so that when the hair is styled off the face, the colour can be seen but when it is styled on the face, the colour will diffuse through the rest of the hair which falls on top.

◆   More interest can be added to a graduated cut by colouring the shorter hair in the nape a different colour to the longer lengths of hair.

◆   On long hair, block colouring can take place on a lock of hair which can be styled off the face, with a side or centre parting. If the client normally wears her hair in a centre parting, ensure that equal sections of colour fall either side of the parting.

Hair courtesy of: Colaura® by Design Essentials®

General hints related to lightening

Removal of lightening products

1   Using the appropriate PPE, remove any lightening product by rinsing with warm water until it runs clear.

2   Give one or two shampoos according to the manufacturer's instructions, taking care not to irritate the scalp, especially if more than one application of lightener has been given.

3   Apply antioxidant conditioner, rinse and style as desired.

> **TOP TIP**
>
> In all cases it is important to advise the client to have regular conditioning treatments.

Additional heat source

It is possible to use an additional heat source when lightening, such as a steamer or accelerator. This cuts the development time in half.

Conditioning

An antioxidant acid rinse may be used to ensure all activity of the lightener has been stopped. However, do bear in mind that the hair will be more porous at this stage so extra conditioning may be necessary.

Problems encountered during lightening

The table below outlines some problems related to lightening, together with possible causes.

Problem	Cause
Skin/scalp irritation	◆ not using barrier cream around the hairline ◆ volume of hydrogen peroxide too high for client's skin ◆ product leakage onto scalp if too much product used or if product if left on too long
Hair breakage/ damage	◆ failure to carry out a strand test ◆ overlapping lightener onto previously lightened hair ◆ lightener applied to hair which has recently undergone another chemical process (relaxer or perm) ◆ volume of hydrogen peroxide too high ◆ lightener left on too long
Hair not light enough	◆ incorrect analysis of natural hair colour, depth and tone ◆ lightener oxidized by mixing too soon and losing its strength ◆ development time not long enough
Hair too light	◆ incorrect analysis of natural hair colour, depth and tone ◆ development time too long
Uneven colour	◆ not enough product used ◆ uneven application of lightener ◆ application not cross-checked properly ◆ incorrect application of large regrowth

Colour correction

Colour correction is usually carried out if the client is unhappy with the end result of the colouring process whether carried out by your salon or not. This could occur as a result of:

◆ hair coming out too light;

◆ hair not light enough – check tensile strength before attempting to gain a lighter colour;

◆ unwanted tones.

◆ uneven colouring creating colour bands in the hair.

Before attempting to carry out any form of colour correction:

◆ Establish what the problem is.

◆ Ascertain the percentage of natural colour and artificial colour on the head.

◆ Check client's hair, skin and scalp for any contra indications.

◆ Discuss with senior member of staff to ascertain the correct product and procedure to rectify the problem.

◆ Agree a course of action with the client based on the results of tests and analysis of the hair, skin and scalp.

◆ Inform the client of any restriction to future services that the planned colour correction may have.

Colour restoration

Colour restoration is carried out if the colour has faded or if the hair is too light for the client. In the case of the latter, the client may want to return to her original colour or several shades darker. This can be achieved by a process called *pre-pigmentation*.

Pre-pigmentation

Lightening removes the natural pigments from the hair. In order to reverse this action, the colour molecules which have been removed have to be replaced, otherwise the colour may look flat or, even worse, appear to have a greenish tinge. Lost pigment can be restored using semi-permanent colourants, quasi-permanent colourants or tints. If tint is applied, do not mix with hydrogen peroxide; mix with a little water, usually two parts water to one part tint. Target numbers in the list below refer to the ICC shade chart.

◆ Final target colour − 1–3; filler colour − red mix.

◆ Final target colour = 4–5; filler colour = 5 R (red).

◆ Final target colour = 6–7; filler colour = 7 (Copper/Copper Gold).

◆ Final target colour = 8–10; filler colour = G mix.

Application

1 Apply pre-pigmentation product to lightened/faded areas evenly using a tint brush. Keep colour well away from any hair which is not to be pre-pigmented.

2 Blot pre-pigmented area and apply target colour which has been mixed with 20 volume/6 per cent peroxide.

3 Leave for 20–30 minutes.

4 Remove and style as desired.

Reduction of colourants

This process is carried out if a client wants a tint removed or lightened and the hair re-coloured/lightened Colour reducing can be achieved by using either:

◆ a bleach-based product; or

◆ a ready-made product.

Bleach-based products will tend to strip out unwanted colour along with some of the hair's natural pigment. This is not suitable for African type hair which is already chemically treated with a relaxer, texturizer or a perm, especially where full head application of colour reduction product is necessary.

Ready-made colour reducers are made of sodium bisulphite or sodium formaldehyde sulphoxylate. They break down the artificial colours locked into the hair during the tinting process into smaller molecules so that they are easily washed out. These products should not be used to remove colour from chemically relaxed, texturized or permed hair.

Colour reducing products will not reverse the lightening effects of pre-lightening the hair, nor will they restore hair to its original colour. They will, however, prepare the hair to accept another colour if the first colour is unsuitable. In all cases check manufacturer's instructions for application procedure and removal and ensure to restore pH balance to hair after removal of product.

If trying to get rid of bands of colour, spot colour/lighten the affected areas by using the relevant tinting or lightening process to achieve the desired result. When correcting highlights/lowlights be sure not to disturb other areas which are still processing when removing product from the hair.

Aftercare

It is important to advise clients on the type of products they should use to maintain their hair in accordance with the services they have had. Ensure that you are knowledgeable about the products and services on offer in your salon so that you can speak confidently about them. Recommend shampoos and conditioners which will minimize colour fade and advise clients about the potential harm to the hair through the excessive use of heated equipment.

As some colouring services may leave the hair feeling dry, it is important to recommend the use of leave-in conditioners and serums to combat dryness. Inform clients about time intervals for future services.

REVISION QUESTIONS

1 What are the primary colours?

1 Red Blue Green

2 Yellow Red Green

3 Blue Yellow Red

4 Orange Violet Green

2 What information should be included in a record card for colouring?

1 Client Name Stylist Target colour

2 Client's Natural Colour Volume Hydrogen Peroxide Colour of eyes

3 Address Client's Name Hair Length

4 Hair Type Full head/Regrowth Density

3 When do you advise the client to report an allergic reaction following a skin test?

1 Within 12–48 hours

2 Within 24–36 hours

3 Within 48–72 hours

4 Within 24–28 hours

4 Which of these tests are not carried out for a colouring service?

1 Strand test

2 Development curl test

3 Incompatibility test

4 Skin test

5 How much 'N' tone is required for a client with 40–60 per cent greys?

1 10 ml

2 25 ml

3 15 ml

4 20 ml

6 Which of these colour options would not be used to lighten hair?

1 Lightener

2 High Lift Tint

3 Semi Permanent Colour

4 Permanent Colour

7 How would you correct unwanted bands of colour in the hair?

1 Apply a toner to the entire head

2 Apply a toner to the affected areas

3 Spot colour/lighten

4 Re-colour the hair a darker colour

8 Which of these could be the result of the client's hair coming out too light when colouring?

1 Natural base shade too dark

2 Peroxide strength too high

3 Insufficient 'N' shade used

4 Too much red tone in the hair

15 Creatively colouring and cutting

LEARNING OBJECTIVES

This chapter covers the following:

Level 3

◆ Maintain effective and safe methods of working when cutting

◆ Cut hair to create a variety of looks

◆ Maintain effective and safe methods of working when colouring and lightening hair

◆ Prepare for colouring and lightening services

◆ Creatively colour and lighten hair

◆ Lighten hair

◆ Resolve colouring problems

◆ Provide aftercare advice

KEY TERMS

Acid balanced product	Dry cutting technique	Marry	Precision
Aesthetically pleasing	Elevation	Mesh	Razor cutting technique
Angles	Fade cut	Neutralize	Section
Blend	Fashion colours	Points/ends of the hair	Subsection
Definition	High lift tint	Pre-lighten	Visual awareness
Disconnected	Look	Pre-pigmentation	

UNITS COVERED IN THIS CHAPTER

◆ Creatively cut hair using a combination of techniques

◆ Creatively colour and lighten hair

INTRODUCTION

Cutting and colouring the hair using fashion techniques allows the stylist to be innovative. It gives you the opportunity to create, combine and develop different shapes, colour combinations, colour techniques, lines and movement. This chapter deals with the art of fashion cutting and colouring on African, European and Asian type hair. The chapter will cover everything a stylist needs to know at Level 3. It provides detailed information on how to achieve a selection of fashion looks with the use of creative cutting and then colouring.

Working creatively

This chapter encourages you to combine existing skills and newly learnt skills to provide modern, tailored, individual colour-and-cut hairstyles for your client.

Creatively cutting hair involves using a combination of different cutting and texturizing techniques which are combined together to create a customized or tailored hairstyle for the individual client. These techniques are also referred to as *fashion cutting techniques*. At this level the stylist must take into account how the hair is reacting to the haircut and falling naturally as it is cut. Based on what is seen, different techniques of cutting and texturizing can be employed. When a stylist does this, it is often referred to as *cutting with feeling and creativity,* so that the finished hairstyle is **aesthetically pleasing**.

For the stylist to be able to design and develop a range of creative/fashion cutting techniques and achieve the final outcome will mean the hairstylist will have to be very visually aware. **Visual awareness** will come from observing a variety of haircuts on people you meet in all types of situations.

To prepare yourself for work in the world of creativity you should use as many different influences as you can to inform, motivate and inspire you:

- ◆ Attend hairdressing workshops, e.g. basic, intermediate and advanced/fashion cutting.
- ◆ Work alongside a session stylist or creative director.
- ◆ Create collections for the British Hair Awards, Black Beauty/Sensationnel Hair Awards or any other hairstyling completions.
- ◆ Theme and create photos for your salon or an electronic hairstyle portfolio.
- ◆ Attend art exhibitions, museums and fashion shows.
- ◆ Shadow session stylists and hair designers who work in film, editorial and TV.
- ◆ You should also draw as much inspiration as you can from your day-to-day life.
- ◆ Watch more experienced stylists in the salon to get tips and expand your skills.
- ◆ Look at fashion and hair magazines.
- ◆ Use newspapers, television, film and the Internet to follow trends.
- ◆ Notice people with fashionable haircuts when you are socializing or clubbing.
- ◆ Sketch or look for images which reflect your final ideas for your haircut inspiration.
- ◆ A research file is an A4 document, which you can use to present your research and final hairstyle ideas.
- ◆ A mood board can be used to present both your research ideas, development of ideas and final inspired **look**.
- ◆ Tear sheets are taken from magazines and can be used for inspiration and ideas.

TOP TIP

A research file is A3 or A4 in size and charts how you research, develop an idea, and the final look to be achieved.

A mood board has the same content but starts to build the design ideas visually using colours and other visual ideas which create the mood of the theme.

A tear sheet is taken from a magazine and used to convey the looks to be achieved.

Creating an image

Reference and inspiration when creating new haircuts can be taken from a number of sources. As discussed these could be magazines, film, TV or a documentary on a related topic. For example, you may want to create a new haircut inspired by the Afro hairstyle which was popular in the late 1960s.

Before the Afro hairstyle became fashionable there is evidence that women would wear their hair natural (as a rest period for the hair in between hairstyles) prior to plaiting the hair in a new style. This was probably the early influence for what was to become the Afro hairstyle of the late 60s and present day. Look at the image of Marsha Hunt, go on to the chiselled flat top Afro of Grace Jones in the 1990s, and the present day modern twist on an Afro haircut carried out by Desmond Murray & Junior Green. This hairstyle has evolved into a twenty-first century natural haircut that can be carried out on hair extensions or natural hair.

Marsha Hunt

Grace Jones

Alternatively look at the 1920s bob of actress Louise Brooks. This was a revolutionary haircut in this decade as prior to this women wore their hair very long. The 20s bob would have influenced the famous bob by Vidal Sassoon seen here on Nancy Kwan in the 60s, and later in 2005 the famous Victoria Beckham bob. Finally, look at the deconstructed bob. You can start your research by sourcing or looking for a deconstructed hairstyle which might have taken its influence from the classic bob.

In the world of creative design it is the norm to carry on historical research to gather information and ideas to influence a final design or look. If we look at some of the great

Louise Brooks

Victoria Beckham

British Hair Awards:
www.hji.co.uk/events
/british-hairdressing-awards/

Hairdressers Journal:
www.hji.co.uk/events/

Sensationnel and Black Beauty Awards:
www.blackbeautyandhair.com
/hairawards2012

designers such as Vivienne Westwood, we can see where her design influences evolve from. We can go even further back when looking at the now classic bob haircut, to Egypt where the wigs and headdresses were geometric shapes, similar to the bob. A key factor in your research in to this time would be to visit the British Museum to look at the pictures of Queen Cleopatra. This way you will start to put together a body of research. Your research can be collated historically leading up to present-day ideas. You can use a mood board for this or your pictures can be scanned and arranged in Word files.

Fashion and advanced cutting techniques

A fashion haircut is one that combines different cutting techniques, **elevation angles**, texturizing techniques and the customizing of the look to meet the needs of the client in creating the finished look or haircut. The following terms are often used to describe different and other forms of haircuts or hairstyles:

◆ A *classic* haircut is timeless and always in fashion.

◆ A *commercial* haircut is worn by a variety of individuals on a daily basis.

◆ A *fashion* haircut is one that is the latest fashion and is worn for a period until the fashion changes or becomes unfashionable.

◆ An *avant-garde* haircut is new, innovative and edgy and is worn by the leaders of fashion.

◆ A *deconstructed* haircut is one which deconstructs the original classic look by using texturizing techniques to create a choppy unblended look.

Cutting angles

Cutting angles are an intricate part of the cutting process. How these angles are used will define the haircut and make it something that is remembered by the client and others. It is this ability to use angles creatively that will develop and create an outstanding haircut. Let us start by remembering the rules regarding angles. There are two angles used when we cut and are as follows:

◆ the angle we hold the hair to cut the hair, e.g. diagonal, straight or concave;

◆ the angle of elevation, e.g. 0° elevation to 45°, 90° and 180° angle/elevation.

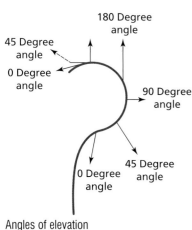

Angles of elevation

Straight   Diagonal   Concave

Held angles

The diagram shows a variety of cutting techniques that can be used to create a fashion cut. In fact, any combination of cutting and texturizing techniques can be mixed and combined together to achieve the desired end result that will become a creative/fashion haircut.

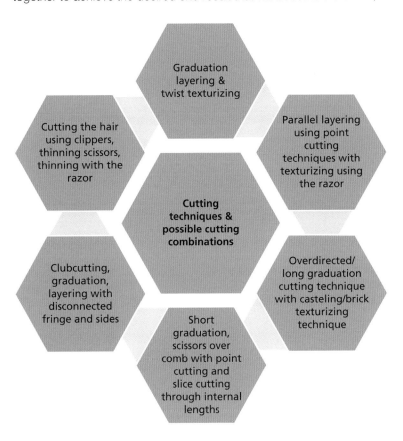

Combining techniques to create a variety of shapes

Technique	Combination techniques used	Effect and tailoring the cut to suit
	Graduation created on the sides and back at a 45° angle. The hair is layered at a 90° angle then twist texturized, slicing or slice cutting through the internal hair lengths adds texture, separation softens and breaks up the finished look for a choppy feel.	The style is suited for shorter or medium length haircuts and thin hair where volume is required. Will help thinner hair look thicker. Suitable for all hair types.
	Cutting the hair with clippers or scissors over comb in the nape and sides of the head at a 45° angle. The outline shape cut freehand 0° angle. Club cutting and parallel layering in the crown and throughout the longer middle channel area. Using twist texturizing, thinning scissors and the razor on the front fringe area to create a choppy, spiky effect through to the back.	Suitable for all thicker hair types. Not advisable for very thin hair as the final result could be sparse.

Technique	Combination techniques used	Effect and tailoring the cut to suit
Graduated bob	Graduated bob. A combination of different movements and outline shapes. Straight blunt cut at the nape area at a 45° angle with reverse graduation to encourage the hair to bevel/turn under naturally on the perimeter. A curved outline on one side of the fringe cut at a 45° angle gives a feel of asymmetry and a straight out line on the other side creates bluntness less movement cut at a 0° to 45° angle.	The overall cut creates weight on the perimeter with movement and body in the finished look. Suitable for all hair types especially medium/thicker denser hair which will give weight and movement on the perimeter of the haircut.
Scissors over comb	Scissors over comb in the nape and sides creates a gentle **faded cut** moving to a minimal graduation in the occipital area. Parallel layering continued through mid-internal **sections**, connecting the sides, crown and fringe areas. Creates volume and fullness on the crown and short nape and sides. The outline nape area can be designed into a V-shape, U-shape, square or round outline.	Creates a nice short neat hairstyle that is low maintenance and easy to care for. Good for active clients. Suitable for all hair types. Will make thinner hair look thicker and fuller.
Texturised sides and internal sections	One-length cut with twist texturized ends/perimeter. The tips of the ends are thinned using thinning scissors to remove the bluntness. The fringe is cut shorter and **disconnected** from the longer sides and twist texturized.	Creates a solid blunt cut with texturizing on the ends and into some of the mid-lengths.

TOP TIP

Freehand cutting techniques can be used to shape around the hairline such as fringe, sides and nape areas to create a more natural look. This technique works better on naturally straight hair. Curly wavier hair can be blow dried and free hand cut but this is not always recommended unless you have excellent control and visual awareness.

Cutting and texturizing techniques

Cutting technique	Technique and look achieved	Hair types and suitability
 Blunt/club cutting technique	Produces a solid blunt line. The hair is cut to one length.	Good on fine hair can make the hair appear thicker. Ideal for geometric cuts/shapes, bobs, layer cuts and graduation technique. Suitable for all hair types. However will make very thick hair appear thicker and denser.
 Cross-checking	Always cross-check the hair during and after you have finished the haircut. Running your fingers down the sides on twisted hair or internally, simultaneously will give an indicator to accuracy in the finished haircut. This will identify if the sides are even. If one hand stops before the other hand then this will give a guide to the section of the haircut that is longer and how much is to be cut off. When cross-checking the hair for evenness and balance, cross check layers and graduation in the opposite way to how the hair has been cut originally, for example if the hair has been cut horizontally at a 90° angle, cross-check vertically. Cross-check one-length haircuts following the same way the hair has been cut, first looking for strands or sections of hair that do not **marry**, then cut so you have a continual blending line if this is what is required.	All haircuts need to be cross-checked.
 Disconnection	A disconnected cut is where one shape does not marry or **blend** in a continual line. The difference in the haircut can be extreme shorter and more sculptured on one side and longer and bob/geometric on the other side. Hair can also be undercut where the hair is cut shorter on the underneath lengths or sections and the hair on top is longer, this is also known as a disconnected shape. You can also have the reverse, shorter lengths over longer. Can also chop into to classic basic shapes to create a deconstructed look.	Suitable for all hair types. May not work so well on very thin or fine hair.
 Freehand cutting technique	Freehand cutting is used without tension from the hair being held between the fingers and then cut. Weight can be removed where required, based on looking at the hair's natural fall once the main haircut is completed. The hair can also be freehand cut by holding the ends of the hair in place with a comb and then cutting.	Good on thicker hair to remove bulk and tailor a cut to suit the client's hair, face and head shape. Better suited to naturally straight hair or very thick relaxed hair after the hair has been blow-dried with a round brush, so that it is easy to see the shape and where the bulk of the hair should be removed to enhance the shape.

Cutting technique	Technique and look achieved	Hair types and suitability
 Concave haircut	A concave is where the hair is cut shorter in the middle and longer on the sides. Known as an A-line bob.	Suitable for thinner to medium density and thickness.
 Scissors over comb/clipper over comb technique	Used to gradually layer cut hair in the nape or sides of the hair, to create a soft fluid line. Clippers are also used for sculpture cutting on both women and men's hair.	Suitable technique used on all hair types. Clippers with an attachment can be used on all hair types. Also used on types e.g. type 1 through to 4b.
 Slice/slither cutting technique	Used to feather cut hair around the face to produce a soft face framing hairstyle. Only very sharp scissors should be used for this technique, to avoid tearing and pulling the hair and discomfort to the client. Open the scissors and slide the back of the scissors through the section to be cut, gradually cutting sections of hair at a diagonal angle.	This technique is suitable for all hair types where shorter layers are required to frame the face.
 Reverse graduation	The hair is cut in the nape area and cut at a 45° angle. The hair in the nape is shorter with this cut graduating to longer up to the occipital bone. This technique encourages the hair to bevel naturally. The longer hair curves over the shorter hair lengths. Can also be done on the sides of a haircut.	Suitable for all hair types especially bobs, where the ends of the hair curl under. Using this technique requires minimal blow-drying as the hair will fall naturally into shape.
 Under-directed graduation	From the centre parting take a horizontal section, under-direct the hair to its furthest point on the right hand side and cut at a 45° angle. This will create a diagonal angle and inverted layers throughout the lower internal section of the haircut. Do the same on the right hand section of the hair, working from the middle parting under-direct to the left hand side and cut. You will now have an A-line/concave shape where the two diagonal lines meet, the hair will be shorter in the middle and longer on the ends.	Suitable for all hair types, ideal for sculptured shorter bob haircuts. **TOP TIP** In a sculpture cut, the hair is cut following the contours of the head.

Texturizing techniques

Cutting technique	Technique and look achieved	Hair types and suitability
Point cutting technique	Point cutting is used to remove blunt lines and create texture on the ends. For fringes the hair can be held with a comb and cut freehand as there is only the tension from the comb holding the hair in place. The technique can also be used to cut a whole head to avoid blunt ends.	Suitable on all hair types to remove blunt ends, weight and create texture.
Twist cutting technique	Twist cutting texturizes the mid-lengths and **points/end of the hair**. Twist the hair in the area to be texturized. Open the scissors and using the back of the scissors run the scissors up and down the twist of hair in a backcombing action. Strands of hair will be removed throughout the length of hair. This will produce shorter and longer lengths, adding texture and separation within the internal haircut.	This technique is suitable for all hair types, better on short to medium length haircuts.
The hair being cut with the thinning scissors at the ends Zigzag placement of the thinning scissors when thinning hair from the middle sections of the hair with hair being removed	**Thinning scissors** Thinning scissors are used to remove bulk from the hair. They can be used to point cut and thin blunt ends (see point cutting above). The technique can also be used to thin extremely thick hair in the mid-lengths taking zigzag or diagonal sections throughout the haircut depending on how much hair is to be removed. Can be used in specific areas of the hair to remove bulk/weight. The technique is best when used on dry hair so that the amount being thinned can be monitored and seen easily.	Best suited for very thick hair or to thin ends/tips of the hair. Works well on straighter very thick hair types. Not suitable for curly hair as the hair may appear frizzier due to shorter sections which may stick out once the hair is dried.

Cutting technique	Technique and look achieved	Hair types and suitability
Razor cutting technique	**Razor cutting technique** The razor should be held in a V-shape with the thumb at the front top of the razor and the first finger behind the razor and the other end of the razor held between the third and little finger. Using this technique will hold the razor securely. The razor is then placed on wet hair only on the top or underside of the section to be thinned. The razor is then glided up and down the section, how many times this is done depends on the amount of hair to be removed. The angle of of the razor to the hair section will increase/decrease according to the amount of hair removed.	This technique is better suited for European and Asian hair type 1 to 2. The technique could damage the ends on tighter, curlier hair.
Castling/brick texturizing technique	The hair is point cut using the tips of the scissors into the selected section/**mesh** of hair. Use the points of the scissors cutting higher and lower in a brick fashion or castling technique. This technique texturizes sections throughout a length of the hair to soften and add volume to the finished haircut.	The technique can be used to soften, tailor and customize a cut in specific areas or to create volume in the overall finished hairstyle. The technique is suitable on all hair types. Works well on short, medium and longer hair.

Using tension when cutting the hair

Due to its curl pattern, natural African type hair requires more control during cutting. This is usually achieved by applying tension and keeping the hair wet throughout the cutting process. This is also true of some relaxed or permed hair. The curlier the hair, the more tension will need to be used to ensure the hair is cut evenly. Do not use too much force on relaxed hair or you risk damaging the hair. On wavier or straighter textures less tension can be used. African type hair can be cut dry after blow-drying or using straightening irons. Once the hair has been stretched and dried average tension is required as the hair is now straighter and in a stretched state. This allows you to control the hair more and using the **dry cutting technique**, you can cut the hair with better **definition**.

Of course you must use some tension on all hair, straighter hair types will require even tension and maybe less tension when working around the ears and nose. In fact this is true when working on all hair types. Facial characteristics must be observed as cutting with too much tension above the ear or nose will, make the haircut shorter in this area in comparison to the rest of the haircut. Do make allowances when working in these areas by using less tension, when cutting around the ears and nose.

TOP TIP

The use of even tension is required more on naturally tight, curly or wavier curl patterns, so that you can see your cutting line easier and balance the haircut. On relaxed or wavier patterns the hair will require less tension. Do remember that chemically processed hair can be damaged easily. Remember excessive tension could lead to alopecia or traction alopecia if excessive tension is placed around the hairline.

TOP TIP

Texturizing is a fantastic method for customizing a hairstyle to suit the client's features, face shape, hair type and to accentuate the haircut. However, do think about the look and effects that you wish to achieve when texturizing. Random removal of hair, using any of the mentioned techniques, could ruin the overall shape of the haircut if too much hair is removed, leaving the hair looking thin, sparse and lacking in shape.

TOP TIP

Using a razor can help you to remove hair from underneath **subsections** of the cut hair, especially in the nape and side areas when cutting bobs where the hair is required to bevel or bend under naturally.

HEALTH & SAFETY

Always take care when using a razor to remove internal and perimeter hair lengths, as the action of razoring must be a gentle, smooth technique of gliding the razor through the section to be cut. A razor with a guard is always better as this will protect both the client and stylist. Work with extra care in areas where the skin, nose and ears are exposed.

HEALTH & SAFETY

Use of the razor technique to texturize or remove bulk and weight from the hair should only be carried out on wet hair, so as to avoid tearing and tugging the hair. Not wetting the hair sufficiently could cause discomfort to the client and also damage the ends of the hair. Sometimes after razor cutting the hair the ends can be left looking sparse. If this happens lightly remove sparse ends to bring back definition to the overall haircut. The exception to this rule is with hair extensions as there is no drag or pull on the false hair. Make sure new razors are used for each new client to avoid any cross contamination.

The consultation and analysis process

The consultation and analysis process is important as it establishes client requirements and allows the stylist to start to develop ideas of the designs that might suit the client. The process allows both the stylist and client to get to know each other better, especially if it is the first time the client has visited the establishment.

Ask your client about their lifestyle. Are they busy, active or sporty? Ask about their occupation and how this might impact on the kind of style they can wear. Individuals in conservative jobs may want something fashionable but not avant-garde. Someone who is sporty may want a short, easy to wear and maintain hairstyle due to exercising and frequent washing. Others may want a hairstyle that is long enough to tie back in the day and style when they are going out. Some clients will give you free rein to give them a creative high fashion hairstyle. Always make sure that such clients are able to maintain such haircuts as visits to the salon may need to be quite frequent to sustain the look.

During the consultation and analysis process discuss the length of time the cut will take and also discuss cost of follow up visits and frequency to maintain the haircut. It is important that the client can relax and enjoy the process and explaining all the factors involved will ensure this happens. The diagram provides a reminder of the points you should cover.

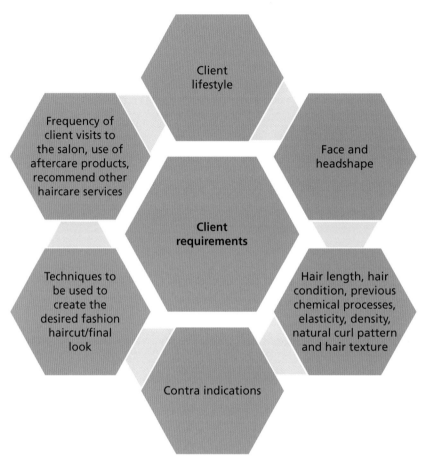

Client requirements diagram

For more information on the consultation and analysis process see CHAPTER 3.

After the cut is finished

You should check that the finished cut is to the liking of the client. Discuss the balance and shape and double check the client is happy.

◆ Discuss when the client should return to maintain the haircut.

◆ Discuss the products to be used to cleanse, condition and style the hair.

◆ Discuss any further services that the client might like such as a perm, colour, highlights, lightener, relaxer and conditioning treatments.

TOP TIP

It is a good idea to give the client a tutorial on how to style their hair and use finishing products. This can be done during or after styling the client's hair.

You can be as creative as you want with the haircut, as long as you work in consultation with your client. Your client will need to make a commitment on the aftercare of the finished cut. You will need to consider your client's lifestyle and ability to recreate the new look you want to give them. Based on this you can recommend suitable products such as gels, mousse, leave in lotion, heat protector, serum, dressing, oil sheen and holding spray. Specialist shampoos and conditioners may also need to be recommended, particularly if your client has permed, relaxed, colour-treated or lightened their hair.

Working safety

Always make sure you leave enough time to set up your work area. Your hair, clothes and self must be clean and tidy. You should be well-rested and prepared for work. Wear comfortable, enclosed toed shoes and stand erect with your feet apart. Try not to stay stationery to avoid later problems with circulation.

This is a reminder of the things that need to be observed in preparation for the client and throughout the process:

All tools, worksurfaces, mirrors and work area are clean, sterilized and fit for purpose

Welcome, gown and protect the client. Make sure the chair is at a height where the client can touch the floor or foot rest and you can work around the client comfortably

Remove all gowns carefully and hair cuttings using a powder puff. Remove all cuttings from the client's clothes using a lint roller

Personal hygiene is observed, your own hair is clean, cut and styled

Remove all hair cuttings from the client as you work and once you have finished the cut sweep up hair cuttings to avoid any hazards

Communicate throughout the process with the client. Check the client is happy with the end result. Update and complete the record card

Any tools that drop during the cutting process are immediately cleaned washed and sterilized

For more information about health and safety see CHAPTER 1.

Safe disposal of sharps

Any razors used during the cutting process should be disposed of in a sharps box. The sharps box is used to house sharp instruments such as razors, which may or may not have come into contact with the client's skin or where the skin has been pierced and to avoid any cross contamination. Razors that have been used to thin the hair are also placed in a sharps box when they have been finished with. A sharps box protects individuals from exposure to cross-infection or injury, from sharps left carelessly lying around. It is the personal responsibility of the user to dispose of any sharps safely and immediately after use. Some councils provide a service for the safe removal of sharp boxes. Always follow the salon policy on the removal of sharps.

HEALTH & SAFETY

Use thinning scissors with caution as chunks of hair can be removed, making the hair visibly thinner.

HEALTH & SAFETY

Take care as you point into the hair when freehand cutting. Think about the angle and positioning of the scissors before placing and point cutting the hair. This will avoid the tips of the scissors being placed too close to the scalp and parts of the face. Remember scissors can be extremely sharp and need to be held firmly but confidently when in use.

For each of the haircuts described below, gown and protect your client, shampoo the hair prior to cutting, condition and apply leave-in conditioner.

Asymmetric cut

For this haircut we are going to use the following techniques:

◆ point cutting;

◆ disconnected;

◆ internal layering;

◆ slide/slither cutting technique;

◆ clipper cutting.

The following tools are required:

◆ scissors;

◆ clippers;

◆ comb;

◆ section clips;

◆ water spray.

STEP-BY-STEP: ASYMMETRIC CUT

1 Designing and mapping out the asymmetric guideline.

2 Cutting the guideline from longer to shorter outline.

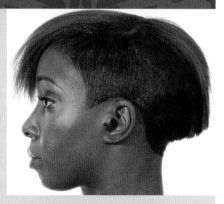

3 Scissors over comb technique is used to cut the hair short into the sides and nape area on the opposite side, forming a disconnection.

4 Blend the internal shape, over directing and point cutting.

5 Clipper cut technique in the nape area creates a double base line and disconnection.

6 Clean up the outline with the clipper using a downward motion.

7 Slice cut the fringe to soften the outline shape.

The finished look.

Cross-check the finished haircut looking for a clean outline, balance, symmetry, shape, design and suitability to the client's face and head shape. Check that the finished haircut is to your client's liking. Provide aftercare advice on maintaining the style, covering frequency of visits and the correct shampoo, conditioner, styling and finishing products.

> **TOP TIP**
>
> A double base line is where you would have two distinct different guidelines within the same haircut.

Geometric A-line bob

For this cut we are going to use the following techniques:

- club cutting;
- graduating;
- reverse graduation;
- concave shape.

The following tools are required:

- scissors;
- comb;
- water spray;
- section clips.

STEP-BY-STEP: GEOMETRIC CUT WITH FRINGE

1 Cut an inverted guideline at a 0 to 45° angle.

2 From the centre parting under-direct the hair to its furthest point and cut at a 45° angle. Repeat the technique on the opposite side of the head.

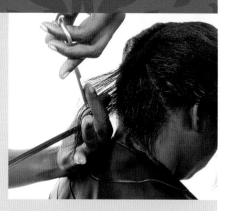

3 Reverse graduation technique to cause the hair to bevel cut at a 45° angle.

4 Take a diagonal section on the sides, use this as a guide to blend the back nape area to the sides. Remember to hold your fingers diagonally so that the sides are longer.

5 Blending the back to the sides holding the hair diagonally.

6 Twist the hair and run the fingers down the sides of the haircut to check balance and that the hair is even on both sides.

7 Start cutting the fringe from the middle of the section for even balance moving to the left and then to the right.

The finished look.

Cross-check the finished haircut looking for balance, symmetry, shape, design and suitability to the client's face and head shape. Check that the finished haircut is to your client's liking. Provide aftercare advice on maintaining the style, covering frequency of visits and the correct shampoo, conditioner, styling and finishing products to be used.

Urchin haircut

For this cut we are going to use the following techniques:

- club cutting;
- graduating;
- point cutting;
- texturizing;
- freehand cutting.

The following tools are required:

- scissors;
- section clips;
- comb;
- water spray.

STEP-BY-STEP: URCHIN HAIRCUT

1 Cut the guideline and outline shape and then use scissors over comb in the nape area.

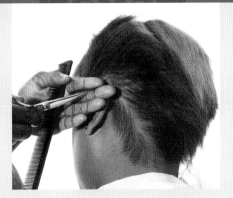

2 Point cut the perimeter guide line to create a softer outline shape. Continue graduation at a 45° angle through the back and sides.

3 Start parallel layering the hair horizontally at a 90° angle throughout the internal sections back and sides and connecting the layers to the graduation.

4 Point cut the crown at a 90° angle.

5 Cut the fringe area at a 45° angle.

6 Free hand cut the fringe by holding the hair in place and point cutting to remove blunt edges and create texture.

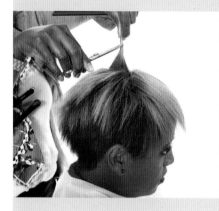

7 Twist texturize the hair on the crown to create shorter and longer lengths to soften and break up the internal shape.

The finished look.

Cross-check the finished haircut looking for balance, symmetry, shape, design and suitability to the client's face and head shape. Check that the finished haircut is to your client's liking. Provide aftercare advice on maintaining the style frequency of visits and the correct shampoo, conditioner, styling and finishing products.

Sculpture cut

For this cut we are going to use the following techniques:

◆ club cutting;

◆ layering;

◆ freehand cutting.

The following tools are required:

◆ Afro comb;

◆ de-tangle comb;

◆ leave-in lotion to de-tangle the hair;

◆ water spray.

STEP-BY-STEP: SCULPTURE CUT

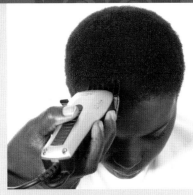

1 Select the grade of the clipper based on the finished length to be achieved. Start by using the clipper at the back nape area.

2 Work up through the sides, holding the clipper steadily and firmly in the hands so that the hair is layer cut to the same length all over. You can fade the sides and back if you want the hair to be shorter in these areas. Cut the front of the hair, following the contour of the head.

Clean up around the hairline if required. The finished haircut.

Cross-check the finished haircut and check it is to your client's liking. Provide aftercare advice.

TOP TIP

If clippers are used to cut the hair short, use a grade 2 or grade 3 attachment on the clippers. A grade 2 will show some skin and a grade 3 will still be short but minimal skin will show. Always clean and remove hair from clippers after use. Sterilize the clipper by using sterile clipper spray to avoid cross contamination.

TOP TIP

A sculpture cut is a hairstyle that is cut short following the contours of the head and is suitable for all hair types when cropping the hair short. It is sometimes referred to as a crew cut in men's hair cutting techniques.

ACTIVITY

Carry out your own research to find out how clients react to questions asked during the consultation process. Write down a series of questions you would ask prior to cutting a client's hair. Get your sample clients to grade your questions from 'Very good', 'Good' and 'Poor' by ticking boxes next to each question. The information gained can be used to collate a range of questions you can ask the client to gain an honest response. This will improve the quality of your questionnaire.

Remember all questions should be anonymous – so do not ask your client to write their name on the questionnaire. Also reassure any client you circulate the questions to that all information is for salon purposes only, is confidential and will not be shared with anyone else.

For information on levelling and testing clippers please see CHAPTER 18 Men's hairdressing.

Fashion colouring techniques

Colouring African type hair is a specialist skill. Creative colouring includes colour correction and creative colour application. The hairdresser specializing in African type hair must be well versed in the world of colour and be fully aware of the susceptibilities and common fragilities of this hair type. African type hair is the weakest of all the ethnic hair types, and it can be easily sensitized, damaged and prone to breakage. Weakening can occur through prior chemical and physical techniques used on the hair such as relaxers, perms and thermal electrical styling irons/tongs. Consideration of these factors will sometimes mean that a client may not be suited to a creative colour service. Colouring should not be carried out on those under 16 years of age as their skin is immature and thus will be more sensitive and prone to damage.

You must ensure that you understand basic principles of colour before practising these techniques. If you are unsure of basic colour selection, application or removal at Level 2, please read the basic hair colour chapter in this book.

The colouring techniques used in this chapter are suitable for use by Level 3 stylists. They will be creative and involve partial colouring methods, using minimal amounts of permanent colour or lightener on smaller sections of hair. They are, however, effective and will avoid further damage to already processed and sensitized hair.

> To remind yourself of basic colouring techniques read CHAPTER 14.

Before colouring

In order to carry out this service safely and effectively a thorough consultation and analysis must be carried out on your client.

There will be a number of additional factors to consider when carrying out a consultation for colour. First it is important to be sure of the client's requirements for the desired finished look and the target shade to be achieved (it is worth bearing in mind that individual perception of colour and tone may vary; for example, a 'plum' tone is often referred to as 'red'). It is best to use a variety of open-ended questions at this stage in order to gain accurate feedback. It will be also helpful to use visual aids such as photographs and a manufacturer's colour chart with hair swatches to give an accurate indication of the end result. You must ensure that you explain all processes involved in achieving the desired look, particularly if you have to **pre-lighten** the hair. Remember that with darker hair tones it is almost impossible to lighten the hair beyond yellow without excessive damage to the hair shaft.

Refer to the hair classification chart in Chapter 2 when advising your client on all chemical services as the effect of the chemicals including colour will vary with each hair type. The more tightly curled the hair, the more susceptible it is likely to be to damage.

Bear in mind the client's lifestyle. Certain colours may not be permissible in a professional working environment, such as a law firm or a bank. Be sure to ascertain this before making suggestions.

> See CHAPTER 3 for details of the consultation and analysis process.

When carrying out a consultation for colour it is necessary to take into account the client's skin tone. As with any other race, skin tone can vary in people of African descent. Therefore, it is important that the chosen colour will not only enhance the cut but also complement your client's complexion.

You will need to establish your client's understanding of the aftercare required to maintain the hair in a healthy state after the colouring service has been carried out. You must be able to recommend a suitable aftercare regime, suggesting the appropriate products to use between salon visits.

The diagram outlines the points you should cover with the client.

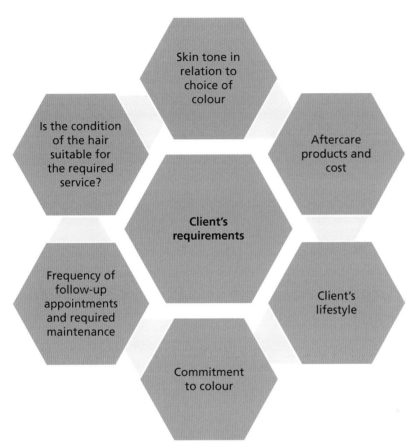

Client requirements diagram

TOP TIP

Be sure to establish whether your client has a history of any allergic conditions or known sensitivities. Do not forget to carry out a skin test on all clients new to colouring services.

Any information obtained upon consultation should be recorded on a record card.

Analysis of the hair

Prior to commencing a colouring service you must carry out a full hair analysis to establish the condition of the hair and scalp, ruling out any infection, infestation or abrasions that may contra indicate this service, and taking steps to avoid cross-infection. If contra indications to this service are found then take the appropriate action and advise your client or refer them to the appropriate specialist recording your findings on the client's record card.

The texture of the hair should be taken into account as this will affect the development time of the colour. Coarser hair will take longer to lighten.

Tests for porosity and elasticity should be carried out to discover the strength of the hair and its suitability for colour. You will need to question the history of any previous chemical

The strand test is described in CHAPTER 14.

Details of the tests are given in CHAPTER 14.

services carried out on the hair, such as relaxer, perming or any previous colouring process and establish whether the client frequently uses thermal styling methods to maintain their hair. All these factors will affect the porosity and need to be considered when selecting the strength of peroxide to be used. Clients should be advised to cut or trim their hair regularly when colouring to avoid split ends and to maintain the condition of the hair. It is also important that you carefully monitor the development time of the process. A strand test should be carried out during the procedure to monitor colour development.

You should carry out the following tests before colouring.

Incompatibility test

This is a test for the presence of metallic substances in the hair which may have come about through use of colour restorers, hairsprays and some vegetable colours. These substances will react with hydrogen peroxide and can cause breakage.

Skin test

A skin test should be done prior to every colour service with reference to each individual manufacturer's instructions. Before applying colour, the client should be asked if they have any known allergies or have reacted adversely to a colour service in the past. If the client is new to you, or has not received a colour service in your salon before, a skin test should be carried out at least 24 hours prior to receiving the full service.

Test clipping

A test clipping should be performed to ensure the hair is strong enough to take the proposed process, that the desired results are achievable and that the condition of the hair will not be unduly compromised. It will enable the stylist to select the best products available for the purpose. This is carried out on a small section of hair that is not readily visible, such as the nape, by taking a small cutting of hair from this area. The client can leave the salon and make a separate appointment for the service dependent on the results.

Strand test

This test will determine the progress of the colour development during the process.

Pre-colour conditioning treatment

See CHAPTER 5 for information on conditioning.

In order to prepare the hair for a colour service, particularly where 'high lift' colours and lightener are to be used, or if the hair has already been chemically treated, it is advisable for the client to undergo a course of reconstructive/moisturizing treatments to fortify the hair and counteract any drying effects of the chemicals. You should use your professional judgement to decide on how many of these treatments are required prior to carrying out the colour.

TOP TIP

Remember that treatments cannot correct previous damage to hair, they can only serve to fortify and strengthen the hair. Any hair that may not be strong enough to withstand the intended service should be removed by cutting prior to carrying out the service.

Selecting colour

In this chapter a combination of colours is used to creatively enhance the overall look and shape of an advanced cut.

First, the client's natural hair shade must be determined as this will act as the baseline in deciding what the target colours will be and the best way to achieve them. This can be done with the aid of the manufacturer's colour chart. If a combination of colours is to be used to achieve the finished look, then ensure that they complement each other and are used effectively.

You must also take into account any previous colour or chemical that has been applied to the hair as this will influence the choices available to your client. Do not take it for granted that the client's hair is in a natural state. It is essential to carry out the testing procedures stated, to discuss this with the client and record your findings.

Permanent colour cannot lighten or lift a previously applied permanent colour. Artificial colour will not lift artificial colour. Lightening over permanent colour can only be achieved with the use of a colour remover which not advisable on African type hair, particularly if it has been previously chemically treated.

Fashion colour

A fashion hair colour is usually a colour that falls outside the spectrum of natural hair colour tones. **Fashion colours** are bold and vibrant and are used to make a strong statement.

It is often necessary to pre-lighten the hair in order to achieve the target shade. Consideration must be given to the condition of the hair and the client's willingness to acknowledge the maintenance involved with this type of colour. More frequent salon visits will be necessary because the colour will tend to fade rapidly due to the increased porosity of the hair, and the fact that the larger colour molecules which make up these tones wash away more easily. Regular conditioning treatments are also recommended to minimize the drying effects of the peroxide. This service is not advisable for clients with relaxed hair as there is a strong risk of over-processing. You should dissuade your client from doing anything that will overly compromise the condition of the hair. However, this type of colouring process does allow the client and the stylist immense scope for creativity.

Colour correction and toning

If the client wishes to reduce the pigmentation of previously applied colour then this can be done through application of a darker colour or toner. This process is described as *neutralizing* and is explained below. In order to achieve this effectively, it is necessary to understand hair colour pigmentation and have a sound knowledge of the colour circle.

Tones at opposing sides the spectrum will **neutralize** each other. Therefore, if a client has a colour that appears too 'brassy' or golden it can be toned down with the application of an ash-based colour and vice versa. Green bases can be neutralized to a more natural looking tone by applying a purple based tint.

Artificial colour can only be removed with the use of a professional tint remover or with the use of an oxidizing agent. These will have been designed to diffuse the colour particles from the hair and may require mixing with either peroxide or water. Extreme caution must be exercised when using such products as they can strip and significantly weaken the hair.

The hair has been pre-lightened in varying degrees throughout the cut to produce a multi tonal effect.

Go to **CHAPTER 14** for a more detailed explanation of the colouring processes.

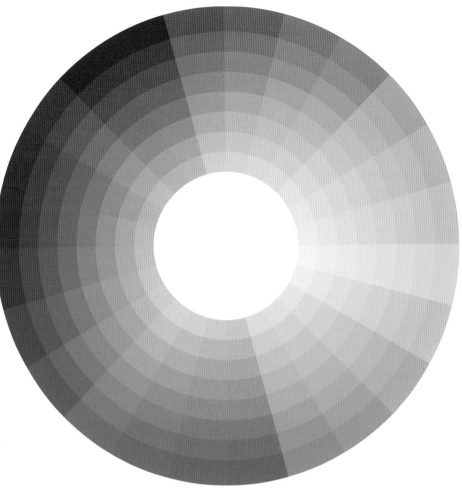

Colour circle

ACTIVITY

Familiarize yourself with the colours of the advanced colour wheel.

TOP TIP

Always remember that a tint will not remove a tint. In other words, a tint will not lighten a previously applied tint that is darker. However, a tint will darken a previously applied lighter toned tint.

The manufacturer's instructions must always be followed carefully. For clients wishing to return to their natural colour, always inspect the hair growing closest to the root. Repeated and long-term use of colour will make the hair very porous and it may not be possible for the hair to be stripped in this way. Colour removal is not usually advised on African type hair and should only be attempted by a very senior stylist.

Lightening and pre-lightening

During the lightening process the hair will go through several colour changes before reaching the target shade. This is because each hair contains molecules of differing colour pigment. It is the presence and ratio of this pigmentation that determines an individual's hair colour.

The lightening process lifts and removes these colour pigments leaving the hair pale yellow if maximum lift is achieved. Prior to reaching this stage, black hair will lighten in the following order:

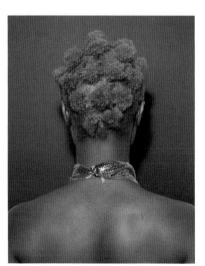

Black ⟶ Brown ⟶ Red ⟶ Red gold ⟶ Gold ⟶ Yellow ⟶ Pale yellow

Client requirements diagram

Darkening hair or returning to the client's natural colour

Pre-pigmentation

Before applying a darker colour to hair that is grey or very light blonde through lightening, it will be necessary to restore some of the red pigment to the hair in order to achieve the target colour. We call this technique **pre-pigmentation**. Hair that has been pre-lightened with lightener or **high lift tint** will have a dull ash green tone if the hair not pre-pigmented before darkening.

Pre-pigmenting can be achieved in two-ways:

◆ application of a red or gold semi-permanent colour to the hair, depending on the depth of the target shade;

◆ application of a red or gold base shade in a permanent colour using 3–6 per cent peroxide.

When covering partially grey hair, then the target colour should be mixed with a natural base in order to achieve the correct tone and depth. The ratio will depend on the percentage of grey hair present.

Colour correcting banding of the hair

If the desired colour is darker than the band you can apply the desired colour to the affected area. If there is the need to lighten a band of artificial colour then only carry out the removal process on the affected area before re-colouring.

Colour correction of lowlights/highlights

If colour has seeped from foils or meches during application then it may be possible to correct this by spot colouring the affected areas with a darker colour. If the hair is excessively light it may be necessary to pre-pigment the hair first.

The table below illustrates peroxide strengths and the levels of lift that can be obtained. It is worth noting that the use of peroxide on African type hair will relax the curl pattern slightly.

Strength of peroxide	Level of lift and use
3%	Used for toning after lightening and is sometimes the strength used in quasi colours.
6%	Can be used to lighten base shade 1 level or to deposit colour or change tone in permanent colour e.g. on blonde or white hair.
9%	Used when up to two shades of lift is required.
12%	Will give up to three shades of lift usually mixed with high lift tints or used for highlighting.

Some peroxides can be diluted to obtain a lesser strength where the required strength is not available, e.g. 6 per cent can be diluted 1:1 distilled water to produce 3 per cent.

For further information on colouring see **CHAPTER 14**.

Before commencing, the client should be given an accurate pricing of the desired service and an indication of the need to perform the service.

Be sure to advise the client on suitable products to use at home. These could include shampoos and conditioners that have been formulated for use on coloured hair. Remember that retailing of products can be a valuable source of income to the salon and you are in the best position to guide the client. Encourage your client to book an appointment for a treatment within the fortnight and if necessary inform them of when the colour will need retouching. Advise the client that coloured hair has a tendency to become dry if not well cared for. Also advise on the adverse effects of overusing heated styling tools and how to protect the hair with suitable heat protective products. Remember to record your service on the client record card.

You should ensure that you have organized yourself with all equipment and products to hand before starting. Ensure that the work station is kept clean and tidy and carry out the service efficiently and safely, in a well-ventilated space. Take particular care when working with powdered lightening agents as these are easily inhaled. Be sure to reseal any containers firmly. Always follow the manufacturer's instructions for all products used, being sure to keep wastage to a minimum.

Equipment and products used in creative colouring process

Equipment	Correct use
Towels	Gown and protect client's clothing. Place a towel around the client's neck and secure. Where necessary also use a plastic cape to provide further protection.
Gloves	Wear gloves throughout application and rinsing process.
Barrier cream	Apply barrier cream to client's hairline.
Pintail comb	Used for neat section of the hair.
Section clips	Used to secure sections in place.

Equipment	Correct use
Foils	Used to separate lower section of halo application and to apply slice colour.
Cling Film	Used to prevent colour from bleeding onto further sections.
Tint bowls and brushes	Used to mix and contain each colour to be used.
Colour and developer	Selected colour and appropriate developer used according to manufacturer's instructions.
Shampoo and conditioner	Used to remove the colour completely from the hair and restore the normal pH balance.

For each of the techniques that are described below, gown the client, taking care to protect the clothing.

It is advisable not to shampoo the hair prior to colouring as the natural oils will protect the hair and scalp. However, if the hair is heavily coated with product a light shampoo may be necessary taking care not to aggravate the scalp, then place the client under a warm dryer.

Position the client comfortably and at the correct height enabling you to work without stooping or slouching. Position your products and equipment so that they are within easy reach to avoid overstretching or bending. If necessary ask for assistance from another colleague.

Be sure to follow your timings carefully, it is advisable to use an alarmed timer rather than a watch to avoid distraction.

HEALTH & SAFETY

Be sure to wear gloves throughout the entire colouring process.

Slice colouring

The steps below illustrate the use of foils to apply high lift tint to the hair with use of a toner to enhance the dramatic look of the cut without compromising the condition of the hair.

STEP-BY-STEP: SLICE COLOURING USING HIGH LIFT TINT AND TONER

1 Select foils appropriate for the length of the hair to be coloured, section the hair neatly and secure with clips.

2 Working upwards from the nape take clean slices approximately 3 mm (⅛") deep, place the foil beneath the section with the edge touching the scalp.

3 Apply high lift tint with a brush taking care to leave approximately 5 mm (¼") gap from the scalp to prevent bleeding of the colour onto the rest of the hair as the colour expands during development.

4 Use the tail of the comb to crease the foil and carefully fold closed, taking care not to drag the foil away from the scalp as you work.

5 Continue applying the colour in this way working towards the crown.

6 Once all foils have been applied, allow the colour to develop according to manufacturer's instructions.

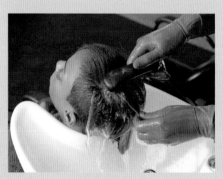

7 Check the development of the colour.

8 If the desired level of lift has been obtained rinse all traces of tint from the hair.

9 Check the tone of the colour once tint is removed.

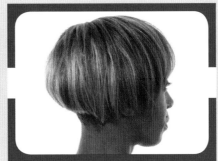

10 If the colour needs to be neutralized or toned down, apply correcting toner and develop according to manufacturer's instruction.

11 Shampoo using a pH balanced product, followed by moisturizing conditioner to return the hair fully to normal pH. Rinse the hair. Style as desired.

Halo colour on geometric bob

The steps below illustrate a technique that can be used to apply one or more blocks of colour around the circumference of the head in order to accentuate the features and geometric line of this cut. A high lift tint was chosen in preference to lightener to minimize the damage to previously relaxed hair.

STEP-BY-STEP FOR HALO COLOUR ON GEOMETRIC BOB

1 Take a circular section just below the crown area extending forward to just above the temples and across the top of the fringe, extending backward, to just above the occipital area. Secure this section in a top knot with a band or section clip.

2 Apply tint to the lower section and comb out of the way.

3 Cover this section with foil to protect then wrap with cling film to prevent the colour from bleeding out onto the rest of the hair while processing.

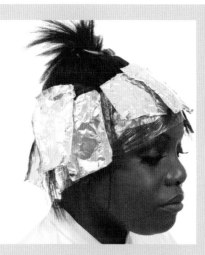  

4 Working around the circumference of the head upwards towards the crown, take slices in a brick formation applying high lift tint for two rows.

5 Allow the colour to process according to the manufacturer's instructions. Once development time is complete, remove the foils and the cling film.

Rinse all traces of the tint from the hair. Shampoo the hair twice. Check tone of the hair and apply toner if necessary. Rinse the toner from the hair, shampoo with an **acid balanced product** and apply the appropriate conditioner according to manufacturer's instruction, then rinse. Style hair as desired.

Once hair is dried, smoothing irons or tongs can be used to add sheen to the finished look.

The finished look.

Using block colour and foil slicing technique to apply colour to the ends of the hair

Using the following technique the stylist can add texture and dimension to a short sharp cut, such as an urchin cut. It also enables the stylist to offer an effective service that is not too time-consuming to carry out. Application of the high lift colour only to the ends of the hair produces a dramatic and modern effect. It also reduces the risk of damage to the root area when the relaxer is to be retouched.

Technique

1 Section the hair in along the crown area in an elongated horseshoe (a).

2 Secure using clips.

3 Apply chosen block colour to the lower section.

4 Using the slice technique demonstrated on the asymmetric cut apply high lift tint, leaving a gap of approximately 10–15 mm (⅜" to ⁹⁄₁₆") from the root free of colour (b).

5 Process according to manufacturer's instructions.

6 Rinse all traces of tint from the hair.

7 Shampoo and condition appropriately.

8 Hair is ready for styling.

(a) Section the hair along the crown in a horseshoe shape.

(b) Leaving the root area of the hair free of colour, apply high lift tint and place foils.

The finished look.

Lightening and toning of natural hair that has been sculpture cut

Lightening hair can require an excellent understanding of the principles of colouring hair, in particular the natural elements of pigmentation and how they affect the colouring process. Having applied lightener to lighten a very dark shade of hair; it is often necessary to apply a toner to the hair in order to achieve a more natural looking colour.

The steps below illustrate the process.

1 Gown to protect the client's clothing and protect the client's skin by applying a barrier cream to the hairline particularly around the face as lightener can be caustic (a).

2 Mix lightening agent with appropriate developer.

3 Apply the lightener mix to the whole head with a tint brush, starting at the nape (b).

4 Take care to cover all the hair in order to ensure an even finish, paying particular attention to the hairline (c).

5 Allow to process checking every five minutes until desired shade of lift is achieved.

6 Follow on from step 9 of the slice colouring with high lift colour and toner technique.

7 Apply styling products.

TOP TIP

Be sure to mix permanent colours to a consistency that does not run.

Products should be mixed and applied according to the manufacturer instructions. Do not overload the hair with colour as permanent colours and lighteners will swell and may seep onto areas where colour is not wanted.

TOP TIP

Work quickly and carefully when applying colour to ensure even processing.

ACTIVITY

Create a montage using pictures that show examples of various creative colouring techniques. Choose two of them and write a description of how these might be achieved.

(a) Gown and protect the client's clothing.

(b) Apply lightener starting at the nape.

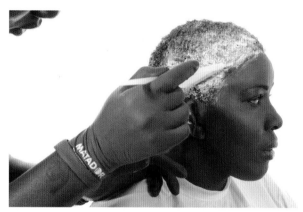

(c) Take care to cover all the hair, particularly the hairline.

(d) The finished style.

In order to neutralize the brassy tones that remained in the hair after lightening, a corrective colour was applied using an ash-based colour, which gave a chocolate toned finish.

REVISION QUESTIONS

1 Why would you razor cut hair wet?

1 To avoid the hair becoming frizzy

2 To keep the hair moist

3 To see the shape

4 To avoid pulling the hair and discomfort to the client

2 What does texture create in a haircut?

1 Movement, volume and separation

2 Creates a hard finish

3 Makes the hair difficult to style

4 Movement

3 Why is it important to stretch curly/wavy African type hair while cutting?

1 To create an even and balanced result

2 To test elasticity and the condition of the hair

3 To see if the hair will bounce back into shape

4 To check the cut

4 On which hair types would you sculpture cut the hair?

1 All hair types

2 Asian hair

3 European hair

4 African type hair

5 Which hair types would you not use a razor on?

1 Asian

2 European

3 Straight

4 African

6 What does the term avant-garde haircut mean?

1 A modern hairstyle

2 A hairstyle that is before its time

3 A long hairstyle

4 A commercial style

7 What techniques does creative cutting cover?

1 All techniques

2 Basic cutting techniques

3 A combination of cutting and texturizing techniques

4 One-length cutting techniques

8 Why would you cross-check a haircut?

1 To cut more hair

2 To cut the hair shorter

3 To test the quality of the cutting edge of the scissors

4 To ensure the haircut is even and balanced

9 How many shades of lift would you expect to achieve using 9 per cent peroxide?

1 1–2

2 2–3

3 3–4

4 Minimal 9 per cent is only used to change tone

10 Which base tone would be used to neutralize orange pigment in the hair?

1 Yellow

2 Purple

3 Ash

4 Green

11 Is it better to use high lift tint or lightener on relaxed hair?

1 High lift

2 Lightener

3 Either

4 You cannot lighten relaxed hair

12 Why is it better to use partial colouring techniques on African type hair?

1 To create a more dramatic effect

2 To give a greater choice of colouring techniques

3 To decrease the risk of damage to the hair

4 Because it saves time

13 Why is it important not to drag on the foils while folding them during slice colour application?

1 To prevent damage to the hair

2 To prevent the colour from seeping onto the surrounding hair

3 Because the tension on colour might straighten the hair

4 So that you don't split the foil during application

14 How long to you wait before rinsing off a lightning product?

1 Follow timing on the packaging

2 5 minutes

3 When desired shade of lift is reached

4 30–40 mins

15 What is the effect of applying a toner?

1 To make the colour brighter

2 To darken the hair

3 To add colour pigment to white hair

4 To neutralize unwanted colour pigment present in the hair

Notes

PART FIVE
Natural Hair

Natural hair is a skilled and specialist area that requires in-depth knowledge of working with a variety of natural curl patterns and hair products as well as the imagination to explore and develop current as well as new hair designs. You will learn how to care for a range of curl types, twist, sculpt, plait, braid and style to create a range of natural hairstyles for a variety of clients and curl patterns. As a natural hair exponent an awareness of issues around sustainability, a product selection and usage is of the utmost importance.

ROLE MODEL

CHARLOTTE MENSAH Award winning hairstylist and salon owner

" I like celebrating the versatility of natural hair with bodacious fro's, beautiful braids and tempting twists that can be therapeutically good for the hair, aesthetically ethnic and in accordance with nature and good common sense. When my mother and aunties didn't have time to braid my hair, they would whip in a few fluffy twists instead, or make two big bouncy ponytails. At other times they would do a bunch of springy spongy twists wrapped in thread or colourful rubber bands.

I did a shoot in Elmina, Cape Coast, Ghana that focused on the art of hair threading; the feature appeared in both *Blackhair* and *Blackbeauty & Hair* and it put me on the map as a natural hair guru. I have since travelled the world, won many awards and teach natural hair care in many parts of the world. All hairdressers specializing in natural hair must learn to style and manage natural hairstyles with confidence by attending training courses. Braiding, twisting and styling natural hair are healthy options that physically change the appearance of the hair but do not change the texture.

16 Maintaining and styling natural hair

LEARNING OBJECTIVES

This chapter covers the following:

Level 2

◆ Maintain safe and effective methods of working when shampooing and conditioning the hair

◆ Maintain safe and effective methods of working when using twisting and wrapping techniques

◆ Style hair using various twisting techniques

◆ Style hair using wrapping techniques

◆ Provide aftercare advice

◆ Maintain effective and safe methods of working when cutting hair

◆ Cut hair to achieve a variety of looks

◆ Maintain effective and safe methods of working when styling and finishing natural hair

◆ Dry hair to create a style

◆ Dry hair to prepare for styling

KEY TERMS

Cane-rows
Contra indication
Double strand twists
Heat protector
Pressing

Product selection
Senegalese twists
Single plait
Single twists
Thermal styling

Traction alopecia
Transitioning
Twist outs
Zulu knots

UNITS COVERED IN THIS CHAPTER

Level 2

◆ Cut natural African type hair using
basic techniques

◆ Dry natural African type hair to create and
prepare for styling

◆ Style natural African type hair using
twisting and wrapping techniques

INTRODUCTION

This chapter is about working with natural hair.
It builds on the earlier chapters of the book that
deal with specific techniques and provides the
additional information you need when working
with natural hair. At the end of the chapter there
is a useful table which summarizes the care
and maintenance requirements of the styles
described. The chapter is designed for Level
2 stylists, but will also serve as a reminder for
stylists studying at Level 3.

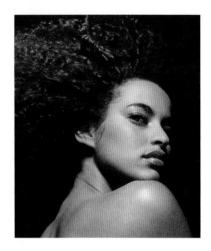

The history of African type hair

In the western world, and in particular in the UK, very little seems to be documented on black people's experiences with hair before the 1980s. What is known, however, is that product development for African type hair started in America with tools such as **pressing** combs, and later on with products such as relaxers, which eventually made their way onto the British market. Although such early items came as a breakthrough in the black hair care industry, it was often felt that the use of chemicals and the pressing of naturally curly hair were carried out to imitate styles worn by Europeans.

The late 1960s saw the emergence of a black consciousness in America, through political activists such as Angela Davis and Stokely Carmichael and with this, the 'Afro' hairstyle, sometimes called the 'natural' look was born. The Afro was considered a militant style declaring that black people were proud to wear their hair in its naturally curly state. It gained in popularity throughout the world as actors, actresses and models sported this new look, and by the 1970s had become a mainstream fashion statement also worn by some Europeans. During this period, the Afro transformed into Afro puffs with zigzag partings, asymmetric cuts, block colouring and eventually the short Afro sculptured cut that is still worn today.

Over the years, there has been a rise and fall in the number of people with African type hair wearing their hair in its natural state. In more recent times, there has been a quiet revolution taking place with a move back to natural hair (hair without the use of chemicals such as relaxers and perms). For the stylist nowadays, the ability to style natural hair is a must as clients are choosing to opt for more natural hair styles such as the Afro look, **cane-rows**, plaits, twists, **twist outs**, dreadlocks and spiral sets using a variety of tools and equipment.

For the purposes of this chapter, wherever the word 'natural' is mentioned, it denotes hair which has not been treated with either a relaxer type product or a curly perm product but may be colour treated.

Working safely and efficiently

See **CHAPTER 3** for more information on the consultation and analysis process.

Before carrying out any work on natural hair, it is necessary to conduct a thorough consultation and analysis of the hair and scalp. Remember that all health and safety regulations must be complied with, both those generated by your salon along with the legal obligations you have as a stylist. As a reminder, make sure that the client is seated comfortably, that your tools are clean, sterilized and fit for purpose. Ensure that you use clean resources (gown and towel), your work area is kept clean and tidy; protect self and client before starting service.

Length of time of service and price

Some of the styles discussed in this chapter may take a while to produce and will vary in price so it is important that you discuss with the client before you begin the service. Do not forget to take into account any additional service the client may have, such as treatments or colouring services, and any aftercare products your client may need to help to maintain their style.

Positioning tools and equipment

Once you are ready, make sure that you position your tools and equipment for ease of use so as not to waste your time (and the client's time). As most clients tend to book services beforehand, prepare yourself well in advance, making sure that you have everything to hand for when your client arrives – this includes a selection of magazines with hairstyles suitable for natural hair.

Consultation

Working with natural African type hair can be an exciting challenge as there are many variations to the texture and curl pattern, as African type hair can range from tight curly to wavy in curl pattern. In its natural state, African type hair has a tendency to be dry. Because of this, many clients tend to overcompensate by applying heavy dressings or hair oils. When there is a large amount of product build-up on the hair, it is sometimes difficult to assess whether the hair is actually dry or porous. Some aspects of your analysis of the hair may have to wait until you have shampooed the hair as the natural curl pattern will become more apparent then. Try to get as much information as you can from your client about the history of their hair and what they would like to achieve by attending the salon. Record the most relevant information on a record card for future reference.

Analyzing hair, skin and scalp

You will need to analyze the hair, skin and scalp to ascertain whether the client's desired style can be achieved and to check for any **contra indications**. The following points should be noted:

◆ *Comb the hair carefully*. Unless the hair is worn in locks, use a wide-toothed comb and, starting from the nape, comb the hair carefully as natural hair has a tendency to tangle easily.

◆ *Check the hair for any split ends or hairline damage* (otherwise known as **traction alopecia**) which can occur with natural hair which has been braided or plaited over long periods. Also check the hair for breakage where the hair has become too brittle or where there are two different textures on the hair shaft, e.g. where the client is growing out a chemical process (known as **transitioning**) and there is both natural hair and chemically processed hair along the hair shaft.

◆ *Remove braids plaits or weave with care*. If the client attends the salon wearing braids plaits or weave and has asked for them to be removed and the natural hair to be shampooed and conditioned, extra care has to be taken when combing hair once plaits have been removed as the scalp could be quite tender. In addition, a build-up of dirt and oils may have collected at the base of the plait forming a knot. This knot must be loosened carefully to avoid breakage and hair loss. It is worth noting here that when combing hair, some shedding will take place. This is simply because the hair has not been combed for a while and hair which would naturally have shed over the course of the wearing of plaits will now be combed away.

◆ *Check the curl pattern of the hair*. This will help to inform you about the type of style that the client could have and the type of product you will need to use to achieve the style.

◆ *Know your client's hair type.* With access to the Internet, clients are very well informed about products and the latest news about what's happening in the hair care industry. Hair 'typing' has become part of the 'natural hair' language so be prepared to communicate with clients in this vein especially when dealing with natural hair as some clients will refer to their hair type in terms of number and letter (i.e. ranging from 2A – wavy to 4C – coily ziggly) – see chart below.

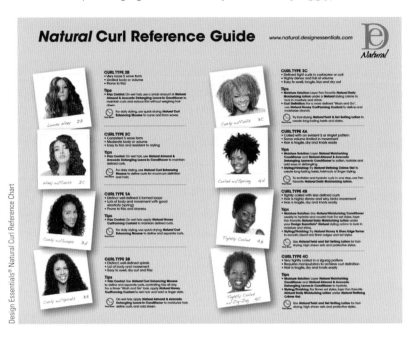

Design Essentials® Natural Curl Reference Chart

Some of the more common problems noted when working with natural hair are:

◆ split ends;

◆ dryness of hair;

◆ dry scalp;

◆ the use of heavy dressings which leaves a build-up on the hair;

◆ styling and controlling hair in its naturally curly state;

◆ working with a client who is changing over from chemical processing to wearing natural hair (transitioning).

Recording information

Once analysis has taken place, record the most relevant information on a record card so that you or another stylist can follow up on services at a future date. Agree with the client what service is to be carried out and discuss any aftercare products which the client may need to factor into their budget and the costs involved. These too need to be recorded on the record card for future purposes.

Shampooing and conditioning

See **CHAPTER 5** for more information on shampooing and conditioning.

As mentioned above, some clients tend to apply a lot of maintenance product to the hair. This results in either a very oily or sticky feel, which can attract more dirt particles to the hair. The shampooing process therefore needs to thoroughly cleanse the hair to remove any maintenance product without stripping the hair of its natural oils.

See **CHAPTER 6** for more information on blow-drying hair.

TOP TIP

Be sure to handle wet hair with care as, once wet, natural hair springs back to its natural curl pattern and this could range from wavy to very curly. The more tightly curled the hair is, the more susceptible it is to breakage if not handled correctly.

If maintenance products are not shampooed out of the hair properly, this can affect styling processes such as blow-drying and **thermal styling** and the hair will have a tendency to smell unpleasant and emit smoke during any blow-drying, pressing or thermal straightening processes. So, the challenge is a dual one: to clean the hair from any heavy oils used and also to ensure that the cleansing agent does not leave the hair dry by stripping it of its natural oils. It may be wise to use a two-pronged approach. If there is a lot of build-up on the hair, use an adequate shampoo which will remove the build-up then use a shampoo with moisturizing properties to infuse moisture back into the hair and leave it feeling soft.

If the hair does not have a lot of product build-up on it, a gentle cleansing shampoo such as a sulfate-free shampoo which also moisturizes the hair will be adequate. When shampooing natural hair, avoid excessive agitation as this may cause the hair to tangle.

Depending on the hair type and curl pattern, you may need to use additional conditioning agents. If the hair is fine, avoid heavy conditioners as this will weigh the hair down. If the hair is dry ensure that the conditioner is hydrating.

Drying natural hair

Towel drying method

Some clients do not want the application of heat on their hair and simply require the hair to be towel dried to remove excess water before styling. If this is the case, part the hair in sections and towel dry it, ensuring that you work on the root area as well as the lengths of the hair. Whether the client is going to have the hair braided, twisted into a style or styled naturally, it is important to moisturize the hair using a leave-in conditioner or a combination of serum, liquid leave-in conditioner or moisturizing hair butters. Work the product through the lengths of the hair to ensure that the hair is well moisturized, then prepare the hair for styling as required by the client. If the hair is going to be twisted, section the hair starting at the nape and apply product, combing product through each section making sure that the strands are well covered. The product will dissipate during drying.

Most of the styles available for natural hair (without extensions) tend not to last a long time unless some type of gel, wax or styling cream is used. Discuss with the client the type of product you would need to use to create the style as some clients may not want alcohol-based products to be used in their hair. If this is the case, then there are other non alcohol-based products which can be used, although when used, the style may not last as long.

Blow-drying natural hair

Blow-drying natural hair can be carried out in several ways depending on the finished result the client is aiming to achieve. Again, some clients do not want the application of high heat on the hair and only require the hair to be air dried, diffused or finger dried to remove some of the water after shampooing. Others require the hair to be blow-dried as straight as possible so that it is more manageable for them.

Design Essentials® Natural—Curl Cleanser Sulphate Free Shampoo

Design Essentials Sulphate Free Curl Cleanser. Ideal for wavy, curly and coily textures

Design Essentials® Natural—Curl Stretching Cream for curl definition, Ideal for coily textures

Design Essentials® Natural—Daily Moisturizing Lotion for coily textures

Design Essentials Natural Daily Moisturizing Lotion for wavy, curly and coily textures. Design Essentials Curl Stretching Cream for curl definition, Ideal for coily textures

ACTIVITY

Draw up a table of leave-in conditioners and moisturizers from different manufacturers that are suitable for use on natural hair and state the benefits of each of them.

ACTIVITY

Draw up a table of serums, hair polishes, waxes, pomades and oils from different manufacturers that are suitable for use on natural hair. State the texture of hair they are suitable for and the benefits of each product.

See **CHAPTER 7** for more information on setting hair.

TOP TIP

When hair is wet, it is in an alpha keratin state. Setting or blow-drying will stretch the hair and, once dried, the hair will take on a new shape and it will now be in a beta keratin state.

Hair smoothed showing how straight the hair could become on blow-drying or setting

Finger drying, blow-drying or diffusing

Before finger drying, blow-drying or diffusing, it is advisable to use a non alcohol based leave-in conditioner, conditioning mousse and/or serum or hair polish. The leave-in conditioner can either be liquid or cream depending on whether the hair is going to be blow-dried straight or not. With more natural styling looks which require the hair to be finger dried or diffused, it is better to use a cream leave-in conditioner which helps the hair to be more pliable and which will add texture to naturally curly or wavy hair. These products tend to lock moisture into the hair before the application of heat from the blow-dryer or diffuser. If the client requires the hair to be finger dried then use your fingers to separate the natural curls in the hair while applying low heat from a blow-dryer to add volume and texture to the hair.

If the hair is going to be blow-dried straight, once leave-in conditioner has been applied, section hair into four and start blow-drying from the nape. Use water or leave-in conditioner to mist the hair if it starts to dry out while blow-drying. If you are working on very long hair and you know that the hair is likely to dry out before you are finished with your blow-drying technique mist the hair which is still to be blow-dried with water taking care not to wet the hair which has already been blow-dried.

If the hair is more curly than wavy, a blow-drying pick attached to the end of the blow-dryer would help to make the blow-drying process easier, after which a paddle brush, Denman or round brush may be used to achieve a straighter finish. If the hair is more wavy than curly, the hair can be blow-dried using a brush rather than the hair pick then curled or flat ironed.

Design Essentials® Natural—photo of Ribbon Curl being diffused

Ribbon curl being diffused

Wavy hair which can be blow-dried with a round/paddle/Denman brush

Setting

As an alternative to blow-drying, hair can also be set on rollers, perm rods, straws or Curlformers, depending on the wave pattern in the hair. These will allow the client to have greater curl definition. Some hair will straighten easily on stretching. Because the curl structure is loose rather than tight, this type of hair can be set on rollers, rods, straws or Curlformers. A roller set will create smooth bouncy curls while the other tools will create a tighter curl which can last up to a couple of weeks.

When setting, use a brick formation for curl uniformity and to avoid channels in the hair. With any of these set styles, the curl can be separated to add volume and texture to the hair and to rid the hair of any partings.

Straw set

1. Shampoo and condition hair using a good moisture-balanced shampoo and conditioner.

2. Towel dry hair lightly and apply leave-in conditioner, setting lotion, mousse or a light hold styling gel to the hair ensuring that it is evenly distributed throughout lengths of hair.

3. Starting at the nape, take either small 6 mm (¼") rectangular, triangular or diamond shaped partings. Place end papers at the points of the hair and wind hair onto straw in an upward motion finishing at the root of the hair. For clients who are transitioning from chemical to natural hair, and where there is at least 25 mm (1") of regrowth, it would be best to twist the hair first with a two strand twist before setting with straws. Twisting the hair will help to stretch the new growth.

4. Use a kirbigrip across the top of the straw to keep hair and straw in place and stop hair from unravelling.

5. Mist hair with water using a spray bottle to stop hair which has not yet been set from drying out.

6. Once completed, place client under a hood dryer or Climazone to dry hair. Ensure client's comfort as the straws may jut out at all different angles making it awkward for the client to sit under the dryer comfortably. Drying time will depend on length of hair.

7. Before taking client out of the dryer completely, ensure that the hair is dried fully. Check different points on the head by unwinding the hair from the straw and making sure that the hair is not still damp and that you have well formed curls.

8. Remove straws and leave curls in place or separate curls carefully to create more volume.

9. Apply dressing to the scalp. Spray oil sheen over entire head and mist with holding spray if desired.

Double strand twist before straw setting.
Stylist: Charlotte Mensah

Complete straw set

Finished look straw set

Setting the hair using perm rods

Follow Steps 1–9 above for straw set, winding the hair from points to root on the rod in a spiral fashion.

Various types of which can be used to set natural hair (foam curlers.)

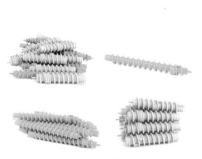

Various types of rods which can be used to set natural hair (spiral)

Various types of rods which can be used to set natural hair (normal perming rods)

Curlformer and hook

www.youtube.com/
watch?v=yJf2czv6M3E

TOP TIP

Do remember that once the hair becomes moist from damp conditions in the atmosphere, exercise or shampooing, it will revert back to the alpha keratin state.

Setting the hair using Curlformers

Curlformers can be used on hair textures from tight to wavy and will create a spiral type curl effect on the hair. These provide definition and natural hold to curls and waves without the need to always use a styling product.

1 Shampoo and condition the hair. Prepare the hair for setting using selected product or a variety of products; such as leave-in product, setting product **heat protector**, mousse and any serum or moisturizing oils/creams.

2 Comb the hair through thoroughly from ends up the mid-lengths to the root area until the whole head is tangle free.

3 Put together the two parts of the styling hook and then, holding the handle, feed the selected size Curlformer onto the styling hook in advance.

4 Starting at the nape of the neck and with the rest of the hair secured out of the way, divide the hair into 6 mm (¼") or 12 mm (½") subsections depending on the thickness of the hair.

5 Gently give the hair a quarter turn twist at the root and holding the handle higher than the hook, slip the twisted section into the hook of the Curlformer.

6 Open the base of the Curlformer with the thumb and forefinger and pull the hooked hair gently through into the former.

7 Apply Curlformers to the entire head of hair, or wherever texture, curls or waves are required.

8 Ensure all the hair is in the former and no ends are left out as hair not in the Curlformer will not be curled. Hair at the root area not secured in the Curlformer can be twisted at the root to avoid the hair becoming frizzy. Avoid twisting the root too tightly to avoid traction alopecia.

9 Depending on the thickness and length of the hair, dry the hair for half an hour for shorter hair and 45 minutes to an hour for longer hair.

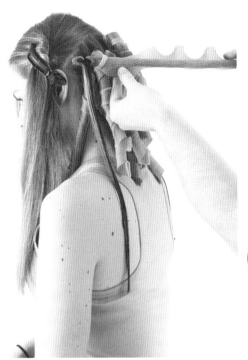

Hair placed in hook and twisted before being pulled through to Curlformer

Hair set on Curlformers

Finished look

10 Check to ensure the hair is dry before taking out all the Curlformers. If the hair is limp and the curl is not bouncy and fully formed, put the Curlformer back using the same technique as described above and place the hair under the dryer until the whole head is completely dry.

11 Apply dressing to the scalp, serum or oil sheen finishing sprays to the hair and separate the curls, styling the hair to create a suitable look for the client. Apply finishing products as required to the completed styled look.

Aftercare (hair oils or dressings)

Once the hair has been blow-dried or set, the hair and scalp can be treated with hair oils or dressings. This should effectively moisturize the hair and scalp, making the hair easier to work with. It should not be too heavy as this will weigh the hair down and eventually attract dirt to the hair. Hair oils and dressings can be applied directly to the scalp and the hair or you can opt for simply using a shine spray to add gloss to the hair. This can be used before or after the finishing process if the hair has been set. If the hair has been blow-dried in preparation for another service, it is best not to use too much finishing product as this can make the hair difficult to work with. The hair is now ready for cane-rowing, braiding, twisting, weaving, thermal styling, pressing or natural styling as the client desires.

HEALTH & SAFETY

Avoid any additional pulling of the hair on the hairline and internally when setting the hair as this could cause traction alopecia.

TOP TIP

Always ensure that the hair is completely dry when setting natural hair, as if the hair is damp the finished combed out hairstyle will become frizzy.

Nutriment Rx Crème Hairdress for hair and scalp

ACTIVITY

Compile a list of natural hairstyles. Alongside each, state how you think the style was achieved and what tools and equipment were used. Using your tuition head, choose one of the styles and recreate it using the tools and equipment you think most suitable for the hairstyle. Working with your colleagues, do a small presentation of your hairstyle, explaining how it was achieved. Be prepared to answer their questions.

Pressing or thermal styling

The art of pressing, as it is known today, dates back to the early 1900s. Prior to this, there was a very crude method using knives or forks which were heated over open fires and then applied to the hair in order to stretch it.

Pressing, along with curling, became increasingly popular and rose to its pinnacle in the 1960s. The demand for press and curl slowed down in the 1990s as the relaxer and perms markets increased. In more recent years, as the natural hair market has steadily increased again, the demand for pressing has also increased. However this time round, with more advanced products on the market, it is possible to achieve the same degree of straightness that one would get from a pressing comb by thermal styling the hair using flat irons.

Technique

1 Starting at the nape, take small horizontal partings (a).

2 Using either an electric flat iron or flat iron which has been heated up in the thermal ovens, place the flat irons near the root of the hair and smooth downward two or three times to straighten the hair (b). Take particular care not to burn the client's scalp. Use heat testing material to check that the iron is not too hot for the hair.

See **CHAPTER 9** for more information on thermal styling.

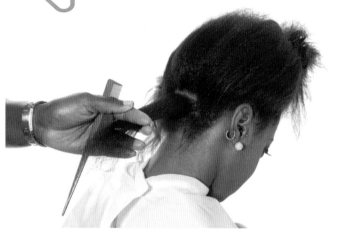

(a) Sectioning hair before thermal smoothing

(b) Hair being smoothed with flat irons

Cutting natural hair

See **CHAPTER 13** for more information on basic cutting techniques.

All hair types need to be cut regularly to avoid split ends, whether worn naturally or not. African type hair has a tendency to be dry and therefore can break more easily than other hair types. Due to this, many clients shy away from having their hair cut regularly because they feel that the length would be compromised. It is up to you, the stylist, to educate the client, letting them know that cutting their hair will keep split ends at bay. This will mean that the hair will not tangle as much, making it easier to comb through. The hair should be cut every six to eight weeks to keep it in optimum condition.

When cutting natural hair (unless you are cutting an Afro style), it is best to blow-dry the hair first, if possible, to help to straighten it out. If not, the finished look may be uneven as it may be difficult to maintain the same tension throughout the whole haircut. Once blow-dried, the same principle applies for cutting as if the cut was being carried out on straight hair. If you or the client has opted not to blow-dry the hair, it is best to comb the hair through first to ensure that there are no tangles, then cut the hair freehand to avoid uneven tension when holding the hair. Remember that curly hair shrinks when dry so it is wise to bear this in mind when deciding what length to cut natural African type hair. Do not forget to take into consideration your client's face shape when deciding on what type of haircut they should have.

Colouring natural hair

Colour added to natural hair does help to bring it alive. While this can be done quite safely because there are no other chemicals on the hair, there is one pitfall to be aware of: colouring hair can make the hair dry. As African type hair has a tendency to be dry anyhow, this can make the situation worse.

There are oil based products which can be used to protect the hair before colouring/lightening and which will minimise the harsh effect of colouring/lightening products on the hair. Please check manufacturer's instructions for guidance.

Cap method

Transitioning clients

More and more clients are making the decision to stop chemically processing their hair and to wear their hair natural instead. So, what can be done for the client who has a relaxer or perm and now wants to go natural? The options available are:

◆ waiting until sufficient new hair grows and cutting off all existing chemically processed hair;

◆ **double strand twist** hair then set on straws or perm rods;

◆ carrying out full head extensions until sufficient new growth is present for the client's desired style;

◆ simply shampooing and conditioning hair, gradually cutting processed ends until only the natural hair remains;

◆ treating the new growth with a chemical free keratin straightening system until all of the old relaxer has been cut out of the hair.

In most cases, if the client's hair is already short, there may be little or no objection to cutting off all of the existing chemically processed hair. However, it is more difficult if the hair is long and the client does not want to lose too much of the length. As mentioned above, one of the options is to wear the hair in extensions until there is sufficient new hair for the client to feel comfortable with wearing their own hair natural. If the client opts for extensions, it is important that the hairline is not compromised with constant use of extensions, which can lead to traction alopecia.

If the client does not opt for extensions but wishes to allow the natural hair to grow through while the rest of the hair remains processed, this can pose problems for both the stylist and the client. The two different textures of hair can cause uneven tension and the hair can begin to shed at the point where the natural hair meets the processed hair.

If the client's natural hair is of a wavy texture, there may be minimum breakage because the two textures may not be very different. As an alternative, the hair can be thermal styled but this can be onerous if the hair reverts and the client has to continuously straighten the hair. In addition,

See **CHAPTER 14** for more information on basic colouring techniques.

See **CHAPTER 13** for more information on creative cutting and colouring techniques.

TOP TIP

When working on hair with a tight curl pattern and, if the hair is long, do not use a highlighting cap as it will not sit snugly on the head. If the client requires highlights, use foils.

See **CHAPTER 10** for more information on hair extensions.

Weaved extensions which could be used while growing out chemically processed hair

ACTIVITY

Make a collage of styles suitable for natural hair and list the type of product which would be suitable to create the styles.

Plaiting from roots to ends

the application of heat to the hair on a regular basis can also damage the hair. The hair can also be pressed to even out texture. This should not be done too often, however, and only carried out with extreme caution, taking care not to overlap too much into the processed hair with the pressing comb as, over a period of time, this will cause too much stress to the processed hair.

Clients who opt to wait until there is sufficient new growth while keeping the hair that is already processed sometimes become tired with the waiting process and, more often than not, opt for chemical processing again. It is the duty of the stylist to have another consultation with the client and to make alternative suggestions. These suggestions could include setting techniques such as the use of perm rods, straws or Curlformers to create curls with an option for separating the curls at a later stage for a more varied look.

If the client opts for the chemical free keratin staightening system, then it is best to advise the client to wear the hair straight until she is happy that she has sufficient new growth to allow her to cut off the old relaxer. If not, and the client decides to wear the hair curly, this could pose a styling challenge as the roots will be curly and the ends straight. Wearing the hair like this can also cause breakage at the point where the natural hair meets the processed hair.

Discuss the best option for your client bearing in mind the client's lifestyle.

Styling hair using plaiting techniques

For years Africans have plaited their natural hair into intricate hairstyles, which very often related to special events in their life such as births, deaths, marriages, coming of age and cultural events.

Single plaiting

Single plaiting without extensions is an old technique for grooming hair, not only for people of African descent but across many cultures. The single plaiting technique could involve the designing of a new hairstyle with lots of plaits or only a few.

When African type natural hair is plaited without extensions, the plaits can last for anything from one day to several weeks, depending on the length of the hair. On longer hair the plaits may last for quite a while, but they will begin to look shabby after about two weeks so it is advisable not to leave them in for longer than that. Removing this type of **single plait** is less time consuming than those using hair extensions.

The technique for single plaiting is described in Chapter 10, Hair extensions. Follow the same procedure, without using extensions.

Cane-rows

This style is ideal for natural hair as it can be worn with or without extensions. The lifespan of cane-rows (without extensions) is not very long and can last from one to four weeks, depending on the length and texture of hair. Ideally, cane-rows should not be kept for more than two weeks as the hair begins to look untidy after this. The removal of this type of look is usually an easy process. This however will depend on the thickness and the number of cane-rows carried out. The smaller the cane-rows, the longer they will take to remove. It is not uncommon to see some shedding of the hair at this stage. This is because the hair would not have been combed for several days or weeks and it is hair which would have been lost naturally through daily combing.

Follow the technique for cane-rowing as described in Chapter 10, Hair extensions, using the three-stemmed technique, without using extensions.

French plait

A French plait can be created by using the same technique to braid the hair in a single plait from the crown to the nape.

Technique

1 Brush the hair to remove all tangles.

2 Divide the hair into three equal sections (a).

3 Starting from either the left or the right, cross an outside strand over the centre strand. Repeat this action with the opposite outer strand (b).

4 Section a fourth strand (less thick than the initial three strands) and incorporate this with an outside strand (c).

5 Cross the thickened strand over the centre, and repeat this step with the opposite outer strand (d).

6 Continue this sequence of adding hair to the outer strand, before crossing it over the centre (e).

7 When there is no more hair to be added, continue plaiting down to the ends and secure them (f).

You can add variety to the finished plait by plaiting the hair under rather than over. This is the reverse of the technique described above and will cause the finished plait to be raised.

Hair cane-rowed with zigzag partings

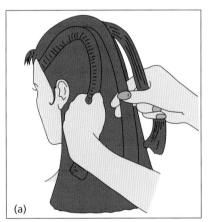

(a)

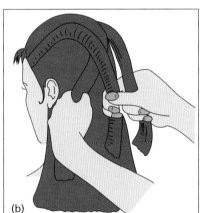

(b)

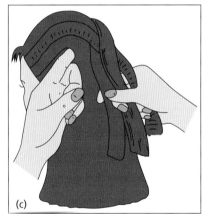

(c)

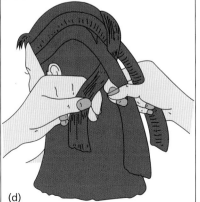

(d)

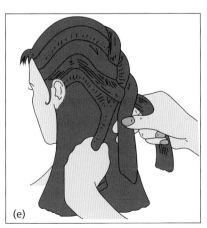

(e)

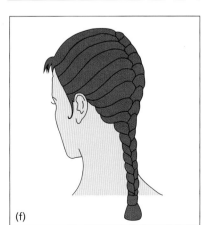

(f)

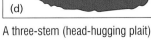

A three-stem (head-hugging plait)

Zulu knots originated from the South African Zulus

Zulu (Bantu) knots

Zulu knots originated from the South African Zulus. The hair can either be twisted or plaited and then twisted round itself to form a tight coil or knot. Today, Zulu knots are worn as a fun style with an avant-garde feel to it. The style is suitable for relaxed or natural hair or dreadlocks. The hair can be divided into squares or asymmetric shapes to create variety and individual flair.

Technique

Prepare the hair according to the hair type and style requirements. Select a suitable dressing or oil sheen spray depending on the hair type as discussed previously.

Equipment needed:

◆ Denman brush;

◆ de-tangling comb;

◆ tail comb.

1 Gown the client.

2 Comb or brush the hair through thoroughly and section the hair as required.

3 Plait or double twist each section from roots to ends making sure that the tension is even throughout (a).

(a) Plait or double twist a section of hair

(b) Wrap the plait or twist in a circular fashion

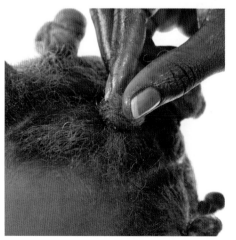

(c) Tuck in the end of the plait or twist

(d) The finished look

4 Wrap the plait or twist in a circular fashion, working from the roots to the ends (b).

5 Tuck the ends under the plait and secure with a bent pin or a kirbigrip (c).

6 Continue sectioning, plaiting and twisting the hair, taking uniform sections until the whole head is complete.

Single twists (comb/finger curl)

Single and double twists help to keep natural hair neat and well groomed. They can be kept for up to one month before the style begins to look untidy. Hair that is short and coarse in texture is unlikely to last as long as one month. However, because no chemical product is used, hair can be shampooed, conditioned and re-twisted as often as necessary. Twists can be carried out using a small toothed comb (comb twists) or simply by using the index finger to create a drop curl by wrapping the hair round the finger starting from the root and working your way down to the ends of the hair (finger curl).

Depending on the curl pattern in the hair, twists can be done using a cream-based product which will help to stretch the hair, a pomade, a gel or a pomade and gel combination. When using a gel and pomade mixture, the gel ensures that the style can be maintained for at least a couple of weeks and the pomade provides sheen and prevents the hair from drying out with the use of the gel.

Technique

1 Prepare client for service in accordance with salon policy (gown/towel).

2 Shampoo, condition, towel dry and section the hair into four.

3 Using a tail comb, section the hair horizontally starting at the nape of the head. Keep the rest of the hair out of the way using section clips or butterfly clips.

4 Divide horizontal sections into subsections, which should be about 3 mm (⅛") in diameter for effective twisting.

5 Apply product for twisting or finger curling to entire length of hair.

6 Using the tail comb, start twisting or finger curling the hair from the root by placing the comb or forefinger close to the root and rotating it clockwise, sliding down the hair with each rotation until the end is reached (a).

7 Continue working up the head, taking diagonal sections and placing each twist in brick formation so as to avoid gaps appearing in the hair style (b).

8 Once all the hair has been twisted, arrange twists neatly in the direction in which it should fall, then place the client under a warm dryer to dry the hair. This process usually takes about 20–40 minutes depending on hair texture, length and thickness of each twisted section (c).

9 Once completely dried, spray hair with a sheen spray and separate curls if desired for texture and added volume (d).

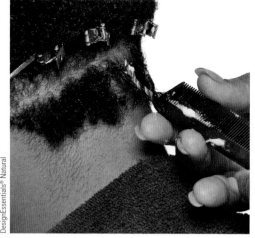

(a) Comb twist

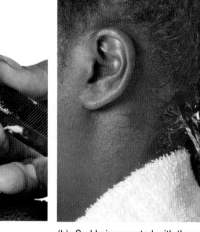

(b) Curl being created with the use of the fingers

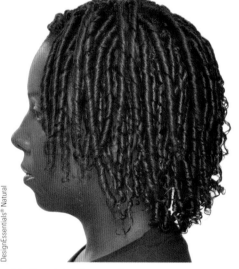

(c) Completed finger curls

(d) Finger curl separated with lots of volume

See **CHAPTER 17** for more information on cultivating and maintaining locks.

If the client intends to grow locks from twisting, the stylist must advise the client to return to the salon every six to eight weeks in order to have the hair re-twisted, until locks are formed.

Double strand twists

Double twists employ the same technique as **single twists**, except that each section is sub-divided into two strands which are then wrapped around each other.

Technique

1   Follow the same procedure for single twist up to step 4.

2   Instead of using a tail comb, divide the subsection into two and, using fingers, twist one section over the other in a clockwise fashion, always taking the left section of hair and twisting it over the right section.

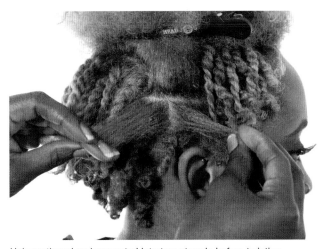

Hair sectioned and separated into two strands before twisting

Hair being double strand twisted

3 Continue working up the head in a brick formation until all double twists are completed.

4 Continue as for single twists steps 8 and 9. Alternatively, the hair can be left to dry naturally or placed under a hood dryer until completely dry and then the strands can be separated in what are called 'twist outs'.

Senegalese/root twists

As the name suggests, this style has its origins in the West African state of Senegal and can be used to create intricate patterns on natural hair or chemically processed hair. Today it is created using styling gel or a mixture of styling gel and hair pomade which is used for creating single and double twists. It can be carried out using the fingers or a tail comb. When the twists are completed, the ends of the hair can be maintained by single strand twisting, double strand twisting, setting or using curling irons to create curl clusters and add variety to the style.

The finished look

Technique

1 Prepare client for service and carry out a consultation and analysis to ascertain the desired style.

2 The hair should then be shampooed, conditioned and blow-dried in preparation. Blow-drying natural hair prior to Senegalese twisting helps to control the hair.

3 Once a desired style is chosen begin to map out sections of hair for twisting.

4 Using fingers, start close to the root, taking a small section of hair and twisting it in a clockwise fashion (a). Work along the channel, taking up more sections of hair as the twists form.

5 When one channel is finished, a band can be used to hold hair in place. Continue until all twists are completed.

6 At this stage, the ends of the hair can be single or double twisted or the client may opt for the ends to be set on rods or thermal styled with curling irons. If the ends are to be set or thermal styled, first place the client under a dryer to dry twists in place (b).

(a) Senegalese twists being carried out

(b) Ends of twists set on perm rods

The finished look

7 Once dried, the ends of the hair can now be styled as desired.

8 Spray a sheen spray over entire head to keep hair pliable.

Hair wrapping

Wrapping the hair with the use of thread is another way of keeping the natural hair neat and tidy. This method is not to be confused with hair wrapping which is a technique used to dry the hair or the method used by clients on a daily basis to maintain their hair style. Wrapping the hair using thread has been carried out in Africa for centuries and is still practised today.

Technique

1 Prepare client for service.

2 Carry out consultation and analysis, in particular check hair for any signs of traction alopecia as this can occur as a result of constant tension on the hair and scalp through the use of extensions.

3 Shampoo, condition and blow-dry hair in preparation for styling.

4 Agree with client the number of sections of hair to be wrapped.

5 Part the hair in squares or triangular sections and using the same thread which is used for weaving, hold the hair close to the root area, placing one end of the thread at the root area also and holding firmly. Take the loose end of the thread and wrap around the hair in a circular fashion working along to the ends of the hair.

6 At the end of the hair, create a knot with the thread so that the hair does not unravel.

7 When removing this style, ensure that the thread is loosened first which will allow it to unravel quickly.

Twist outs

Twist outs can be done from single strand twists, double strand twists or **Senegalese twists**.

Technique

1 Carry out twists to the hair using one of the techniques mentioned above.

2 Dry hair under a hood dryer ensuring that the hair is completely dry before removing twists.

3 Undo twists and use fingers to separate twisted sections and to remove any partings from the hair.

4 Spray with sheen spray.

Hair separated for a 'twist out' look

Aftercare

The client should be advised how to care for their new style. It is important that, as a stylist, you are familiar with the aftercare products that your salon retails and also the aftercare products which will help your client to gain the most out of all your hard work. In order to protect the hairstyles from becoming dishevelled quickly, clients (especially those with twists), should be advised to cover their hair when they go to bed to keep the hair in place.

Clients should also be advised as to the type of hair oils and sheen sprays which will help to maintain their style in optimum condition. For more information on aftercare, see the chart below.

Natural hair care, maintenance and equipment table

Technique	Equipment	Aftercare	Shampoo	Conditioner
Natural Afro style	De-tangling comb Afro pick	Use hair polish and/or sheen spray daily to add gloss to the hair.	Shampoo as often as desired using a hydrating or de-tangling shampoo. If there is a lot of product build-up on the hair, use a cleansing shampoo first.	Use a hydrating conditioner. Use as recommended by manufacturer or, if the hair is excessively dry, leave on for longer.
Thermal styled	De-tangling comb Tail comb Blow-dryer Pick Thermal irons	Avoid getting hair wet or damp environments otherwise hair will revert. Use hair polish or serum and/or scalp oil.	Shampoo hair when required. Avoid excessive agitation of the hair as this could cause tangling.	Use a surface conditioner which enables the hair to be combed easily or, if the hair is damaged use a reconstructurant. Apply leave-in conditioner just before blow-drying.
Twist out	De-tangling comb Tail comb Section clips	Styling gel, shea butters, pomades. Use desired product for twisting. After twisting allow hair to dry either naturally or under a hood dryer. Separate twists with fingers.	Comb hair thoroughly from ends to root removing all tangles and knots prior to shampooing. Avoid excessive agitation of the hair as this could cause tangling.	Use a surface conditioner which enables the hair to be combed easily or, if the hair is damaged use a reconstructurant. Apply leave-in conditioner just before styling.

Natural hair care equipment and maintenance table

Technique	Equipment	Aftercare	Shampoo	Conditioner	Removal
Cane-row **Single plaits** **Zulu knots**	De-tangling comb Tail comb Section clips	Spray with oil sheen or apply light hair oil to the scalp. Do not use liquid braid spray because of added water which would revert hair which was previously blow-dried or thermal pressed.	As this style is done fairly often, shampooing usually takes place once the plaits or knots have been removed. However, if client wishes to shampoo while wearing the style, use gentle movements. Use a cleansing then a moisturizing shampoo.	Use a liquid leave-in conditioner. Avoid using cream conditioner as it may not be rinsed out fully and therefore becomes trapped inside styled hair. After conditioning, place client under a warm dryer.	Use a metal end tail comb to loosen end of the plait if necessary. Use a larger comb to comb through the rest of the hair until all plaits or knots have been removed. A deep penetrating treatment should be given at this stage. If hair is styled in Zulu knots, first take out pins which are holding knots in place, unwind knots and undo plaits.
Single or double Senegalese twists		Use oil sheen or light hair oil or dressing. No liquid sprays should be used as this will loosen twists.	Unless twists are to be removed, shampooing should be avoided as this will loosen the twists.	To be avoided unless twists are removed completely.	Dampen hair first to loosen gel used for twisting. With Senegalese twists, cut bands used to keep hair in place using a pair of regular scissors and taking care not to cut the client's hair. Comb hair with a wide-toothed comb and proceed to shampoo and condition. A deep penetrating treatment should be given at this stage.

REVISION QUESTIONS

1 Which of the following are NOT all natural hairstyles?

   1 Zulu knots, twists, cane-rows

   2 Double strand twists, single plaits, cane-rows

   3 Zulu knots, Senegalese twists, keratin treatment

   4 Single plaits, cane-rows, single strand twists

2 To create Zulu knots, what does the hair have to be?

   1 Tied into a knot

   2 Twisted or plaited then wound into a knot

   3 Plaited from the front to the back of the head

   4 Twisted or plaited in a 'z' formation

3 What can traction alopecia be caused by?

   1 Braiding hair too tightly

   2 A fungal infection

   3 A bacterial infection

   4 Shampooing the hair too often

4 Why is it important to position yourself and your client accurately when working on natural hair?

   1 To ensure partings are neat

   2 To get the right tension when plaiting or cane-rowing

   3 To minimize fatigue

   4 To enable the stylist to create the style more easily

5 What are cane-rows carried out with?

   1 Three-stemmed technique

   2 Two-stemmed technique

   3 Four-stemmed technique

   4 As many stems as the stylist desires

6 What is the art of straightening the hair without a chemical currently known as?

   1 Twist outs

   2 Thermal styling

   3 Pressing

   4 Sculpting

7 What is the key benefit of a leave-in conditioner?

   1 To add gloss to the hair

   2 To make the hair easier to comb through

   3 To tame fly away hair

   4 To lock in moisture and protect the hair from heated styling tools

8 What is the most likely reason why heavy dressings or oils should not be used on the hair?

   1 It builds up on the hair and attracts dirt

   2 It makes the hair difficult to style

   3 It takes longer to shampoo out of the hair

   4 It makes the hair too greasy

9 What is the best type of shampoo to use on African type hair?

   1 Two in one shampoo and conditioner

   2 Moisture balanced shampoo

   3 Anti dandruff shampoo

   4 Deep cleansing shampoo

10 How is hair wrapping carried out?

   1 Take sections of hair and wrap them around the head for a smooth finish

   2 Take two strands of hair and use one strand to wrap around the other

   3 Wrap the hair in a circular manner at bedtime to protect the hairstyle

   4 Take desired sections of hair and use thread to wrap around each section to keep the hair neat

17 Cultivating and maintaining locks

LEARNING OBJECTIVES

This chapter covers the following:

Level 3

◆ Maintain safe and effective methods of working when locking hair

◆ Cultivate locks

◆ Maintain locks

◆ Repair locks

◆ Maintain effective and safe methods of working when styling and dressing locked hair

◆ Creatively style and dress locked hair

◆ Provide aftercare advice

KEY TERMS

Traction alopecia
Re-twisting
Light oil

UNITS COVERED IN THIS CHAPTER

◆ Cultivate, maintain and repair locks
◆ Creatively style and dress locked hair

INTRODUCTION

Locks have a tradition that goes back centuries, but they are now very much part of contemporary styling for African type hair. Once locks are established, they require considerable maintenance and cannot be removed. It is essential that you are able to advise the client before they commit to locks. This chapter covers the cultivation, maintenance and repair of locks and is designed for Level 3 stylists.

The history of locks

'Locks' have been worn by people with African hair types throughout the diaspora for centuries. Maasai men in Tanzania and parts of Kenya are thought to have been wearing them for thousands of years. Artefacts depicting locked hairstyles have been recovered from archaeological sites in ancient Egypt and the Hindu deity Shiva is also described in the scriptures as wearing twisted locks of hair.

The term 'dreadlocks' appears to have originated in the Caribbean and has mainly been associated with the Rastafarian movement, where the cultivation and grooming of locks is considered to be sacred. Reference is drawn from the biblical text 'Judges 16'. Samson's strength was lost when Delilah cut off his locks. The length of a person's locks is also thought to be a sign of their spirituality and wisdom as it takes many years to grow a head of long, healthy locks.

Today locks are very much a part of contemporary styling. Adopted by both men and women, they are a popular style of choice for people with African and combined hair types who want to wear their hair in a 'natural' look. Contrary to popular belief, locks are not a low maintenance option for the unkempt. The cultivation and grooming of a healthy head of locks requires time and patience.

Salon and legal requirements

Consultation

The decision to lock hair is one which should be given a great deal of consideration. Naturally established locks are achieved once the hair has effectively twisted and fused together. Once the locking process has taken place, there is no turning back and any change of heart will result in the client having to cut off all the locked hair and start afresh. Adequate time should be set aside during consultation and analysis to discuss the different locking processes. This should include:

- the time that the service will take;
- the cost;
- the length of time it would take before the hair begins to lock and a permanent set of locks is established; (this will vary depending on the chosen method and the texture of the client's hair)
- the maintenance of hair before and after the locking stages.

You also need to establish whether or not the client has any particular sensitivity or allergy to any of the products which are likely to be used and if there are any contra indications to carrying out the service on a particular client.

You can use open ended questioning to elicit information and gain feedback from the client, such as:

- 'How much time do you generally spend on the maintenance of your hair on a daily basis?'
- 'What problems (if any) have you had in the past with your hair and scalp related to hairdressing or anything else that might affect your hair or scalp?'

When dealing with the client, be sure to project a professional manner at all times.

HEALTH & SAFETY

Be aware of the risks associated with establishing locks. If you are in any doubt about whether the client is suitable for this service, seek guidance from an experienced member of staff.

Working safely, effectively and hygienically

Before carrying out the service, make sure that you have reduced the risk of injury to yourself and the client. Your nails should be short and clean as long nails may catch easily in the hair or on the scalp during the locking process. Minimize the risk of cross-infection by ensuring that any tools and equipment have been properly cleansed and sterilized. The client's clothing should be properly protected before you begin.

This is a long and time consuming process so it is important to ensure that both you and the client are positioned comfortably. You should adopt a good posture and adjust the styling chair to the correct height so as to avoid any excessive bending or stretching.

Any equipment to be used should comply with health and safety regulations and manufacturer's instructions must be followed for all products used. Always follow health and safety guidelines for potentially hazardous substances and check that any electrical equipment to be used is in good working order. Keep your working area tidy and clear up any spillages immediately in order to avoid subsequent accidents. A messy work space does not reflect professionalism.

HEALTH & SAFETY

It may be a good idea to take breaks during this service to allow the client to adjust position at regular intervals.

See **CHAPTER 1** for more information on health and safety.

Potential risks when establishing locks

During consultation the stylist can identify any potential risks in carrying out this service. A record card should be completed clearly noting any previous hair or scalp problems that the client may have suffered which may be a contraindication to this particular service. Once a decision is made then the stylist can proceed with the locking process of the client's choice having taken the hair type into consideration.

Any issues or contra indication identified during the consultation which may affect the outcome of the service, or cause concern, should be discussed with the client and/or referred to the appropriate specialist.

For more information on contagious and non-contagious conditions see **CHAPTER 2**.

Previous history of skin conditions such as ringworm or recurrent yeast infections may make this service inadvisable as it can be difficult to dry the hair thoroughly after shampooing hair in locks, making the client more susceptible to repeat episodes of such infections. Clients with eczema may not be able to wear their hair in locks due to excess dryness, itching and flaking caused by the condition. A history of **traction alopecia** may indicate a weakness in certain areas of the hair and scalp make this style unsuitable.

Traction alopecia

Traction alopecia is probably the main risk and concern when locking or **re-twisting** the hair. Significant hair loss can be caused from excessive and prolonged pulling on the hair close to the scalp. If this type of traction is sustained the resulting hair loss can be permanent.

The hair around the hairline is usually finer and more fragile than the rest of the hair and therefore particular care should be taken when placing locks in this area. While forming locks, caution needs to be exercised when applying tension to the hair and scalp. The scalp should not appear raised or irritable at any time during the service and the client should not complain of any discomfort.

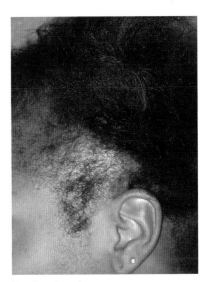

Traction alopecia

Lauryn Hill

Techniques for establishing locks

Locks can be started using a variety of techniques. The method chosen should have been established during consultation with the client. The main factors to take into consideration are:

- the texture and density of the hair;
- the condition of the hair and scalp;
- the client's requirements;
- the client's face shape.

Texture and density of the hair

The texture and density of the hair will determine the method used to establish the locks. Softer hair textures may easily be twisted using single gel twist. The double twist is probably more suited to longer, coarser hair. With either of these methods the client must be advised of the need to revisit the salon to continue the twisting process in the root area as the hair grows. In the interim, the hair should not be shampooed until the locking process (fusing of the hair) has taken place, ensure that the client is comfortable with this before proceeding. Once this has been achieved, the client must be encouraged to return to the salon at least once a month to separate the locks and re-twist the root area in order to prevent the hair from matting.

If desired by the client with fine hair it may be possible to add additional fibres such as wool or synthetic hair to the locks to create a fuller look.

This method illustrated in the step-by-step guide (see page 374) may also be used to establish longer locks for a client who does not want to wait the necessary time for the hair to grow and lock.

HEALTH & SAFETY

Care should be taken not to place stress on fragile hair by making locks too long and heavy.

Condition of the hair and scalp

If during the consultation the stylist feels that the condition of the hair and scalp contra indicate proceeding with this service, then it may be necessary to postpone to a later date to allow the problem to be dealt with. It may simply be that the client may benefit from a course of treatments before having the locks started or there may be a more serious condition that requires referral to a specialist.

See **CHAPTER 16** pages 361–366 for twisting methods.

Client's requirements

During consultation you should establish the client's hair maintenance habits and lifestyle. You should have a clear idea of the client's personal preferences regarding the technique to be used to establish the locks, the finished look and the relevant aftercare. Be sure to bear in mind any previous information held on record or offered to you by the client when making these decisions. It can be useful to use visual aids such as photographs to clarify what the client's expectations are.

You should have an excellent knowledge of the products used when carrying out this service and be aware of the aftercare products available to the client for home use. You must be able to answer the client's questions satisfactorily or know where to go for further advice.

Kimberley Hay

The information gained and choices made should be noted on the client's record card.

Client's face shape

As with all hairstyles the astute stylist must take into consideration the client's facial shape and features to ensure that the finished look is complementary.

ACTIVITY

List the pros and cons of having locks.

Cultivating locks using yarn or wool extensions

You will need the following tools, equipment and products:

- gown;
- towel;
- section clips;
- scissors (for cutting yarn);
- tail comb;
- shampoo;
- conditioner;
- hood dryer.
- **Light oil** for the scalp

HEALTH & SAFETY

It is important to position the client and yourself safely and comfortably as this is a lengthy procedure.

Technique

Having established that the client's hair and scalp are suitable for this service you should gown and protect the client. Shampoo the client's hair to remove any product build-up, comb through with a moisturizing conditioner, then place the client under a warm dryer until the hair and scalp are thoroughly dry.

With this technique, the client must be advised to return to the salon after six to eight weeks so that any new hair which is growing in the root area can be twisted, thus starting off the locking process in their own hair. With each visit to the salon, the hair must be separated at the root and re-twisted, encouraging the growth of individual locks rather than a matted look. By the sixth month most, if not all, of the wool can be cut from the nape area or all over if the client so desires. At some point there will be a significant amount of the client's own hair in its twisted shape showing in the root area. At this point it will be necessary to advise the client to cut off the wool extensions.

By the time all of the wool has been cut, fusing should be taking place in each twist. This will be apparent because the twists will not unravel or be able to be combed out. The strands in the twists will have enmeshed themselves around each other causing fusing. The client must be advised to return to the salon regularly for the maintenance and upkeep of the locks.

TOP TIP

There are now many synthetic hair types available on the market that resemble natural hair. These may be used instead of wool for this method. Ensure that any additional hair or fibre used match the client's hair and that the client does not have a history of sensitivity to any such product.

Eric Benet

STEP-BY-STEP: CULTIVATING LOCKS USING YARN OR WOOL EXTENSIONS

1 Section hair for single plaiting technique. Locks are usually started using diamond or brickwork sectioning as this will produce a more aesthetically pleasing finished look. When deciding on the size of the sections, bear in mind that broad sections are not ideal on fine hair as the locks will appear sparse.

2 Add yarn or wool to client's hair in the form of single plaits or twists. When selecting the fibre ensure that it closely matches the client's hair texture and colour and the amount used should give a consistent and even lock that is not unnaturally bulky. This method can also be used on straighter hair textures using hair extensions. However the client's hair may require some backcombing first.

3 As an additional process, one strand of the yarn may be left out during plaiting. This is then used to wrap around the plait to give a more dense and authentic dreadlock.

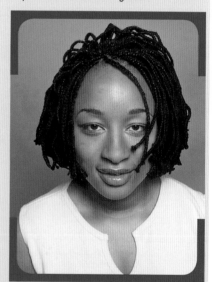

4 Once extensions are completed they can be moulded with the fingers. Ensure that your finished look is balanced. It is not necessary to apply gels or waxes when establishing locks in this way as the addition of wool yarn or hair will hold the locks in place. However a light oil can be applied to the scalp to prevent drying of the skin.

	Single twist	Double strand twist	Wool or fibre method
Which hair type is this method of establishing locks suited to?		Thick coarse hair	
Approximately how long should the client wait before washing the hair?	6–8 weeks		

ACTIVITY

Complete the table.

Maintaining locks

In order to advise the client and carry out the maintenance of locks effectively, you should be aware of the products available on the market that are appropriate for each of the locking techniques.

It is no longer necessary to maintain this look using heavy and often messy waxes. In fact it is advisable to keep the use of this type of product to a minimum in order to prevent irritation to the skin and scalp and prevent build-up of product dust and dirt on the hair itself. Once locking is established and the hair has fused, it is no longer necessary to refrain from shampooing. A small amount of light natural oil may be applied to the scalp in order to prevent dryness of the skin. A light loose fitting cap may be worn at night, but bear in mind that at night we perspire considerably as we sleep, as a way of cooling the body. Excessive use of head coverings particularly when tight can result in the build-up of bacteria on the scalp causing odours. Longer locks may be secured loosely at night with a hairband or in large braids. The client may need to be educated with regard to the importance of regular maintenance and grooming.

Re-twisting of any loosened hair at the root after washing is strongly advised to keep the hair neat and prevent unwanted matting. This should be done by an experienced stylist in order to prevent unnecessary traction and damage to the hair and scalp.

Shampooing locks

Once locks are established they should be shampooed on a regular basis in order to prevent the build-up of products and dirt in the hair, otherwise they will begin to look lifeless and unkempt. When shampooing locks, care needs to be taken not to cause any unnecessary unravelling or matting of the hair. A gentle petrissage motion is sufficient. Shampoos must be soap free and prolonged rinsing of all products from the hair and scalp is recommended to prevent product build-up and skin sensitivity.

See **CHAPTER 5** for more information on shampooing and conditioning.

Maintenance of locks

Treatments and conditioners

The client with locks will need to treat and condition their hair in order to maintain elasticity, moisture balance and pliability of the hair. However, due to the fact that this style does not permit combing or ease of rinsing, products used should be of a light consistency.

After shampooing and conditioning the locks should be separated (to prevent matting) and re-twisted at the root using the finger twisting or palm rolling method; taking care not to apply too much tension. If placing under a hood dryer, a hairnet should be placed over the head with the locks hanging freely as this will allow the locks to dry close to the scalp and prevent unravelling. The client should then be placed under a warm dryer until all moisture is removed from the hair and scalp. If desired, a light oil or hair dressing may be applied to the scalp at this stage. This is purely to counteract drying and flaking of the skin and should be done very sparingly.

Consultation and analysis for re-twisting or tightening of locks

During consultation the stylist should first refer to any previous record held by the salon pertaining to the client.

The following factors should be taken into consideration when deciding on the maintenance to be used:

◆ method used to establish locks;

◆ how long ago the locks were first established;

◆ texture and density of the client's hair;

◆ condition of the hair and scalp;

◆ choice of products;

◆ time required and pricing of the service.

The method selected for the re-twist or tighten should correspond with the method used to establish the locks.

Extreme care needs to be taken when shampooing if the locks have only recently been established. You will need to ensure that fusing of the hair has taken place before shampooing. Massaging too aggressively will cause new locks to unravel.

If the locks are long and the hair is naturally fine then the client may be advised to trim the locks at the time of re-twisting to prevent excess drag on the scalp and to prevent the locks from looking too thin.

Examine the scalp for abrasions or signs of excess dryness and itching which may require treatment or further referral to a specialist. Check for signs of traction alopecia, particularly around the hairline.

Discuss with the client any preference in choice of method or products used for re-twisting or tightening and the reasons for this choice. Give the client a quote for the timing of the service and the price. Follow the procedures outlined earlier in the chapter for working safely and effectively and identifying potential risk.

When tightening locks established by the single twist, double strand twist or wool technique the methods shown below may be used.

Finger/comb twisting

You will need the following tools, equipment and products:

◆ towel and gown;

◆ shampoo;

◆ conditioner;

◆ tail comb;

◆ section clips;

◆ light oil or product of choice.

Technique

Starting at the nape, separate locks by easing them apart from each other in the root area. If separation has been done regularly, there should be minimum matting in. Once all separation has been carried out, shampoo and condition hair using the appropriate shampoo and conditioner.

Towel blot hair, apply spray-on leave-in conditioner and place client under a warm dryer for a few minutes to remove excess water but do not dry the hair out completely or the twisting will not hold.

Separating locks at the root

STEP-BY-STEP: FINGER OR COMB RE-TWISTING

1 Begin re-twisting starting at the nape and using product of your choice. Keep the rest of the hair out of the way using section clips.

2 Twist hair from the root using a clockwise twisting technique. If preferred, use a fine toothed comb instead of fingers and apply the same technique as used for single twists. The tension should be even and not too tight as this could cause breakage. Apply enough product so as the twist is worked along the length of the lock. Any hair which may have become detached from the lock can be worked back into the locks.

3 Completed back section. Place the client under a warm dryer to set and dry the hair and scalp.

HEALTH & SAFETY

Twisting the hair too tightly will result in traction alopecia or breaking off of the locks.

Palm twisting

Palm twisting

Start by following the same method as for the finger or comb twisting methods. Separate the locks, shampoo and condition the hair with care. Towel blot the hair and apply leave-in conditioner. Start re-twisting at the nape of the neck, keeping the rest of the hair out of way with section clips.

Then follow on by rolling the lock between the palms of your hand gently in the same direction as the twist, using an even tension and maintaining a cylindrical shape along the lock.

Most clients should be advised to return to the salon to have their locks re-twisted about once every four to six weeks, depending on the amount of loosening and regrowth. It is important to re-twist regularly in order to prevent the hair from matting.

TOP TIP

Palm twisting works particularly well on longer locks because it is easier to establish an even tension here.

Tightening locks using micro hook method

The micro locks or hook method

The micro locks or hook method can be used to establish or tighten existing locks. The locks formed are usually much finer in appearance and less heavy, and therefore have the advantage of causing less drag on the hair and scalp. They are also more versatile to style. It is performed using a specially designed hook to loop or weave the lock through the loosened hair at the scalp thus reducing any slackening caused by regrowth. The lock is looped back on itself several times until it rests against the scalp.

This method must be carried out with care as over tightening is difficult to correct and will most certainly result in breakage.

TOP TIP

Care must be taken to ensure that this repair is as invisible as possible and any fibre used matches the client's hair colour and texture.

Repairing locks

Locks can sometimes break or become detached close to the root, particularly if care is not taken when tightening or if the sectioning when forming locks is too thin. If the hair breaks close to the root or has become loose in this area, it can often be re-blended during re-twisting.

If a lock should break or become damaged further down the shaft then it may be possible to repair it by stitching it back together using a darning needle and wool or synthetic hair that matches the colour and texture of the client's hair.

Cutting locks to one length

Traditionally, people with locks do not usually cut them. However, in recent years people have become much more experimental with this look and the cutting of locks is not unusual. Locks are best cut using a freehand technique.

Consultation

Establish the amount to be cut from the locks and discuss the desired finished look with the client. Decide whether locks are also to be re-twisted and include this in the pricing of your service. Offer the client aftercare advice.

You will need the following tools and products:

◆ towel and gown;

◆ shampoo;

◆ conditioner;

◆ scissors;

◆ section clips.

Technique

Gown and protect the client's clothing. Shampoo and condition the hair taking care not to unravel the hair unnecessarily. Position yourself and the client safely and comfortably. Cut free hand following the step-by-step instructions. If necessary re-twist the locks once cutting is complete.

STEP-BY-STEP: CUT LOCKS TO ONE LENGTH

1 Position client comfortably and section the hair as evenly as possible starting in the nape area.

2 Cut locks freehand to produce the desired outline.

3 Bring down each section and follow your guide working your way to the crown.

4 Follow on from your guide at the back and blend each side still cutting free hand. For a more layered look section hair across the crown from ear to ear and direct hair towards the face. Remove the desired length from the ends.

5 Check the balance of the finished look. Ensure all locks remain twisted neatly at the roots. Place under a warm dryer until scalp and hair are dry.

www.collegestudenthaircaretips.wordpress.com

Finished style, French pleat with the use of thermal irons

Creatively style and dress locked hair

In the past locks were not considered to be a very versatile style option. However, with modern heat styling tools and new products constantly appearing on the shelves, the stylist with a flair for creativity can combine any number of techniques to produce an array of looks, from avant-garde to elegant the possibilities are limitless.

Consultation and analysis

Using a series of open ended questions and with help of visual aids, you must ascertain the client's expectation and desired outcome. For this to be achieved effectively, the advice you give should take into account the client's face shape and features.

Factors affecting the styling methods of choice and the outcome will include:

◆ the size of the lock;

◆ the length of the lock;

◆ the density of the locks.

You must give clear advice on the time needed to complete the service and the price. You must also remember to check for signs of traction alopecia or other conditions that may affect the condition of the hair and scalp before commencing this service.

In their natural state, African and combined hair types can be very unstable and susceptible to the elements, especially heat and humidity.

If shampooing and conditioning in your preparation of the hair for this service, be sure that the client's locks are completely dry, especially when heat styling is to be used as the style will not hold if the locks hold on to any traces of water. This is best achieved by placing the client under a warm dryer.

Having decided on a style, ensure that you have all tools and equipment to hand organized in a tidy fashion.

French pleat with thermal styling

You will need the following tools and equipment:

◆ towel;

◆ gown;

◆ hair grips (matching client's hair colour);

◆ long hairpins;

◆ thermal tongs;

◆ tail comb.

Technique

1   Gather all locks into one hand at the nape.

2   Twist hair and pull upwards using the other hand to form a roll Taking care not to pull excessively on the hair and cause tension which may damage the locks or scalp.

3   Secure the pleat with long hairpins and grips leaving the ends of the locks to form a spray at the crown of the head (ensure that the pins are not visible upon completion of the look).

4   Taking small sections and using a large barrel pair of tongs, curl the front of the hair.

5   Secure with pins if necessary.

6   Spray hair with a light oil sheen to finish.

Locks rolled into a French pleat style

HEALTH & SAFETY

Pins placed too tightly or digging into the scalp will cause excessive tension leading to headache and possible damage to the hair and scalp.

Bun with fresh flower ornamentation

You will require the following tools and equipment:

◆   towel;

◆   gown;

◆   hair grips (matching client's hair colour);

◆   long hairpins;

◆   fresh floral ornamentation.

Finished style, hair-up bun

Technique

1   Place hair in a ponytail close to the crown using two to three locks to wrap around the base and secure with a pin.

2   Style the rest of the hair into a bun by twisting and folding under.

3   Pin to secure.

4   Position the ornamentation as desired and secure with pins.

5   Spray hair with a light oil sheen to finish.

TOP TIP

Ensure all locks are neatly twisted before commencement of style.

REVISION QUESTIONS

Level 3

1 What type of hair are locks best established on?

1 Relaxed hair

2 Broken hair

3 Natural hair

4 Permed hair

2 Which method of cultivating locks will give client an instant and more permanent form or lock?

1 Single twists

2 Double strand twists

3 Wool or fibre method

4 Flat twist technique

3 What is the form of alopecia that is caused by too much tension on the hair?

1 Alopecia areata

2 Traction alopecia

3 Alopecia universalis

4 Alopecia totalis

4 What is the name of the fungus that can affect the scalp if hair is left damp for long periods?

1 Ringworm

2 Psoriasis

3 Folliculitis

4 Scabies

5 Why is it preferable to use soap free products when shampooing locks?

1 To prevent build-up

2 Because they are better quality products

3 Because they are more readily available

4 To cleanse the hair effectively

6 What is the best method to use when cutting locks?

1 With tension

2 Scissor over comb

3 Freehand

4 Graduated

7 Why might you advise occasional use of light oil on the scalp to a client with locks?

1 To keep hair soft

2 To give the hair a less dry appearance

3 To prevent dryness of the skin

4 To add shine to the hair

PART SIX
Barbering

Men's hairdressing is a time honoured skill that requires practise and mastery of some highly specialized tools. In covering the elements contained in this chapter you will learn: How to use these tools safely and effectively; combining a number of traditional methods and modern day techniques to produce both classic and contemporary looks. Once acquired, these skills will increase your manual dexterity while enhancing your visual perception, thus increasing the potential to expand your client base.

ROLE MODEL

DESMOND MURRAY Award winning hair dresser and photographer

" Audley Lougheed was my mentor when I first entered hairdressing – what an excellent hairdresser. I absorbed and emulated everything he taught me. My interest in photography started when my first shoot for the British Hair awards went wrong. I joined up with the photography team of Paul Pannock and Max Bradley where I traded hair skills for photography training. I did the hair on their shoots and they taught me photography.

I am a specialist in Afro and European women's hair, but got catapulted into Men's hairdressing when I entered the British Men's hairdressing awards and won. In my opinion the Men's, Avant-Garde and Colour categories allow a stylist to be more artistic, creative and edgy; however the women's category is commercial with a slightly different spin. One of my Men's collections was inspired by a seller of the big issue I would see every day and purchase my copy from. I do a lot of research and preparation before a shoot. With over 34 years' in the industry; my advice to up and coming hairdressers is 'be prepared, or prepare to fail'.

18 Men's hairdressing

LEARNING OBJECTIVES

This chapter covers the following:

Level 2

◆ Maintain effective and safe methods of working when cutting and grooming and finishing hair

◆ Cut hair to achieve a variety of looks

◆ Groom and finish hair

◆ Maintain effective and safe methods of working when cutting facial hair

◆ Cut and shave beards and moustaches to maintain their shape

◆ Provide aftercare advice

Level 3

◆ Maintain effective and safe methods of working when cutting and grooming and finishing hair

◆ Cut hair to achieve a variety of looks

◆ Maintain effective and safe methods when creating designs in hair

◆ Plan and agree hair patterns with your client

◆ Create patterns in hair

◆ Maintain effective and safe methods of working when shaving

◆ Prepare the hair and skin for shaving

◆ Shave hair

◆ Provide aftercare advice

KEY TERMS

3D shape

Blood borne

Cutting tool

Fade cut

Hairdressing cream/pomades

Male pattern balding

Razor bumps

Stencil

Styptic

UNITS COVERED IN THIS CHAPTER

- Cut groom and finish African type hair using barbering techniques
- Cut and shave facial hair to shape using basic techniques

- Creatively cut African hair types to create a variety of looks
- Design and create patterns in hair
- Provide shaving services for African type hair

INTRODUCTION

A regular visit to the barber has long been a tradition among black men. The history of barbering tools can be traced back to Ancient Egypt. These have included razors made from copper or bronze and numerous styles of comb that have been discovered during excavations of the pyramids. In many ancient cultures, there has been a strong association between hair, wisdom, strength and spirituality, thus barbers were well respected and prominent men within their communities. The title barber is itself derived from the Latin word 'barba' meaning beard. Today's barber will pride himself on the skill with which he masters his tools to produce a unique twist on what is often a traditional haircut. The barbering of African hair types has evolved into an art form in its own right.

The barber shop has always been a social hub for the men of the black community. It is a lively and entertaining place, where they will passionately discuss anything from politics to current music trends. Young and old will often patronize the same establishment and traditionally many barber shops operate on a drop-in basis. However, with the ever increasing pace of life in the twenty-first century, the discerning establishment will have an appointment system in place, particularly with the demand for complementary men's grooming services such as manicures and depilation becoming more popular.

Working safely

In order to offer a professional standard of service, the barber must work in a way that minimizes risk to themselves, their clients and their co-workers. To do this effectively he or she must be familiar with the health and safety guidelines which should be set out in the salon handbook, as well as knowing the current legislation which relates to their area of work.

Barbers work in very close contact with their clients often using extremely sharp tools in direct contact with the skin's surface. For this reason, these tools and equipment must be kept meticulously clean and where appropriate, sterile. When working with blades, a new one must be used for each client as this will limit the risks of cross contamination and the spread of life threatening blood borne conditions such as HIV and Hepatitis B, which are easily transmitted via cuts or through the use of contaminated equipment.

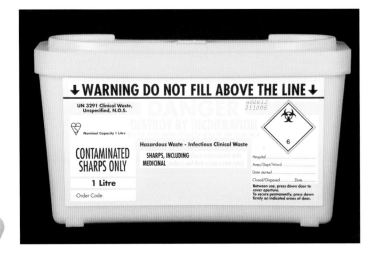

All tools such as combs and brushes should be thoroughly cleansed by removing the hair first and washing with soapy water then rinsed thoroughly and immerse in a suitable sterilizing solution such as Barbicide.

Sterile sprays should be used to sterilize clippers. Remove all hair first by brushing the hair clippings away, wipe tools and then apply the appropriate sterilising clipper spray. This process should be carried out each time the clippers are used.

Avoid cross contamination by checking your client's skin and hair for any of the following contagious infections.

◆ *Tinea Barbae*. Ringworm infestations in the beard also known as barbers itch or barbers rash;

◆ *Tinea Capitis*. Ringworm of the scalp;

◆ *Sycosis Barbae*. ingrowing hairs;

◆ *Impetigo*. A bacterial infection of the skin.

◆ Head lice

The work area should be kept organized and tidy, with work surfaces regularly wiped down in order to keep them free from a build-up of cut hair. Sweep up immediately after each client, placing any cuttings in a covered bin. Every barber must also maintain a high standard of personal hygiene.

For more information on health and safety go to **CHAPTER 1**.

For further information on contagious and non-contagious infections see **CHAPTER 2**.

HEALTH & SAFETY

Always remember to wash your hands before and after each client. Also make sure your hands are clean when moving from working on the client's face to the head and vice versa.

HEALTH & SAFETY

Any discarded sharp implements, such as razor blades, should be placed in an allocated sharps disposal box. The salon owner is responsible for contacting their local authority to establish how this box is to be disposed of.

Tools and equipment

Scissors

Scissors are available in a variety of different designs, sizes, materials (steel, porcelain. Left/right handed), and at a range of prices. A good quality pair of scissors can be quite expensive, but if they are taken care of properly they will last years. Scissors are the most important piece of equipment for a hairdresser or barber to invest in.

Because of diversity of hand and finger sizes, the best way to find the right scissors for you is to hold a pair in order to determine how comfortable they feel in your hands.

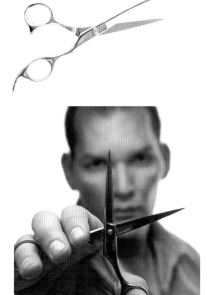

Correct holding of scissors   Hold the scissors with your thumb through one handle and your third finger through the other. Only the blade that is controlled by the thumb should be moved when the scissors are being used. This technique gives control, stability and accuracy.

Thinning scissors   The purpose of thinning scissors is to remove bulk and thickness without affecting the overall length of the hair. There are two main types:

◆ thinning scissors that have one ordinary blade and one notched or serrated blade;

◆ thinning scissors that have two notched or serrated blades. These will remove less hair.

The spaces between the notches can vary in size and determine the volume of hair that is removed each time the blades are closed.

Clippers

Clippers are generally used for short or graduated styles. They are also used for shaping and trimming the hairline and for shaping facial hair.

Electric clippers

These operate with the bottom blade remaining fixed, while the upper blade moves side to side (oscillates) at a high speed. Most barbers choose to use clippers with an adjustable head in combination with graded clipper guards or attachments that can be added to vary the length of the cut where required. The guards range from 1 to 8. The higher the number on the guard that you attach, the longer the hair will be left; the lower the number on the guard, the shorter the hair will be cut. Prior to attaching the guard ensure that your clipper blades are aligned (levelled) by adjusting the screws on the back of the blades so that they oscillate freely. The front blade should be marginally (approx. 1 mm) lower than the back blade to avoid small nicks in the skin while cutting if the clippers are used without a guard.

Rechargeable clippers

These are usually smaller than electric clippers and they give a closer cut. They are used to trim around the perimeter of the head, at the neckline and behind the ears. They are also available with different heads for use in hair sculpting. After use, these clippers must be replaced on their stand for recharging.

Clipper guards and attachments

Make sure that you place guards firmly and correctly onto clippers before use. Clipper attachments should not be used if they have broken or missing teeth as this will result in an uneven haircut and it is also unhygienic as bacteria can multiply in such conditions.

Clipper attachments can be cleaned and sterilized by removing them and brushing away the hair clippings, then either applying recommended sterilizing spray, or by immersing them in a chemical sterilization fluid, such as Barbicide solution, for the recommended time. Remember to remove any fragments of hair from the blades prior to cleaning and sterilizing.

Razors

The two types of razors used commonly are open (or cut throat) razors and safety razors. You should only use razors on wet hair. Using a razor on dry facial hair will cause pulling and discomfort to the client. Always wear gloves when using any type of razor as this will reduce the risk of cross contamination from the smallest of 'nicks'. Talc free non latex gloves are most suited to this purpose so that you can handle the client's skin effectively.

Open razor   The open razor has traditionally been the razor of choice for most barbers for use in shaving. More recently, some areas prohibit the use of this type of blade. It is the responsibility of the barber or salon to check with the local authority to establish their policy on the use of such a blade.

Modern open razors will come with removable blades that must be changed for use on each client.

This type of blade is very sharp and must be handled with great care. Thorough training must be undertaken before attempting to use this piece of equipment on a client.

Open razor

HEALTH & SAFETY

Always store this blade in the closed position when not in use or when passing it from one person to another. Keep it well out of the reach of children. Place any discarded blades in the allocated sharps box.

ACTIVITY

Working in pairs with an open razor and a safety razor, apply shaving foam onto the surface of an inflated balloon. Take it in turns to shave the foam from the balloon while your partner holds the balloon. Repeat this until you can remove all the cream comfortably with either of the razors without bursting the balloon.

Holding an open razor   Hold the razor in the hand which suits you best, depending on whether you are right or left handed, as shown in the illustrations below. Be sure that your hands are dry and free from oils to ensure a firm grip.

Safety razor

The safety razor is more commonly used for shaving today particularly for use at home as they require less skill and the risk of injury to oneself is reduced. The safety razor usually comes with a removable blade encased in the head which when used in a salon must be changed for each new client. However, many men still feel that a closer shave is achieved with the use of an open razor. The skilled use of this tool is not easily acquired and can take years to perfect.

Other tools and equipment

Styptic chalk or matches   These are used to quickly stem the flow of blood in the event of a client sustaining a cut They often contain an antiseptic agent which helps to reduce the introduction of bacteria into the injured area. A new match is used for each client and must be disposed of in a plastic bag and then an appropriate bin immediately after use.

Shaving brush   This is used to apply shaving foam to the area that is to be shaved. The foam should be applied thinly enough to be able to see the skin through it. This minimizes the risk of cutting the client during the shaving process.

Cutting combs   Cutting combs are usually the choice of the individual barber. Most commonly used is a straight comb with fine teeth. They may have slightly larger teeth at one end than the other.

Neck brush   A neck brush is used to remove hair cuttings from the client's face and neck area during and after a haircut.

Cutting cape/gown   This should completely cover the client's clothing in order to protect from hair clippings while cutting or shaving.

Towel   A clean towel is placed round the client's neck and shoulders as protection.

Rubber neck and shoulder cape   The use of this cape is optional. It will further protect the client from small hairs which can travel into the client's clothing and cause discomfort.

Cutting hair

Consultation

For a more detailed explanation of the hair classification and consultation process read CHAPTER 3.

It is always necessary to carry out a full consultation with your client prior to commencement of any service. This will enable you to:

- establish the client's requirements;
- analyze the hair for texture, type, density and condition;
- detect any unusual hair growth patterns;
- analyze the skin and scalp;
- refer the client for further help and advice if necessary.

HEALTH & SAFETY

Before carrying out any service, always examine the scalp and hair for infestation, infection or any lesions that may need to be treated or require specialist referral prior to carrying out your service.

As with any other consultation, the barber will need to gain an understanding of the client's lifestyle when helping them to decide on a look. For instance, if they work in a professional environment then the choice of style may need to be more conservative. Suitability to a certain style may require consideration of the client's hair type, i.e. further services may be required in order to achieve a certain look, such as a texturizer or the use of specific finishing products.

See CHAPTER 3 for more information on infestation, infection or lesions.

Shaving/razor bumps (Sycosis barbae)   Removing curly or wavy hair against the natural growth pattern causes the hair to be pulled out of the hair follicle. The clubbed hair then springs back into its natural curl pattern and lies deeper in the hair follicle. The hair begins to grow into the follicle walls, and beneath the epidermis. The hair follicle may become infected by staphylococcal bacteria. This infection causes raised, pus-filled spots and inflamed skin. This condition is highly contagious and can affect any hairy part of the body. It is common on the face in areas where hair grows, predominantly in African-Caribbean males and is commonly referred to as shaving bumps.

When considering the cut and subsequent styling, there are some additional factors that a barber needs to take into account. It is important to consider the client's facial features, head shape and bone structure, particularly if they are requiring a style that is close cut and sculpted in any way, as all of these factors will have an impact on the suitability and outcome of the chosen style.

When examining the texture and density of the hair, pay close attention to the varying growth patterns found around the hairline and on the crown. Sensitivity with regard to peculiarities such as male pattern balding must be exercised. Some clients may require a style which retains length that will minimize exposure of such areas. In some instances, you will also need to take into account the natural direction of hair growth and the curl pattern of the hair type as this may influence your choice of cutting method and may affect the overall outcome.

You will need to ascertain your client's preference for the shape to be achieved around the hairline. They may wish you to follow the natural growth pattern or prefer that you create a clean neckline area. The most common choices tend to be squared, rounded or tapered. With men's haircutting it is also necessary to balance the sideburns, establish with the client how far onto the face they wish them to extend and the shape required for the finish. Small rechargeable clippers are usually used to tidy the areas around the outline of a haircut. An experienced barber may use the regular electrical clippers or a blade.

Throughout the cutting process you will continue to consult your client to ensure that they are happy with the progress of the cut.

Prior to commencement of the service, ensure that the client has been given an accurate quote on the price and the time taken for their required service, Record the outcome of your consultation on the client's record card.

Barbering techniques

Though men will tend to wear much stronger and sharper shapes than women, cutting techniques remain the same. However, clippers are most frequently used in the barbering of African type hair.

Below is a table illustrating some of the techniques that can be applied to barbering.

HEALTH & SAFETY

Avoid wet or close shaving younger men, as the skin will be soft and more prone to the development of in-growing hairs.

For the natural direction of hair growth and the curl pattern see CHAPTER 2, Hair characteristics.

Techniques that can be applied to barbering	
	**Fade cutting** Also called fade out. Used as a base for many men's haircuts, this is usually tailored to the individual's request and can be embellished with patterns and designs cut into the hair.

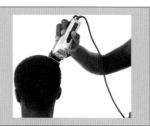

Sculpting
The haircut follows the natural contours of the head. The length of the cut may be varied by changing the clipper guards.

Cutting in channels
This involves working over the entire head with clippers from front to back to remove the desired quantity of hair.

Scissor over comb
This involves placing the comb into the hair to lift it away from the skin or scalp and cutting with the scissors over the top of the hair to remove length. Working in this way will result in very close, short layers.

Clipper over comb
This method is the same as scissor over comb but can be used to get a closer and cleaner cut.

Free hand cutting with scissors
This is usually used to tidy up the silhouette of a cut and remove any stray hairs. This is done in front of the mirror. More experienced barbers will sometimes use unguarded clippers.

Edging
This technique uses small electrical clippers to create or tidy the outline of a cut.

ACTIVITY
Create a style book of at least five different looks for men and annotate each one to show the techniques used to achieve the finished look.

For additional cutting techniques see CHAPTER 13.

Preparing for cutting

Start by ensuring that the client's clothing is adequately protected by covering them with a gown and towel.

Shampoo and condition the hair if necessary in order to remove any excessive product build-up which may make cutting difficult or prevent your tools from working efficiently.

In addition to the gown and towel, some barbers will often place a paper strip around the neck to prevent the very small cuttings from slipping into the client's clothing and causing discomfort.

Prepare your working area in an organized fashion and have all your equipment clean, sterilized and close to hand. Ensure any electrical tools are in safe working order and conform to health and safety regulations.

Your personal appearance should reflect your professionalism. Your clothes should be clean and your nails should be neatly trimmed to prevent accidental scratching of the client's skin.

Always position yourself and the client safely and comfortably, taking care to adjust the styling chair to the correct height, to allow freedom of movement. Ensure that your client is comfortable with both feet either on the ground or on a foot rest. This will minimize the risk of injury and fatigue to you both.

See CHAPTER 2 for more information on health and safety.

Sculpture cut

Sculpture cutting is a technique that follows the contours of the head. It can be used to create either short or long styles. The sculpture cutting technique was used in the 1960s and 1970s, when the Afro hair style was very popular. It allowed the stylist to create a variety of shapes such as round, oval, oblong, square and asymmetric. The technique is a classic method used for cutting men's hair.

Scissors or clippers can be used to achieve the finished look.

◆ *Scissors* are used to layer-cut the hair between the fingers. This technique is particularly suitable on texturized or wavy hair which is worn short.

◆ *Clippers* are good for cropped looks where a more defined look is required. The stylist can select a variety of attachments which can cut the hair shorter or longer. Tapered guards are also available for graduation and blending along the sides of the head.

Below is a guide to the length of cut achieved by using the various guards.

Clipper Grade	Hair length required	
Grade 1	1–3 mm	≈ $\frac{3}{64}$ in–≈ $\frac{1}{8}$ in
Grade 2	2–6 mm	≈ $\frac{5}{64}$ in–≈ $\frac{15}{64}$ in
Grade 3	3–9 mm	≈ $\frac{1}{8}$ in–≈ $\frac{23}{64}$ in
Grade 4	4–12 mm	≈ $\frac{5}{32}$ in–≈ $\frac{15}{32}$ in
Grade 5	5–15 mm	≈ $\frac{13}{64}$ in–≈ $\frac{19}{32}$ in
Grade 6	6–18 mm	≈ $\frac{15}{64}$ in–≈ $\frac{45}{64}$ in
Grade 7	7–21 mm	≈ $\frac{9}{32}$ in–≈ $\frac{53}{64}$ in
Grade 8	8–24 mm	≈ $\frac{5}{16}$ in–≈ $\frac{15}{16}$ in

Technique for sculpture cut using scissors

1 Start by shampooing, conditioning and drying the hair, then comb thoroughly.

2 Starting in the nape area and following the contour of the head. Lift hair and hold parallel to the head, club cut to remove the desired amount of hair (this can also be done using scissors over comb). Work through to the occipital bone.

3 Blend from the occipital bone to the top of the crown using the same technique as before.

4 Proceed to the sides, taking horizontal sections and using the back as a guide-line. Continue cutting until you reach the front hairline. Cut the other side of the hair using the same technique as before checking your balance carefully in the mirror as you go.

5 Take or horizontal sections, working from the top of the crown to the front hairline. Blending and balancing each side as you move forward.

6 Cross check the whole cut to make sure it is even.

Technique for sculpture cut using clippers

STEP-BY-STEP: SCULPTURE CUT USING CLIPPERS

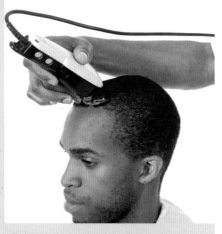

1 Gown and protect the client. Start by shampooing the hair and rough drying using a warm dryer. Comb through the hair to remove tangles and establish the direction of growth.

2 Attach the appropriate clipper guard required to achieve the desired length. Start cutting from the side front hairline and work in channels towards the back of the head. Repeat this action across the entire head. Comb the hair forward and repeat the process in order to remove any stray hairs. Adjust the head of the clipper using the side lever in areas where a closer cut is required.

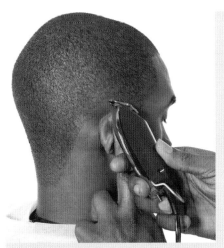

3 Clean up around the hairline and outline of the cut with small edge trimmers. Hold the ear down gently as you work around this area to avoid cutting the ear and to ensure your outline shape is clean and precise.

4 The finished look.

Creating a fade haircut

The fade haircut is a classic look for men with African type hair. The techniques used for this look can be adapted to form the basis of a number of styles worn by black men today. It is a sharp clean look that can easily be tailored to meet the requirements of the individual.

Technique for creating a fade haircut

Begin by shampooing and conditioning the hair, then comb the hair thoroughly and rough dry using the blow-dryer. Comb the hair using an Afro or cutting comb. Keep combing the hair as you proceed through the cut. This will ensure the fade/cut is even and balanced and the required shape is achieved.

STEP-BY-STEP: CREATING A FADE HAIRCUT

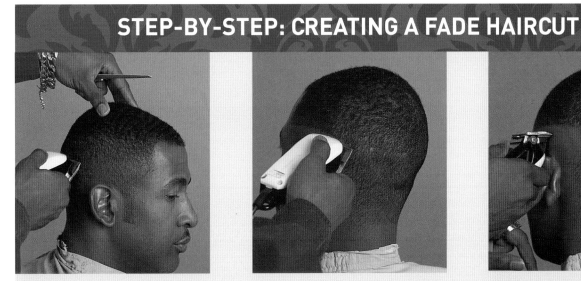

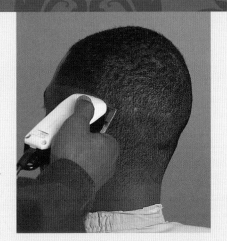

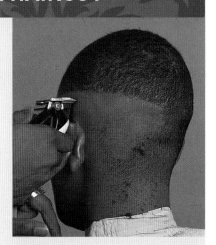

1 Select a suitable attachment for the clippers. Start clipper-cutting the hair from the nape.

2 Proceed to the left and then the right side of the head, taking off excess weight and length.

3 Mark out the area to be faded, working from the nape up to the temple.

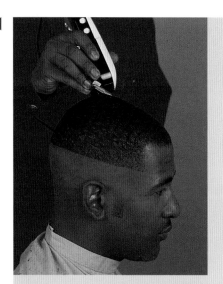

4 Cut the hair on the crown in channels, starting in the middle. Once the desired length has been established, cut the rest of the crown.

5 Blend the faded area to the crown, working in channels.

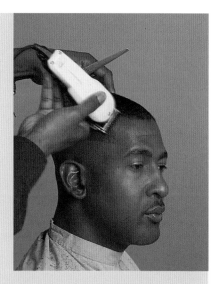

6 Continue working in channels until you reach the front hairline. Cross check by combing the hair after the initial cut. Remove any uneven hair with the clippers.

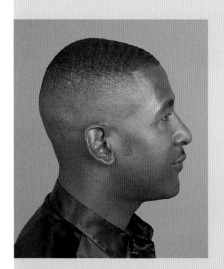

7 The final look – side.

8 The finished style.

Advanced cutting techniques

Having mastered the basic cutting techniques, at Level 3 the barber will be able to adapt them using more advanced techniques to create a range of more sophisticated looks. At this level the creation of designs in the hair is introduced. This can be achieved through use of a stencil. However, the more experienced barber will be able to design a look freehand.

They will understand how and when to combine the various barbering and cutting techniques to create individual looks.

Consultation for cutting a pattern or design in the hair

In addition to the information gained during the normal consultation process, it will be necessary to take a number of other factors into account.

Below is a chart of points to consider during the consultation, prior to creating a design in the hair.

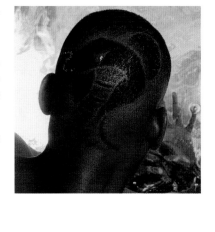

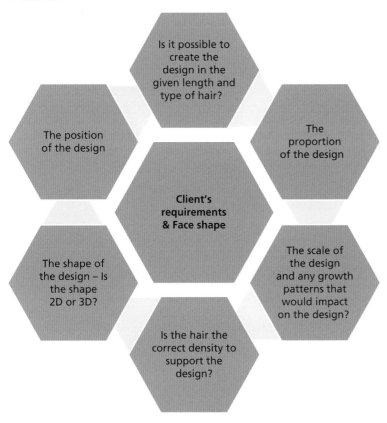

You will need to begin by establishing the client's requirements. This can be achieved with the use of visual aids and questioning. You will also need to think about the following points:

◆ *Face shape and lifestyle*. Have you considered and discussed them with the client?

◆ *Shape*. Is the client requesting an intricate design, e.g. a 3D effect?

◆ *Scale*. This is the size of the design in relation to actual objects, such as a face, flower, symbol, etc.

◆ *Proportion*. This relates to the amount of space on the head that is to be filled by the design.

◆ *Position*. Where exactly the design is to be placed?

◆ *Density of the hair*. Is the hair dense enough for the design to be effective?

◆ *The Hair type*. See classifications; does this support the chosen style or design?

◆ *The client's natural hair growth pattern*.

◆ *Length of the hair*. It is difficult to create a 3D effect on hair that is shorter than 5 mm (¼").

Document your findings and outline them on the client's consultation and record card.

STEP-BY-STEP: CREATING A DESIGN IN THE HAIR

1 Prepare the hair by smoothing over the area to be designed in the direction of the natural hair growth with the clippers using a guard No. 1 attachment.

2 Remove the guard and adjust the clipper blade by turning the small lever at the side upwards to allow maximum hair removal. Begin marking up your initial design.

3 Complete your initial design using large clippers.

4 Brighten, enhance and redefine your design using small electrical clippers.

5 Complete the look with the fade technique to add depth and dimension according to the client's preference.

Technique for creating a design in the hair

Begin by gowning and protecting the client. Shampoo and condition the hair to remove any build-up of product.

Comb hair through in order to determine the pattern of hair growth and identify the natural growth pattern, taking care to look out for anything that may impact on the desired outcome, such as a scar, a piercing or excessive thinning of the hair in a particular area.

Creative cutting techniques

The use of the clippers can be combined with more conventional cutting methods such as club cutting, layering and texturizing, to create more advanced and individual looks that allow the barber plenty of scope for innovation.

It will pay dividends to keep abreast of current styling trends and to take every opportunity to experiment (within reason). You should keep an up-to-date portfolio of looks that can be used to help your clients visualize a new look.

The style below combines the use of clippers, layering and graduation to produce an adaptation on a timeless trend.

Technique for Mohican type fade

Begin by gowning and protecting the client. Shampoo the hair to remove any excess product build-up.

STEP-BY-STEP: MOHICAN TYPE FADE

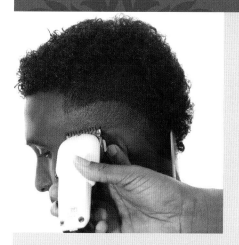

1 Using the clippers with a guard No. 1, remove the hair from a channel over the ears and working into the sides of the nape. Be sure to cross check and balance on both sides.

2 Change the clipper guard to a No. 3. Remove the hair in a channel from the temporal area working towards the nape area.

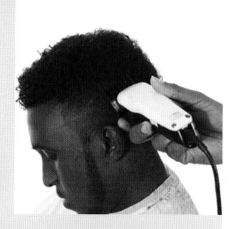

3 Blend the two areas together, by working with a guard No. 2, then a guard No. 1, in upward strokes, adjusting the clipper blade using the small lever as you go, until no lines can be seen.

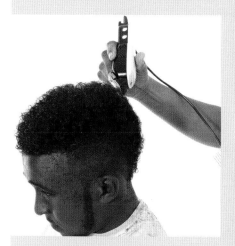

4 Using a Guard No. 4, blend and trim the hair on top and blend into the sides. Comb the hair out with an Afro comb as you work to ensure even hair removal. Tidy the top by either layering or cutting freehand with scissors. Clean up your outline with the small electrical clippers. Check that the look is balanced.

5 The finished look.

Hairstyles must be designed to take into account the client's face shape, curl pattern and lifestyle. Some Mohicans can be narrower, higher or flatter. The outline shape in the nape can be pointed, round, oval or square. The decision on the outline shape will depend on the client's personal preference, head and neck shape. You must always discuss the finished design to be achieved with the client first. Develop a catalogue of different designs that you can show your client as a reference point. Spray on hair colours are sometimes used to enhance a creative design temporarily. Check that your client is not sensitive to such products before using them.

Aftercare advice

Having completed your cut, the service that you offer should extend beyond the chair.

You can help to promote customer loyalty by advising the client on how best to care for their hair in-between visits. Be sure to inform them of roughly when they will need to return in order to ensure that their look is maintained in tip-top shape. Offer advice on how best to care for the hair and scalp in order to maintain their look, for example the use of **hairdressing cream/pomades** or gels ensuring that they understand the importance of shampooing regularly to avoid product build-up.

Your salon should stock a range of products suitable for you to retail to your clients for use at home (who better to recommend this than you, the professional?). In the event that your salon does not stock anything appropriate, you should be aware of the brands that are available to purchase locally. Always allow time when booking your appointments to be able to offer aftercare advice and reassurance.

Record your service and the aftercare advised on the client's record card.

Clients can enhance their chosen style with the option of an additional service, such as a texturizer or colour. You should always bear in mind that you client may want to try something new.

You may find some inspiration for texturizing and colouring in **CHAPTER 14**.

Cutting and trimming facial hair

The removal of facial hair is as much a part of barbering services as haircutting itself. Trends in the way that men wear their facial hair can vary from culture to culture and at times will be dictated by fashion.

The tools that men use for shaving have also evolved, particularly with more men choosing to shave themselves at home, where the use of traditional razors (open and safety) is often replaced by electrical shavers and disposables. However, shaving and trimming of facial hair will always remain an essential part of male grooming. Your establishment should have a clearly set out Health and Safety procedure for this service, which should include the correct use and disposal of sharp implements.

Consultation

In order to be able to offer this service with confidence the barber should be aware of, and proficient in, cutting the traditional, popular and current beard shapes. The names of the shapes tend to vary, therefore it is probably best to use a visual reference when deciding on a shape for your client. As with beards and moustaches many men have a preference as to how they wish to wear their sideburns and this needs to be taken into account when discussing any particular requirements.

These preferences should all be established during consultation and noted on the client's consultation card.

TOP TIP

Keep a selection of images of beard and moustache shapes along with your visual aids.

Dwayne Johnson

Ben Affleck

Mark Wahlberg

Lewis Hamilton

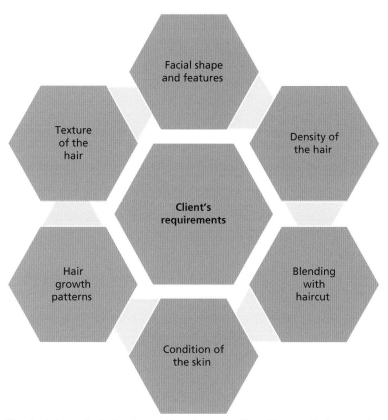

The chart shows the factors to consider when consulting with your client on how to shape his facial hair

You need to take into account the following points:

◆ *Hair growth patterns*. The hair growth pattern will determine the shape and possibly the technique that is to be used to cut the hair. It is important to identify any irregularities in the hair growth that the client may wish to conceal. Cutting certain hair textures against the natural growth can result in pulling and cause in-growing hairs. Tightly curled hair is more prone to causing in-growing hairs.

◆ *The condition of the skin*. Does the skin look healthy? Are there any signs of infection that may be aggravated by the service or need to be treated prior to the service? As discussed earlier in this chapter, men with African type hair tend to be prone to in-growing hairs.

For hair growth patterns refer to the hair classification table in CHAPTER 2.

◆ *The texture type and curl pattern of the hair*. This will influence the choice of **cutting tool** and method to be used. Facial hair tends to be coarser in texture. Therefore, it is recommended that the eyes be covered with a damp cotton wool pad so that it adheres to the skin around the eye area during shaving or cutting as the hair cuttings tend to be springy, sharp and can flick into the eyes or become embedded in the skin and cause irritation.

◆ *The density of the hair*. The density of the hair may vary around differing areas of the face. Some men will have very thick facial hair growth, particularly as they get older, while younger men tend to have softer, sparser distribution of facial hair.

◆ *Facial shapes and features*. It is important to take note of the shape of the mouth and the contour of the top lip in particular in order to prevent injury while cutting. The client's jawline and the shape of the nose are factors that will influence the chosen finish. Depending on how far down the face and neck the beard is to extend, the thickness of the neck should be observed to ensure that the shape is flattering.

◆ *Blending with the haircut*. Hair growth in men tends to extend beyond the natural hairline; often there is no clear distinction between hair on the head and facial hair. The sideburns can be incorporated as part of the desired look. Ensure that your chosen look complements the client's haircut and facial contours. It is sometimes necessary to create a clean shape using a blade or small electrical clippers.

Working safely on facial hair

Because the face is a highly sensitive area, all tools used must be meticulously clean and, where possible, sterile. You should ensure that your tools and equipment are used in a way that contributes to the comfort and safety of the client:

◆ *Scissors* must be sharp and properly balanced to avoid pulling and tearing the hair.

◆ *Clipper blades* must be cleaned to remove any traces of hair and sprayed with the appropriate sterilizing agent. They should be oiled to avoid catching and pulling on the client's hair.

◆ *Razors* (either open or safety) must be used with a new sterile blade for each client. Most modern open razors now come with detachable blades.

◆ *Cotton wool pads* should be used to cover and protect the eyes for flyaway hairs while working.

◆ *Barbers chairs* are designed with a head and foot rest to stabilize the client while working and can be adjusted to a comfortable height for the client that will also allow you to work safely and comfortably. Always ensure that you adjust the height of the chair to ensure that you are not overstretching or bending to perform the shave and that the client is comfortable. This will minimize the risk of injury to either of you.

There is more information on health and safety in CHAPTER 1.

You must adhere to all health and safety considerations while carrying out your service. Work in an organized and tidy manner. Check that your tools are in safe working order and always work with caution when handling sharps. Take every precaution to protect yourself and the client from injury.

Cutting facial hair

Level 2

STEP-BY-STEP: CUTTING FACIAL HAIR

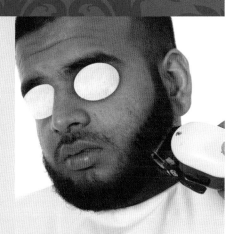

1 Gown and protect the client's clothing, position them in a height adjustable chair with the head supported on a headrest and the eyes protected with moistened cotton wool pads. Comb the hair of the beard to remove any tangles.

2 Using the appropriate clipper guard, work against the natural hair growth to remove the bulk of the unwanted hair. Work through the entire beard area until the length is satisfactory. Check that your client is comfortable throughout the service.

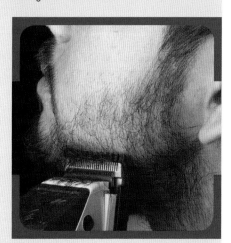

3 Tidy any remaining hairs by using the scissor or clipper over comb method, lifting the hair with the comb and cutting over the top. This method is most effective when the hair is taken in small sections. Holding the comb closer to the skin will remove less hair, while lifting the combed hair away from the face will remove more.

4 Complete the look by tidying the outline of the shape using the clippers. Ensure that your look is even and balanced and that your client is satisfied.

TOP TIP

A razor should never be used on dry hair as this causes discomfort.

Preparing for a wet shave

Hot towels Prior to shaving make sure that the client's face and beard are clean, if necessary this can be done with a mild facial wash; using an effleurage motion. Untangle and remove hair that is excessively long using the clippers. Beard hair can be

Level 3

Wrap the towel around the client's face leaving the nose exposed so that the client can breathe. Let the towel cool then remove it and repeat the process. The client should be shaved while the face is still warm.

quite coarse and it should be softened prior to shaving. This is usually done with the application of hot towels. This also relaxes the facial muscles, which helps the client feel comfortable and makes shaving easier. The towels must be meticulously clean and prepared either by heating them in a steam cabinet or soaking them in hot water and wringing them out.

Lathering
Lather is applied for several reasons. First, it lifts any unwanted dirt from the skin's surface and also helps the hairs stand away from the skin for ease of shaving. Again the effleurage motion of the brush or hand application will help to relax the facial muscles The consistency of the lather will help to lubricate the face so that the razor can glide over the skin and keep it hydrated throughout the shaving process.

The lather should be applied thinly enough to be able to see the client's skin to avoid cutting them by accident. Take care when applying lather to the top lip not to get lather into the client's nostrils or mouth. Work in with the brush using a circular motion to cover the entire area to be shaved. Take care to avoid the eye area do not allow the lather to drip.

Start the shave on the side closest to you and work your way across the face following the direction of the hair growth (this is known as the 'once over'). For a closer shave the work against the hair growth going over the face a second time. This is not recommended on clients with tightly coiled African type hair because it can cause susceptibility to in-growing hairs/razor bumps. Ensure that the sideburns are balanced.

Shaving

The skin is stretched and held with tension to allow the razor to glide smoothly and get a close shave. Only with experience will you fully understand how much tension to apply and how much pressure to put on the blade.

Finishing the shave and grooming

Once the shave is complete, the face should be wiped clean with a fresh warm facecloth or patted dry. Some barbers will apply a cool towel to close the pores and freshen the skin.

Following this, a small amount of moisturizer or talcum powder may be applied according to the client's preference. If an astringent is desired then an aftershave lotion can be used to help lessen the risk of infection.

Full beard

Chin puff

Vandyke

Handle bar moustache and chin puff

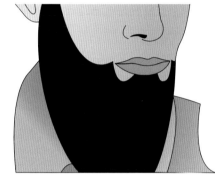

Shenandoah

Box beard

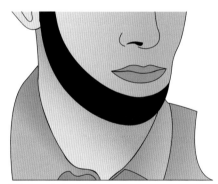

Chin curtain/beard

Napoleon imperial

Mutton chops

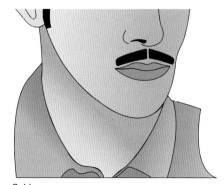

Gable

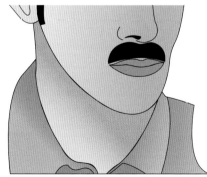

Copstache

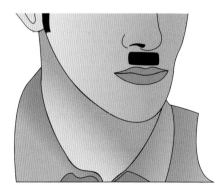

Toothbrush moustache

Table of common beard shapes some of which may be requested by name

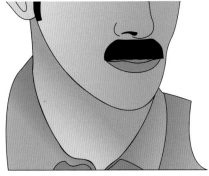

Moustache

Mexican Moustache

Horseshoe/biker moustache

Pencil Moustache

Dali Moustache

Table of common beard shapes some of which may be requested by name (Continued)

Aftercare advice

The client should be told when to return to the salon for a repeat service or be given advice on how to maintain his beard at home. The rate of growth of hair on the face differs with each individual and is much faster and coarser than the hair on the head, and therefore will need more regular shaving. The salon should retail a range of products suitable for use by men, in which case you can guide his choice as to what might be best for him. If the client is prone to in-growing hairs then he should be given advice on how to minimize them, such as keeping the facial area clean and taking care to ensure that any razor he may use at home is sterile. It may be helpful to recommend an exfoliating product to minimize the growth of skin over the hair follicle. Record the services advice given and the cost on the client's record card.

REVISION QUESTIONS

1 What clinical condition are men with African type hair susceptible to?

1 Head lice

2 Ringworm

3 In-growing hairs

4 Acne

2 Where do you dispose of sharp implements?

1 In a sharps box

2 In the general waste bin

3 Take them home

4 In the recycling bin

3 Which of these will sterilize your equipment safely?

1 Washing with soap and water

2 Soaking in salt water

3 Autoclaving

4 Wiping with a damp towel

4 What will using a razor on dry facial hair cause?

1 Pulling and discomfort

2 A smooth close shave

3 Cuts and abrasions

4 No difference

5 What are Styptic chalks or matches used for?

1 Drawing patterns

2 Stemming the flow of blood from cuts

3 Cleaning tools and equipment

4 Close shave and razor work

6 Which of these is a blood borne disease?

1 Hepatitis

2 Influenza

3 Candida

4 Staphylococci

7 What is the correct name for a cut throat razor?

1 Safety razor

2 Bic razor

3 Open razor

4 Disposable razor

8 What is the name given to a cut that follows the contour of the head?

1 Fade

2 Sculpture cut

3 High top

9 Which tool is used to define and brighten a design that has been cut into the hair?

1 Razor

2 Shaper

3 Small clippers

4 Scissors

10 It is difficult to create a 3D effect on hair that is shorter than?

1 10 mm (⅜")

2 20 mm (¾")

3 30 mm (1⅛")

4 5 mm (3/16")

11 When thinking about the size of the design in relation to actual objects, what do we refer to this as?

1 The scale

2 The proportion

3 The shape

4 The position

12 The application of hot towels is used to do what?

1 Maintain a professional barber image

2 Soften hair and relax facial muscles

3 Clean the client's face and neck

4 To act as a head rest for the client

Glossary

45° angle angle used when cutting hair to create graduation

90° angle angle used when cutting hair to create a cut of the same length all over

180° angle angle used when creating an over-directed haircut keeping longer hair on the outside of the cut

3D shape a shape that gives the appearance of being solid

Above shoulders describes a hairstyle that is shoulder length or shorter

Acid balanced product a product is of similar acidity to that of the hair and scalp

Activator a product used to add moisture to permed or naturally curly hair to promote curl

Aesthetically pleasing describes a haircut where the fall, movement and design are pleasing to the eye and suit the client's face and head shape

Albinism a congenital condition that is caused by the failure of melanocytes to produce colour pigment in the hair, skin and eyes. The condition results in a pale, white or creamy skin tone with yellow/red to yellow white hair. The eyes can be pink/red due to blood in tissues. Blue/grey/brown or hazel eyes are not uncommon.

Ammonia a colourless gas with a pungent smell that produces a strong alkaline solution when dissolved in water; found in permanent tint. Helps to open the cuticle of the hair during the colouring process

Analysis examination of the scalp and hair, including specific tests, to ensure that the desired end results can be achieved

Angle the degree of elevation at which the hair is held when it is cut

Arrector pili muscle a muscle that contracts in response to cold or fear, causing the hair to stand up to help keep the body warm

Balance and shape the overall look of a hairstyle in conjunction with the contours of the face and head shape that makes it aesthetically pleasing

Base shade depth of natural hair colour (from 1–10) before consideration of tone

Basic perm winding nine section perm wind using basic perm winding techniques e.g. directional and brick wind techniques

Below shoulders describes a hairstyle that sits below the shoulder

Blend to bring together or marry one section of a haircut with another

Blood borne describes infections transmitted via contact with blood

Blow-dry products products used on hair prior to blow-drying

Bonding a method of extending hair with the use of bonding glue

Bonding glue a liquid, either black or white in colour, which is applied to hair wefts to secure them to the scalp

Cane-rows three-stemmed plaits, plaited close to the scalp in a crossover fashion, finished off with a single plait at the ends

Cap weave a stocking-like covering to which hair wefts are attached and which can either be removable or bonded to the hair

Case study an extended example that can be analyzed to decide on a course of action or to solve problems

Classic cut a style that never dates or goes out of fashion

Client requirements the client's wishes about what they want to have done to their hair

Clip-on extensions wefts of hair attached to a snap-on clip

Closed questions questions which promote a one word answer such as yes or no

Colour correction correction or removal of unwanted colour pigment from the hair

Colour swatches swatches or samples of nylon/hair colour choices/shades, usually found in the manufacturer's colour chart

Comb attachment an attachment to the hand-held dryer used to comb through and straighten out natural or relaxed hair while drying

Complementary colours colours that enhance or balance one another

Compound dyes dyes which contain metallic salts such as compound henna. These are often known as progressive dyes which colour the hair over a period of time by working on the sulphur within the hair turning it into the desired shade

Consultation a discussion with the client to find out their needs and requirements

Contra indication something relating the hair, scalp or previous services which makes it unsafe to carry out a hairdressing service or treatment

Corrective relaxer a relaxer applied to areas that were under-processed by previous relaxers

Creative advanced perm winding technique fashion perming techniques

Crest the raised part of the wave

Curved needle embroidery needle used to stitch hair wefts to a plaited base. A curved needle minimises the risk of injury to the scalp

Cutting cape a protective cape placed over the gown to prevent hair cuttings moving down the neck and to keep the area around the shoulders flat

Cutting terminology professional vocabulary used to describe the cutting process

Cutting tools tools used specifically for cutting the hair

Damaged brittle hair hair that is prone to breakage because of previous chemical or physical over-processing

Definition clean, strong lines within a haircut

Demographic a sector of a population that has its own characteristics

Diagnostic tests tests carried out to confirm the compatibility of treatment to be used

Disconnected describes a cut in which different angles or shapes do not connect

Disulphide or sulphur bonds bonds that are broken when the hair is relaxed

Double strand twists two strands of hair looped over each other in a twisting fashion from roots to ends

Dry cutting technique a technique that involves cutting the hair when it is dry, used to get precision in the final haircut

Dual action perms perms that consist of two phases, first smoothing and straightening the hair and then winding the hair to produce a wave or curl

Effleurage a stroking movement used in massage

Electrically heated straightening irons electrical tools used to straighten both natural and relaxed hair

Electrically heated styling wands electrical tools used to curl the hair from roots to points

Elevation the angle or degree of lift

Emergency numbers phone numbers ready for use in an emergency, e.g. 999, 112, local police, local hospital, manager's contact numbers

Enhance the shape make the cut look better or strengthen the look

Eumelanine Dark pigment found in black and brown hair

Evaluation a written assessment of an activity or task

Fade cut a haircut that graduates from very short around the nape and sides of the head to longer length on the crown

Fashion colours bright and vibrant colours, or other colours that are currently in fashion

Final finished look the agreed hairstyle or look to be achieved

Finger wave a setting and styling technique which follows the movement of waves in the sea and is shaped by the stylist's fingers

Finished look look achieved when all styling is complete and to the satisfaction of the client and stylist

Friction used during massage to stimulate the scalp and new growth

Gesticulation movement of the arms and hands accompanying speech

Growth pattern how the hair naturally grows on the head

Hairdressing cream/pomade a product used to moisturize the scalp or to calm itchy dry scalp, may contain special additives such as tea tree oil

Heat protector a cream or serum which is applied to the hair prior to the application of heat in thermal styling

High lift tint a tint that can be used to lift hair more than three shades, usually used in conjunction with 12 per cent peroxide

Holding spray a product used to protect the hair from the elements and atmosphere as well as holding the hair in place; comes in light to strong hold

Hydrogen bonds bonds that break during the thermal process and reform once the hair becomes wet

Hydrogen peroxide a chemical compound mixed with hair colourant or lightener to activate the lightener/tint/dye prior to the application of the product

Hydrophilic attracted to water

Hydrophobic repelled by water

Hygroscopic able to absorb moisture

Implementation putting into action

ICC (International Colour Chart) international colouring system used to denote synthetic hair colour/dye. Sometimes the system is made up of only numbers or has letters as well

Incompatibility test test carried out to see if there are any metallic salts (e.g. henna) on the hair that could react violently with hydrogen peroxide

Irons electrical or thermal instruments used to temporarily straighten the hair or curl it

Job description an outline of the responsibilities for a given role in the salon

Keloid a rubbery, itchy growth due to injury or scarring, found on people of African, Asian or Mediterranean descent

Lanthionine bond when the hair is sufficiently relaxed, one disulphide bond changes to a lanthionine bond; the other disulphide bond remains intact after the process

Legislation a legal regulation or requirement, passed by the Government

Lifestyle how the client lives on a daily basis, including their job or profession, family responsibilities, socializing

Light oil clear oils that can be easily shampooed from the hair

Lime scale a white deposit left by hard water

Litmus paper used to measure acid or alkaline products

Look the haircut to be achieved

Male pattern balding a pattern of hair loss around the temples and crown area, usually occurring in men

Manual handling moving by hand

Marry to blend the hair from one section of the haircut to another

Melanin a natural colour or pigment found in the skin or hair

Melanocytes cells which produce melanin

Mesh a section of hair

Mesh weave a hairnet-type covering which is either sewn to a cane-rowed base on the head or set on the head with the use of spritz and added heat

Metallic salts salts found in compound dyes such as compound henna and some over the counter hair dyes.

Micro bonding an extension method using small strips of hair, which may or may not be pre-bonded

Moisturizer a product used on natural hair or permed hair to maintain moisture levels and stop the hair becoming dry

Neutral product a product that is neither acid nor alkaline; a product with a pH of 7

Neutralize apply a tint in order to tone down the pigmentation of the hair

Off-base a placement of rollers or pin curls which decreases movement at the crown and creates movement on the mid-lengths and ends

Off-base thermal curl a curl that creates no volume at the roots and curl on the perimeter

Oil sheen spray a product used to give the hair sheen during or after styling

On-base a placement of the rollers or pin curls at the crown of the hair in order to create fullness and volume

On-base thermal curl a curl that sits on its own base and produces an open curl movement and volume in the finished hairstyle

Ortho-cortex the inside of the wave on a strand of curly hair

Oxidation the process by which the colour molecules of a dye are deposited and trapped within the cuticle

Para dyes dyes which contain Para-Phenylenediamine (PPD) such as permanent hair dyes and some quasi colourants

Paracortex the outside of the wave on a strand of curly hair

Pediculosis capitis head lice

Permanent hair colours synthetic colours which penetrate the cuticle to permanently change the melanin/pigment in the hair when mixed with hydrogen peroxide

Perm burns damage caused when perm lotion is left on the skin

Perming a method of curling or waving which uses a chemical to process the hair

Petrissage a circular lifting massage movement

Pheomelanin the yellow-red pigment found in blonde hair

pH scale the measurement of how acidic or alkaline a product is

Physical effect the effects of heat on the hair

Pigment the molecules present within the hair that give the hair its colour

Pigment granules small particles of colour which mass together to form pigment granules within the cortex of the hair

Pin curling a technique used to create soft curls and movement in the hair

Pityriasis capitis dandruff of the scalp

Pliable easier to mould into a new shape

Points/ends of the hair the perimeter of the haircut

Policy procedure that should be followed when dealing with certain situations

Potential likelihood that something could happen

PPE personal protective equipment

Pre-relaxer treatment a procedure applied prior to a relaxer in order to even out the porosity and to coat the cuticle, protecting against damage to the hair

Pre-lighten to chemically lighten the hair through the use of bleach or high lift tint before applying the target shade

Pre-perm test curl a test taken prior to a perm to see which products, perm rods, rollers or formers are best suited to create the end result

Pre-pigmentation the application of a base tone to white or lightened hair before applying the target colour

Precision even blunt ends that are all the same length

Pressing the technique of straightening African type hair using pressing combs

Primary colours Red, Yellow and Blue. These colours can be mixed to form all other colours

Product selection the series of tests and questions asked during consultation to select a suitable product

Productivity the amount of work carried out by the staff

Protective base a product used around the hairline and applied to the scalp as a protection

Pull burns damage to the scalp caused when the hair is pulled too tightly in the rod or former during perming

Quasi permanent colours colouring agent which will deposit a small amount of colour pigment just within the cortex but which will not lighten the natural colour of the hair

Radial or spiral brush a tool used to smooth out, stretch and straighten the hair and create movement in the final blow-dried look

Razor bumps a colloquial name for in-growing hairs

Razor cutting technique a technique used to thin and texturize the hair when cutting

Re-twisting a process to tighten locks that have grown out or loosened at the scalp

Record cards cards used to record services carried out on the client including relaxing history, tests and contra indications

Regrowth relaxer a relaxer applied to the regrowth area only

Relaxer a cream-based hydroxide product that is alkaline, used to remove natural curl from the hair

Relaxer application the method of applying relaxer

Retro hairstyles hairstyles that are based on older, historical looks

Reverse pin curling technique arrangement of the pin curls in alternating rows in order to create waves

Risk assessment working out the likelihood or potential for harm

Rotary circular massage movement that stimulates the scalp to improve blood supply to the follicle and hair growth

Sebaceous gland a gland that produces natural oil in the skin and hair

Seborrhea an oily scalp and hair condition

Secondary colours colours which are achieved by mixing two primary colours together

Seborrhoea the excessive production of sebum

Section the main sectioning of the hair prior to cutting

Semi-permanent colours colouring agent that last 6-8 weeks, fading with shampooing, and which does not alter the chemical structure of the hair

Senegalese twists a technique where hair is styled using a two stemmed crossover technique from the roots to the ends

Serum a product used to add moisture and sheen to the hair, improve the condition and diminish static electricity

Session stylist a very experienced hair stylist who works on magazine shoots, commercials, catwalk and hair shows, sought after on an international level

Shade charts a chart usually provided by the colour manufacturer which illustrates the colours available within their range

Single plait a three stemmed plait, plaited off the scalp

Single twists sections of hair twisted using either a comb or the fingers, rolling the hair in a twisting fashion from root to ends

Skin test a test carried out on the skin before a service to rule out allergy or intolerance of a product

Stencil a template used to trace the initial design in the hair

Straightening the hair a temporary and physical process which will only last until the hair absorbs moisture and reverts

Strand test test carried out on a small section of hair during the colour or lightening process to check development

Stray ends ends of hair that may have been missed during the cutting process

Styptic a product used to stop bleeding

Subsection a section taken from the main hair section

Sudoriferous gland a gland that produces sweat

Surface tension the property of water that prevents it from wetting the hair before shampoo is added

Target the expected amount of work to be completed, or sales to be made, within a given timeframe

Target colour the intended colour to be achieved for a finished look

Tea tree oil a natural product used to soothe and heal, which is a natural antiseptic and is found in some (where listed) hairdressing products such as scalp creams, shampoos and conditioners

Template a cut section of hair which is then used as a guideline to ensure that the remaining sections are cut to match

Temporary effect non-permanent colour which gives the client time to decide whether or not they would be happy with that colour permanently

Tertiary colours colours achieved by mixing primary and secondary colours together

Thermal tools that use heat in order to straighten or curl the hair

Thermal pressing comb a tool used to straighten natural or semi-relaxed African type hair

Thermal styling a physical technique used to temporarily straighten or curl the hair

Thermal styling stove/oven a device used to heat thermal tools

Thinning scissors scissors used to remove hair or weight on the tips or from internal lengths of hair

Tinea fungal infections such as ringworm, which can be found on any part of the body

Tints permanent hair colourant which requires the use of hydrogen peroxide for the product to work

Tone colour which can be seen on the hair in conjunction with the main colour. These can be warm or cool tones

Traction alopecia a form of hair loss caused by the constant or excessive pulling of the hair, particularly seen on hair which has been braided too tightly

Transitioning the process of going from chemically treated hair to non-chemically treated hair

Trichosiderin red pigment found in red hair

Trough the dip of the wave

Twist outs hair which is separated after it has been twisted and dried

UVA ultraviolet light

Viable capable of working successfully

Virgin relaxer a product applied to natural hair that has never been chemically processed or relaxed before

Visual awareness experience and creativity in relation to the haircut or hairstyle, aesthetics and how this influences each stylist's approach to cutting

Weft a strip of hair (synthetic, human or blended) which can either be sewn or bonded to the client's hair

Wet set a technique used to create solid curls and movement

Working environment place of work, e.g. the salon or client's home

Wrap set a setting technique used to create a freer, smoother finish

Zulu knots hair which is twisted or plaited and rolled back on itself in a tight coil to form a knot

Answers to revision questions

Chapter 1

Health and safety pp. 20–21

Q1	1	Q10	3
Q2	2	Q11	1
Q3	3	Q12	2
Q4	3	Q13	1
Q5	1	Q14	4
Q6	2	Q15	3
Q7	3	Q16	1
Q8	3	Q17	2
Q9	1		

Chapter 2

Hair characteristics pp. 42–43

Q1	2	Q7	3
Q2	1	Q8	1
Q3	4	Q9	3
Q4	2	Q10	2
Q5	1	Q11	1
Q6	2	Q12	4

Chapter 3

Client consultation pp. 60–61

Q1	1	Q7	1
Q2	2	Q8	4
Q3	3	Q9	1
Q4	3	Q10	4
Q5	1	Q11	2
Q6	3		

Chapter 4

The successful salon p. 75

Q1	3	Q6	1
Q2	3	Q7	3
Q3	3	Q8	3
Q4	1	Q9	1
Q5	1		

Chapter 5

Shampooing and conditioning pp. 93–94

Q1	2	Q6	4
Q2	1	Q7	2
Q3	2	Q8	1
Q4	2	Q9	2
Q5	1	Q10	3

Chapter 6

Blow-drying pp. 112–113

Q1	1	Q7	1
Q2	3	Q8	1
Q3	3	Q9	3
Q4	1	Q10	3
Q5	2	Q11	1
Q6	1		

Chapter 7

Setting hair pp. 132–133

Q1	3	Q7	3
Q2	2	Q8	1
Q3	1	Q9	4
Q4	1	Q10	3
Q5	1	Q11	1
Q6	2	Q12	3

Chapter 8

Styling and finishing p. 151

Q1	4	Q3	4
Q2	2	Q4	2

Chapter 9

Thermal styling pp. 168–169

Q1	3	Q8	1
Q2	4	Q9	3
Q3	1	Q10	2
Q4	1	Q11	4
Q5	3	Q12	1
Q6	3	Q13	4
Q7	3		

Chapter 10

Hair extensions p. 198

Q1	2	Q8	1
Q2	3	Q9	4
Q3	1	Q10	3
Q4	4	Q11	1
Q5	3	Q12	4
Q6	2	Q13	4
Q7	1		

Chapter 11

Perming p. 227

Q1	3	Q7	1
Q2	1	Q8	3
Q3	2	Q9	1
Q4	4	Q10	3
Q5	1	Q11	1
Q6	1		

Chapter 12

Relaxing hair pp. 250–251

Q1	4	Q7	1
Q2	1	Q8	4
Q3	3	Q9	1
Q4	2	Q10	2
Q5	4	Q11	1
Q6	1	Q12	4

Chapter 13

Cutting hair using basic techniques pp. 276–277

Q1	1	Q8	3
Q2	4	Q9	1
Q3	1	Q10	2
Q4	1	Q11	4
Q5	3	Q12	1
Q6	3	Q13	2
Q7	4		

Chapter 14

Colouring hair using basic techniques pp. 308–309

Q1	3	Q5	4
Q2	1	Q6	3
Q3	4	Q7	3
Q4	2	Q8	2

Chapter 15

Creatively colouring and cutting pp. 342–343

Q1	4	Q9	1
Q2	1	Q10	3
Q3	1	Q11	1
Q4	1	Q12	3
Q5	4	Q13	1
Q6	2	Q14	3
Q7	3	Q15	4
Q8	4		

Chapter 16

Maintaining and styling natural hair p. 367

Q1	3		**Q6**	2
Q2	2		**Q7**	4
Q3	1		**Q8**	1
Q4	3		**Q9**	2
Q5	1		**Q10**	4

Chapter 17

Cultivating and maintaining locks p. 382

Q1	3		**Q5**	1
Q2	3		**Q6**	3
Q3	2		**Q7**	3
Q4	1			

Chapter 18

Men's hairdressing pp. 406–407

Q1	3		**Q7**	3
Q2	1		**Q8**	3
Q3	3		**Q9**	3
Q4	1		**Q10**	4
Q5	2		**Q11**	1
Q6	1		**Q12**	2

Index